COLD WAR IN A HOT ZONE

Cold War in a Hot Zone

*The United States Confronts Labor and
Independence Struggles in the British
West Indies*

GERALD HORNE

TEMPLE UNIVERSITY PRESS
Philadelphia

Gerald Horne, Moores Professor of History & African-American Studies at the University of Houston, is the author of many books including *Black & Brown: African-Americans and the Mexican Revolution, 1910–1920* and *The Deepest South: The U.S., Brazil and the African Slave Trade.*

Cover photograph: Demonstration against British colonialism in St. Kitts, early 1950s (from far right: C.A. Paul Southwell, holding placard ; Joseph Nathaniel France, wearing light colored suit with white hat; F.T. Williams, to France's left) Courtesy National Archives of St. Kitts-Nevis.

Temple University,
Philadelphia 19122

The paper used in this publication meets the requirements
of the American National Standard for Information Sciences—
Permanence of Paper for Printed Library Materials, ANSI Z39.48-1992

Library of Congress Cataloging-in-Publication Data

Horne, Gerald, 1949–
Cold War in a hot zone: labor and independence struggles in the
British West Indies / Gerald Horne.
p. cm.
Includes bibliographical references and index.
ISBN 13: 978-1-59213-627-8   ISBN 10: 1-59213-627-3 (cloth: alk. paper)
ISNB 13: 978-1-59213-628-5   ISBN 10: 1-59213-628-1 (pbk.: alk. paper)
1. Labor movement—West Indies, British—History.   2. West Indies, British—
History—Autonomy and independence movements.   3. United States—
Foreign relations—West Indies, British.   4. West Indies, British—
Foreign relations—United States.   I. Title.

HD8242.H67 2007
331.8809729'09171241—dc22   2006034694

2   4   6   8   9   7   5   3   1

CONTENTS

LIST OF FIGURES

INTRODUCTION

CHEDDI JAGAN WAS STUNNED.

It was a bright sunny day in early October 1953 in Georgetown, British Guiana, the only predominantly English-speaking nation in South America, not far from the Caribbean Sea. He had only recently come to power—or as much power as this man of South Asian origin could assume in a British colony. But now, as he recalled later, London had had quite enough of his months in office, as "the cruiser 'Superb' and the frigates 'Bigbury Bay' and 'Burghead Bay' were steaming from Bermuda. Troops were being flown from Jamaica. The aircraft carrier 'Implacable' was to bring further reinforcements from the United Kingdom towards the end of the week." Thus, as he stood there in disbelief in his pajamas and slippers, police raided his home, taking away "papers, books and a recording machine," while "downstairs, said Jagan, the police were digging up the floor of my garage."[1]

If there was any consolation, Jagan's was not the only home ransacked, as "about 40 homes and offices" of other leaders of his People's Progressive Party were invaded. To be on the safe side, the authorities with guns "at the ready" not only made a forced entry into his home at 97 Laluni Street but also his office—Jagan was a dentist trained at Northwestern University in Illinois—at 199 Charlotte Street. Streets were cordoned during these raids at the break of dawn.[2]

What prompted this extraordinary measure that led to the dislodging of the Jagan administration and his eventual incarceration? As Jagan saw it, his overthrow was of a piece with the June 1953 coup targeting Mohammad Mossadegh in Iran and the 1954 coup against Jacobo Arbenz in Guatemala; "the three deposed governments had all been popularly elected at free and fair elections," he said. "In fact, the PPP, though dubbed 'Communist' won three consecutive elections in 1953, 1957 and 1961."[3]

Jagan was on target in pointing to the specter of communism as the ostensible basis for his being toppled. In the runup to his removal from power, the Executive Council in British Guiana, which included Jagan and London's representatives, debated intensely whether a travel ban that barred various reds and radicals from entering Georgetown should be continued. This ban included the Jamaican-born former leader of the National Maritime Union of the United States—Ferdinand Smith—who only recently had been expelled from that nation, not least because of his ties to communists[4] and to various leaders of the Caribbean Labour Congress (CLC), which since its auspicious start in 1945 had been spearheading a dual agenda of organizing workers and pushing for independence from various European powers, particularly Great Britain. The ban was lifted in the face of fierce opposition from London's man, who "stressed the need for creating conditions which would dispel distrust and encourage the investment of capital and gave his opinion that the removal, at this time, of the ban against persons who were known to have connections with Moscow, could only have a prejudicial effect."[5] Strikingly, other than the travel ban, the most contentious issue debated in the Executive Council prior to the ouster of Jagan's administration was Jagan's introduction of a bill to make it easier for labor unions to organize. As the minutes of this momentous meeting indicated, "Dr. Jagan then stated that it was his Party's declared intention to introduce legislation based on the American pattern to compel employers to recognize any trade union which commanded the support of the majority of the workers." This démarche came in the midst of a highly contentious strike by sugar workers.[6]

The United States, already the dominant power in the hemisphere, was dumbfounded by this turn of events. *TIME*, the magazine that was the centerpiece of the publishing empire of the influential Henry Luce, observed nervously that Jagan's electoral triumph months earlier was "the first time that the Reds reached power in the British Empire,"[7] while the State Department was "bewildered" by Jagan's victory. "How could a party with leaders suspected of ties to Moscow be elected in a freely contested election in an English-speaking colony?"[8]

The ouster of the Jagan regime in 1953 also foreordained the 1961 collapse of federation in the British West Indies that sought to unite the far-flung colonies of the region. It had been organized a few years earlier but the overthrow of Jagan crippled the regional labor-left that had pushed the notion of federation in the first place. As Jagan later observed, when a federation of sorts was "born in 1958, it had not only a weak centre but a crown colony status. Britain retained powers of foreign affairs and defence [*sic*]," which suggested the scope of London's 1953 triumph. This was a turnabout from the early postwar era when the labor-left, as represented by Jagan, crusaded for sovereignty. "What precisely went wrong?" asked Jagan plaintively in 1972. "The Cold War intervened and the West Indian leadership joined the bandwagon," he answered.[9]

I N PART THIS IS A BOOK about the Caribbean Labour Congress, which, propelled in 1945 by a wave of labor unrest, sought to organize the working class—especially in the former British West Indies—as it pushed for independence for these postage-stamp-sized islands, in the form of a federation. This is also a book about how anticommunism proved notably useful in blunting the thrust of the CLC's twin objectives.[10] It ranges from the high tide of labor unrest in the 1930s, which paved the way for Jagan's rise, to his overthrow in 1953—which was an early signal that meaningful independence and federation would not be allowed to emerge. In sum, this is a book about the impact of the early Cold War in shaping today's former British West Indies, which is characterized by the continuing influence of labor (in Barbados, both the ruling and opposition parties are known as "Labour" parties), which has proven instrumental in insuring one of the most pervasive regional democracies in the developing world. In fact, the relatively small British West Indies exemplifies the relatively grand idea that a precondition for a thriving democracy is the organization and influence of what is the majority in most nations: labor. This book also sheds light on the origins of today's CARICOM or Caribbean Community, which is a form of federation—and, again, a powerful voice for regional democracy, as exemplified by its principled response to the 2004 ouster of the democratically elected government in Haiti[11]—but its loose bonds are not precisely what the labor-left had in mind.

Though these colonies were struggling for independence from London, this book reflects the dominant fact of the second half of the twentieth century: how a diminished London was replaced by a rising Washington in its Empire—and elsewhere. However, this reality was noticeably evident in the Caribbean. Why? The West Indies was the "third U.S. border." These "islands form a semi-circular outer ring around the Panama Canal. It is through these islands and the Canal that much of U.S. imports flow."[12] This region was the "outer defence [sic] ring covering the soft underbelly of the United States, as well as being the lynch pin for control of the Central Atlantic." Washington's strategic dilemma was exposed as the CLC was coming into existence, for during the war, the German navy waged a "Caribbean U-boat campaign" that "was the most cost-effective campaign fought by Germany anywhere during World War II," inflicting considerable damage on the interests of both the United States and the United Kingdom.[13]

Consequently, after the war, as the CLC pushed for federation, Washington, from its colony in the Virgin Islands, sought to exert more influence in the region, pushing for "the creation of a Caribbean Commission Secretariat" with a "suitable staff."[14]

Hence, despite the relatively small size of the jurisdiction encompassed by the CLC, this region was of enormous strategic significance to Washington, a fact which became clear after the Cuban revolution of 1959. What was called the "Commonwealth Caribbean" consisted of "seventeen territorial units. Fifteen of these are islands or groups of islands. Two are mainland states. Together, these territories encompass a land mass of 105,325 square miles" and, as of 1971, "a population of five million people." The region forms a "vital land-line between the two American continents," and, concluded one analyst, this "link . . . gives to the area a preeminent economic and strategic value."[15]

One problem for Washington was that the CLC—as the prominence in Jamaican labor ranks of Ferdinand Smith suggested—was welcoming of the radical left, and the influx of Caribbean nationals into the United States itself had created a progressive link from there to the former British West Indies. Thus, these Caribbean migrants raised thousands of dollars for the financially strapped CLC and constituted a domestic U.S. lobby on their behalf.[16] Not least because of the economic misery that gripped the islands during the 1930s—which also propelled a wave of strikes—migrants from the British West Indies poured into Harlem particularly, where they organized the Jamaica Progressive League, the West Indies National Council, and other groups that took a decided interest in their old homeland.[17]

These migrants quickly became incorporated within a larger African American community that too was hardly indifferent to the Caribbean. As early as 1927, the journal of the NAACP "urge[d] the peoples of the West Indies to begin an earnest movement for the federation of these islands," an unsurprising development given the Caribbean roots of its leader, W.E.B. Du Bois.[18]

By the same token, in December 1948, in a "confidential" message, U.S. diplomat Nelson R. Park reported nervously to the secretary of state about the Jamaican visit of Paul Robeson, the performer and activist known to be close to the U.S. Communist Party. He was "feted by official and civic organizations," he said disconsolately, though he brightened when noting that Robeson was "under discreet surveillance" by the authorities. At times this surveillance was not difficult since at one concert "some fifty thousand persons" attended and there was blanket press coverage of his visit.[19] Robeson had long held the Caribbean dear, stating words at one juncture that were not comforting to his opponents. "At this moment in world history," he told Jamaicans, "nothing could be more important than the establishment of an independent Negro country to the south of us." This was of monumental Pan-African significance, since such a nation could "help show the way to Negro peoples in Africa," which was why "Negro Americans must join with their West Indian brothers."[20]

A significant reason why Washington was so concerned about developments in these microscopically small nations was their direct influence on a vital sector of the U.S. population: African Americans.[21] Historian Winston James is correct in asserting that migrants from these nations arrived in the United States with a "long and distinguished tradition of resistance with few parallels in the New World." The Father of Harlem Radicalism, Hubert Harrison, who hailed from the Caribbean basin, was largely accurate when he asserted in 1927 that "almost every important development originating in Harlem—from the Negro Manhood Movement to political representation in public office, from collecting Negro books to speaking on the streets, from demanding federal control over lynching to agitation for Negroes on the police force—every one of these has either been fathered by West Indians or can count on them among its originators." These migrants were a vector of influence for Bolshevism, influencing the Communist International on the so-called Negro Question, not least since West Indians were "simultaneously much more nationalistic, class conscious and international-minded than were American-born blacks." Indeed, Harlem's widespread influence and pre-eminence in Black America is inseparable from this profound impact of migrants from the Caribbean. This became clear during the early stages of the Harlem Renaissance when "eighty thousand copies of radical print [was] pouring out of a couple of Harlem blocks each month," not to mention the journal of the NAACP, which had a circulation of 104,000. The presence of the *Challenge*, the *Negro World*, the *Emancipator*, the *Messenger*, and the *Crusader* were intimately tied to the presence of West Indians like Marcus Garvey, Claude McKay, and Cyril Briggs.[22]

Given its strategic significance and its ability to influence an influential bloc of voters—African Americans—it was not surprising when the region was engulfed by a tidal wave of red-baiting that eventually capsized both the CLC and regimes friendly to it, such as Jagan's. As hysteria rose accordingly in November 1948, the prominent Trinidadian politician Albert Gomes denounced what he saw as a red offensive in the Caribbean. "Unless we can rally democratic, anti-Communist sentiment in the [region]," he said, "we shall be rudely awakened one fine day to find that the Red termites whose headquarters are in Jamaica have gnawed their way into all the West Indian territories . . . they have a well-thought out plan for infiltrating into all the West Indian territories and have found a convenient vehicle in the Caribbean Labour Congress." Their "aim," he said, was to "destroy British rule in the West Indies and to establish a Communist West Indies in its stead." This was possible since they had "henchmen in every West Indian territory."[23]

Gomes had a point in that the CLC had affiliates—or at least sympathizers—throughout the region, which was no small thing considering the diversity of the region. For though at times these colonies were spoken of as a monolith, there were distinct differences between them sufficient to flummox the most astute of organizers. The scholar Robert Alexander has opined that "the Jamaicans are a people who are colored and have no inferiority complex about it . . . when the Jamaicans go into Florida to work during the harvest time, they cause all kinds of ruckus. And the British Colonial Office would tell anyone who asked that the Jamaicans are the most unfriendly people in the Empire."[24] Jamaica, a former Spanish possession before becoming part of the British Empire, was the most populous nation in the Commonwealth Caribbean, while

Trinidad—which was influenced profoundly by French Catholicism—was just off the coast of South America and second in population to Jamaica within the former British West Indies. It was, in turn, "the very opposite of Barbados"—whose ties to the Empire were encoded in its nickname "Little England"—in terms of "climate, soil, [and] population." Trinidad contained "an area of 1,287,600 acres, of which about 60,000 only are under cultivation. Barbados, covering some 106,000 acres is cultivated from end to end like a garden. Trinidad, even under slavery, never had anything like an adequate labouring population. Barbados is so thickly inhabited that work or starvation is the labourer's only choice . . . the only similarity between the two islands is that sugar forms the stable production of both."[25] Barbados, said Trinidad's George Padmore, was "the most patriotic of all the West Indies, and, incidentally, the poorest"—a dubious designation whose accuracy its neighbors could rightly challenge.[26] British Honduras—now Belize—is on the mainland of Central America and historically has faced aggressive territorial claims from neighboring Guatemala, while British Guiana (now Guyana) is on the mainland of South America and faces similar claims from neighboring Venezuela. Both British Guiana and Trinidad and Tobago have sizeable populations of South Asian origin, while Jamaica, Antigua, St. Kitts-Nevis, Barbados, St. Lucia, Grenada, Dominica, St. Vincent, etc. do not. Eric Williams, the Caribbean intellectual who became the leader of his homeland, Trinidad and Tobago, once commented that Trinidad and Tobago is "to Grenada and St. Vincent" as "Antigua is to Dominica and Montserrat," that is, a big brother and a little brother, a dominant cultural influence and those it influenced.[27]

To a degree, Trinidad, St. Lucia, Grenada, and Dominica can be grouped together. Why? Though all were "only under French domination for a few years" more than two centuries ago, "a French patois, the Roman Catholic religion and many of the old French customs have vigorously survived"—including a "style of building construction"—to an extent.[28] St. Lucia was notably unique in that it "always looked to France" and "Martinique . . . for their intellectual life," while maintaining a high level of economic concentration. In 1946, U.S. diplomat Charles Whitaker reported that "about three families . . . control most of the economic life of the island."[29] In turn Grenada—which produced some of the most militant of Trinidad's labor leaders—had a uniqueness all its own. The writer Alfie Roberts may have been thinking of the tumultuous 1951 Grenada strike and the turn to the left that culminated in a U.S. invasion in 1983 when he said that Grenada "seems to have something in its body politic that has pushed it, even politically, in a direction more advanced than some of the other islands.[30] A "fashionable West Indian saying of the 17th and 18th centuries," said a writer in St. Kitts, "was that the noblesse were to be found in St. Kitts, the bourgeois in Guadeloupe, soldiers in Martinique and peasants in Grenada."[31]

The relatively small "white" communities varied from island to island too. As Margaret Locket recalled her native Antigua, "there were then three distinct white societies . . . the Portuguese, the Arabs who had come mostly from Syria, and the rest mostly of British descent. These groups remained almost completely separate socially in the 1920s and early 1930s." Unlike St. Kitts, "a far richer island with many absentee owners, the Antiguan planters were for the most part resident on their estates."[32] Barbados, which was the antipode to British Guiana's vanguard radicalism, also—not coincidentally—contained one of the largest white communities in the region.

Richard Hart, a leading Jamaican lawyer and union leader, remarked in 1947 that in "St. Vincent, Grenada, Dominica and St. Lucia wage earners form a relatively small part of the population and trade unionism cannot be expected to present an appeal to the broadest masses in exactly the same way that it does in Trinidad, Barbados or Antigua." In Antigua, Barbados, and St. Kitts, wage earners were in the majority. "But the overwhelming majority" of these were "sugar workers and it is notorious," he opined, "that agricultural workers are more difficult to organize than urban industrial workers." Meanwhile, in Jamaica, the heavyweight of the British West Indies, "the principal obstacle in the way of the growth of the democratic socialist workers' organization" was "the existence of [a] strong active fascist movement." Trinidad and British Guiana were plagued by rifts between workers of African and South Asian origin.[33]

The Leeward Islands, with a population in the early 1950s of about 100,000, were treated as a cohesive unit, though the constituent islands were "widely scattered" and "intercommunication" was "not easy," which facilitated uniqueness even in these small territories. At first glance, St. Kitts resembled Antigua except that "it is mountainous instead of flat" and its soil was "so much richer" and thus had "no peasant proprietors and the estates are owned by individual planters." Nevis was characterized then by "sulphur baths, still in excellent repair," and "Obeah," a form of religion with African overtones, flourished. Tiny Anguilla had "never known prosperity" as its climate was quite dry and its soil "too stony." While considering reasonably distant Tortola and St. Thomas of the Virgin Islands, these islands had a singularity all its own, with a closer resemblance to the Anglo-French condominium that prevailed in the New Hebrides than to its Caribbean neighbors.[34]

That is, within the broader region there were distinct miniregions and cultures that complicated the push for federation.

But with all this variation, there were certain blanket verities within the former British West Indies. The peasantry and working class were subject to crass exploitation, which included a heavy dose of racism. Events in the more populous territories—Jamaica, Trinidad, and British Guiana—tended to shape trends and tendencies regionally. And Barbados, "Little England," tended to have a conservative influence regionally. In some ways, this is not unlike the United States today where California, New York, Texas, and Florida tend to have an outsized influence on the nation, with the former two pulling the country to the left and the latter two to the right.

Still, the differences in the region were not unknown to outsiders. As the CLC was getting underway, the U.S. vice consul in Trinidad explained that "because of social and economic differences between the two islands, Barbados labor was 'definitely preferred' to Trinidad's." He claimed that "the Barbadian developed a reasonable amount of industriousness, was willing to work and exhibited a respectful attitude toward his employer, whereas the reverse was true of the Trinidadian." Most feared of all were the Jamaicans, as a State Department official feared that a "'large influx of Jamaican Negroes for employment would cause repercussions of a political nature' in the United States," because of their reputation for militancy, "but also because it was suspected that funds from [them] would be used to finance an extreme left wing party in the Caribbean."³⁵ U.S. diplomat Henry Taylor argued in 1944 that "Grenadians will regard an inhabitant of St. Vincent as a resident of Boston would regard a Canadian. They would regard a St. Lucian or Dominican as a Bostonian would look upon a Mexican. There is very little concern in Grenada," he thought, "for the welfare of other islands."³⁶

At the same time, there was considerable movement and migration between and among the Caribbean nations—and to the United States. This meant that the dual notions of labor radicalism and sovereignty—which the CLC embodied—were difficult to quarantine. Clement Osbourne Payne, the "John the Baptist" of labor radicalism in a Barbados which had a justifiable reputation for conservatism, hailed from Trinidad. Indeed, his "arrival on Friday, March 26th, 1937 . . . was the beginning of the upsurge of radicalism" regionally.³⁷ Maurice Bishop, the Grenadian leader whose murder was a factor in a 1983 U.S. invasion of this spice island, "frequently stated that Brooklyn was Grenada's largest constituency." From 1888 to 1911 at least "one quarter of the forty thousand inhabitants of St. Vincent were reported to have emigrated . . . and between 1911 and 1921, out-migration was so heavy that Grenada actually experienced a reduction in population." Part of the purpose of the CLC was to provide the protective cover of a union for workers as they moved around the region, which was good since in 1951 the colonial administrator of St. Vincent publicly proclaimed that "the employment of workers outside the colony assists the social and economic well-being of the people." This helped to foment a pragmatic culture of migration. As one Vincentian put it, "'if you go to a "swearing-in" [of] citizens, you see people from the other nations moved to tears. West Indians don't have that feeling. Quite the contrary.' Many West Indians think that U.S. citizenship will enable them to better represent the interests of their home countries."³⁸

This also contributed to a progressive cosmopolitanism that made it easier for outsiders like Payne or Ferdinand Smith—along with their labor radicalism—to be welcomed. It facilitated the very notion of a pan-Caribbean labor federation, such as the CLC, and paved the way for various forms of federation. Thus, Barbados, which was said by its colonizers in 1944 to face the problem of "continuously increasing population,"³⁹ was "investigating the prospects of [mass] emigration to Brazil and other South American countries" in 1947.[40] In a "private and confidential" report, the British Labour Party—patiently waiting to resume power—in early 1938 explored the "question of finding an outlet for the surplus population of some of the West Indian islands," which was a "serious problem which ought to be faced immediately." To cite one example, St. Lucia—"definitely the poorest of the Windward Islands" with "economic conditions" that were "very bad"—consisted "largely of steep hills and owing to unwise deforestation in the past, erosion" had taken hold and "the actual amount of cultivable land" was "decreasing in consequence." Previously, "West Indians in search of employment were able to find it on the oilfields of Venezuela and on the estates of Cuba and San Domingo," but now these lands had "refused to allow West Indians to enter their territories in search of employment." In a labor-based version of beggar-thy-neighbor, "many of the West Indian islands" had "taken steps to prevent the natives of other islands coming to them in search of work." On the other hand, British Guiana could withstand a "large increase of population." British Honduras had a "very small population in a colony of which the area is three times as large as the areas of Barbados, Trinidad and the Windward Islands combined"—so why not move labor to where it was needed?[41]

If that did not occur, it would be akin to trying to keep a lid forced down on a pressure-filled steaming pot. Given such a state of affairs, it was only natural for West Indians to keep an alert eye on regional, hemispheric, and, indeed, global developments as their residence was not certain from year to year.

West Indian wanderlust accelerated in the wake of the labor tumult of the 1930s, perhaps the most serious challenge to British hegemony in the region since the inception of colonialism. It occurred as London itself was under immense pressure from Berlin and Tokyo, thus providing West Indians with even more leverage. In fact, argued Jamaica's People's National Party, "the condition of the working classes in Jamaica which led to the disturbances of 1938 were regarded by the Royal Commission of the West Indies as so shocking that the British government decided not to publish the report lest it make useful enemy propaganda."[42] World War I and the onset of the Great Depression "shrank opportunity for mobility" and, as a result, may have contributed to labor unrest, and it was feared, quite properly by the colonial authorities, that another war could induce a similar result.[43] Mass migration away from the West Indies could ease the pressures, it was thought.

Thus, according to one account, "between 1943 and 1947, 116,124 agricultural and industrial workers recruited in the West Indies worked in the United States, earning approximately $100,000,000 of which $40,000,000 was remitted to the West Indian states." This included about 14,500 workers from Jamaica, 3,000 from Barbados, and 500 from Belize.[44] This migration transformed the region as it occurred as Washington was beginning to challenge London's preeminent role in the British West Indies, thus buoying challenges by the colonized to colonial rule. And as these nations surged to independence, they were hardly prone to accept passively the kind of bestial Jim Crow they were compelled to endure in the United States, which meant the Colossus of the North too was transformed.

One of the reasons that Caribbean nationals were so footloose and so prone to migration was the staggeringly horrendous living conditions they had to endure. That this state of affairs also paved the way for labor radicalism is also true. During the 1930s, for example, blacks in Barbados—where those of African descent made up more than 90 percent of the population—faced "mountains of discrimination . . . when they walked into the 'Mutual Building'" in downtown Bridgetown in the 1930s. "[W]hite officers refused to attend to them until all the white clients had [conducted] their business, even though they had arrived at the office before the whites." This imposing edifice on Broad Street "symbolized economic and social apartheid"—but it was not particularly unique in a land that, evidently, took its sobriquet of "Little England" quite seriously.[45]

This monstrous apartheid was hard to disentangle from the oppressive poverty that reigned in the region. George Padmore, who hailed from Trinidad, observed in the 1930s that "throughout all of the West Indies one is confronted with the shocking spectacle of whole populations living on the verge of starvation." There were "thousands of pauperized, downtrodden natives, huddled together in company-owned barracks on the sugar plantations or scattered around the countryside in mud shacks." There was mass "starvation and disease" that was "causing havoc in depopulating entire sections of the population." There was "forced labor," a throwback to the bad old days of slavery, remnants of which had yet to disappear. There was "all kinds of repressive legislation, such as vagrancy laws," which were "enacted in order to enable the imperialist rulers to find a pretext to force the Negroes to work." The colonized were "arrested on all kinds of framed-up charges, thrown into prison and there assigned to chain gangs and made to build roads and do other forms of public work."[46]

As late as 1970, a Jamaican journalist commented that residents of St. Vincent "were living in a way which, in terms of material and environmental conditions, could scarcely be far removed from the situation as it was under slavery." Unlike, say, Barbados, it "lacked white sand beaches and certainly was not the most favoured of places [for] the development of a tourist industry." There was "untreated water" in "use" and the "state of housing was rapidly [getting] worse."[47]

The Caribbean nations were routinely referred to as the "slums of the Empire," while Padmore once said that the "West Indies could briefly be described as the sugar section of British imperialism."[48] This was no accident. The scholar James Walvin observes that "the main engine which drove boatloads of Africans across the Atlantic was cane sugar. Of the 12 million Africans loaded into the potential hell of the slave ships, some 70% were destined to work in cane fields."[49] Subsequently, in Barbados, "almost the entire working population was directly or indirectly dependent on the sugar industry for a living."[50] In

Jamaica, said Padmore, there was a "government of sugar for sugar by sugar." Something similar could be said about British Guiana and Trinidad and Tobago and the other major colonies of the region. Still, the banana moguls could well object to this characterization of sugar hegemony, since in Jamaica this fruit "accounted for 55% of the values of domestic exports" in 1937, "while sugar accounted for 18%."[51] In St. Lucia, St. Vincent, and Dominica, bananas constituted the "primary export industry throughout most of the second half of the twentieth century, accounting for as much as 80 percent of . . . total exports from the 1960s onwards," and slightly less before then. This "industry also had important linkages to the transportation, domestic marketing, employment, regional trade and other agricultural sectors. It was so integrated into the life of the country that it was virtually impossible for anyone in St. Lucia to remain untouched by it."[52]

Subsequently, tourism surged in importance in the region, while in British Guiana and Jamaica, bauxite zoomed in importance, which accentuated the role of Kaiser, ALCOA, and Reynolds Aluminum; as late as 1950, Trinidad was the leading crude oil producer in the Empire.[53] ALCOA began trying to control bauxite in British Guiana as early as 1914, which "in time" brought "British interests . . . into open conflict with ALCOA and the U.S.A."[54] By 1942 Reynolds of the United States was eagerly seeking to get its hands on Jamaican bauxite, which it linked to Washington's wartime needs and long-term strategic goals—which, again, was not pleasing to London.[55]

The unvarnished dominance of capital—often foreign capital—combined with a crisis of everyday living that was of major ideological consequence. As the Cold War was launched in the aftermath of World War II, Caribbean nationals were being instructed that they had to align with the forces of "freedom" and reject the myrmidons of "totalitarianism," as exemplified by the CLC. But when a labor leader in tiny and depressed Dominica was fed this line by H. V. Tewson, general secretary of Britain's Trade Union Congress, he resisted. "Conditions of Dominica today [are] worse than ever before," it was said in late 1951. "[T]oday when you tell the man in the street that there will soon be war," the "answer they give is 'whether they are going to fight to strengthen the capitalist exploitation.' Our working population is about 20,000 but it is only about 7,000 who are employed. . . . We in Dominica today," he reported, "are just like the people of England in 1833. Hundreds of acres of land are wasted land; people are crying in want of land to make gardens"—and many more were barely hanging on.[56]

This Cold War in the hemisphere was headed by Washington, though the U.S. presence became a roiling factor even before the post-1945 onset of this conflict. When the U.S. flag rose in Antigua on the first day of spring 1941, Washington moved "from the wings to center stage in Antiguan life." This U.S. base—one among a number that arose with the onset of war—"immediately became an enormous labor market," and for the "first time since the early 1700s, the planters no longer controlled access to work, and therefore to livelihood, for the mass of the population." This had a contradictory impact. The undermining of planter hegemony gave a palpable boost to labor organizing and to the idea that the majority should rule. After all, those within the majority were overwhelmingly part of the laboring classes and were overwhelmingly absent from the ruling elite. But then there was the "introduction of American style racism" on this tiny island. Euro-Americans "brought to Antigua a consciousness of race and a level of racial discrimination and hostility, that was far greater than any that Antiguans"—or, for that matter, Trinidadians and the others subjected to U.S. praxis—"had known, at least since slavery ended—it was so strong and so different that many people [asserted] that it was the Americans who had *introduced* racism to Antigua" (emphasis in original). For it was they who "introduced Jim Crow practices at the base and separate buses took whites and nonwhites to and from town." They "brought with them racially based violence, verbal and physical; filthy language, drunken driving, fist fights, brawls and shooting incidents"—"all became commonplace." They were "trigger happy and prone to pulling out knives and guns."[57] This conservative and racist militancy helped generate a correspondingly antiracist and progressive militancy that helped drive labor organizing—and, ultimately, independence.

Yet emblematic of the pervasive exploitation faced by West Indians was that many welcomed the arrival of a sizeable U.S. presence as a counterweight to British colonialism, with the latter viewed as cash-strapped and penurious and the former as cash-rich and wealthy.

Of course, the colonized were largely deprived of the right to vote and generally had no say in the selection of the Windsors of London as their sovereign. "I lived through a period in St. Vincent and the Grenadines," said the activist intellectual Alfie Roberts, and "up to 1951 you were only able to vote if you had access to property and a certain monetary income."[58]

Perhaps not accidentally, 1951 was the key year for many in the Caribbean, for it was then that London, as a way to blunt the thrust toward sovereignty and workers' rights spearheaded by the CLC, began to make critical concessions. Certainly this was the view of Richard Hart, the radical Jamaican lawyer who in many ways was the sparkplug of the organization. As he saw it, beyond its contribution to labor and sovereignty, the CLC had other benefits, for when it convened for the first time in Barbados in 1945 "this was the first time that popular organizations in Jamaica had established contact of any kind with popular organizations of the eastern Caribbean islands and British Guiana." The walls between these small nations had benefited London; breaking them down—which the CLC pioneered—benefited independence. There were gaps in the organizing scheme, however. "Trinidad was well represented" but the "messianic movement of Uriah Butler, already dissolving into confusion, was excluded," as was the Barbados party led by W. A. Crawford, and "no one had been invited from the French and American colonies." At the CLC council in

Antigua in 1947, Hart officially became the chief executive of the organization, and the ranks were broadened as Crawford came on board; representatives of the French colonies and Puerto Rico were invited "but did not respond. No representatives came from Suriname . . . it is probable that the letters to Puerto Rico were intercepted by American authorities," thought Hart. "A reply was received from the Communist Party of Martinique but they were not then interested in participation as their policy was then one of 'assimilation' with France. The Socialist Party in Martinique did not even apply. No reply was received from Guadeloupe and here again interference with the mail" was "suspected."

Despite these setbacks, the very organization of the CLC was a step forward for the region. "The first official conference on federation of the [British West Indies] and British Guiana [was] convened by the Secretary of State for the Colonies"—said London's man—and "was held in Jamaica shortly after the CLC 1947 Congress." This was the beginning of London's successful crusade to "wean" the region "away from the CLC line and [obtain] . . . approval for a federal constitution which differed materially from the CLC's proposals." By 1948, one of the CLC's founding fathers, Grantley Adams of Barbados, turned to the right and renounced his former alliance with the left, which was a wicked blow to the organization's fortunes. CLC persevered, however, but by the time of the toppling of Jagan in 1953, the organization's initial promise had dimmed significantly.[59]

Yet Jagan eventually did come to power, albeit after the collapse of the Soviet Union when the possibility of realizing his most radical dreams had diminished. The relatively tiny nations in the Caribbean basin found it difficult to stand up to the major powers, notably London and Washington. Still, the legacy left by the CLC was nearly unique on a global scale in that there are few regions on this planet where leaders of labor played such a huge role. Though trained as a dentist, Jagan was a union leader, as were the founding fathers of virtually all of the nations within the former British West Indies. Even those who were to the right of the CLC in the aftermath of the bitter split in its ranks—such as Norman Manley of Jamaica, who sided with Adams—were Social Democrats. Then there were the unrequited radicals like Richard Hart and Ferdinand Smith, both of Jamaica, who never renounced their core left-wing beliefs. This was nothing new in that the earliest black members of the U.S. Communist Party were disproportionately from the Caribbean basin. The cosmopolitanism induced in part by a culture of migration, combined with the harsh conditions in the region, all contributed to a culture that created tropical radicals—radicals like Cheddi Jagan, who was deposed unceremoniously in 1953.

The scholar Constance Sutton is largely correct in asserting that "more than in most world regions, labour and the control over labour has shaped the contours of Caribbean societies." It "has been the defining element and main player in Caribbean struggles for freedom and equality."[60] It remains true that "just as the black church provided black political leadership in the United States, so did the trade union movement provide political leadership in the Commonwealth Caribbean."[61] The British West Indies, consequently, was a transmission belt for labor radicalism to Harlem—as exemplified by the life of Ferdinand Smith— and to the United States as a whole.

These labor radicals in turn became the primary victims when the Cold War took hold in the Hot Zone that was the British West Indies. Nevertheless, the bold radicalism of the region meant that Washington had to devote consider- able time and attention to this region—particularly in the runup to Jagan's ouster in 1953—which could have been directed elsewhere. Thus, despite its relatively small size, the British West Indies did not play a tiny role as the Cold War was launched.

CHAPTER 1

Early Organizing

A S EVIDENCED BY THE COMING to power of the radical Cheddi
Jagan in 1953, British Guiana had long been in the vanguard of the
movement in the former British West Indies for sovereignty and labor
rights. Thus it should not be overly surprising that Hubert Nathaniel Critchlow,
a man of African descent though indigenous to British Guiana, could well be
deemed the modern Father of Caribbean Labor.[1] The Caribbean Labour Congress (CLC) had its origins in the "First British Guiana and West Indies Labour
Conference," hosted by him in 1926.[2] Born in 1884 and deceased by 1958,
Critchlow was an "excellent singer" and often captivated the assembled by croon-
ing hymns at meetings.[3] He often wore a suit and cap, "except on May Day when
he wore a red shirt and white trousers." He passed on his belief in trade unionism to his children, which included three sons, two of them becoming active
trade unionists in their own right.[4]

But what set Critchlow apart was not his velvet voice or his sartorial splen-
dor but his devotion to the working class. With the waterfront workers in the
forefront, he founded an omnibus union in British Guiana in the aftermath of
World War I; by some accounts "he became in the Colonial World the first professional trade unionist," earning a paltry $20 per month. In its first year the
union had 13,000 members, but what distinguished this body was its militancy.
Critchlow was "committed to the socialist ideal" and it was he who introduced
the term "Comrade" after his return from the Soviet Union, just as his penchant
for red clothing emerged during this journey. He was at the founding of the left-
led World Federation of Trade Unions (WFTU) in Paris in 1945—but also
attended the founding of its ideological polar opposite, the International Confederation of Free Trade Unions (ICFTU), in 1949. More important than any
of these gatherings was his organizing a conference of workers and unionists

from British Guiana and the region in January 1926 in Georgetown. Here he was "able to successfully cause the formation of a Caribbean Labour Movement—the B.G. and W.I. Labour Federation."[5]

Always "regionalist in his thinking," Critchlow was "responsible more than anyone else for the establishment of a Caribbean-wide labour movement. As early as 1920 he had invited West Indian delegates to a Labour Conference to be held under the auspices of the British Guiana Labour Union." Naturally, the press "viciously attacked him as a Bolshevik and from 1930 he began to speak in terms of socialism."[6]

At the WFTU founding, Critchlow explained how and why he took the lead in labor organizing. "As a boy I was an athlete," he said, then he "went to a foundry to learn engineering. But I left there and went to my uncle, who was manager of a cigar factory, which was worse. Seeing me on the wharf, Mr. Mackey, who was the manager, got me an all-round job. But the hours were long and I began to want to know why we, who worked hardest, could not knock off at four o'clock like the Europeans. Because," said this budding sports star, "I wanted to get to my cricket and running." Management ignored him—but his fellow workers did not; "the people began to listen to me," he said, referring to his reasoned arguments. "On April 5th, 1919, I called a mass meeting for the eight hour day. I was arrested because I gave out a handbill with a verse from the 'Marseillaise' [the rousing French anthem] and was charged with sedition." In response, "between then and January 1st, 1920 we gathered 13,000 members and [placed] $9700 in the bank . . . between 1919 and 1930 I roped in nearly the whole country, every estate, and I had to travel night and day to keep in touch."[7]

Critchlow learned a crucial lesson from this early experience, which underscored the necessity for a Caribbean Labour Congress—lessons he articulated at the 1947 meeting of the CLC itself. For "when the British Guiana movement fought for the eight-hour day, the shippers of that colony brought waterfront workers from Trinidad and Barbados to discharge the ships." Now, said Critchlow, "if there was better communication between the waterfront workers of the different islands, that would not have happened."[8]

Critchlow may also have been inspired by his attendance at the summer 1925 confab of the "First British Commonwealth Labour Conference" in London's House of Commons, where he was the only delegate from the Caribbean. There he laid out the region's grievances and hastened the day when sovereignty and labor rights would arrive. "The franchise" in British Guiana, he complained, "was based entirely on property qualification," and "for a man to be able to sit in the Court of Policy he had to possess property worth 5000 dollars." At this juncture, his union "had only a financial membership of 1100," and though he insisted that "they did not pay much attention in his country to the question of color," it was apparent that fissures between African and South Asian workers were hampering unionism. Critchlow disagreed, arguing that "it was the capitalists" that "raised the colour question when they wanted to create dissension amongst the workers." Yet it was at this august gathering that Critchlow announced that "the East Indian labourers were rather a menace to the other workers of the country," since supposedly they were "willing to work cheaper than the colored man"—a point that did not augur well for labor unity and, in a sense, paved the way for Critchlow's future marginalization and the rise of the "East Indian," Cheddi Jagan. All of Critchlow's points concerning ruptures among labor were not misguided, for he also stressed that unions "had to contend with a certain section of white labour. On one occasion they had a general strike, but the white men jumped in and worked the electric cars. They were not blacklegs but whitelegs," he said sarcastically amidst an eruption of laughter. Moreover, "the coloured militia did the same." Strikingly, "when there was a strike" and "they appealed to the English seamen they found that they were always willing to give assistance, but it was different with the men on the Canadian boats."[9]

His militancy notwithstanding, Critchlow's apparent animus to his "East Indian" compatriots was not without consequence. As the scholar and activist Walter Rodney put it, "the two main groups of involuntary immigrants—African and Indian—having arrived at different times, had developed competing interests," and Critchlow's rhetoric was not helpful in bridging this gap. Afro-Guyanese, said Rodney, "displayed the same animus towards all labor competitors, irrespective of whether they were Hindus, 'Bajans' or islanders from elsewhere in the West Indies. Nevertheless, the prejudice against Barbadians virtually disappeared over a period of time," but the same could not be said of those from India. Inevitably, "planters took advantage of the possibilities of manipulating racial separation or tension between Africans and Indians" to the detriment of both.[10] Ironically, Forbes Burnham, the pre-eminent leader of the nation that came to be known as Guyana, had roots in Barbados yet was accused repeatedly of stoking "racial separation."

London was becoming increasingly concerned about the ability of labor organizers and radicals to meet in its own backyard. A few years after Critchlow's sojourn in London, an "International Trade Union Conference of Negro Workers" was being planned there. This meeting raised the probability of further contact between West Indian unionists and their African American counterparts, not to mention allowing the exploited from Brazil, Haiti, Cuba, and Colombia to compare notes. William Patterson, the fiery black communist who was later to lead the campaign to save the Scottsboro defendants falsely accused of raping two white women, reminded Whitehall that "approximately 85 million of the 150 million Negroes in the world inhabit those regions over which His Britannic Majesty's Government holds economic and political sway" and that "forced labor as a means of securing native labor power still obtains" there. This, he said, was "closely analogous to slavery, while in some instances remnants of slavery itself are still in existence." The "specific purpose" of this transnational organizing of black labor was "to link up the movement of the Negro workers nationally and internationally."[11] Aghast, London noted that this meeting was "being organized under Communist influence & is intended to be productive of subversive movements in [the] British [Empire],"[12] but it thought better of banning the event, observing that "if we don't let them meet here they may meet somewhere else—probably Moscow."[13]

Though Critchlow and his native British Guiana may have been premature in its labor organizing and militancy, soon it was not alone, not least due to efforts such as Patterson's. Between 1918 and 1924, Jamaica, British Honduras, St. Lucia, St. Kitts, Anguilla, and Tortola, among other territories, "experienced strikes and disturbances." This time frame was not accidental in that the aftermath of world war had much to do with this unrest. Thus, "ex-servicemen in Trinidad were affected by news of racial attacks on veterans in Liverpool and Cardiff in June 1919 and near-pogroms in many U.S. cities," which "left hundreds of black people dead." Similarly, the Bolshevik Revolution created tremendous ripples and an early attractiveness of Communist parties, as Critchlow's early career exemplified.[14]

In Barbados, the "Workingmen's Association" (WMA), the "industrial wing of the Democratic League," was founded in 1926. The WMA worked together with Marcus Garvey's forces during the early 1930s to the point where, according to the scholar Hilary Beckles, the Garveyites had "temporarily taken over leadership of the workers' movement."[15] No doubt inspired by the dual jolts of war and revolution, it was in 1919 that stevedores in Trinidad shook colonialism by striking.[16]

Still, at times it seemed that the authorities were more exercised by the rise of Garvey than of Lenin. Certainly that was the import of the "secret" message from the governor of British Honduras to the secretary of state for the colonies in 1920. Striking a repetitive theme, he was gravely concerned with how Garveyism, refracted through the prism of the United States, might influence the Caribbean basin. Apprehension was expressed about the "status of the West Indian Protective Society of America" (WIPSA). Their "attitude," he announced worriedly, "in some directions, is born of race prejudice, so rampant in the United States against the Negro. It is possible that the whole movement underlying the Universal Negro Association and African Communities League was originated by German propaganda and money, and probably is still supported by German Americans." Yet, as worrisome as the apparition of Berlin was, there was something even more troublesome to this colonial bureaucrat. "One danger in the Colony," he said of this territory on the Central American isthmus, "is the fact that cut off as we are from any direct connection or communication with any British possession, the sympathies and connections of the Negro population are to a very large extent American. They look on New Orleans and New York as the great centres of civilization; and look at political questions mainly from the aspect of the American Negro."[17]

Though WIPSA was viewed negatively by this bureaucrat, this group's leader was closer to London than might have been realized, for he too blamed "recent bloody strikes in Trinidad" on Garveyites. Though the stevedores' job action in Trinidad had all the earmarks of Bolshevik influence, with its invocation of working-class radicalism, WIPSA's executive secretary was of a different opinion. "I am calling the attention of the several consuls of the United States," he told London, to this alleged baneful influence from the north, "to the end that they might scrutinize all coloured persons applying to them for passports to the British possessions with a view of finding out if they are members or stock holders, readers or subscribers to . . . [Garvey's] 'Negro World.' "[18]

There was a certain contagion in the region as the spark of labor organizing tended to spread from territory to territory from the northern tip of South America to the eastern coast of Central America. Ultimately, this trend settled on tiny St. Kitts, with a contemporary population of less than 40,000. By 1932 the Workers' League was well under way and one reason was the visit of T. A. Marryshow of Grenada, whose "lecture at the Apollo" was deemed a rousing "success."[19] Labor in St. Kitts also consulted with A. A. Cipriani of Trinidad, the leading figure on that island.[20] Though ostensibly isolated in the eastern Caribbean, with miles of open sea separating them from their nearest neighbors, workers in St. Kitts managed to stay in touch with others in the region—and beyond. Early in 1933 the Workers' League was instructed by their counterparts in equally minuscule St. Vincent that "a branch of the West Indian National League was organizing in British Guiana and asking what was being done at our end." This was then "discussed," followed by a "motion that the political organization of all islands of the Eastern Caribbean be approached with the object of forwarding a united petition to the Colonial Office praying for Constitutional Reform." But this estimable gesture, strikingly, "found no seconder"—and immediately spoken of was the "desirability of the members of the League being encouraged to read the newspapers as a means to educating them and arousing their interest along political lines."[21]

As the Great Depression began to bite in the hemisphere in 1933, the Workers' League received two letters. "[O]ne was from the Committee of the Negro Workers Trade Union of New York and the other from Mr. Harold Wilson of the 'Antigua Magnet' announcing the good tiding that an organization had been started at Antigua known as 'the Antigua Workingmen's Association,'" which "was received with general expressions of pleasure." But the Workers' League remained "cautious" about the former group due to its alleged "strong communistic tendency," though they were in touch with the "League of Coloured People" of London, which was accused of similar tendencies.[22]

In the mid-1930s, unrest was to blossom in St. Vincent and St. Lucia, then Trinidad and the entire region. As this tumult approached, a delegation from the British Labour Party gave a glimpse as to why this turmoil was to unfold. From Antigua came the report that the "field work of labourers" did "involve harder and heavier physical labour than is demanded in St. Kitts or Barbados," which were not known to be worker havens either. The "wages" were "lower" in Antigua too, as this island was deemed "more poverty stricken than that of Barbados," and the "housing [was] extremely bad."[23]

Despite this dire situation, as Labour saw it, organizing was tepid. There was a "Trinidad Working Men's Association" and a "Labour Party" led by A. A. Cipriani, but he was "absolutely king of the movement" and the organization, as a result, was shallow. "If 'the captain' "—as he was called—"were removed, I do not see anyone who could take his place," said Labour's representative. Typically, Grenada was seen as more advanced, with a "really good party," while nearby there was a "very weak St. Vincent Working Men's Association. I am quite sure," it was reported, "it has no real contact with the masses or any influence over them. In St. Lucia I found one good comrade" and "at Antigua I found a very small Working Men's Association" but a "fairly large (800 members) and very interesting Friendly Society" that "sprang spontaneously from the people." But there was one constant that augured for change: Throughout the region "the interest taken in the Abyssinian question" was "very great," though "education" was "excessively backward."

But there was another sign of something new. In October 1934 there were "riots" in St. Vincent that kicked off a wave of unrest.[24] A "deputation of strikers came to see me today demanding double wages," said the governor a year later; yes, they were "orderly"—at least so far—but not reassuring was that the "ringleaders" were "men with criminal records. I am continuing to maintain precautions against sabotage," he added forlornly. He "declared a state of emergency which will be maintained until [the] strike is over."[25] A few days later the "Commander in Chief, America & West Indies" remained worried, though it was "all quiet" in St. Vincent and the "strike" in St. Lucia continued with "no disorders." He was worried especially since there were "48 police in St. Vincent and 60 in St. Lucia, which appears to be barely adequate for normal duties."[26] As his subsequent peregrinations were to reveal, Sir Cosmo Parkinson was most concerned about an event in St. Lucia planned for 2 November 1935, sponsored by Garveyites, whereby "Negroes [were] invited to attend the fifth anniversary of the Coronation of the Emperor Haile Selassie," and "a silver collection will be taken," it was added.[27] Concerned about the implications of such potentially explosive activity, the authorities "emphasized the undesirability of fomenting racial animosity" and sought to steer their efforts toward the "laudable object of raising funds for [the] Red Cross and ambulance work in Abyssinia."[28]

Writing from the commodious Governor House in St. Lucia, Sir Cosmo Parkinson's interlocutor remained concerned when he "heard that special meetings over this Italy/Abyssinia business here were being staged over the weekend." So he "chartered a small motor vessel, 'an ex rum runner,' " to explore the island further. He "purposely staged an official landing, which," he said, "had its effect and the following morning I had conversations with the local orators and the editors of the two local papers" and was "subsequently told that the situation had cleared." Then, "all of a sudden"—as if the workers decided to accord him a proper greeting—"everybody working on unloading the coal suddenly struck." That was eventually settled, then this unnamed bureaucrat "promised to go to a concert got up by some local African society for the benefit of Red Cross work in Abyssinia," but he continued feeling unsettled. "[A]part from Baynes . . . and my Police Officers and myself, the Chairman, who is a member of the Legislative Council, was the only white man in the crowded hall" where passions already ran high because of Italian aggression in an Ethiopia that historically held a dear place in the hearts of Africans globally.

His unease continued when he met with strike leaders that included an "ex BWI soldier with a thoroughly bad record" and, he added dismissively, "an ex-prize fighter who is at present out of prison on ticket of leave." Thoroughly unimpressed, he asserted that "some of the remarks addressed to me might well have been made by a Communist agitator in England." In Castries, St. Lucia, and Kingstown, St. Vincent, he was "quite convinced that there has been some subversive influence at work which has taken advantage of the intense racial feeling engendered by the Italy/Abyssinia war." Precisely, who was the culprit? "The notorious Marcus Garvey," he said, "whom I thought to be thoroughly discredited is again much to the fore. The St. Lucians have enlisted in his latest organization . . . [and] receive his literary productions."[29] But Sir Cosmo's colleague was not without proposed remedies. As he saw it, "the administration of St. Lucia has been too much influenced by the landlord class and that our one hope of stable condition in this and other islands is the creation of a much larger peasant proprietor class."[30]

It might have helped as well if London had paid more attention to the professed cause of this conflict—the plight of the workers. Coal workers received "metal discs as evidence of the number of loaded baskets of coal carried by them," which could be "exchanged for money" and could also be "accepted in payment for drink or provisions supplied to the workers by local shops." And, yes, they could also be used "for the purchase of rum," not a negligible consideration for the most unscrupulous among the ruling elite. Inexorably, the workers wanted a raise—in real money. But the authorities remained seized not by the legitimacy of the workers' demands but the alleged manipulators of the workers. "The main speakers on behalf of the strikers," it was reported, "was a man who had apparently been in Cuba for some years and who attracted my attention by phrases which showed that he had been influenced by Communistic propaganda." The existence of "bitter racial animosity" was acknowledged, which existed in "St. Lucia to a marked degree and must necessarily be a potent source of danger." The "sullen hostility" that graced the visages of the workers was not soothing, nor were "the obscene threats against whites in general which have been used to [intimidate] residents of long standing in this Island and the fact that anonymous threats against the 'whites', the police and all who side with the 'whites' have been sent to a well-known sergeant of the constabulary is significant. One of these documents ended with the words, 'Hail Selassie our King,'" which was notably disconcerting. With sobriety, London's man concluded, "My anxiety about the future would be less if I had not formed the opinion that there is some organization of definitely subversive character at work in these islands," suggesting that the "possibility of open disorder, in any of the smaller islands, where the police force is inadequate, will remain."[31]

It wasn't just presumed communists, actual Garveyites, and nascent Rastafarians that were making for sleepless nights in London. In St. Vincent, S. M. Grier complained of the "unwise speeches" of the bishop of the Windward Islands, who was "most imprudent in his last farewell speech" with his "impetuous verbosity." This audacious cleric "boasted of the fact that he was a politician and then gave it as his opinion that any Priest who was not a politician was not worth his salt. He then proceeded to inform his audience that he was a fighter and that any time he wanted anything he fought for it," and he "advised the St. Vincentians that they must fight for what they wanted." Again, a distinction was drawn between what was allowed in London and what was allowed elsewhere in the Empire, particularly in the West Indies; democracy was acceptable for the former but not the latter. "This sort of stuff may be quite harmless when spoken to an English audience," Grier huffed, "but it is not suitable for a St. Vincentian audience at a time when racial feeling is running high." Also worthy of note was the presence on the island of a "mysterious alien who has been particularly active in these islands and on whom no proper check was kept."[32]

Exasperated, the authorities chose to squash this unrest. There had been "rioting" in St. Vincent that was "serious," and "seven rioters were shot before order was restored," said one colonial official. The HMS *Dundee* steamed to the island, though it was troubling that "few of the coloured population removed their hats on the arrival of His Excellency." After this was "remarked on," it was reported that "under normal conditions the population were most punctilious in removing their hats," which made this incipient display of sedition even more troubling.[33]

No doubt this incipient sedition would persist as long as the de facto "wage of a penny a basket" was "paid to coal workers unloading ships."[34] Finally, by the end of 1935 a kind of quiet had descended on St. Lucia. Detectives had been dispatched from Barbados but they "failed to discover anything of much value"— not necessarily because nothing was going on but because they were "under the great handicap of not being able to talk the French patois which is virtually the language of St. Lucia."[35]

However, events in another French-inflected island—Trinidad— provided the kind of proliferating contagion that was characteristic of the region's history. This vanguard role of Trinidad was shocking in a sense in that there was an early spate of labor organizing in 1929 spawned by Hubert Carrington and Helena Manuel, who were "living together" at the time and formed a "trade union centre" that, in essence, was "not a bona fide trade union in any sense of the word"— or so thought British unionists. "It will accept anyone who will pay a few contribution[s]," it was said, and "its few officials are almost all people who have been expelled from the Trinidad Workingmen's Association for monetary irregularities. Hubert Carrington has been convicted six times for petty swindles and assaulting the police. His general record is bad. He has got money from people, professing to tell fortunes on some system of Negro 'Black Magic.'"[36] Actually, the idea of a union as a business or fraud was not unique to Trinidad. It was common in the region and was an early barrier to successful labor organizing as workers had to be convinced that this time they would not be swindled.

Yet Trinidad and its twin island of Tobago not only had the sugar fields that characterized the region, but they also had ample oil and gas reserves, the energy that would be needed desperately as the war machine geared up in the perilous 1930s. Trinidad and Tobago "produced some 62.8% of the British Empire's refined oil, it also produced 25% of the aviation fuel required by the Royal Air Force" if it were to have a wisp of a chance of defeating the German air corps.[37] Thus it was in 1937 that the Oil Field Workers Trade Union, what Jamaica's *Daily Gleaner* later characterized as "the single largest proletarian grouping in the West Indies," called a strike. This strike was symbolized by one man, Tubal Uriah "Buzz" Butler, born in Grenada in 1897, a war veteran who served London in North Africa, then decamped to Trinidad and Tobago in 1921.[38] He was a powerfully built man of medium height, dark-skinned with a generous beard and an even more generous head of hair; this head sat on a massive neck that, in turn, rested upon thick-set shoulders. He possessed a powerful vibrant voice of great emotional intensity, a booming baritone that could be heard over great distances—no small factor when public address systems were not commonplace. He was a master showman and psychologist, always commencing his meetings with "Lead Kindly Light," often with a Bible in hand. During tense moments he was liable to raise his hand and ask for prayer, to be followed by mass signing of a hymn. His meetings manifested certain characteristics of Father Divine, the charismatic preacher who at that precise moment was riveting attention in Harlem—which may not have been accidental given the back-and-forth between the Caribbean and New York. He caught the popular imagination of the Trinidad and Tobago public, much after the fashion of a romantic knight of previous centuries. His followers were not only in the oil fields but also amongst the peasantry.[39] Yet Butler had an indelible anticommunist streak that hampered the ability to build labor unity in the region.

An oil worker himself, Butler was injured in 1929, which left him permanently lame. He first came into prominence in 1935—just as strife was percolating in St. Vincent and St. Lucia—when he organized and led to Port-of-Spain a hunger march of some 120 men. In 1936, following his expulsion from Captain Cipriani's Labour Party, he formed a party of his own known as the British Empire Workers and Citizens Home Rule Party, which by the 1940s claimed to have about 100 paying members and 900 others. He struck fear in colonial bureaucrats.

This was not surprising, for the conditions that workers and peasants alike were compelled to endure was no prize, and it was still that way a decade after Butler was catapulted into prominence and had forced concessions from the authorities. Though this Caribbean island—like its counterparts—was routinely thought of as a lush paradise in London and elsewhere, actually workers usually lived in shacks, often with two families sharing a single room. It was not unusual for a family of ten to be crowded into a single squalid room in a wooden hovel with a tin roof. Living conditions were so grim and overcrowding so intense that even the colony's fiercest critics were pushed to concede that prison cells where three thrust into a space designed for one were a vast improvement over these shacks.[40] This gave an added jolt to workers' desperation and militancy, as prison held no terror.

Indeed, conditions were so desperate in this nation that it should not come as a surprise that organizing came well before the era of Butler. As in Georgetown, stevedores in Port-of-Spain were pioneers in this regard, with Charles Phillip leading a strike there in December 1905. And even as early as 1844, in the aftermath of slavery's abolition in 1838, there were "attempts at organizing workers in a trade union in Trinidad" when a "freed slave by the name of Charles McKay led 600 fellow labourers on the banks of the Couva River with the formation of the Trinidad Free Labourers's Society."[41]

As ever, within Trinidad and Tobago there was a struggle within the struggle. Being a diverse society, this nation featured a number of leaders—besides Butler—who were politicized. There was the heroic Elma Francois of the Negro Welfare Cultural and Social Association, who paved the way for accelerated labor organizing in Trinidad. There was Adrian Cola Rienzi, for example, born in 1905, widely regarded as "Trinidad's first Communist." Born as Krishna Denarine, he changed his name "after the hero of the same name who had staged a successful revolution in Italy in May 1437."[42] As the Barbados activist Wynter Crawford recalled him, "his father was a white man" and his "mother was Indian." He was associated at one point with Ireland's Sinn Fein, indicative of his militancy.[43]

According to a colleague, he changed his name "to gain easier acceptance in the United States where he had planned to go. This is understandable," according to the writer Brinsley Samaroo, "for as late as the thirties, a Hindu name in Trinidad or elsewhere in the western world was a sure means of personal derogation and refusal of even one's legitimate privileges." Whatever the case, the farsighted Rienzi was an early advocate not only of labor rights but its twin, sovereignty, as he clamored for "the idea of a federation of the British West Indies" and "saw federation as the logical development of working class unity." He worked closely with Butler in organizing both oil and sugar workers, though Samaroo blames Trinidad and Tobago's perennial—a "racial split"—for ultimately driving him out of the movement.[44] Yet during his heyday, he symbolized a militancy that was widely influential since it was manifested among the strategically significant workers of the oil fields. These laborers "used to wear a special black shirt uniform," recalled Wynter Crawford, "and he used to drill them every afternoon with military precision" as "they used broom-sticks like guns, marching like soldiers. The British were a bit afraid of them."[45]

Then there was the aforementioned A. A. Cipriani, born in 1875 into a "white creole family of Corsican descent," a reflection of the nation's historic ties to France. His family included leading landowners and businessmen, but he earned his spurs among the Africans when, while serving with a British regiment during World War I, "he was able to defend the black soldiers against discrimination."[46] Arthur Andrew Cipriani was "below middle height" and "very solidly built" with a "big fleshy, clean-shaven face" and eyes of a "peculiar greenish colour." His martial mien was maintained by his preference for khaki suits of "military cut, brown boots and a white helmet." Yet when traveling to London he would "don the regulation tweeds." This quiet man spoke with a drawl, though he excelled as an orator, often delivering stem-winding perorations without the benefit of one note. Perhaps religion explained why he opposed divorce.[47] He never was able to jettison all of his class accoutrements, as his "hobbies were cocoa-planting and horse-racing."[48] But he was sufficiently militant to have a "long talk with the Secretary of State" in London, informing him in June 1937 that he "felt that Trinidad got too little out of oil."[49] Similarly, as early as 1932 he was arguing that the "movement towards Federation . . . like the incoming tide, has gathered strength at every turn. It may now be regarded as inevitable."[50] The representative of Britain's Labour Party, in a "strictly private and confidential" message, asserted, "I think Captain Cipriani rather over-estimates the maturity of any movement for political federation of the West Indian colonies," since he underplayed "inter-colonial rivalry and inter-colonial differences." But Cipriani bluntly disagreed.[51]

As evidenced by the pre-eminent presence of Butler and Francois (of African descent), Rienzi (of South Asian descent) and Cipriani (of Corsican origins), Trinidad and Tobago exhibited a diversity in leadership second to none—which makes their pioneering role in the labor unrest of 1937, in a sense, all the more surprising. For it was a colonial official writing from Government House in August 1937 who remarked—seemingly without a tinge of regret—that the "most marked feature of Trinidad's social order is the sharply defined colour bar. The whites, including the near white Creoles"—the group that was said to include Cipriani—"keep themselves fastidiously aloof from the Negroes and East Indians." Though Cipriani was viewed sympathetically among the masses of Trinidad and Tobago, this official was less positive, averring that he was, "as I see him . . . a lonely and a rather pathetic figure. He, a white man, has thrown in his lot with colour. He leads Negro and East Indian labour, and he is the only white man in the Municipal Council of Port-of-Spain. He is therefore an outcaste." It was "alleged that Cipriani is corrupt where money is concerned" though "he lives in a most frugal manner, and is a teetotaler and non-smoker and . . . is chronically hard up." He was a "ready and fluent speaker but he is no orator, and he relies for his effect upon a spate of words and a truculent tone rather than upon reasoned argument." As this official saw it, "the secret of Cipriani's influence, lies not so much in any personal ability, as in the color of his skin. The Negro community is still permeated with the stagnation of the old slave mentality," he thought, "and the East Indians have retrogressed in sympathy. Labour, formerly accustomed to cringe before the white slave-driver, found in their strong and forceful white champion as it were a demi-god," but now "they are beginning to find that their idol has feet of clay." For now, as a result of his conflict with Butler, "the workers in the oilfields repudiate Cipriani and will have nothing to do with his Labour Party" and "his star is definitely waning." Almost giddy, the official added, "Trinidad holds that it has nothing to gain by federation, and much to lose, and the movement has no support here."[52]

The disparagement of Cipriani was a reflection of the fact that he "must be considered the first true Trinidad and West Indian socialist," a man—it was thought—who spelled doom for the amassers of excess wealth. He was also involved with worker organizing, and "the real growth of socialism in the West Indies started with the trade unions."[53]

In part, these colonials were whistling past the graveyard, trying to reassure themselves—in the face of evidence to the contrary—that all was well. For a few weeks before this analysis, a police officer in Fyzabad, in the heart of the oil belt, provided a clearer picture of what was developing. It was mid-June 1937 and darkness had descended. The hall was crowded with 300 people straining to get seats. Butler's words were not at all reassuring. "The signal for the strike," he said, "will be a big oilfield [fire]." Why such bold tactics? "All is fair in war," he thought, "there will be a hell of a . . . fire right round the oilfields," "houses will be burnt down," and "we are going to set up a new Jerusalem." Mixing his religious imagery liberally with current political concerns, he too sought to capitalize upon the conflict raging in Africa, asserting ominously that "the Abyssinians are taking the Italians' arms. We have no guns or bullets, so we must take example."[54] Repeatedly, Butler stressed that "your conditions are like slavery and we are prepared to fight like hell." "We have no fear," he emphasized, and "they could call it Sedition if they like," for he thought it was the "fascist imperialist" that was "sinking us into slavery." "Let the police arrest me," he cried. "I am prepared to die."[55]

Though willing to assist in fulfilling his latter musing, London hardly desired to confront militant oil workers with arms in hand led by a charismatic and messianic Butler. The officials' opinion of him quickly soured. One official had spoken to Peter Bushnell who "told me as follows. 'I know Butler since he was a boy in Grenada. We played cricket together and we even went to the last war together, he is the third child of a mother of six children and he is the only one who was sent to the asylum, he sucked mad milk and he is mad.'"[56] Another who knew Butler in Grenada recalled that when he returned from the war, "he organized a gang [there]" and "their activities were famous," though "after a while the activities of this gang broke up and the members traveled to different countries," namely Trinidad. He concurred that "Butler is insane." After all, his "sister-Adina Butler" had been committed to a mental hospital, so it ran in the family.[57]

Certainly Butler's militancy seemed mad to many in London. "If we are British subjects, we must enjoy British rights," he insisted in 1937, which included the right to organize. "Do you know a few weeks ago that black rig[-]men were laid off at the Leaseholds Company and white boys were taken on, boys who do not know need, who were never hungry; and starving black men who have nowhere to lay their heads were turned away; and starving black men who have nowhere to lay their heads were turned away." Perhaps worse, the colonials were "draining all the oil and riches of your country," he told the oil workers, "and putting it into foreign countries." Striking a nerve, he added that "we are more slaves than our forefathers owing to the high standard of living today." Then one of his comrades added threateningly that labor's leaders "have failed with white leaders and that it is time to follow their own race."[58] Perhaps he was referring to Cipriani, but even the esteemed Captain, after a "long talk with the Secretary of State," acknowledged that Trinidad's benefit from a lush oil industry was nominal.[59]

This Garveyite and black nationalist appeal was potently combined with the new internationalism that focused on Ethiopia. At one gathering of oil workers, a representative from the Negro Welfare Association of Port-of-Spain read a letter from the International Committee of Negro Workers, who wanted "you all as workers and Negroes of this community to support us in passing a resolution that no part of Africa in possession of the British Empire, be given to Germany." But this speaker, identified as "Comrade Ashby," "referred at length to the Abyssinian and Italian war, also to the Spanish war."[60] Once Caribbean workers began taking on a global perspective, they could not help but wonder why a tiny island nation off the coast of Europe should control their region and so much else.

Many Trinidadian workers had come to see that their exploitation was not altogether unique. At the same time they could hardly ignore the specificity of their own exploitation. Most could not purchase a bicycle and, thus, "had to walk distances of from five to eight miles to get home" from work. "Squalor, prostitution and hooliganism" were the three horses of the apocalypse with which they had to contend. They were treated with utter "contempt" by "members of the managerial staff" in the oil fields, "a number of whom were recruited from South Africa."[61]

Finally, the authorities had had enough and determined that any protest of the status quo was verboten. On 19 June 1937, warrants were issued for the arrest of Butler "on charges of using violent language," and "it was the attempt to arrest Butler on the evening of the 19th June," said a colonial bureaucrat later,

"that caused the immediate outbreak of the riots," uproarious disorder that
shook the nation. Butler was arrested, tried, and "found guilty of sedition and
sentenced to two years' imprisonment." Again in 1939 he was detained as he
was perceived to represent a "danger of dislocation to the oil industry" and
"finally released in April 1945."[62] But as the Trinidadian Joseph Richards put it,
"Comrade Butler . . . invented a new electricity called 'the electricity fever' and
in 1937 when he pressed the button, Grenada, St. Vincent, Barbados and the
whole of Trinidad"—not to mention the entire region—"received the shock."[63]

CHAPTER 2

Big Islands/Big Problems

"THE WEST INDIES COLONIES with which we are in touch by correspondence," said the International Department of the British labor movement in July 1938, "are practically confined to three—Trinidad, Jamaica and British Guiana. Trade union development," it was added not inaccurately, "is naturally most advanced in Trinidad."[1]

Obviously, it would have been preferable for British labor to be in touch with every nation in the region, as St. Lucia and St. Vincent had demonstrated that disturbances among workers were not limited to the "Big Three" of the region. Yet if resources were limited, it is understandable why these three nations would be the focus, for Jagan's rise clearly showed that Georgetown was a locus of radicalism; Butler's activism and the presence of strategically important oil fields demonstrated that paying insufficient attention to Port-of-Spain made little or no sense. But it was Jamaica that was the most populous nation in the former British West Indies and it was Jamaica that contained the precious deposits of bauxite and the location near the most populous nation in the Caribbean—Cuba—that guaranteed careful scrutiny.[2]

The Jamaican Marcus Garvey, whose organization and words had inspired a good deal of the disquiet regionally, in the spring of 1938 told the secretary of state for the colonies directly that "it may be stated very frankly that Governors in Jamaica do not understand the situation of the common people," for there were "more than seventy per cent of Jamaicans unemployed" in this "island Poor House." It was, he spat out, a "country of social inhumanity where the class that is above shows absolutely no interest in the class below."[3]

Garvey had taken notice of an extraordinary upsurge of labor activism in the region that had both presaged and fed into the electrifying events in Trinidad in 1937 and similarly jolting events that were to occur in Jamaica in 1938. This was why the *Negro Worker*, for which Trinidad's George Padmore toiled—and thus was pored over avidly by the Colonial Office—termed "1937 a new year of struggle for the West Indian masses." It was "glorious" in that "never before within modern times did the discontent of the West Indian masses assume such forms." There was a "strike of plantation workers in St. Kitts in the early part of 1936," while "several cocoa plantations in Trinidad went on strike" as "the workers burned two plantations to the ground. They were savagely attacked by the armed forces of the island." There were also "splendid demonstrations of unemployed as well as the Ex-Servicemen" and a "revolt of the unemployed in St. Vincent" in which "thousands" participated. The "marines were landed and opened fire on the unarmed masses. Five workers were shot dead, eight were wounded." For the future, exhorted this journal, labor should raise "the right of the people to elect their own candidates," as the right to organize merged almost effortlessly with the right to independence and sovereignty.[4]

Actually, driven by desperation, workers in the Caribbean were on the march in the 1930s. "The six year span 1934–1939 is indeed remarkable," asserts the scholar Francis Mark. "It began in 1934 with a sugar workers' strike in Trinidad. In 1935 there was an oil workers' strike and hung[er] march in Trinidad, a wharf labourers' strike in Jamaica, a sugar workers' strike in St. Kitts and British Guiana and St. Vincent. 1937 witnessed another oil workers' strike and general disturbances in Trinidad, a sugar workers' strike in St. Vincent and July disturbances in Barbados. In 1938 sugar workers and dockers went on strike in Jamaica," while "the disturbances at Leanora in British Guiana in February 1939 mark the end of this chronicle."[5]

The attention paid to the region by the *Negro Worker*, which had ties to the Communist International, indicated that that the triumph of the Bolshevik Revolution and the onset of the Great Depression were creating enormous opportunities for organizing labor. The theory emanating from Moscow held that the worker was paramount and that organizing this class should be a high priority. This message found a receptive ear in the Caribbean.

As it turned out, just as 1937 was a turning point for Trinidadian labor, the key year in Jamaica was 1938. That year, said the U.S. diplomat Hugh Watson, "saw the beginnings of changes in Jamaica more widespread in their ultimate effect than any that have occurred since the emancipation of the slaves one hundred years ago." What were these changes? "In brief," he said, "these were the birth of trade unionism, the commencement of an upward movement of the lower classes," and this all "sprang from the riots of last May."[6] That this occurred in Jamaica was bound to have impact on the rest of the British West Indies. The Trinidadian politician Albert Gomes once remarked that "perhaps because they occupy the largest of the islands, Jamaicans have always seemed rather superior in their attitude to other West Indians," and, he adds, "this feeling was not always without justification."[7] This was so because Jamaica's size and heft meant that it was easier for it to influence the other nations in the West Indies than vice versa.

Garvey had a point too—at least the Workers and Tradesmen Union of Montego Bay thought so. Shortly before his anguished protest, they complained that the "labourers of Westmoreland working on the estate of Messrs. Tate and Lyle [have] not been properly treated by their employers." Moreover, the police had just killed "six labourers of both sexes and more than fifty wounded and approximately one hundred arrested. . . . this meeting held in Montego Bay on this third day of May 1938 in the presence of over two thousand persons bitterly protest."[8] Often described as "riots," these forceful and militant labor protests forced to the forefront of Jamaican political consciousness the dueling cousins—the more progressive Norman Manley and the regressive though flamboyant Alexander Bustamante—who were to dominate politics on the island for decades to come.

George Padmore was of Trinidadian descent but even he recognized that "as bad as conditions" were in his homeland, "in Jamaica they [were] much worse, for unlike Trinidad with its petroleum and asphalt to supplement agriculture, Jamaica is entirely agrarian" in that the exploitation of bauxite deposits and the tourist industry were in their infancy in 1938. "In proportion to its size— 4450 square miles, Jamaica" was "more thickly populated than many European countries," and the agony of poverty was thus harder to hide. Movingly, Padmore noted that "things have gotten so bad that a short time ago hundreds of ragged men, women and children marched to the doors of the prison in Kingston, pleading for admittance, so that they might get food." Meanwhile, "the United Fruit Company of America, the Standard Fruit and Steamship Company and Elders and Fyfe Limited control the export market and dictate the price of bananas," and they profited handsomely. Workers were demanding an increase in wages from such giants, and they were met with cold police batons and hot lead. Hundreds had amassed and at least one old woman was bayoneted to death, which led to a familiar and time-honored tactic—setting the cane fields ablaze. Then a general strike hit Kingston. The governor of the island, Sir Edward Denham, notorious for his ruthless crushing of a seamen's strike in Gambia, transferred this approach to Jamaica. The British navy, whose mission was to intimidate in such a situation, steamed into the island.[9]

As so often happened in the region, a contagion was spreading, this time from Trinidad. Inspired by the example set by oil field workers, Jamaican workers were taking up the cudgels, and as a result, in the spring of 1938 Governor Denham noted almost casually that "four persons were killed (one of whom was a woman), while only [sic] nine were severely wounded" and "eight other persons received minor wounds."[10] The League of Coloured Peoples in London captured this tense moment in May 1938 when they met with high-level London officials. "They had followed carefully events in Trinidad and a similar state of affairs having occurred in Jamaica." There were "extremely bad conditions of labourers in Jamaica," it was reported, "where conditions, particularly as regards housing, resembled those in Trinidad." There were intensely "low rates of wages in Trelawney" that was like kindling just waiting to be ignited. "In view of what had happened in Trinidad," there was reason to believe that "there would be a similar outbreak in Jamaica," not to mention "British Guiana and possibly Sierra Leone." In other words, the contagion could press across the Empire.[11]

London had a problem. The flames of protest, buoyed by legitimate grievances about paltry wages, horrendous working conditions, and awful housing, were spreading like wildfire. "The only means of quelling them," the colonial secretary was told chillingly, "is by declaring open war on the rioters regardless of loss of life among them." It was conceded that "the labourer is made to feel that because he is black he is little better than an animal," which provided the colonials with a convenient rationale for slaughtering them correspondingly. Yes, said R. S. Peat, a Jamaican writing from the relatively safe distance of Aberdeen, it was shameful that in the British colonies one should be made to feel that it is a disgrace to be black and, he added pointedly as the colonized were about to be called upon to defend London itself against aggressors, "it is more shameful still that those of us who are coloured [are] made to feel in coming to England or Scotland that we are totally inferior." "In the event of war," he asked querulously, "how would Britain fare if her coloured population decided that 'niggers' are not wanted." There was "ignorance on the part of those in the country," referring to the United Kingdom, "who regard even cultured Jamaicans as 'natives' such as there are in the wilds of Africa." Moreover, though Tokyo inexorably would be a target of this forthcoming conflict, as Peat saw it, "the influx of Japanese goods [into Jamaica] was a boon to the poor who were then able to wear shoes and improve their general appearance." London did not win his amity when "Japanese goods" were "prohibited" and a "Buy British' campaign" was instituted. Jamaicans were being exploited shamelessly, he thought, since there were "labourers who walk approximately 15 miles daily to and from work and after working for some 10 hours in the boiling sun receive one shilling and sixpence." Illiteracy abounded as a result of British shenanigans, as "far too many" were "unable to read or write." Illnesses proliferated, with astronomical rates of tuberculosis and venereal disease, with "infant . . . mortality" rates jeopardizing generations to come. All this was occurring as "we are made to believe that it is the Americans who are colour prejudiced." This displacement was not minor since Washington would be needed ultimately to repel Tokyo; stirring sentiments against the United States was thus quite typical of London's misfeasance.[12]

Peat remained unmoved by London's pleas of fairness in the Caribbean. How could the United Kingdom "boast of 'British is best'" when "conditions of modern slavery" persisted in Jamaica. These conditions were such that "frankly," argued Peat, "I am ashamed to be British." The "riots" that were tearing his homeland apart were the "direct result" of "colour prejudice!" he exclaimed. For "during the years 1914–1928 Jamaicans to a man offered to fight for 'King and Country'. Conscription was not necessary." But times had changed and this could make the fate of the Empire itself more perilous. "Today, I am convinced," he insisted, "that Indians, Africans and West Indians would only be too glad to stand aloof in order to expose the folly of this underhand British prejudice in an empire which is made up of some 70% coloured peoples. Britain is fast becoming the laughingstock of the world" as a result, all to preserve the rampant privileges of "cane and banana companies that exploit cheap labour."[13]

London's ally-cum-rival in Washington was watching these developments with growing alarm. A sense was growing that the United Kingdom was not up to keeping a lid on a vast Empire, and, maybe, things would run more smoothly if London were to be replaced—say, by a budding North American superpower. Even before the 1938 eruption, in a "strictly confidential" missive, the State Department was concerned about the "smuggling of aliens into the United States from Kingston, Jamaica," not to mention the "smuggling of narcotics."[14]

Worse was the fact that there was "noticeable" in this capital city a "constant endeavor on the part of government officials—who are English not Jamaicans—through law, regulation and action to turn both thought and trade away from the United States and toward England." There was an "Empire Preference in trade," which gave a decided advantage to the British, and had a "distinct" and negative "effect upon American exports."[15]

A "serious handicap to the welfare of Jamaica," thought Washington's man, "lay in the extent to which benefit to English interests is given precedence over the interests of Jamaica . . . motor buses in Kingston are all to have 'British diesels', a restriction which can be of no possible benefit to the people of Jamaica." There was a strict "monopoly or extreme advantage to one English firm or group of firms." Thus, a "practical monopoly of the condensed milk business [was] granted to Nestle's," which provided that "company fabulous profits" and tended to "wipe out established channels of distribution and leave the company with no legally enforceable duties."[16] The chief of New York–based Brimberg Textile Corporation, whose "main exports" were to "the British West Indies," railed against a "new sort of discrimination against American cotton goods in favor of the British product," which was "in effect" not only in Jamaica but "also in St. Vincent."[17]

London saw it otherwise. In a "private and confidential" note, London was informed that U.S. merchandise was all too prevalent in the Caribbean. "I can see no reason," said the writer Harold Mitchell, "why the Jamaican should not use a British motor car etc. instead of an American, as he does almost entirely at present." Concern was expressed over the growing "tourist trade," which had to rely upon the nearby U.S. populace. "[T]housands of Americans who would normally go to Europe are reluctant to cross the Atlantic" and were streaming into the Caribbean, though the "lack of an island telephone service" was a "real handicap" for those interested in accelerating hemispheric ties—which may not have been a bad thing in the eyes of some in London.[18] Washington was learning what Jamaicans already knew: Colonialism was a rigged system crudely designed to benefit the colonizer and loot the colonized. Given that anti-London anger and distrust were rising in the region, it was understandable that workers and peasants of the Caribbean would begin to smile bountifully upon the United Kingdom's rival in Washington, which too had a desire to witness the Empire take a nasty pratfall.

Years later the renowned Antiguan writer Jamaica Kincaid could not contain her anti-London fury. "The English have become such a pitiful lot these days," she wrote in 1988. "[T]hey don't seem to know that this empire business was all wrong and they should, at least, be wearing sackcloth and ashes in token presence of the wrongs committed, the irrevocableness of their bad deeds, for no natural disaster imaginable could equal the harm they did. Actual death might have been better."[19]

Likewise, Washington could afford to be as blunt as Kincaid in detailing the proliferating anger in the region. "Discontent is widespread throughout the island," said the U.S. consul Hugh Watson in May 1938, speaking of Jamaica. "The Governor is unpopular, his methods and his objects are disliked." Watson also noticed the regional implications, observing that "agitators were quick to learn from the Trinidad difficulties." But above all he stressed that the "root of this trouble lies in poverty, which comes from low wages and unemployment . . . serious undernourishment among school children is prevalent."[20]

Weeks later, Watson had become concerned with the notion that *"race hatred"* (emphasis in original) was "probably in the long run the most serious and the most lamentable outcome of the happenings of the last six months." The "police inspectors of English origin have been openly attacked and beaten; white people of both sexes are being continually subjected to insults." Again, there were implications that stretched far beyond the shores of Jamaica itself since "authorities suspected that money and arms were being sent in for the use of rioters from foreign countries, the United States being thought to be the origin of the money and Cuba the immediate source of the arms."[21]

Actually, despite the comparative isolation of the region—poor telephone service, inadequate flight service, relatively slow boats, an infrastructure that could hardly handle adequately an influx of visitors—there was a growing concern outside of Jamaica about the mushrooming troubles there and the regional implications. In June 1938, London consented to meet with "representatives of the Methodist Missionary Society of Jamaica," and what they heard was not pleasing. "Import duties on clothes was specially mentioned as a hardship because many Jamaicans rely for their wardrobe on discarded clothing sent by their friends in America," which reminded London once more that the island's orientation northward was irresistible. "Communist agitation, though often asserted, was non-existent," it was said, "the only Communists being a few clerks in Government employment whose communism was quite academic." What was of concern was an issue that was to become even more pronounced in coming years, the "rapid rate at which the prolific Negro population was increasing."

"[O]utlets should be found for them in vacant lands in British Honduras or British Guiana," but exporting Jamaica's "problems" could only exacerbate tensions in other parts of the Empire.[22]

Yet when the Colonial Office met with Hugh Clarke of Westmoreland, Jamaica, and an accompanying "solicitor of Montego Bay," they heard a contrasting message. The "troubles at Frome," said Clarke, speaking of a prominent plantation, "were not [due] to local people but to extraneous agitators." It was a "happy-go-lucky" community in which, in spite of bad housing and low wages, most people were contented. Now there was a real issue that was inevitably tied to the fate of their neighbors: "unemployment among students who had recently left secondary schools and were unable [as in] the past to get employment in America, Cuba or Panama" and, as a result, had plenty of time on their hands to stir up trouble. This was combined with a general "ignorance of the people" due to inadequate education and a derisory infrastructure. "[I]n the hot months many people had insufficient water for drinking, let alone for washing" and "even towns like Montego Bay"—which had to accommodate a growing stream of tourists—"had inadequate supplies."[23]

Writing from Morant Bay, the scene of a major uprising in Jamaica decades earlier, Helen P. Hyatt-Short told Prime Minister Neville Chamberlain that she was not pleased that "the affairs of this very small portion of the British Empire seem to be engaging a great deal of time on the part of the British Press and the sentimental part of the British public." This was unwarranted, she thought, not least since "the Jamaican Negro is vain," was a "coaster and credulous especially of the incredible." Besides, "he is a coward" who "does not want to live like a European" and "would rather be black than white," amazingly enough. "This of course does not refer to half castes who spend all their time trying to prove that they are free from any trace of color." As she saw it, the "struggle" was "resolving itself into one between Capital and Labour. This is complicated with race hatred for though scarcely any of the property owners are of pure English, Scotch or Irish extraction, they are sufficiently fair-skinned to be described as 'dem white people' and these chiefly were attacked and beaten up by the strikers. But for the police and the garrison," she concluded, "it is not likely that any white man would now be alive in Jamaica." As she saw it, "if the West Indies are of real value to the British Empire, now is the time to realize that lenience does not impress the 'Black Man' as the Negro calls himself. He laughs at it as a confession of Fear."[24]

Prime Minister Chamberlain, under pressure from Germany and Japan and wary of his erstwhile ally in Washington, hardly wanted to hear that the Empire's most populous Caribbean island was descending into turmoil leavened with generous dollops of race and class antagonism. Similarly not reassuring was that besides seeking to contain a growing regional revolt, he had to contend with the fact that this rebellion was being materially assisted by Jamaicans and their allies in the United States. This was a double-edged sword: Washington could

justifiably plead freedom of speech in allowing for a rising chorus of protest
against British colonialism, allowing Jamaicans to develop a well-honed appreciation for this major power—but what would be the impact of this crusading
on the United States itself?

Already nationals of the West Indies had developed a well-deserved reputation for radicalism in the United States. The "only black charter member of
the American Communist Party," Otto Huiswood, hailed from Surinam and
was in and out of the region repeatedly in the 1930s spreading the gospel of
revolution.[25] Returning the favor, it was acknowledged that the "viewpoint" of
the U.S. Communist Party had an "influence" on Trinidadian society. "This
was through the part played by the Negro Welfare Cultural and Social Association, which had been founded by Rupert Gittens . . . [who] had spent several
years in the United States."[26] George Padmore, born in Trinidad, studied at
Columbia, Fisk, New York University, and Howard—before becoming a
renowned communist, then Pan-African writer.[27] W.E.B. Du Bois aside (who,
after all, had Haitian roots), the man who could justifiably be deemed the
"Father of Pan-Africanism"—Henry Sylvester Williams—was born in Trinidad
in 1869, then studied in Canada, settled in London, practiced law in South
Africa, and developed a philosophy that shook the foundations of colonialism.[28]
Ferdinand Smith, perhaps the most powerful Negro trade union leader in the
United States in the 1930s and 1940s and certainly one of the more influential
communists in that nation, hailed from Westmoreland, Jamaica.[29] Generally,
nationals from the Caribbean played an outsized role in their contribution to
radicalism in the United States particularly.[30]

This was an outgrowth of the fact that there had long been an intense traffic between the islands and the United States. It is estimated that "70 per cent"
of black New Yorkers "came from Caribbean and American sources" before the
mid-eighteenth century, "with thousands arriving from Barbados and Jamaica,"
including some from the latter nation who had been knee-deep in slave revolts.[31]
During the war of 1812, for example, the last time conflict between London and
Washington was terribly inflamed, an estimated 3,600 enslaved Africans from
Maryland, North Carolina, Louisiana, and Georgia escaped behind enemy lines
and 781 of them, along with others, including former members of the "Corps
of Colonial Marines" that had fought alongside the Redcoats, were brought to
Trinidad to live.[32]

On the one hand, Washington, for its own purposes, could allow Caribbean
exiles to protest vigorously against British colonialism, but on the other hand this
ran the risk of uncorking more than a whiff of radicalism on its own shores.
Moreover, as war clouds loomed and as it became evident that London would
be its ally against Berlin and Tokyo, did it make sense to upset this ally unduly?

Thus it did not take long before London began to monitor carefully the
activities of nationals from the Empire who had migrated to the United States.
In July 1937, shortly after the disturbances in Trinidad, the Colonial Office

began to receive reports about the Jamaica Progressive League (JPL), which was holding meetings in Harlem at St. James Presbyterian Church at 407–9 West 141st Street, though the JPL was "now located at 210 West 129th Street, which is a private house." At the church, the "Rev. Imes is the pastor" and "on several occasions" he had "addressed members of the Communist Party." Now the members of the JPL were "not Communists," actually "these people were former members of the Garvey Association"—but that did not make them necessarily less dangerous in the short term.[33] The JPL, however, was buoyed by the same currents that had led the Communist Party to surge in the mid-1930s, for it was founded in July 1936 in Harlem.[34]

The Jamaican governor, Sir Edward Denham, regularly received "confidential" reports about the JPL and its publications. The governor was informed reassuringly in early 1938 that W. Adolphe Roberts, JPL president, was recently in Jamaica, but "owing to his long absence from the island he does not appear to be in touch with the local situation."[35] The JPL condemned the "economic and social conditions of labourers of Jamaica," which had "been for many years unbelievably and deplorably unsatisfactory," with "low wages of 18 pence a day." Then there were massive civil liberties violations, such as the barring of "meetings, gatherings or assemblies of persons and all processions and marches in any public place."[36]

So moved, in October 1937 the Defense Council of the West Indies met at the Elks Auditorium in Harlem at 160 West 129th Street in a "protest conference & public meeting to consider measures for assisting over 50 Trinidad . . . workers indicted for trial in November and hundreds awaiting trial in Barbados." They insisted that "the mockery of 'British liberty' for West Indian Negroes must be exposed."[37]

Jamaicans in the Diaspora had good reason to organize, for their plight abroad, though a mite better than at home, was hardly commodious. And it would be even harder for them to secure better treatment as long as their homeland was a slum of Empire with those emerging from there seen as deserving no better treatment than slum dwellers. W. A. Domingo, a leader of the JPL, observed in early 1938 that "at least some 200,000 Jamaicans" were "domiciled in Cuba, Central America and the United States," with "those who travel between Jamaica and the United States" facing a "very humiliating situation. They are not allowed the same free choice of cabins that is accorded white passengers. The obviously colored passengers are segregated in the least desirable sections of the ships." The "Standard Steamship Company, owned by Italian Americans," did not "accept any noticeably colored passengers on their newer and larger boats." Now the "Columbia Line" made "an exception in the case of Haitians because the Government of Haiti, composed of people of the same racial stock as the population, defends the human rights of its nationals"—which in itself was a powerful argument for sovereignty, particularly since "Haitian citizens travel as first-class citizens on the Columbia Line while unmistakably colored British subjects

are denied their ordinary human rights." Such a policy was guaranteed to foment
enmity between the lighter- and darker-skinned of Jamaica, which may not have
been an unintended consequence since this color conflict proved to be a major
barrier to independence. "The situation, like practically all those conditions
affecting color," said Domingo angrily, "is stupidly ignored by Jamaicans who,
though the sufferers, regard it as an act of supreme 'good taste' to pretend that
they are not mistreated." But Domingo saw a glimmer of hope in all this for "with
Self-Government," he concluded, "we would not need to depend upon indifferent white men to see that our ordinary human rights are protected."[38] But if
this dream were to become reality, those who heretofore had been viewed as so
many labor units would have to organize, which is why the JPL placed so much
emphasis on assistance to ordinary workers.

External assistance from the likes of the JPL was one reason why otherwise
poverty-stricken labor in the former British West Indies was able to make such
gains. This was not only true for Jamaica but also for Trinidad and Tobago,
which in many ways had initiated this new era for Caribbean labor. However,
here there was a related external factor that was bothering London: What would
be the reaction of this colony in case of a widely expected pan-European war?
The reports from the oil fields were not encouraging. "If Britain goes to war,"
said one intelligence report in May 1939, "they [West Indians] should through
patriotism enlist but they would only do so under the command of coloured com-
manders," and "in the absence of this they were not prepared to enlist and perform menial services as was done by West Indians in the Great War." It was
apparent that the old model of the colonized as a horse to be mounted by the
colonial rider would have to undergo severe readjustment. Meanwhile, Butler
was surging in popularity; his jailing had won few fans in the oil fields and talk
was rife of his "martyrdom." An emotional leader, at this gathering where antiwar
sentiments reigned, "Butler cried and his audible sobbing . . . brought tears to
the eyes of sentimental individuals." He was also gathering ever wider support,
having "received numerous cablegrams from white workers of Europe, Canada,
America and far off Australia and New Zealand,"[39] while back home in La Brea,
"about five hundred men, women and children" amassed to greet him upon his
arrival—"most of the women kissed Butler on his arrival."[40]

But distressing for those who saw discord within the labor movement as self-
defeating, Butler scorned "not only Hitlers in Germany but local Hitlers like
Rienzi," adding forebodingly, "I will not [be] afraid to term myself Hitler to overthrow them." Trinidadian official Tilbert St. Louis cited Butler as asserting that
his "chief aim throughout was to overthrow the Oil Field Workers Trade Union
and to set up a second union" with himself in charge.[41] The feisty Butler routinely referred to other trade unionists as "crooks" and called the progressive John
Rojas a "traitor; I told him so to his face. . . . He has to die a traitor's death."[42]

In sum, Butler was idiosyncratic and not necessarily a force for union solidarity. He was not alone. Rienzi, a frequent target of Butler's invective, "had been

expelled by Cipriani" from the latter's organization "on the specious ground that he was a Communist."[43] This lack of uniqueness did not prevent Butler from coming under severe scrutiny by the authorities. "Butler's reported speeches contain nothing of a seditious nature," the colonial secretary was informed, "as they seem to open with expressions of extreme patriotism and loyalty to His Majesty." Butler tended to "claim divine guidance"—then swiftly launch into "violent attacks upon the Oilfield Workers' Trade Union . . . A.C. Rienzi and the other permanent officials." Yet he was a force to be reckoned with and this would lead him to be detained at length, for "most of his meetings are well-attended," though "two-thirds consist of women who may be attracted by an evening's free entertainment." So, it was concluded, "his activities should continue to be carefully watched."[44]

For despite the fractiousness, union organizing in Trinidad and Tobago began to increase in the 1930s and this trend suffered no surcease. Thus, "starting out with some 8000 members in 1938 trade union membership increased to 20,000 by 1947 and finally to 50,000 by 1957" as sovereignty loomed.[45] Suggestive of how far-reaching this trend was is the fact that it reached Barbados, the conservative anchor of the region. The Trinidadian intellectual and leader, Eric Williams, argued that "Barbados with its uninterrupted and unchanged Constitution and its land and industry almost exclusively in the hands of European large proprietors was, historically, socially and politically, poles asunder from the Crown Colonies of St. Vincent and St. Lucia where [there] was a considerable coloured and Negro peasant proprietary." Thus, when the "first formal proposal" for federation was "made by the British government in 1876" involving federation of the Leeward Islands and the Windward Islands, there was considerable "opposition of vested interests," and the "Barbadian planters" were "the first in the field. They objected to federation with Crown Colonies and refused to surrender their ancient Constitution under which they enjoyed a large measure of self-government." These planters, "sticking at nothing in their opposition to federation, unscrupulously told the workers that federation would mean the restoration of slavery."[46]

Given this history, the colonial authorities were comforted by their assumption that Bridgetown was an anchor of stability in a sea of brooding turbulence, though there was a "daily wage of 20 to 24 cents for labourers" which was "given after Emancipation" and "remained practically the same until 1937, even though the cost of living had risen significantly during that time."[47] An outsider, Clement Payne, played a role in rousing the disaffected; his flaming oratory, combining a "visionary socialism and fiery rhetoric," was so effective that ultimately he was deported to his native Trinidad. Among the worst-treated group of workers were the bakers, whose onerous conditions had led them to form a trade union in early 1937. These conditions still remain difficult to grasp. "[B]akers were locked into the bakeries at night by the proprietor and could not get out in case of fire, illness, or emergency." They were exemplars of the nation's dominant trend, an

economy based "on the exploitation by white capital of coloured labour." For in
Barbados, "10% of the population were classified as white, a greater proportion
than was to be found in any other British West Indian territory"—and this was
a key to the island's conservatism.[48]

Finally, in that epochal year of 1937, disturbances erupted in protest of
inhumane treatment. Then in the dying days of February 1939, at the height of
the sugar harvest, cane cutters went on strike, crippling the island's most vital
industry. In a tactic that was the hallmark of protest in the region, "the sky was
a red glow as cane fires parched the rural districts."[49]

CHAPTER 3

The Labor of War

A S THE HOOFBEATS OF WAR approached ever more insistently, London—and its erstwhile ally, Washington—had a security problem in the Caribbean. It was not only that Britain's rules mandating preference for those of "pure European descent" were not designed for mass appeal in the West Indies[1] and made the nationals of this region susceptible to the blandishments of London's opponents (especially those in Japan who purported to be the "champion of the colored races"), it was also that these small islands were stepping-stones from which the security of the United States itself could be challenged. Antigua, for example, was "an ideal place from which air surveillance of the whole of the north-eastern Caribbean could be mounted," and after war commenced, "German submarine activity in the Caribbean was greatly intensified."[2] In January 1940 the U.S. Consulate in Jamaica expressed fearful concern about the alleged increase of German influence on the island. The "German Legation in Haiti and certain influential Germans there are planning to foment a revolution in Jamaica in the interest of Germany," it was stated with the utmost sobriety.[3] Yet "surprisingly," says one scholar, "the Germans seemed to have recognized the strategic importance of Trinidad even before the Americans and the island always figured prominently in their wartime political writings." Berlin "broadcast propaganda towards Trinidad, aimed at causing disunity between the troops of the various nationalities and the local population. This forced the Americans to retaliate" by launching their own radio station, thus perhaps increasing the audio options of the Trinidadians. Rumors were so rife about spies in the region that a "witch hunt" ensued.[4]

To bolster its own security, Washington, which was widely viewed as the logical inheritor of the various pieces of an overstretched British Empire, moved rapidly to broker a "lend-lease" agreement with London, which provided the

United States with bases in various Caribbean islands, a development that dramatically transformed the region.

To that end, in November 1940, the White House dispatched a team led by
Charles W. Taussig to investigate the region, and this team produced a report
that was to shape U.S. policy for years to come. The security question was rarely
far from their contemplation; already there was a "considerable emigration of
deserters from the French forces in Martinique (followers of De Gaulle) to
St. Lucia," though rather easily Vichy or pro-Berlin forces could be infiltrated
likewise. A similar situation obtained in Dominica. Because of London's abys-
mal neglect of the infrastructure in this area, "any minor enemy activity in some
of these remote islands that have neither telegraphic or steamer communication could well go on undetected for a period of five days or weeks." Like those
who had studied Barbados, they concluded that the "major problem" regionally
was "over-population," though it was wisely conceded that this might be "misleading" and "we must not overlook the possibility that the fault lies in the economics of the island and not in the birth rate"—that is, the skewed concentration of wealth in a few hands was the Caribbean problem, not too many people.
Still, there existed an "ambitious resettlement project providing for the emigration of urban Barbadians to View [sic] Fort in St. Lucia." Refusing to view
the region as a monolith, Taussig's delegation observed that there were a "wide
variety of economies operating in the islands, ranging from relatively pure Communism in a part of the British Virgin Islands" to the "plantocracy of St. Kitts.
In some of the smaller islands such as Tortola, Anguilla and Carriacou, we found
a primitive peasant economy." Like legions of observers before them, Taussig
and company were stunned by the degree of underdevelopment that obtained
in the region after years and years of misrule by the Empire. "We visited the
island of Anguilla," it was noted, "an island of five thousand inhabitants," which
then had "no communication, either in the form of steamship service, radio or
cable. It has poor soil, deficient rainfall and inadequate water supply. There is
practically no money on the island." The descendants of Africans, cruelly
scooped up via an inhuman slave trade and dumped on this less-than-arable
patch of territory, barely scraped by.

The nationals of the region hardly had the vehicle through which to profoundly alter this sad state of affairs since there was a "property and income qualification for enfranchisement," though it was not pointed out that this underscored
vividly the need for labor organization as a means of change. Thus in Barbados,
with "two hundred thousand population, only about six thousand are qualified to
vote"—again, it was not added, that even these were disproportionately white.
And, yes, Taussig too found this island nation "probably the most conservative"
in the region.

But these were not anthropologists or even disinterested political observers.
They were men with a mission to assess security matters, and what they
found was not comforting. There were a "large number of organizations" in the

United States "and to a limited extent in South America, which, to a greater or lesser degree, maintain contacts in all or some of the islands," and it was "obvious" that "subversive purposes" were on their agenda. For example, there was a "definite campaign in the West Indies for federation and self-government," and the "headquarters of this movement is apparently in New York City." There was grave concern that radical labor in the region—which was intertwined with the movement for sovereignty—could impact the "construction of the Caribbean naval and air bases," whose importance was increasing with every passing day. "Even now," it was stated with trepidation, "work is being interfered with by shortage of skilled labor and strikes."

Looming menacingly were *"problems of race and color"* (emphasis in original). "It is essential that the United States give this matter the most careful consideration in order to avoid unnecessary friction and disturbance." It would be "unfortunate if Americans with extreme color prejudice and antagonism were placed in important positions in the construction of the West Indian bases," for a "very unpleasant and difficult situation could be created."[5]

It was this latter concern that was to drive racial reform in the United States itself, as Washington, intensely worried about the global ramifications of Jim Crow, had to make concessions to African Americans. These newly empowered African Americans could then press their homeland, which was gaining influence in the region as London was forced into a helter-skelter retreat, on the pressing matter of independence and sovereignty for the West Indies. Then, as nationals from the region began visiting the United States more frequently as Washington gained in prominence in the West Indies, their often bracing encounters with the cruel domestic folkways that constituted Jim Crow led to their own protests targeting this devilish system, thereby leading to an improved situation for African Americans. This virtuous circle led the United States itself to retreat from de jure to de facto racial segregation and in the Caribbean from colonialism to neocolonialism.

But these developments were to emerge full-blown much later. In the meantime, Taussig and his cohorts had to grapple with the immense security implications of the "slum" that had been allowed to fester in Washington's neighborhood. The problem the United States encountered inhered in geography; that is, these Caribbean islands were so small, so scattered, and so heterogeneous that they presented an enormous challenge. For reasons of security, if nothing else, it made sense for Washington to approach them with a coordinated policy, which in turn increased the islands' cohesion and push toward federation.

Across the region, there was a challenge to ensure that morale did not dip dangerously to the point where security might be endangered. Thus, in St. Kitts, it was noted that the "labor situation is in bad shape," and there was "considerable ill feeling between the labor leaders and the planters and the central sugar factory. St. Kitts is one of the more prosperous of the British West Indies. The soil is fertile, rainfall good and the cane fields well cultivated." Still, there was "much discontent in the island," not least since "housing ranks with the poorest in the entire" region. If "discontent" prevailed in a relatively prosperous St. Kitts, might this be an indication of fertile possibilities of labor advance or security dangers in the Caribbean, and what did this augur for global powers who sought to inflict damage on Washington and London?

St. Kitts was colonized by the British in 1623 and rapidly became one big "sugar plantation par excellence." It rivaled Barbados as a "striking example of [a] one-crop economy" with a "land holding system dominated by estates." It "has maintained cane production for almost centuries without serious deterioration of its soil," concluded a 1980 analysis, as the island was deemed "the most agriculturally efficient and prosperous of the Leewards and Windwards."[6]

Yet this prosperity came at a major cost for a nastily exploited labor force. There were failed strikes in 1930 and 1932, but that could not halt the eruption of major labor conflict in 1935, and, as was typical of the region, this "produced the same exaggerated fears in the white community as had those of 1896," which too were viewed apocalyptically. "On the night after the [obligatory] riot in Basseterre," a report emerged from a "very reliable source" that "'attempts were going to be made that night to burn down the town of Basseterre' and that the labourers 'were going to descend . . . and exterminate the white people.'" The St. Kitts Workers League, belying its name, "stood firmly on the side of the colonial authorities in their effort to restore order."[7] In other words, discontent certainly was not absent in tiny St. Kitts, particularly in the turbulent decade of the 1930s, when labor strife spilled over the entire region.[8]

The St. Kitts Workers League (SKWL) was akin to a mutual or benevolent society rather than a union, but that did not prevent it from hosting advocates like Cipriani and the independence-minded T. A. Marryshow of Grenada. A resolution was carried unanimously hailing the former since "for the [third] time in succession [he has been] re-elected Mayor of Port-of-Spain." It "spoke in glowing terms" of that gentleman's merits. But the SKWL was not in tune with rising sentiments in the Caribbean, as was made clear at this very same November 1935 meeting when much was made of "the ignorant remark that Selassie of Ethiopia is our King." The speaker who "brought up" this notion was "rebuked . . . and the President took the opportunity [of] condemning such ignorance on the part of any individual; he stressed the fact that West Indians have one King—George Fifth and to him alone must homage be paid."[9]

Still, it does not take much teasing of the record to uncover that the otherwise staid SKWL was being affected by the currents rippling from East Africa, as was the rest of the region. Before those assembled were reminded to pay homage to King George, the organization's leader "and others expressed the view that while we are wholly in sympathy with the Ethiopians from a humanitarian and racial feeling yet we must not give cause for its being made to appear that the League is overanxious to thrust its activities unreservedly to public notice. There are other sources from which such action should emanate, let us give them an opportunity to do something without the League's initiatives."[10] This oblique endorsement of pro–Addis Ababa activity that the SKWL felt it could not easily spearhead was followed by a formal message to London "expressing appreciation [for] Britain's stand in the Italo-Ethiopian conflict" and their "willingness to cooperate in any measure found by His Majesty's Government for bringing the aggressive invasion of Ethiopia by Italy to an end." This was accompanied by a "donation to the Ethiopia Red Cross Fund."[11]

In retrospect, this internationalism on the part of workers in tiny St. Kitts should not be seen as overly surprising in that there was a transmission belt from there to cosmopolitan Manhattan that regularly deposited West Indians in this metropolis. This trend embraced virtually the entire leadership of the island. Robert Bradshaw, a founding father of independence and a charter member of the Caribbean Labour Congress, had a mother who was a domestic servant and a father who migrated to the United States when Bradshaw was nine months old. Edgar Challenger, another leader, studied biology at the Harlem-based City College of New York, then migrated to the study of Caribbean history. In 1933 he married Rubina Ginyard of South Carolina and returned home. Their predecessor as a labor leader was Joseph Nathan, "the most militant of the union organizers of 1917." Born in 1880, Nathan had migrated to the United States as a child in the 1890s before returning home in 1912. "Strongly anti-colonial" and "an admirer of German militarism and efficiency," he was also in close touch with U.S. labor leader Samuel Gompers.[12]

Throughout the 1930s, besides hosting visiting dignitaries from Grenada[13] and Trinidad, the SKWL often hosted guests from the United States, particularly successful migrants.[14] These visitors often came bearing gifts that meant the organization did not have to rely wholly on its financially strapped membership.[15] Sustained by such external support, St. Kitts was able to inspire young workers to seek to educate themselves further about a wider world.[16]

It was good that St. Kitts received such assistance, since it needed all the help it could get. That it was viewed in Washington as one of the more prosperous Caribbean colonies of London only served to reveal how the Empire had sucked the region dry. Homes of microscopic size with outdoor latrines were the fate of many. The aforementioned Edgar Challenger is an example of this. Tall and aristocratic in his bearing, he smoked a pipe, "walked barefoot and used bad words." His lack of footwear was designed to signal his "identity with the people he was trying to lead," who were similarly shoeless. "It did not work. The barefooted people wanted shoes, cheap Bata shoes; they did not want a leader who pretended to be a companion in distress."[17] There were all too many in this parlous category and more were not needed.

This combination of relative prosperity—compared, say, to an Anguilla that at times teetered on the brink of starvation—and terrible material conditions was combustible. There were significant industrial disputes in St. Kitts in 1940, 1943, 1944, 1946, 1947, 1948—then again in 1958 and 1969.[18] The conflict in

1940 was noticeably difficult. A strike meant a cessation of work, which meant penalties for those so bold as to depart the workplace and a desire for gainful employment for those unable to withstand the burden of enforced idleness. It was not long before the call arose that had dogged Caribbean workers over the decades: migrate to greener pastures. This trend could also increase the level of militancy in the countries receiving strikers and those with the gumption and self-assurance to embark on a new future.

Certainly the labor unrest roiling St. Kitts was sufficient for the authorities to take reprisals, thus spurring migration. In early 1940, "a strike was contemplated among factory workers" at the island's main "Sugar Factory."[19] A few weeks later there was a proposed "strike of porters and lightmen." This was "regarded" as "being serious, because the detainment of a steamer transporting sugar to England would interrupt the proper operation of the convoy system," thereby potentially complicating the war in Europe,[20] enraging the colonizers, and possibly igniting migration by intimidated workers.

In July 1941 the St. Kitts-Nevis Trades and Labour Union made a "proposal to send a delegation to St. Thomas, V.I., U.S.A., to investigate the labour situation in that island with a view to finding out the conditions of work and to ascertain what possibility existed from tradesmen and from labourers from St. Kitts-Nevis to obtain work there." This was being proposed even though a "large number of British subjects" that "had entered St. Thomas illegally by vessels and had obtained employment there had now to be repatriated"—an indicator of how desperate things had become in Basseterre. Thus, it was "suggested that officers" of the union "should make periodical visits to Antigua, St. Thomas, St. Domingo [sic], Curacao and other places to which workers from [St. Kitts-Nevis] emigrated."[21]

Soon there was "much talk of the effect of large numbers of workers leaving these shores to seek employment in Antigua, St. Thomas, [and] Trinidad." According to the Workers' Weekly, published in St. Kitts, "we have seen an outward stream of tradesmen as well as workers from the fields, factory, and business houses in Basseterre." Such compelled migration disrupted labor organizing by forcing out some workers while bringing in others who required time to get acclimated to their new setting. This was rationalized and viewed as a righteous struggle against provincial barriers. The claim that "[w]e are all one West Indian family and all the members of the family should be at home in any part of our West Indian country" had a ring of truth to it—but it also underscored the need for a Caribbean Labour Congress that could encompass the region; "ordinarily a West Indian cannot travel from one country to another unless he is able to make a deposit of a sum of money." A "Kittitian cannot normally travel to Trinidad without depositing a sum of money," for example, while an "American can travel from Texas to Tennessee or St. Thomas."[22]

This latter aim was driving the desire for federation, but in the meantime, "work men" from St. Kitts in the Virgin Islands were "suffering much inconvenience" as the "endless drift of the working class in search of a liveli-hood tells a story which reflects no credit to anyone in this country," said the *Workers' Weekly* of Basseterre.[23]

Shortly thereafter, "two natives of Dominica arrived" in Basseterre "and were not permitted to land until they deposited the sum of fifteen dollars each with the port authorities. They were persons of the labouring class and had left their homes to take up residence in Antigua where they expected to earn a livelihood." This was all well and good but it was a "puzzle to some" in the Car-ibbean "that West Indians were virtually barred from emigrating to Canada, South Africa and other parts of this blessed Empire of ours." This was due of course to the machinations of white supremacy, but the *Workers' Weekly* nev-ertheless found it hard to fathom—it was "entirely beyond the bounds of pro-gressive thought and sober reasoning"—why "one West Indian group should be [content] to have its doors virtually closed against their fellow island[ers]." This did not "make sense," not least since "the world looks at the islands, broadly speaking, as a single West Indian unit; but some West Indians seem to view each island as a house which he must close against his brother."[24]

That any workers would flee to St. Kitts for work was even more remark-able given the harsh climate for labor that existed there. It was not unusual when a "threat to shoot" a "domestic servant" arose, as there was a "feeling in some quarters that certain classes of workers are 'inferior creatures.'"[25] "Unpleas-ant situations" that were "arising between employers and employees" abounded, with the former "threatening to kick" the latter.[26] The conditions in the sugar fields, it was reported, "suggests a system of slavery of which even the slave mas-ters of about a century ago would have been ashamed. The Empire is fighting against Hitler in Germany," it was noted. "But here we have a sample of Hitlerism in St. Kitts."[27] This was in early 1942 as the Empire was suffering rever-sal after reversal, particularly in Asia, where Tokyo was challenging the predi-cates of white supremacy. This unfortunate situation was worsened by the encroachment of technology, it was thought. "Here in St. Kitts," it was said in the spring of 1942, "we already had examples where machines are forcing men out of work. Tractors are used on some estates for drawing ploughs, haul-ing canes from field to siding, etc." "What will the future bring? Will there be thousands of people out of work in this island some day?"[28] With workers stream-ing in from other islands as labor machinery was taking hold and the environ-ment ringing with cries of "freedom" and "democracy," it was little wonder that labor in St. Kitts chose this moment to down their tools.

Ironically, the war, which was a long hard slog of massive bloodletting and political repression, had opened space for Caribbean labor, not least since Washington was becoming increasingly dependent upon this force. On the one hand, there were jailings of various leaders on spurious grounds, including But-ler in Trinidad and Richard Hart in Jamaica. This left aching feelings; in early 1942 Hart told his "own darling wife" from the discomfort of a detention camp that "the act of separating me from my sweetheart, my own wife, when we were just settling down to a married life & we were so very happy, is one thing that [I] shall never forgive."[29] Hart, president of the newly formed Government Railway Employees Union, was accused in a "secret" report of using his "superior education"—he was also a lawyer—"to influence and train others in extreme Marxist and Leninist doctrines and their application to Jamaica during the difficult conditions arising out of the war." Hart's "bitter hatred of Britain" was supposedly "surpassed only by his fear of the United States which he regards as the supreme Imperialist menace to the future of the coloured man."[30]

On the other hand, jobs were being created on the various U.S. bases that were popping up on various islands, not to mention posts in the United States itself as the military draft and recruiting cut a huge swath through the domestic work force. Thus, in a "strictly confidential" missive, the U.S. consul in Kingston, John Lord, told Washington in May 1943 that "during the current month approximately 10,000 Jamaican agricultural laborers will have been recruited to the United States. To date over 5000 have already been embarked." Even then Lord recognized that this would have impact beyond the immediately visible, as he remarked on the "considerable speculation" as "to the effect upon local labor when they return to Jamaica after having worked abroad at wages fully 300 per cent higher than those prevailing here."[31] He was prescient. Weeks later Lord mentioned that "upon the return of a small group of Jamaican laborers from the [United States] who for one reason or another had been found unsatisfactory, certain labor leaders in Jamaica started a campaign criticizing the conditions under which Jamaican laborers were working."[32]

The introduction of the dynamic force that was the U.S. economy into otherwise somnolent Caribbean colonies shook up the region. As early as March 1943 the House of Assembly in Barbados was complaining that "the return to this colony of large numbers of Barbadians who were previously engaged on construction work on United States bases in the Caribbean and the increasing decline in sugar production, must result in increasing considerably the already large numbers of unemployed in the Colony," hence they made a "request that Your Excellency [the governor] will take the necessary steps as expeditiously as possible to endeavour to have some portion of our unemployed recruited for work on United States farms."[33] But sending West Indians into the maw of a bruising Jim Crow could alienate those needed to join the war effort, radicalize those not accustomed to the unique folkways of the United States, and produce higher expectations for wages in Barbados itself. In sum, the impact of the United States on the region was dynamic.

But Bridgetown had few good choices. A "serious situation had arisen with regard to labour employed in the sugar industry; the reaping of the 1945 cane crop had been delayed through absenteeism and the unwillingness of labour to settle down to steady work. The cause of this unrest was attributed to the calling up of would-be emigrants for registration and medical examination and the position had been aggravated by rumours of further call-ups. The sugar crop which was urgently needed by [London] had already been reduced by the large number of cane fires." The island's sugar producers were upset, feeling "they should have been consulted by the Government before it was decided to allow recruits to leave for the U.S.A. during the crop season." Labor was needed at home—but it was also needed abroad and this could increase the leverage of unions. "After discussion it was agreed that it would not be advisable to cancel the whole programme of recruiting, indeed it was considered that the consequences of such a step would be disastrous."[34]

The impact of importing labor from the Caribbean into a wartime United States was exposed when Jamaicans—who had an Empire-wide reputation for militancy—arrived. Typical was the arrival of "about 100 Jamaicans" in Centreville, Maryland, slated "to work for farmers in the neighborhood," though their "camp" was "not completed" and "proper arrangements for feeding them [also] had not yet been completed." As a result the Jamaicans had a rather bad time for the first day or two. They had an unpleasant voyage to Norfolk; their ship was chased by a submarine and they were kept below as a result, which contributed to their seasickness and general unhappiness. In addition, much of the food on board spoiled so that when they arrived they were ravenous. Indeed they were so hungry when they got to their camp "they broke into a neighboring orchard and consumed large quantities of green apples thus making themselves thoroughly sick." Thus, "at the moment the men are not too happy and some of them are very homesick," particularly since they were "promised $5 each on arrival" and "they did not get the $5."[35]

By the summer of 1943 a group of them had arrived with a cohort of nationals from the Bahamas with the aim of "helping to harvest vital war crops." But even Sherman Briscoe of the U.S. Department of Agriculture, whose agency had oversight of these workers, was concerned with how they were treated and was involved in "improving" their "living and working conditions," though he confessed candidly, "I don't seem to be getting to first base." He asked the crusading black journalist Claude Barnett to "make no mention of my name in connection with this program," but he admitted that more public focus on their plight—perhaps in the "white press so that white people can be more effectively informed"—was a must.[36]

The problem was that laboring in the sugar cane fields of the southern United States was no picnic in the best of times, and bringing those who were both foreign and black into the picture only exacerbated an unfortunate situation. Some "600 Jamaicans," for example, "were lodged in the county jails at Miami and Tampa and in the Florida state penitentiary at Raiford," which did not improve their mood.[37] And, unbelievably, housing may have been the prime asset of this forsaken job. After making keen "observations" at what were called euphemistically "labor camps," the writer Frank E. Pinder detailed the "poor food" served, the "discriminatory wages due chiefly to labor auctions," the "discrimination faced

in public places"—and worse.[38] "At present we have 1700 Jamaicans in the state,"
said Pinder in early 1944, reporting from Azucar, Florida, "harvesting something
like 33,000 acres of sugar canes. Very few domestics," meaning U.S. nationals,
"were working for the United States Sugar Corporation due to the terrible name
they have carried in the past—peonage," namely bonded labor. Thus, the war-
pressured United States was thankful for the arrival of the Jamaicans. "I do not
know what would have happened to this large sugar crop," said Pinder, "had this
company been unable to secure the services of the West Indian workers."[39]

Barnett, who conducted his own investigation into the "camps belonging to
the United States Sugar Corporation," discovered that the Jamaicans were "doing
a good job" and were "in excellent spirit." These Caribbean workers "were the
residue of those who were imported in May 1943 to augment the farm labor
needed to harvest current crops—work for which the normal supply of labor was
not available." The catch was that "originally the Jamaicans were recruited for
work, which it was agreed would be largely, if not wholly, above the Mason-Dixon
line." Why there? "This is because," added Barnett, "the Jamaicans are a rather
high-spirited people not accustomed to color prejudices of the type sometimes
found in the southern areas of this country." They tended to "enjoy," he noted
with more than a hint of yeast, "complete manhood and citizenship status at
home and are not accustomed to the restrictions, segregation, and racial treatment accorded in the Deep South." This situation was worsened when bosses
in the North spread negative "propaganda" about the South to compel the
Jamaicans to stay above the Mason-Dixon line. Still, when they did move southward they were hardly prepared to countenance the casual racism that had
become ingrained in the Old Confederacy. "These Jamaicans," he said, "have
intelligence far superior to that of the average southern farm worker or that of
the Bahamian. They are independent and proud and will not tolerate mistreat-
ment." Hence, the white South was about to get a foretaste of the militancy that
was to seem endemic by the 1960s.

African American workers "almost unanimously . . . praised the coming of
Jamaicans and Bahamians. Their reasons were simple: wages and working conditions have both been improved by the advent of the foreigners," even though
the "Bahamians while more numerous, do not appear to have quite as much
quality as the Jamaicans." Indeed, "some planters" were "said to prefer them
because they are quite as docile as the Southern Negro worker." Moreover,
"unlike the Jamaican government," that of the Bahamas had a profound "weakness," that is, an "almost total lack of supervision by their own government,"
which was like a green light for exploitation by the planters. Still, it was felt that
it "would add materially if the Jamaican government might receive the suggestion that a distinctly Negro personality might be added to their overall liaison
group sent here."[40]

As it turned out, the purported lack of docility of the Jamaicans proved their
undoing. They cast a militant cloud over the "Sunshine State" to the point where

their presence proved incompatible with the dictates of Jim Crow. "Jamaican farm workers who were unyielding in their demands to receive the going wage and who refused to submit to discrimination are not going to be brought back this year to meet farm labor shortages," announced the Associated Negro Press of the United States in February 1944; Washington would now "have to look to 'other West Indian islands.'" The United States was considering the "importation of 66,900 workers with the bulk, 52,000, coming from Mexico. The Bahamas will provide 5000. Jamaica will be credited with 2000 and the balance of 7900 will be gotten in Puerto Rico, Cuba, and possibly Barbados." Consider that in the previous year "8826 Jamaicans were brought in." But things had changed. Now Washington felt compelled to make an "oral agreement" with London mandating that "the Jamaicans would not be required to work beneath the Mason-Dixon line"—though it was not clear if the now chagrined and frustrated devotees of Jim Crow were behind this maneuver.[41]

The invasiveness of U.S. personnel and bases in the region was also having unintentional consequences. Lionel Hurst, for example, was born in Antigua in 1912. Both of his parents had lived in the United States "without the accompaniment of children," so he was "reared by a grandmother." Perhaps weaned on stories about the Colossus of the North and the pervasive influence of neighboring Jamaica, he was "attracted to the Garvey movement when it was unpopular to be so." As an adult he was "passed over for a promotion at the U.S. Naval Base" in his homeland "where he was employed. His view of the world was thereafter irrevocably changed," as he "joined the trades union movement" and became one of its more esteemed leaders.[42]

The U.S. bases that had begun to mushroom in the region were becoming nodes of resistance, not least due to the often burdensome conditions that prevailed there. The base in Trinidad and Tobago had a "tremendous impact on not just Trinidad alone," according to the writer Nyahuma Obika, "but affected the entire British West Indies as well," for "wages offered on the base were so extravagant in comparison with the highest paid labourer of the day that workers from Barbados, St. Vincent, St. Lucia and Grenada rushed to Trinidad to get 'a piece of the action.'"[43]

Quintin O'Connor, general secretary of the Federated Workers' Trade Union in Trinidad, was not so sanguine about the arrival of a critically strategic U.S. base in his homeland. In fact, he chose to "protest vigorously against what is considered brutal fascism exercised upon the workers employed at the American base in different parts of the island." They were "beaten on their heads with truncheons without justification and . . . if they resist, revolvers are pushed in their bellies and they are sometimes kicked by their bosses." Worse, he lamented, "we have not been treated in this way up to the present by the British government." Why such ugliness? "Negro haters are employed at the bases," he insisted, "men who believe Negroes are dogs to be brutally kicked, men who get drunk and then want to beat up Negroes. We cannot have an ally fighting a war for freedom and committing acts worse than slave owners," he bellowed. He warned London, already reeling from war reversals, that "we must face the fact that today the task of the democracies has been made difficult in the Far East, because of the native populations going over to the Japanese. There must be some cause for this, and"—he pondered pointedly—"will the native population of Trinidad and Tobago help the Americans if we are invaded or will they help the invader as in Burma?"[44] O'Connor's view was not his alone. At best it could be said there was a mixed opinion of the invasive presence of the United States.[45] For on the one hand, compared to the receding power—London—Washington seemed to represent an improvement, but its more determined Jim Crow policies suggested that the arrival of the United States brought new complications.

This was understandable as tumultuous events in St. Lucia in 1944 indicated. Harsh conditions meant that "looting broke out in Castries when a mob overpowered the police while foodstuffs were being conveyed from a ship to a warehouse and stores." Then "United States Marines" intervened, "called out at the request of the British authorities. One native was shot," but things did not end there. "Several weeks ago," it was said just after D-Day, "the local authorities were worried about reports that the unemployed people of Vieux Fort planned to burn the village down so that the British Government would be forced to put the people to work building up the village again." An impotent London would be compelled to "call upon the Americans for help in case of need." Charles Whitaker, the U.S. vice consul, was not pleased. "Vieux Fort is one of the most disreputable towns that I have [seen] in traveling on six continents," he contended in a "confidential" message. "The outlook for the people here at present is hopeless."[46]

British Guiana was hardly better off. For beginning in 1942, a U.S. base was constructed there; "80 per cent" of the laborers were "coloured" and their experience was not uplifting. "They worked in downpours of rain, in knee-deep mud. They worked with swarms of mosquitoes and sand flies swarming about them, and sometimes they cried out as they worked to relieve the sheer agony of the flies." There were "poisonous snakes" that were seen as workers "walked miles to reach the [construction] site . . . carrying their equipment the entire way through swamps waist-deep. They disregarded pimpler bushes which bore thorns so sharp that the men would receive cuts as they walked by. Other workers were cut badly by the razor grass—not cuts that were mere surface scratches either, but some which cut deep to the bone." Those "men unable to find a place to sleep at the base, rode back and forth to Georgetown every day by bicycle— two hours of pedaling each way to top off a ten-hour working day. Others piled 20 into a building no larger than a living room and slept in hammocks."[47]

As horrendous as these workers might have had it, at least they received wages—which was more than could be said for some. For as one London exposé put it in 1943, "today forced labour is the subject of much propaganda in this country; but only when it is exacted by the German authorities from the inhabitants of occupied territories. This is denounced vigorously. But what then are

[we] to say of the arbitrary resumption of forced labour for a similar reason (i.e. to win the war) in our own colonies?" Worse, this bondage was "often for the benefit of private employers."[48] So Washington, in offering wages, represented something of an improvement over London, which at times winked at bondage.

Despite the higher wages it could offer, the United States was at a competitive disadvantage since its peculiar customs did not go down well in the region. A report from St. Kitts objected that their "farmhands" were "given 'colour wages'" in the United States, which was "blamed . . . primarily" on an "ingrained . . . practice that a coloured worker should not receive the same rate of pay as a white one." The "majority of our farm workers," it was added forlornly, "are not happy in their new environments despite the admittedly high rates of pay they receive."[49] Speaking in "strictly confidential" terms, the U.S. consul to Jamaica, John Lord, pointed to a "prominent notice that appeared in the leading local newspaper advertising 'help needed white male and female,'" for the U.S.O. that for some reason "evoked a great deal of unfavorable comment." Suggestive of how Jim Crow was compelled to retreat due to the restraints of war and the desire not to unduly alienate those whose labor was needed, "on the following day the offending word 'white' was omitted." But "the damage had been done," and Washington's reputation plummeted further. "The whole incident only goes to show," said Lord, "how extremely careful one must be in dealing with the susceptibilities of the local inhabitants. Although," he added quickly, "several long-time residents of Jamaica have pointed out to me that in the past private advertisements for white domestics have elicited no such unfavorable comment."[50]

What was not grasped as well, perhaps, was that one of Jamaica's leading political forces was the People's National Party (PNP), led by the accomplished lawyer Norman Manley. He and his party both had a Social Democratic orientation similar to the outlook of Britain's Labour Party, but to the left of respectable discourse in the United States. Even before these engineered migrations, a U.S. consul was complaining that "labor leaders and the heads of the [PNP] constantly inveigh against communism, yet it is found in widely separated social levels." Thus, "many school teachers, particularly in the country districts, are Communists and through them communistic principles are being sown among the young."[51] In a "Top Secret" message, the State Department instructed "American Diplomatic and Consular Offices" to be alert to the "distinction between Social-Democratic and Communists." There had "been instances recently in which officers construed replies by Social-Democratic applicants for visas as making them ineligible to receive such visas on the ground that they were Communists, whereas in fact, they are almost the direct antithesis."[52] If a Jamaican might have gotten hold of this message, she might well have asked why Washington, in an alliance with communist Moscow, was so exercised about communists and, in any case, why the controversy about Social Democrats whose collaboration with the United States during this war was also widely known.

The sharp challenge to the British West Indies colonizer provided by Tokyo, in particular during the rout in Singapore in early 1942, eroded whatever illusions may have remained about the potency of "whiteness," and it emboldened the colonized. Months after this huge setback for the Empire, Washington's Office of Naval Operations, in a "confidential" dispatch from Jamaica, rued the fact that the "political situation on the island is most precarious." The "natives are unruly, very anti-Government and anti-American. An open break is expected at any time, and violence and bloodshed are feared. The blacks have openly stated they will try to overthrow the Government by force and do away with all the whites." The police were "apathetic and will do nothing in the event of a gang attacking a white," something of more than academic interest in a U.S. Consulate overwhelmingly led by whites. It was "not safe to go out on foot in certain sections after dark" and, thus, "riots" were "expected to be even worse than the riots of 1938." Yes, it was concluded with a sigh, "very serious trouble is definitely brewing among a very large percentage of the natives of Jamaica."[53]

The almost casual exploitation to which Caribbean nationals had been subjected hardly prepared them for the combined rhetoric of sacrifice and freedom they were expected to ingest. The Trinidadian leader Albert Gomes recalled later that he was "present on occasions when cinema audiences generously cheered appearances of Hitler and Mussolini; and later, when the Russians so heroically repulsed Nazi invasion, Stalin became a figure of awe and veneration among the masses. I was daily in close contact with the ordinary people," he said with assurance, "and knew their reactions well. When Hitler seemed to be succeeding, they experienced a feeling of satisfaction that someone was getting the better of the English." Gomes was "often surprised to find this even among trade unionists who had profound ideological reasons for hating the Hitlers and Mussolinis of this world."[54] Grantley Adams, the Caribbean Labour Congress founder from Barbados who later turned sharply to the right, "had frequently expressed his admiration for Soviet Russia . . . during the years of the Second World War." He "persuaded the Labour Party and the Workers' Union to sing the 'Red Flag' on all public occasions and to fly banners with the Hammer and Sickle prominently displayed."[55] Generally in Barbados, according to the scholar David Browne, there was a decided "lack of enthusiasm" for the war.[56] In "the case of the British, Dutch, and French colonies," says the scholar Gaylord Kelshall, "there were elements who did not care for colonial repression and considered German brutality in the event of a German victory, as similar to colonialism. In all cases, they looked to America as the great leveler who would change the area, but their dreams were not to be fulfilled. The prejudiced behaviour of many of the inexperienced American troops quickly soured relations and there were elements of the population who ended up not caring which side won the war."[57]

Washington was coming to find that taking London's place—and supplanting other colonizers—in the region was not simple opportunism. It was survival, since the malfeasance of the Empire was increasingly seen as creating a security threat in the backyard of the United States. At the same time, despite Jim Crow, on balance the advent of Washington—generally—was seen as a step forward from London's malfeasance.

Militant Jamaica was something of an exception that validated the rule. There was present in Jamaica, Washington was informed during the war, "an anti-Government Negro movement which finds expression at the moment chiefly in anti-Americanism." The "unemployed element in Kingston" were fingered as a major culprit and were seen as "ready to make trouble for the Americans at a moment's notice." Notably worrisome was that "the view is being sedulously put about among the native population that the Japanese are colored people and therefore may be considered as fighting the local coloured man's battles."[58]

When Labor Organizes

T HE WAR HAD A SEARING IMPACT on Caribbean labor. Workers were being moved around the hemisphere like so many pieces on a chessboard, which exposed them to stimulating experiences as it enhanced their internationalism and reduced their provincialism, making them more susceptible to regional forms of organization. The rhetoric of the war, with its impassioned calls for democracy, freedom, and self-determination, would have been exposed as empty if they had been applied solely to those of "pure European descent"; inevitably those of the Caribbean began to think that such uplifting sentiments also applied to them. Given the outstanding role played by the Soviet Union during the war, inexorably the profile of communists generally was burnished, along with their ideology, which gave pride of place in its theory to the power of labor. The region was racked with labor unrest during the war as the colonial masters were quite busy trying to save their own hides, and the experiences learned were not to be easily forgotten once the war ended. Caribbean labor was influenced by all these currents and had the advantage of having within their ranks sophisticated Marxists like Jamaica's Richard Hart and British Guiana's Cheddi Jagan, men who were quite capable of taking advantage of the propitious historical moment.

Looming above all was realizing the promise of a war to which the region had contributed so much. The Fifth Pan-African Congress, which had significant input from the Caribbean, met in Manchester just after the Caribbean Labour Congress (CLC) gathering in 1945, and the opinions expressed were parallel. One was that during the "war of 1914–1918 coloured workers had taken a very major part in the defence of Britain and were given all sorts of promises of employment and benefits, which were not fulfilled. In fact, they were in many instances the victims of riots. Despite any technical qualifications they had, it

was impossible for them during the inter-war period to secure employment"—
and they were determined to ensure that history did not repeat itself.[1]

This was an era when the working class recognized that a turning point in
the planet's evolution had been reached. The millions of corpses that littered
graveyards and battlefields alike were sufficiently convincing proof, and, consequently, there was a felt desire to confer and plan for a brighter tomorrow.
That was also why delegates from the colonized world met with their counterparts from the metropole in July 1945 in London in a meeting that contributed
to the formation of the World Federation of Trade Unions—a kind of global version of the CLC—and viewed widely in London and Washington as little more
than a "Communist Front" due to the significant participation of Moscow-backed
radicals. "This is the first time that we have been able to gather under one roof
such a large and representative body," said Georgetown's Hubert Critchlow. "In
the past," he added with asperity, "the International Labour Movement was too
much a European movement—a white movement," but the war had inflicted
heavy damage on this kind of thinking. "So strongly do the workers of my country resent racial chauvinism," Critchlow asserted, "that they feel that governments of all countries in which racial discrimination is legalized . . . shall be
debarred from taking part in the World Peace Conference, unless they take
steps to annul such legislation before victory." This was a double-barreled blast
at both London and Washington, with the latter—being simultaneously the
ascendant power, a nation not afraid to tout its own alleged virtues while marred
by officially sanctioned racism—resting directly in the crosshairs.[2]

Preceding this auspicious gathering was a confab in early 1944 that included
T. A. Marryshow of Grenada, Grantley Adams of Barbados, A. A. Cipriani of
Trinidad, Robert Bradshaw of St. Kitts and Nevis, V. C. Bird of Antigua, Eric
Gairy of Grenada, Eric Williams of Trinidad, and others, with the prime demand
on the agenda being a "political federation" in the British West Indies.[3] This
"British Guiana and West Indian Labour Conference" was convened in Georgetown and, inter alia, addressed the pressing question of "colonies with surplus
populations, especially Barbados and Jamaica." The conference chose to "join
with British Guiana in calling upon the Imperial Government to undertake and
pursue the development" of the South American nation "systematically" by, for
instance, allowing the "free and unimpeded movement between the population
of the British West Indies and British Guiana," which would be a concrete step
toward pan-Caribbean unity. Befitting the era, there was also a certain militancy, with the session chaired by Cipriani demanding freedom for "Buzz" Butler
and other jailed labor leaders. Symptomatic of the objective push toward
sovereignty was the "urgency" with which the presence of U.S. bases was viewed,
even though the war was ongoing. Conferees viewed "with abhorrence the agreement whereby without consulting the views of the peoples concerned such bases
are to be of a permanent character for 99 years." A "plebiscite" was suggested.
Also symptomatic was the "deep appreciation of the brilliant successes of the

Red Army" and the proto-independence viewpoint that analyzed with "grave concern the position of the colonies in relation to the principles enshrined in the Atlantic Charter" and the fact that conferees chose to "place no confidence in the hope held out that such principles will be extended to them."[4]

This pro-sovereignty demand too was to be pre-eminent at the CLC gathering, which convened in Barbados in September 1945. It was "the first deliberative assembly of freely chosen political representatives of West Indian peoples," said the Jamaican lawyer and labor leader Richard Hart. The region was presented with a dramatic choice of organize or starve—literally—since the West Indies, he noted, "were brought to the very verge of famine during the war when our lines of foreign food supply were cut."[5] Grantley Adams, the host of this meeting, was enthusiastic in greeting those assembled, noting that "this is, I believe, the first occasion on which delegates from outside the British colonies have attended a Caribbean labour conference of this kind." He was referring to the participation of delegates from other European colonies, as representation was envisioned from Puerto Rico, the U.S. Virgin Islands, French colonies, the Bahamas, etc. Present were delegations from nine British colonies and one Dutch colony, along with Bermuda. Adams felt that whatever the ostensible colonial master, they had much to learn from one another. "I have visited France," he said, "and seen a black man who was Secretary of State for the Colonies and I think something like that should take place in the British Colonial Office."

As this comment suggests, all were not of one mind on the matter of sovereignty and independence. At one point Hart "refuted Comrade Gomes' statement that self-government meant severance of ties with Britain. What it did mean was passing from the 'Empire' into the 'Commonwealth.'" Still, more than one present pledged "undying affection and unswerving loyalty" to London. The logic of events, however, was pushing inescapably in Hart's direction. For example, there was much consternation expressed at the CLC founding about the presence of U.S. bases, installations whose presence had been negotiated in London. Would not such developments continue to occur as long as the residents of the region did not hold firmly the reins of power?

Given the intensity of the remarks, it would be easy to conclude that the existence of U.S. bases in themselves were sufficient to impel the CLC headlong toward a full-throated endorsement of independence. Albert Gomes of Trinidad captured the opinion of many when he announced that he was "resentful in the extreme of the attitude adopted by the U.S. on the question of bases." Another delegate proclaimed sadly that these bases "had caused a deterioration in status and morals." U.S. forces in British Guiana, said A. A. Thorne, had been told to associate solely with Europeans there and next the apparent analytically distinct category of "Portuguese," "but on no account with the coloured people or the Indians." Concurring, a delegate from Antigua, which had a U.S. naval and air base, observed that the "behaviour of the U.S. troops had been bad. They had accentuated racial feeling, demoralized the people and shocked their British training" with their raw crudities in language and attitude. Yes, said a delegate from St. Vincent, "women were debased by visiting U.S. troops even though there were no bases" in his homeland. At this confab, the added wages brought by these bases were not seen as sufficient to vitiate their downside.

Marryshow of Grenada was elected president of the CLC, a reflection of his own eminence and also the militant example historically displayed by his tiny homeland. Adams was selected as vice president, along with Hubert Critchlow of British Guiana; Vivian Henry was secretary and was assisted by Hart. In focusing a searchlight on the question of federation and independence and privileging the role of labor in this process, the CLC had performed a major service. Small polities like St. Kitts, Nevis, Anguilla, Antigua, St. Vincent, etc. hardly had the heft to stand up to London—or Washington—but yoked into an alliance with others similarly situated, they at least had a fighting chance. Yet for various reasons, the founding CLC meeting did not establish a sufficiently staffed or funded Secretariat to carry out the burdensome though important tasks of information sharing, collecting of dues, producing publications, etc. that the times demanded.[6]

Besides, it was hard enough for this fragmented polity that was the Caribbean to confront major powers in London or Washington, but this formidable task was complicated further by the abject lack of unity that prevailed in their ranks—a disunity that was exacerbated further when the Cold War erupted almost simultaneously with the conclusion of the Pacific War.

Moreover, the CLC met under the shadow of a leveraged takeover of the region by the power that saw itself as the logical inheritor of the Empire—the United States. As it became clear that it would be difficult—at best—for a bloodied Empire to maintain control in the region, public opinion began to consider the alternatives. In St. Kitts there was serious discussion as to whether the British West Indies "should be taken over by the United States of America in liquidation of debts incurred by Great Britain for financing the war."[7] As early as November 1940, the Jamaican president of the New York–based National Council of the West Indies, W. A. Domingo, observed that at a hemispheric gathering in Cuba, Washington had "proposed that in case of a British defeat European possessions in the Western Hemisphere should be placed under the collective trusteeship of American nations. This proposal was resisted by Dr. Leopoldo Melo, Chief of the Argentine delegation, as well as by our Council" and its representative in Havana, attorney Hope Stevens of New York. This "received considerable publicity in the Cuban press"—and, perhaps, sheds light on Domingo's own subsequent problem in retaining his immigrant status in the United States. But at this juncture, Domingo was seized with the idea that in the "document and the Convention implementing it, West Indians are guaranteed the right of self-determination and self-government by the 21 American nations." This was a "significant victory for the peoples of the Caribbean, a

majority of whom are [of] Negro blood." Ironically, U.S. secretary of state
Cordell Hull "was obliged, through our activity, to concede to Black West Indians
rights which up to now the Negroes of his state, Tennessee, have not gained"—
a contradiction that only began to resolve itself when the Caribbean marched
toward sovereignty and African Americans marched away from Jim Crow.
Domingo, whose lobbying extended to Buenos Aires, also received a letter from
Dr. Melo, who told him to "rest assured that I will continue working with all my
strength" in "fighting for the realization of the ideals which the West Indies
National Emergency Committee is defending so courageously." Similarly,
Dr. Melo reassured Ethelred Brown of the Jamaica Progressive League that his
"ideals were listened to at the Convention."[8]

London chose to take all of this seriously. Hubert Young, the governor in
Port-of-Spain, confided that he had "recently received information from a reliable source that the [British West Indies Labour Party] has addressed from
Cuba what purports to be a 'declaration of independence' on behalf of the British West Indies," which was "addressed to the Secretary of State, Washington,
and requests the United States government to give protection to the independent West Indies." Cipriani, the president of the party, was seen as the
culprit.[9]

Reporting from Havana, Sir G. Ogilvie Forbes had a differing view. He was
informed indirectly by a "delegate to the Havana conference who is quite reliable that Jamaica had lodged a petition for autonomy" that was "intended to be
kept secret from His Majesty's Government,"[10] words that he in turn enclosed
in a secret report. The worried colonizer cracked down. "No exit permits have
been asked for or given to anyone likely to be behind such a movement," it was
stated coldly. "Censor has been watching correspondence with Cuba carefully
since conference started and has nothing to report."[11] Digging for information,
London was not altogether reassured when it found that it was actually the
"Argentine delegation" that "introduced the subject [self-government in the
Caribbean] to the conference," for that suggested that the colonized might
be able to call upon hemispheric allies.[12] But this rapidly dissipating reassurance
was brief, for London then had reason to believe that stirring up trouble for the
Empire were Jamaican exiles in Manhattan. Exiles in the Jamaica Progressive
League were the "authors of the declaration" that was "claiming [the] right to
self-determination and appeal to the Monroe Doctrine," it was reported—a bla-
tant attempt to enlist Washington in this crusade.[13]

This concern also reflected the fact that the United States, which countenanced anti-Empire propaganda within its borders, not least because it had
its own problems with London, was now having this tendency "blow back" in
Washington as those like Domingo sensed that the Caribbean might be passed
on to another "master." "We did not wholeheartedly approve the destroyer-
naval and aerial bases deal," said the West Indian columnist A. M. Wendell
Malliet. Putting his New York audience on alert, he reminded them that the

"West Indian situation is the most ominous of the several vexing problems now facing the non-white people anywhere."[14]

So moved, these U.S. residents and nationals sprung into action as the war was ending, knocking together a "Provisional World Council of Dominated Nations," which not only included the relatively small Caribbean territories but such giants as India and Indonesia—though Richard B. Moore of Barbados chaired this New York–based entity.[15] Moore was also "duly elected and delegated" by the National Council of the West Indies "to present its appeal on behalf of the Caribbean people of the British, French and Dutch West Indies, the Guianas and British Honduras" at the founding 1945 meeting of the United Nations to be held in San Francisco.[16]

Moore made quite a splash in the perpetually fog-bound city by the bay. Born in Barbados in 1893, he came to the United States sixteen years later, and eight years after that became a U.S. citizen.[17] He was a Communist Party candidate for attorney general in 1930 and the "only Negro delegate from the United States to the Conference of Oppressed Peoples called by the League Against Imperialism and Colonial Brussels at Brussels in 1927."[18] He had become a Communist Party member seven years earlier, part of the West Indian wave that flocked to the red banner. The FBI, which gathered this data on him, also was of the opinion that he "was given [a] course of training in Russia."[19]

Thus, as world delegates conferred on the shape of the new world order, Moore was "asking" for a "wire" of "a hundred immediately. This is an SOS," he added breathlessly, "for I have spent everything I had—$625 up to the moment. But the results accruing show this to have been more than warranted. Proportionately, our Council," he added not incorrectly, "has achieved more in ratio to its expenditure than any other groups here, I am sure." He had made "very important contacts" and "significant opportunities" were "opening up."[20]

London's consul general in Manhattan told his superiors that "you may be surprised as I was that a comparatively small and particularly wealthy community such as the West Indians in Harlem should find it worth their while to incur heavy expenses to present their views at San Francisco."[21] It was dawning that this force of the hammer that was Africans in New York and the anvil of labor unions in the Caribbean could inflict mighty blows on the Empire.

Thus, the British Consulate in Manhattan expressed interest in "A.M. Wendell Malliet, a British West Indian known to this office for many years and a feature writer for the 'New York Amsterdam News,'" which targeted the city's burgeoning African American population. They were interested in his participation in the upcoming Pan-African Congress, and they expressed interest in exploiting perceived rifts between him and the NAACP.[22] A "secret" 1945 request from the Colonial Office sought "information about West Indians in the United States and American Negro movements generally." Reference was made to the participation of Caribbean nationals in the recently concluded Pan-African gathering in Manchester, with special reference to the roles of Jamaica's "Ken Hill" and a "Miss Alma la Bardie representing" Garvey's movement, and, one bureaucrat was told, "your old friend Mrs. Amy Garvey also played quite a prominent part at the Congress."[23]

Yet the fact that the war had devastated both the rivals and allies of U.S. imperialism—particularly Britain, Japan, and the Soviet Union—meant that Caribbean nations were at a noticeable disadvantage. Moreover, Washington— well aware of the U-boat threat posed by Berlin only recently—was determined to maintain a chokehold on military bases that many Caribbean nationals saw as a threat to their sovereignty. Early on there was awareness of the dilemma posed by these facilities in Bermuda, Jamaica, Antigua, British Guiana, Trinidad, St. Lucia, and elsewhere, particularly the dilemma involving the "handling of a situation which many Americans refer to as the 'color line.' In all these places a large proportion of the native population is wholly or in part Negro," President Franklin D. Roosevelt was informed. "All officers on duty . . . should be instructed that in all official relations with the governments of these places, they must conform with the practice and usage of these governments." Mention was made of an analogous situation that exploded when the "Marine Corps . . . took charge of order and supervision of many government functions in Haiti in 1916," which was viewed as an example to avoid.[24] However, it would take more than a presidential memorandum to compel an officer corps that was steeped in the racially offensive traditions of the Old South to update their questionable practices.

Then there was the similarly sensitive matter of labor imported from the Caribbean to the United States and its possessions. At one point the United States desperately needed workers in the Canal Zone—they needed "six hundred Jamaicans at once." But the "War Department in cooperation with the Government of Panama" wanted to "accept labor brought from Spain or Colombia [or] Puerto Rico," even though one U.S. official did "realize that Jamaican labor is highly efficient." So what was the problem? The "Republic of Panama" had an "insistent desire . . . that the bulk of labor brought in should be of white or near white blood."[25]

This importation of labor had also increased the base of support for U.S.–based Caribbean radicals such as Richard B. Moore of Barbados and W. A. Domingo of Jamaica. In the West Indies they had been practicing their political craft against some of the most retrograde forces to be found on the planet and thus—even given the disadvantages provided by U.S. Jim Crow— they found themselves very much up to the task of moving an agenda when residing in New York City. For as one paper in St. Lucia concluded bitterly, it was "common knowledge that the plantocracy in the West Indies is the most reactionary group to be found in any part of the world. They have always opposed adult suffrage."[26] Moore and his comrades were sufficiently sophisticated—and bereft of narrow provincialism—to realize that it was not just a "scarcity of labour in the South" that motivated the arrival of West Indian workers. One Barbados newspaper quoted the New York–based West Indian Wendell Malliet, who "flatly" agreed and "suggested that the importation of labour from the West Indies was an attempt to discriminate against the [U.S.] Negro and the poor white worker of the Southern States and the Pacific Coast"—a trend that did not augur well for his desire to build an alliance in the United States in favor of Caribbean sovereignty.[27]

Moreover, those elites dreaming of playing off one sector of the work force against another encountered a crude surprise when even workers from an otherwise conservative Barbados began to organize and strike.[28] Interestingly, just as the CLC was convening in Barbados, Washington was giving "five thousand West Indian Negro workers in Wisconsin only five days in which to leave this country and go home to Barbados and Jamaica." On the one hand, the war's end meant their labor was needed less; on the other hand, employers were becoming increasingly fed up with these workers' militancy.[29]

For Washington was beginning to realize that the mass importation of Caribbean workers was something of a Trojan Horse. "West Indian Negroes are restless and dissatisfied as a group and are the first to agitate among themselves," announced the FBI as the war hung in the balance. No doubt referring to entities headed by the likes of Moore and Domingo, it was stated that "many organizations reported to be un-American in tendencies are largely made up of West Indian Negroes." These migrants were happy to "secure better wages in the United States and better living conditions than in the British West Indies," but they were enraged to find that "there is allegedly more discrimination in the United States than in the homeland." Worryingly, a "large percentage" of these sojourners had flocked to the nation's key city: New York. And since they were part of the Empire's heritage, they naturally followed carefully events in other parts of this sprawling conglomeration, notably in Asia, and "had alleged sympathies for Eastern countries." "Negro publications have followed closely Eastern affairs dating back prior to the last World War, especially as to those matters affecting colored races," which may have suggested a like sympathy for the alleged champion of these races: Japan. The arrival of English-speaking foreigners in Black America had aroused internationalist predilections that were not greeted with equanimity in Washington. "The recent action of Britain with regard to India is said to have created considerable comment among Negroes and their reactions allegedly reflect a certain amount of unity with the other colored peoples of the world."[30]

Moreover, the war also dispersed West Indians to the headquarters of the Empire itself, and there they encountered a vulgar awakening upon discovering that their presence was something less than desirable. "The better dance halls in Liverpool" were "closed to the West Indians and feelings of bitterness" were increasing.[31] There was also a "colour bar on Merseyside," though it was "clear that the problem" was "undoubtedly caused by the presence of the

Americans," that is, the "prejudices of individual white American personnel" [32] in the United Kingdom.

H EMISPHERIC AND GLOBAL SUPPORT ASIDE, prospects for the kind of progressive, labor-centered federation envisioned by Hart and others may have been overly ambitious, particularly given the existence of conservative forces in Barbados, an island that would have to play a prominent role in the CLC, as evidenced by their founding meeting occurring there. If Barbados could not be won over, it could be a thorn in the sacroiliac of the CLC and a base for subversion of any labor-left regimes that might emerge in the region. The problem was that there was a "deep-seated white racism and economic domination" in this nation, although—according to one informed analyst—"these things cannot be said in public."[33] In the postwar era "there was whites only housing in the capital; and it was next to impossible for the Black Barbadian to get a job as a bank clerk or a jockey, let alone a manager or accountant." In the latter part of the twentieth century, it remained true that "young whites" would "sometimes get promotion over experienced blacks."[34] There was "legend of sort, that in Barbados only Euro-Barbadians or Caucasoid Barbadians can manage and run business enterprises."[35]

Wynter Crawford, one of the most eminent sons Barbados has produced, has spoken forcefully in a like fashion about his native soil. A man of socialist orientation—"Garvey had no influence on me at all," he says—he founded the Barbados Labour Party (BLP) in 1938, then departed and founded the West Indian National Congress Party in 1944, where it quickly became "fully a match" for the BLP, not least because of its leading role in organizing agricultural workers. "It is in Barbados," he says "that the racial contract of white dominance and black accommodation has been experienced in its most extreme form." Barbados, he asserted, was "perhaps the only country in the entire West Indies that preserved the rigid racial discrimination after emancipation because so many whites remained and controlled the land and commercial enterprises." It was "impossible," as a result, "for any coloured person to get a job in a bank or big business." He contrasted "Grenada or Dominica or St. Lucia"—for example, in Marryshow's homeland, Crawford expressed "doubt if there are six white families." The presence of a sizeable European population not only pushed Barbados to the right as this group strained to preserve the privileges bestowed by white supremacy, but it also meant attracting capital from the like-minded, who—after all—continued to control this precious resource disproportionately. Thus, when he visited Kingston, Jamaica, in 1947 for a CLC conference, Crawford was dumbfounded as he "toured a place called Denham Town. We had never seen such poverty in all our lives. Jamaicans were living in boxes, in trees and in holes dug in the earth lined with cardboard. Living down there was actually horrid. I had never seen anything like it in Barbados," he said.

Yet despite the clear import of "Barbados exceptionalism," even "Little England" could not stand apart altogether from pervasive regional and hemispheric currents. For as in other Caribbean territories—such as British Guiana—the stevedores were a major force to contend with. They were the "backbone of unionization for a long time," says Crawford. "[Y]ou see," he continued, "the port had to be kept working all the time so, if they said they wanted a certain wage, it was paid to them after a little struggle and then the additional costs would be put on the price of goods." And just as in Jamaica, external forces intruded on London's reverie in Barbados. New Yorkers of Caribbean extraction—Hope Stevens, Richard B. Moore, W. A. Domingo, et al.—were instrumental in the founding of the Barbados Progressive League in 1938, which became the Barbados Labour Party.[36]

But even here, "Barbados exceptionalism" intruded, for the BLP was "torn by ideological conflict over the question of ideological representation," with Grantley Adams on the right of this scalding issue. That he could be elected a leader of the CLC did not bode well for the group's future.[37]

In fact, the antipodes of the CLC and the region generally were Adams on the right, Cheddi Jagan of British Guiana on the left, and others—Manley and Bustamante of Jamaica, Eric Williams and Albert Gomes of Trinidad, T. A. Marryshow of Grenada, et al.—falling somewhere in between. In a simplified sense, the fate of the region turned on the contrasting fortunes of these two men, and, as it turned out, Adams was on the winning side of history—at least to this point—and that spelled doom for the CLC and its version of federation.

Of Jagan and his long-time Euro-American spouse, Janet Jagan, Wynter Crawford argued that "the two of them almost single-handedly spread communism right through the British West Indies and the Caribbean, starting with small cadres in different islands . . . all the little Communist cadres that existed in the other islands in the West Indies were almost all created by the Jagans," though they did so in a noninvasive, nonconfrontational manner. "[F]or all the years I knew them," says Crawford, "we never once discussed Communism or Marxism or any politics."[38]

As for Grantley Herbert Adams, born in 1898, he exhibited tendencies toward both "Asquithian Liberalism" and "Socialism" befitting his training in the United Kingdom,[39] though charges of his "seemingly conservative approach to politics" and being "less than sensitive to the needs of the poor and marginalized"[40] can be ascribed to his deep immersion in the marrow of his homeland. The son of a primary school teacher, he had won scholarships to Harrison College and to Oxford before becoming a leading member of the Bridgetown bar. His purported socialist leanings notwithstanding, he was the lawyer that forced the "radical" Clennel Wickham "out of political life in Barbados." Yet when the Barbados Progressive League began to surge as a result of the unrest of the 1930s—at one point it had an estimated membership of 20,000—there was Adams in the forefront of its ranks.[41]

Like many of his Caribbean counterparts, he too had ties to the United States. His brother Stanley was an official at the historically black Johnson C. Smith University in Charlotte, North Carolina. As for the man who became Sir Grantley, a title richly deserved given his service to London, he returned from his training in the United Kingdom allegedly with the firm opinion that liberalism was a "spent force" and was drawn to the then existing viable alternative: socialism. It is arguable whether he continued to adhere to this view upon ascending to the CLC leadership in 1945.[42]

T HE BAHAMAS TECHNICALLY was not part of the Caribbean lineup of nations, resting as it does in the Atlantic off the coast of Florida, yet it is worth scrutinizing since it tended to reflect influences from both the United States and the British West Indies, and perhaps this closeness to the U.S. mainland sheds light on why its politics and composition were closer to those of Barbados than to, say, British Guiana. Yet it too was affected profoundly by the war and presented a distinct challenge to its powerful neighbor in Washington. Like the Caribbean, this was nothing new but, in a sense, was an extension of what had occurred during World War I. For it was in 1918 that Washington recruited 2,000 men from the Bahamas and took them to Charleston, South Carolina, where they were paid $3.30 for a ten-hour day, with living quarters provided. As the workers saw it, this was gross exploitation. Thus there were lingering and unpleasant memories when again during World War II the United States began to rely on Bahamian labor once more, as well as moving more of its personnel onto the islands where a potential security threat was thought to exist. These dueling occurrences contributed to violent riots in the Bahamas in June 1942, and a Commission of Inquiry concluded that this conflagration was the "natural outcome of the narrow economic, political and social policies pursued by a small but dominant political group in this Colony during the last quarter century."[43] Centered in Nassau, the "labour disturbance" erupted when "unskilled labourers in the large American project staged a demonstration" that quickly descended into "smashing shop windows and looting fashionable stores." They were "protesting against wages,"[44] concluded a paper from St. Kitts that was grappling with similar issues.

This disturbance was described as "the biggest and most disastrous riot in the history of the Colony." Considerable damage was inflicted, and armed troops were called in that eventually fired on the crowd. Five men were killed and forty-six were injured, and thirty-seven were arrested. The immediate cause of the rampage was dissatisfaction with the wages paid by a U.S. enterprise. This was not unique to the Bahamas as grievances about the rates of pay paid by the United States was a regional concern. There were strikes in Jamaica spurred precisely by this point. There were rumors that the United States was prepared to pay higher rates but that the colonial governments had prevented this—one more blemish on an already blotted colonial record of London. The Duke of

Windsor immediately made a number of concessions to the workers, but since there was no labor legislation or effective trade unions in the Bahamas, riots became the vehicle of change.

Like Barbados, a good deal of this elite were of European extraction, and, buffeted by the strong and bracing winds of Jim Crow blowing from Florida, had little incentive to change their ways. Dr. Roland Combebatch had practiced in the Bahamas for seventeen years and, when queried in the aftermath of the riots, spoke movingly of an "underlying sense of injustice." "[O]ffices in the Government service"—at least "some of them"—"could not be filled by a Negro, and there were certain offices where a Negro could not be employed, for example, the hospitals." There was "no black officer in the police force" and the nation "had never had a black magistrate." Dr. C. R. Walker, a doctor and member of the House of Assembly, agreed. "The Coloured man made all the concessions," he maintained. "He challenged any man in the Colony to say that he was wrong there. The Coloured man was discriminated against in the churches, in the theatres, in the private schools—there was harmony at the expense of the coloured population."[45]

Though some in the Bahamas were pointing the finger of accusation at Washington for their difficulties, the real culprits may have been closer to home. The visiting British dignitary, Creech Jones, agreed that the colonial "authorities in the West Indies were determined that the work on the American bases . . . not disturb the miserable standard prevailing. The Americans were prepared to pay what standards were declared by the British to be reasonable and proper. They were prepared to pay more & said so publicly. I discussed all this at great length with the Colonial Office at the time," he said, "[and] deplored the exclusion of trade unions in the wage determination. I spoke to the highest American authorities in Washington recently," he continued, "who strongly resent my suggestion that the wretched rates in the Bahamas were due to them. I suspect that the British authorities were influenced in their policy by the big economic interests in the colonies. I can say privately that the Americans would welcome an independent enquiry by the ILO [International Labor Organization] into the whole problem of wages."[46]

It could not be reassuring to the Empire that Creech Jones—albeit not a Tory—was breaking ranks. Others were vainly seeking to uphold the prevailing line about the beneficence brought to the region by London, particularly in the face of Washington's undisguised challenge. Yes, "the condition of the West Indians is deplorable enough," said the British official Alan Dudley, and, yes, the situation in the region was "less exciting than might be imagined." Still, "the photographs, for example, show housing conditions no worse than those which are common in the southern parts of the United States"—at once a curt slap at a rival and a damning capitulation to the hard bigotry of low expectations.[47]

Fortunately for the colonizers, the lid was placed back on the Bahamas, but insurgencies of various sorts continued to simmer in the scattered island nations south of Florida. The Bahamas revolt was one more bit of evidence that the very existence of the Empire and its template of rampant underdevelopment, super-low wages, and gross exploitation—combined with shooing away other powers via "imperial preference"—presented a clear and present danger to the security of the United States. First there was concern about Berlin and its seemingly ubiquitous U-boats and noisy propaganda. Then after the war concluded there was Moscow and its rhetoric about class exploitation—which was not a chimera in the Caribbean. The press of war had handcuffed Washington to a degree. Labor was needed, so even after the 1942 riots, the War Food Administration "announced that its Office of Labour would begin to bring 1300 additional workers from the Bahama Islands" to Miami to toil on "Florida truck crops."[48]

There was a contradictory response to the war-driven incursion from the United States into the region. The overstretched Empire could hardly compete with the United States in terms of wages. But as a Kittitian working on the U.S. base in Trinidad put it, "the Americans employ hundreds of persons to finish a certain job quickly and as soon as it is done they knock off those labourers."[49] Generally, as a St. Kitts journal put it, "emigration to the United States is a welcome 'break' to West Indian labour . . . who would . . . prefer to be able to earn a decent livelihood and remain near to family and friends."[50] If Jim Crow Washington was perceived as a benevolent alternative, this was more of a statement about the parsimoniousness and crass exploitation of London.

Yet, if the otherwise drowsy Bahamas was up in arms, then what about, say, Trinidad, home of the most advanced proletarians, as evidenced by the revolt in the oil fields in 1937 that had kicked off the current wave of labor militancy? In brief, things were not going very well in Trinidad and Tobago. Albert Gomes was to become a fierce anticommunist after the war, but when U.S. personnel began to flood into his nation in the wake of World War II, he was not necessarily enthralled by their presence. When unions sought to organize at the military bases, "we soon learnt," he recalled with enduring irritation years later, "that the United States authorities were insisting that the base was a military installation and, therefore, particularly in wartime, entitled to regard its employees as subject to military discipline, which was incompatible with membership of a trade union." They then met with these officials and discovered to their dismay that "their attitude was hostile from the very beginning. They would not hear us"—and, just in case, they were "accompanied by a uniformed marine who was heavily armed." Their U.S. interlocutor was the embodiment of "red-hot resentment during the first half-hour of our meeting," Gomes recalled. "He protested wildly," and the West Indians were taken aback further when "the seemingly trigger-happy marine who accompanied him also joined in the argument."

This unforgiving atmosphere was not just a product of the U.S. arrival. As Gomes recalled it, the colonials "kept a watchful eye on all we did." Workers "were paid by the security branch to spy on us" and "even when we spoke to the trees and grass in the Square we were sure of an audience of one—the security officer, in plain clothes and somewhat shamefaced, lurking furtively behind some tree and nervously recording everything we said."[51]

Both London and Washington were finding out that it would not be easy to maintain white supremacy in the face of the stiff challenge it had received from all sides during the war. As this titanic conflict was winding down, a page-one banner headline in the newspaper of Trinidad and Tobago unions blared, "Colour Bar on Oil Fields Must Go!" Jobs had been allocated on the basis of color and the "natives—East Indian and Negro Workers" had had their fill of this. "They are never permitted to hold any of the jobs" that were preferred, such as "Senior Operator" or "Operating Superintendent." "Those jobs," it was stated with rancor, "are reserved for the white people and their children. The natives do the actual operations but they are never called operators."[52] This issue was not going away with the war's end. Later the Trinidad and Tobago unions cited the words of the African American activist and scholar W.E.B. Du Bois, who asked a question to which the war had provided a definitive response: "Is it democracy," he inquired, "for whites to rule dark majorities?" An accompanying article assailed U.S.-style racism and the concomitant deprivation of the right to vote and how all this was reinforced by similar ideas emanating from the "great nations in Europe." This must end, it was thought,[53] and increased organizing and the resultant power of unions and federations like the CLC would guarantee this outcome.

For the conclusion of the war had presented what was viewed as the region's most sophisticated unions with a fresh set of challenges. David T. Pitt, a surgeon and president of the West Indian National Party, was based in Trinidad. As the war was lurching to a close, his morose demeanor belied the ecstasy of the moment. One problem: It seemed that the only thing worse than hosting U.S. bases was their downsizing. "As a result of cessation of work on the U.S.A. bases," he lamented, "there are approximately 20,000 people unemployed in Trinidad." He was reduced to "trying to secure a quota for Trinidad workers for the U.S.A." Initially, "the government refused," and Pitt was "afraid of the possible dangers that may result from allowing the unemployment situation to get out of hand." He was banking on the return of the Labour Party to power in London, hoping they could alter power imbalances in the colony that, he thought, allowed for a nonresponsive government. "At present," he said, "Trinidad has the worst constitution of all the West Indian colonies," with only British Guiana being able to challenge for this dubious title. Perhaps it was not coincidental that these were the two nations with the most militant unions, yet Dr. Pitt did not list Jamaica in this questionable category—and, according to some, their unions were the most militant of all.

But if there was any consolation, things were bad throughout the region. Seamen arriving in St. Kitts from Anguilla in October 1945 told of a "spell of hardship which has overtaken the island," including a "continued drought," "not much money in circulation," with the residents being in a "bad state." Basseterre was no prize, as "water scarcity" was "again the cry" there.[54] For in St. Kitts "1500 labourers" were "idle" after the sugar cane crop was harvested in that same year. Generally, "about 7000 labourers" were "employed in the sugar industry and in the dull season about three quarters of these are more or less regularly hired."[55] Just before then, "many fields of potatoes" were "now ripe" but were "not reaped because the market" was "flooded."[56]

CHAPTER 5

Militant Jamaica

T HE CARIBBEAN LABOUR CONGRESS (CLC) had gotten off to a slow start since its euphoric founding meeting in Barbados in 1945. With an understaffed and underfunded Secretariat, it was unable to effectively meet the challenge provided by its twin goals of coordinating labor organizing while pushing for a federated independence for the British West Indies. But the sum of its parts was considerably more than the whole, for the affiliates of the CLC were waging ferocious and militant battles throughout the region in a manner that in many ways exceeded the now fabled battles of 1937 and 1938. Hence it was entirely appropriate that the CLC chose Jamaica for its 1947 meeting, for it was here in the most populous island in Britain's hemispheric possession that labor was both powerfully sophisticated and intensely militant.

A major problem in overcoming the underdevelopment of the region was—precisely—this very same underdevelopment. To begin with, travel and communication were exceedingly difficult, which made organizing regionally problematic at best. Weeks before the convening of the CLC convention in Kingston, Jamaica, "delegates from British Guiana, Suriname and Grenada" were "requested to advise immediately whether there is any steamer or other sea transport which they could use to get to Trinidad in time to make the plane connection." The "delegates from St. Lucia and St. Vincent should likewise advise on their transport to Barbados or whether alternatively it is easier for them to get to Antigua or St. Kitts." Fortunately, "all transportation and maintenance expenses" were to be "paid here in Jamaica by the CLC," but that did not make the process of getting there less complicated.[1] But, as CLC leader Richard Hart pointed out, "there is no sea communication between the other islands and Jamaica by which it would be possible for the delegates to travel."[2] Not only were the territories of the British West Indies relatively isolated from each other, but, as Hart observed, "it is a peculiarity of the British possessions in the Caribbean that they have developed practically no connections or economic relations with the Latin American republics in close geographic proximity."[3]

The vast blue sea that separated one colonial appendage from another was not easy to bridge. These distances were exacerbated by differences that complicated the stated goal of federation. These ranged from the pervasive British influence in Barbados to the lingering French influence in Trinidad to Iberian influence in British Guiana, a reflection of its South American location. Of course, British Guiana and Trinidad and Tobago contained huge South Asian populations, which distinguished both nations mightily. Nearly half the population of the British West Indies was Jamaican, and the distance from Jamaica in the north to Trinidad in the south was roughly a thousand miles. In an era when travel was not easy, at times it seemed that these two regional leaders were as far apart as Perth and Paris.[4]

Logistical complexities were bad enough, but when combined with administrative incompetence, it meant that any progress by the CLC was virtually miraculous. Months before the slated confab in Kingston, V. C. Bird of Antigua was complaining that "we wrote about three letters to the President and Secretary that are still unanswered and we were wondering what has gone wrong."[5] The secretary—or chief administrative officer—was Vivian Henry, but according to his second in command, he was not meeting his responsibilities. "We have absolutely no progress with the formation of the [CLC]," said Richard Hart, but "rather than make a scandal," he was trying to find ways to work around Henry's weaknesses.[6] Henry, a solicitor in Port-of-Spain, confessed candidly that he was "very hard pressed with both professional as well as civic duties" and hardly able to perform his assigned tasks.[7] "How pleasantly surprised I was to learn that you still maintain an interest in the CLC," said Hart with more than a tinge of sarcasm. "All previous letters which have been sent to you by main connection with CLC business have been unanswered."[8]

Hart was already seen as the rising luminary in the region. After the first CLC gathering in Barbados, one Kingston periodical rhapsodized that "Richard Hart stars at West Indian conference," as he "made world headlines with a careful analysis of the case for West Indian federation."[9] Norman Manley, who later was to engineer the expulsion of Hart from the People's National Party once the Cold War heated up, earlier was unstinting in his praise of him. "We do not have in our ranks," he gushed, "anyone who has more closely studied West Indian history or kept himself better informed as to the course of events in recent years in other West Indian countries."[10] This was true. Unsophisticated telecommunications and general difficulties in communication combined with riotous heterogeneity made it difficult for any but the most dedicated to get a grip on the entire British West Indies—Hart was one of the few in this charmed circle.

Finally at a prefatory meeting in Antigua on Saturday, 12 January 1947, action was taken to smash the administrative logjam. Present were members from fifteen colonies representing about 200,000 workers from various trade unions.[11] It was a solemn occasion as the meeting was opened at 2:20 P.M. Prayers were said by the island's leading cleric, V. C. Bird, soon to be the founding father of independence, spoke amid loud cheers, and the "Council Chamber in which the meeting was held was packed to its capacity." Then the report on the work of Henry was provided and it was devastating. "The results of the inactivity of the Secretary was that (a) no invitations to join Congress were extended although a list of names of organizations within the Caribbean were sent to him." So the hammer fell. It was "agreed that Comrade [Henry should] be suspended" and it was "unanimously agreed" that Richard Hart of Jamaica should replace him. Robert Bradshaw of St. Kitts was approved as assistant secretary. Discussion then followed about the prospects of raising funds for the CLC in the United States. Norman Manley "felt that Paul Robeson and others would attend" fund-raisers, and he was correct. Indeed, the success of the CLC was heavily dependent on material support from within the West Indian community in the United States, for it was there in particular where sectarian differences between Barbadians, Jamaicans, Trinidadians, and the rest were submerged, as they were viewed either as "Negro" or "West Indian." It was there, consequently, that there was noticeable enthusiasm for the "blueprint of West Indian federation" that was "drawn up" in Antigua.[12]

It was also in Antigua that the work of the CLC took a quantum leap forward by the simple act of promoting the administrative virtuoso, Richard Hart. Imbued with tireless energy and a diplomatic mien—not to mention being a relentless letter writer—Hart was the right man in the right place at the right time. Earlier Hart had referred to "jealousies concerning Jamaica," touching pointedly on a major barrier to federation, the tensions that existed in an incredibly diverse array of territories that, after all, were for the most part islands unto themselves. Hart, however, was determined, stressing, "I am willing to work and work like hell to build up the CLC," but "six months have passed since the conference in Barbados and we have not taken one step in the direction of organizing the CLC. Are we fit for self-government," he asked querulously, "if we can't do better than this?"[13]

The professionalism and political vision Hart brought to the CLC answered his rhetorical question decisively. For more than most, he targeted for coordinated assault the essence of British colonialism. "Imperial trade preference," he told Albert Gomes of Trinidad shortly after being appointed CLC secretary, "is a means whereby having conspired together tacitly to rob and exploit primary producing countries as a whole by paying too little for their agricultural produce as compared to the price paid for manufactured goods, the industrialized countries then turn around and harness various primary producing countries to themselves economically and politically. By getting self-government and federation," he concluded, "we will be able to bargain for better terms (e.g. Cuba gets better terms from America than we do from Britain for sugar)."[14]

"I am delighted to see that you have now been installed in the post of Secretary," said George Padmore. "I feel that your services will be invaluable to the organization." Then he apprised him of an important initiative that, no doubt, would have fallen by the wayside if it had been raised pre-Hart. The soon-to-be prime minister of India was organizing an "Inter-Asian Conference" in New Delhi that "envisage[d] the unity, first, of the peoples of Asia . . . with the coloured peoples throughout the world." "I have been asked," said Padmore, "to extend an invitation to your Congress," which was no minor matter given the weighty presence of South Asian migrants in the West Indies.[15] Brimming with enthusiasm about Hart's appointment, Padmore's Pan-African Federation congratulated the CLC directly "on its good fortune in having secured so able and energetic a secretary as Richard Hart who has enabled West Indians abroad to keep intimate contact with Congress activities." He went on to indicate that his group "unanimously" endorsed "Caribbean federation and political self-determination based [on] Dominion status," and "strongly warn[ed]" against "accepting any compromises that may nullify immediate transfer of political power from Whitehall to West Indian people."[16]

Another heavyweight from the Pan-African world, W.E.B. Du Bois, reached Hart about another important initiative that would surely be ventilated at the CLC convention slated for the late summer of 1947. It concerned a "proposed petition" to the United Nations raising sharply the pressing matter of human rights violations against African Americans, and "we wish very much to have the support of the Caribbean Labour Congress."[17] Recognizing that the Caribbean's fortunes would be measurably improved if the African Diaspora could be enlisted, Hart moved to ensure that the NAACP petition would receive exposure in organs in the United Kingdom with which he had more significant contact than did his New York counterparts. Hence, *Pan-Africa: A Monthly Journal of Life, History and Thought*, published in Manchester by the legendary T. R. Makonnen, "reproduced . . . in full" the petition and then, in response to Hart's initiative, expressed gratitude "to receive your Bulletin," speaking of the CLC newsletter, "more especially since we get little news from the West Indies."[18]

Still, despite Hart's prestige and competence, the CLC still had a steep mountain to climb, for he was trying to run a far-flung organization from his inadequately staffed law office. Moreover, his predecessor, Vivian Henry, had "failed . . . to surrender all correspondence, funds, etc." from his reign, thus deepening the hole the CLC found itself in.[19] Nonetheless, one man could make a difference, as Hart exemplified. "Thank you for all the material," Padmore enthused shortly after Hart's ascension; in return he was "trying to collect a little extra funds" for the CLC, suggesting how competence, like yeast, could cause the bread of money to rise.[20]

Thus it was in September 1947 that the CLC demanded "federation," a "federal constitution," and a legislature with proportional representation for the British West Indies. The leadership reflected the region as it included Marryshow of Grenada, Gomes of Trinidad, Manley of Jamaica, Critchlow of British Guiana, and V. C. Bird of Antigua. Suggestive of the radicalism that was de rigeur then, "at the conclusion of the Congress, 30,000 people demonstrated through the streets of the city in support of the CLC demand for Dominion status for the Caribbean and for socialism." The many resolutions passed focused on issues such as labor's right to organize, sugar prices, racism, international human rights—especially support for struggles in Vietnam, Burma, and Nigeria—and attacks on the primary local foe of this agenda: Jamaica's own Alexander Bustamante, who headed an eponymous trade union federation that was viewed by the CLC as precisely how not to go about building workers' strength.[21]

Simultaneously, London was not happy with the CLC's left-wing politics. It was a "political organization and not, as it purports to be a labour congress," it concluded in May 1947. The "actual work" was "being done by Richard Hart," who already had a well-merited reputation for radicalism. Hart was also active in the People's National Party (PNP) of Jamaica, which had a kind of Social Democratic orientation, though it had distinct wings, and it was the "left wing" of the PNP, thought London, which "contains individuals who are members of the Communist Party and the group as a whole is very definitely influenced by the West Indian National Council and the Jamaica Progressive League, both of whom in turn are absolutely controlled by the Communist Party of America." Yet somehow the CLC had "noticeably increased its influence during recent months." The "Manpower Citizens Association" of British Guiana had "just been affiliated" with the CLC, and it was "now by far the most important and powerful trade union in the colony." Bermuda, which was more akin to the Bahamas or Barbados than to British Guiana, had recently seen its "Workers Association . . . become affiliated to the Caribbean Labour Congress" and it too was the "largest and most powerful labour organization in that colony." Kirby Green, senior defense security officer in the Caribbean area, concluded that CLC was "potentially, if not already, a Communist Front organization."[22]

It was understandable why eyebrows would be raised about the participation of Bermuda, which was distant from the Caribbean though similar in many ways to the easternmost island in the British West Indies, Barbados, with a relatively sizeable European population—which seemed to be a guarantee of conservative politics. Ernest W. T. Robinson, secretary general of the Bermuda Industrial Union, told a "dear comrade" of the CLC what he already knew: "There is quite a big difference between Bermuda and the West Indies."[23] Weeks before the CLC gathering in Kingston, E. F. Gordon of Bermuda, with an anguished lamentation, told Richard Hart that "it is unfortunate that the colored people of Bermuda, because of the low standard of education, and the centuries of subjection are very indifferent to the political future. A few of the people who should be in the forefront of the fight"—tellingly—"are hampered by the fact that I am a West Indian and the resultant jealousy leads them to cash in by a concerted attempt to induce as many as they can to pretend that the colored people have no social, economic or political difficulties." Still, he thought it "would be an inspiration to some of our colored members of Parliament to be present at the [CLC meeting]."[24]

The journey to a viable CLC was as remarkable—if not more so—than the journey leading away from it. Consider Bermuda, for example, which—according to one local publication in 1947—saw "nothing good, unless it be rum," emerging from the "West Indies and nothing gives greater offence than the assumption, so generally made by the British, that Bermuda is a member of that congeries of islands. She is a not a West Indian island," insisted the *Bermuda National Review*. But there was something riling the usually complacent island, a sea change of major proportion: "Americans retain their naval base and magnificent airfield on the island and American Senators have not hesitated to ask openly that the Colony should be handed over to the United States in partial settlement for debts owed and likely to increase."[25] Thus—surprising to many—Bermuda unions were found in this same epochal year of 1947 in league with the left-led CLC, meeting in the prototypical West Indian island of Jamaica.

London seemed stunned by the breadth of the CLC, observing that "Bermuda is represented, while Surinam has participated from the first." This was the case even though "the Congress is said to have close Communist affiliations," and even though there were evident trends toward "Fabian Socialism," as evidenced by Manley's critical role. Noticeable also was that like its predecessors stretching back to "1926 the Congress has pressed for West Indian federation."

The Colonial Office also noted in passing that "supporters of the Congress are drawn from Manley's PNP and that Bustamante's Jamaica Labour Party (the government party) will have nothing to do with it."[26] This was all too true, and the prospects for labor gains and federation crashed upon this mighty boulder of difference, as a left-right split developed in the region—not unlike what had occurred in black America when Du Bois was purged from the NAACP[27] or when Ferdinand Smith was ousted from the National Maritime Union.[28]

Yet in some ways this split in Jamaica was deeper, and it certainly had wider regional and hemispheric repercussions in that this island wielded direct influence from the Caribbean to Central America (British Honduras) to South America (British Guiana). Richard Hart was at the epicenter of this political earthquake and he holds that "from the time of the Labour Rebellion in 1938 the trade union movement" in Jamaica "had been plagued by internal divisions." For "most of the workers on the sugar and banana plantations and the vast majority of the unskilled manual workers had supported Bustamante and the JLP [Jamaica Labour Party]. The PNP's numerically smaller working class support had been drawn mainly from skilled, semi-skilled and clerical workers." As a result of JLP influence, the "issue of federation had not been considered in Jamaica" prior to 1944, as the "only Jamaican organizations with Caribbean wide connections being the cricketers and the sugar manufacturers." But by March

1945, when the secretary of state for the colonies inquired about federation, "all the legislatures, with the exception of those of the Bahamas, British Guiana and British Honduras had given an affirmative answer."

The CLC grew out of this consensus and was bolstered by the avid support of West Indians in North America. "Much of the money to finance" the Barbados meeting in 1945, said Hart, "was raised during a speaking tour in the U.S.A. by Norman Manley and Grantley Adams organized by the American Committee for West Indian Federation." Ferdinand Smith's union was also a heavy contributor.

A consummate opportunist, Bustamante sensed earlier than most that a movement backed by London or Washington would wield more heft than one that could only be indirectly backed by Moscow. So he moved with gusto to crush his opposition, a fact that became clear—ironically—when workers at a mental asylum struck in 1946, which was just one among many turbulent events in a turbulent year.[29] As it became clear that Bustamante's approach was emerging triumphant, leaders like Robert Bradshaw of St. Kitts and V. C. Bird of Antigua, who were less committed ideologically to class struggle and socialism, began to backslide, and as they came to power moved away from the politics which had gained them prominence in the first place.

Presumably they did not want to share the fate of those mowed down by the JLP. On one single day in February 1946, three were killed in Kingston when "gangs of men moved through [town]" as a "strike wave" hit "vital services." They were "smashing everything in their way" with a manic "use of force." Finally, at a PNP meeting in Edelweiss Park, "steps were taken to form able-bodied members into resistance groups who" were "to be armed."[30] Richard Hart was ecstatic about the "monster meeting of over 20,000 held at Edelweiss Park" and the "two meetings held during the strike," which were "the largest ever seen in Jamaica." There was a "record collection taken at the first meeting of 166 [pounds]." The "war therefore is not over," Hart chortled, "but we have won a resounding victory in the first battle. We carried a successful strike for 24 days which virtually paralyzed the Departments of Government concerned in the face of an alliance between the official element and Bustamante to crush us." Just as important, he added, "we have demonstrated to the Governor the unreliability of Bustamante's assurances of his power to crush us and break our strikes."[31]

TIME, the popular New York–based magazine, which usually paid as much attention to Jamaica as it did to male pregnancy, this time was captivated by the "turbulent dusky islanders" who during the "last fortnight erupted in chaos of strong-arm politics, union shootings and escaped lunatics" after the mental hospital strike. "Scores of unguarded lunatics yelled 'we are free!'" as they "romped (some naked) into town, looting stores and homes, raping, smashing windows or just wandering aimlessly." As strikes raged among "prison guards, firemen and railroad workers . . . armed mobs of rival unionists prowled the streets. Three men were killed" and "fifteen inmates burned to death." When "American nuns arrived to give their help, one piano-playing lunatic strummed 'Happy Days are Here Again' but surly strikers ejected the nuns with the cry of 'strikebreakers.'"[32]

At the vortex of this raging storm of violence was Bustamante. Light-skinned with a shock of hair that was even lighter, it was possible that he "passed for white" earlier in life, which was ironic in light of his demonizing of those—like his cousin Norman Manley—who were said to represent "brown man rule," or the rule of those who were not seen as part of the darker-skinned folk who, iron-ically, made up the bulk of the Bustamante union's membership. "Tall, tower-ing, angry, his voice staccato, his actions seemingly nervous" is how he was described at one notably tense spring 1947 confrontation. On this occasion he "pulled two guns from his hips, yelled at a crowd that was milling around him, and discharged one of the weapons with electrifying suddenness." Then "some-one in the crowd echoed: 'keep back! The Man Mad. He's going to shoot.'"[33]

Thus, it came as no surprise that the CLC meeting in Jamaica targeted the mercurial Bustamante as a barrier to labor unity. When Richard Hart requested that his union affiliate with the CLC, Bustamante was typically dyspeptic. Speak-ing of the fee requested, he sputtered, "as you know 5 [pounds] does not mean anything at all to me—that I spend nearly every hour, but I cannot send you 5 [pounds] to affiliate with the Caribbean Labour Congress as I cannot affiliate with something of which I do not know its true purpose or the true purpose for which it is intended."[34]

In response, Albert Gomes of Trinidad, who later was to be accused of blaz-ing a trail akin to that of Bustamante, assailed him bitterly as "delegates, observers and the general public packed the Coke Memorial Hall" for the "open-ing sessions." They sat in "enthusiastic attention for two hours while the speech-making progressed." Gomes, a wordsmith of some renown, along with Manley, "had the huge audience applauding loudly and at time deafeningly." V. C. Bird, who likewise was to be subsequently accused of being the Bustamante of his own Antigua, "was bitter about the disunity of workers in Jamaica," due he said to the fault of one man, Mr. Bustamante—though he hoped that "people [would not] misunderstand [his] visit to [Bustamante's] headquarters."[35]

Grantley Adams, who too was to be charged later with following in Busta-mante's footsteps, continued the attack on the Jamaican leader. "There is only [one] obstacle to West Indian unity," he cried, "and that obstacle" was the man known colloquially as "Busta." He was exceeded in vituperation by Gomes, who recounted to delegates his visit to see Busta to try to change his mind about participating in the CLC and their crusade for federation. "As we entered this little den," he said contemptuously, "in which this vain and self-centered crea-ture hides himself out, I saw this little figure sitting at his desk with a bust of himself on the left hand and a picture of himself on the right hand, surrounded as it were by mirrors reflecting his own vanity." Gomes was not impressed. "We were treated to an extraordinary display of maniacal glee, self-satisfaction and, believe me, the atmosphere created in that room was abnormal in the extreme . . . a display of buffoonery such as I have never seen in my life." Busta was afraid of the larger West Indian scene, he charged, afraid that with federation he would lose his "grip" on Jamaica and take on a wider range of progressive adversaries.

It was Gomes who set the tone as he railed against the "grim spectre of starvation" that "is haunting not only Trinidad but the other islands of the West Indies. People are literally starving." Exploitation had accelerated, for "as a result of the building of the American bases in Trinidad, a sum of 200 million dollars came into the island and was passed on to Great Britain." Yet he veered from assaults on London and Washington to a focus on one man: Bustamante. "Some of us have made serious attempts to persuade the labour leader of that organization," he said in a veiled reference to the JLP leader, to attend, but he chose not to. Then it was back to London. Unfortunately, said Gomes, "there are still in our midst certain sentimentalists who believe that a Labour government in Britain will so transform the Empire as to make it possible for subject peoples to occupy an entirely different position in the Empire . . . I do not share that delusion," he sniffed. He complained that instead of aiding the oppressed, the colonizing power was pressuring Venezuela and Surinam "to absorb some of our poor, helpless starving unemployed people," while blocking these West Indians' migration to the United Kingdom itself, since London "cannot conceive of a Negro minority in England."

Bustamante struck back. As the CLC met in one part of Kingston, another meeting was convened "at the corner of Thompson Street and Asquith Street," where a "strong protest" was registered "by the crowd numbering several thousand against the speeches of the Hon. Albert Gomes." The 500 present "expressed the feeling that Mr. Gomes should leave the country."

T. A. Marryshow of Grenada chose to speak of tactics to be used to bring down colonialism with a chief "weapon [being] the boycott. In the United States of America boycott has become a polished blade. I have seen the wheels of industry brought to a standstill by that means. Sometime in 1935, Woolworth's on 125th Street, New York, was under boycott for not employing a proper quota of Negroes"—and they prevailed by the deft wielding of this weapon. Why couldn't West Indians emulate their counterparts in Manhattan?

The teeming ghettos of Kingston were to become the sites of cultural transformations of global import as first the religion of Rastafarianism, then the pulsating music of Bob Marley were to take root there. But in the early postwar era, Jamaican cities were more likely to be seen as dens of vice and iniquity rather than places of enriching enchantment. This misery is what impelled the CLC—which was what made Bustamante's boycott of this organization so maddening. For these communities were not neglected by CLC conferees. "The slums of Denham Town and Kingston Pen were described by Councillor C. B. Mathura of Trinidad . . . as the worst in the West Indies."[36] There were "322,609 dwellings for Jamaica's population of 1,250,000," said a 1945 report. However, "nearly one-half of these dwellings are bad" with "as many as 160,451 of the dwellings consist[ing] of one room, many of these being less than 100 sq. ft. in area," and "only about 10 percent have water closets and 18 percent are without any toilet facilities . . . 98 percent of the dwellings are without washing facilities and less than one-half percent have washing facilities inside." Besides, "many" of the dwellings of Jamaica were "infested by termites."[37] This wretchedness made Jamaica an appropriate launching pad for the CLC's initiatives.

Their important meeting was capped off by the aforementioned "spectacular torchlight march" of thirty thousand striding in "solid phalanx." They "surged through city streets" and "sent crowded pavements into frantic cheering," egged on by a band playing pulsating music. The "vast throng jam-packed the stand enclosure and occupied a large part of the open spaces including the race tracks," where more "attacks were made" on Busta, "who was accused of standing in the way of West Indian unity." Robert Bradshaw of St. Kitts, who was to be accused subsequently of becoming Busta-like during his lengthy tenure in office, then was inspired to avow that "we in the Caribbean islands of the [British West Indies] shall not sit idly by [and] will not be satisfied until a socialist government is returned to the House of Representatives of Jamaica." On a more prosaic note he observed that "from the time he landed in Jamaica, he found a similarity between the people of Jamaica and his own people in St. Kitts."[38]

In response to these militant calls for federation and socialism and worker empowerment, a day or so after the CLC finished meeting in Kingston, London convened its own "momentous conference" on "closer association" or a kind of federation-"lite" in the region. Repaying the favor, Bustamante addressed a rally of 25,000 at a racetrack, where he issued pointed insults targeting Gomes, Manley, Hart—and, of course, the entire CLC.[39]

The underdevelopment in the region where the control of the public sector was a handsome prize, in the face of a private sector dominated by London and resident Europeans, contributed to piercing political battles. Invective and gunplay were not uncommon and intimidation was routine. Grantley Adams, who led the defection away from the CLC in the early 1950s, recalled subsequently that in 1947 during the course of the meeting, "after a night of oratorical onslaughts on Bustamante," he and "Albert Gomes found themselves being shadowed by four men, with heavy truncheons, as they moved from one shop to another in Kingston." The "men approached them and explained that the [PNP] had assigned them as bodyguards for the two delegates." Another evening, Lionel Francis of British Honduras spoke at a meeting supporting PNP candidates for the forthcoming municipal elections. A number of hecklers tried to break up the meeting and in the ensuing confusion Francis was struck by a stone under his eye and bled profusely. Half a mile away, another PNP meeting was in progress with Albert Gomes as the guest speaker. When they heard of the assault on Francis, the meeting was adjourned and the audience, consisting of some 3,000 persons with Gomes at their head, marched to the scene of the attack.[40] Such violence was a prelude to a similar eruption that occurred when Manley's son, Michael, became prime minister of Jamaica decades later.

TWIN DEVELOPMENTS—THE KINGSTON conference and Hart's appointment—gave the CLC a new birth of freedom. This occurred at a propitious moment, for another set of twin developments—labor organizing and the thrust for independence—were surging simultaneously as 1947 drew to a close.

As a successful conference should, delegates had departed from Kingston energized and excited about the CLC agenda. I. G. Fonseca of the Civic League of Tortola, the British Virgin Islands, told Hart that "very likely I am the last delegate to the [conference] to express my thanks and appreciation for the lavish hospitality bestowed on me by the officials and various members of the praiseworthy and indispensable 'Peoples National Party,'" for "daily intercourse with members of the PNP" provided him "with a wider experience and many more progressive ideals than I had hitherto possessed." Now, he concluded, "I am in a far better position to carry-on the fight for the advancement and general improvement of my people in these small islands."[41]

Though personalities like T. A. Marryshow and Grantley Adams were the titular leaders of the organization, it was Hart who was both the face of the CLC and its sparkplug. He was backed up by the PNP, one of the most advanced political entities in the region. It was this Jamaican influence which explained why "in 1947 all the important parties and trade unions had affiliated" with the CLC. As Hart explained, "the national movement is most highly developed in Jamaica and Barbados"—and he was being overly generous to the latter—with both able to "enjoy semi-responsible government and a wholly elected lower house of the legislature. The other colonies are still under crown colony government." There were dangers in Jamaica, such as the "local fascist movement centering around the colorful demagogue Bustamante," but, on balance, optimism reigned.[42]

So motivated, right after the Kingston meeting he reminded A. Creech Jones, secretary of state for the colonies, about the plummeting price of sugar, the crop on which thousands of livelihoods in the region depended. "Various organizations affiliated to the [CLC] protested to you by cable concerning the inadequacy of the price fixed for the 1947 sugar crop and the manner in which it was allocated. We further demanded that organized labor be given a voice in the price negotiations." He also reminded Jones that the "British government in 1946 purchased a considerably larger quantity of sugar from Cuba, the Dominican Republic and Haiti than is purchased from the British West Indies and British Guiana combined and at a price more than four pounds ten shillings per ton higher than was paid for our sugar." Of course, this was a function of colonialism and the special relationship that yoked the British West Indies to London, like an overburdened horse pulling a gold-braided carriage.[43]

Hart kept a close eye on the sugar industry, accumulating data that suggested that the industry in Jamaica was "on its death-bed" and had been for years;[44] that a "glut had been reached in world rum supplies," which was allied to the "surplus" that was "likely in world sugar production";[45] that Britain was buying more sugar from both Cuba and Mexico—and in the latter there would be "no dollar payment," but instead "the price will probably be set off against the compensation due from Mexico to British oil companies whose property was confiscated by the Republic some years before the war."[46] Demonstrating that the unity of the components of the British West Indies were more potent than their separate, uncoordinated efforts, it was not long before Hart was able to announce a preliminary victory. "The advantages of combined effort," he exclaimed, "have been demonstrated very clearly with the announcement of the Secretary of State's decision to convene a conference of sugar interests to consider an increase in the 1948 price and the manner of its allocation." This successful process was "initiated earlier this year through the [CLC]," he announced modestly, "when the details of the price for the 1947 crop were announced."[47]

But even amidst the hosannas and bouquets there were niggling signs of distress. Given limited staff and formidable barriers blocking effective communication and coordination, Hart was wisely trying to unite the CLC and the region around an important commonality—sugar. But then Arthur John Riley, general secretary of the Montserrat Trades & Labour Union, reminded him of how diverse the region was when he told him that "our staple industry is cotton and this being so we did not enroll sugar workers," thus thwarting the attempt to have pan-Caribbean unity around the well-being of the industry.[48]

But the maritime trade was another common linkage regionally, even if sugar was not. British Guiana had demonstrated earlier the importance of stevedores, but this lesson was part of the common wisdom of the region, along with the significance of sailors who were responsible for bringing goods of all sorts—from necessities to luxuries—to territories that were hardly self-sufficient. It was not long before the CLC took up the cause of the Progressive Seamen's Union in Jamaica, which endured an all-too-typical destiny of low wages and bad working conditions. When in 1931 the "Jamaican Banana Producers Line started their fruit and passenger service with four ships to and from England . . . no protection was then made for the seamen of Jamaica with that line of ships," and Jamaicans "were taken on only as Boys in the Steward Department to work at the rate" of a few pounds per month. "During the stay of the ships in London," these sailors "were not allowed to sleep aboard." They "had to find board and lodging . . . for whatever amount of days the ships might remain in port, which was never less than five days." The "Webster Line" particularly was "treating the men as nothing else but slaves." "How much we were badly treated by the English companies," they cried. Hence, in early 1944 they "decided to re-organize a Seamen's Union for the third time in 21 years." The situation was "most abominable with no hope of being remedied unless through action by this Congress," the CLC was informed.[49]

This was the hope that was being placed on the shoulders of the CLC—or in many cases, Richard Hart. New vistas had opened with the weakening of the Empire as a result of the war, and the increased militancy of labor in the region, which, like their global counterparts, was beginning to flex its muscles, propelled as it was by the progressive antifascist atmosphere that had yet to be arrested. Looming above both tendencies was the rise of the Colossus of the North, the United States, which had a burgeoning "Negro" population that in its primary urban center—New York—contained an increasingly influential West Indian community.

CHAPTER 6

Washington Confronts the West Indies

T HE INEXORABLE WEAKENING of a war-ravaged Empire combined with the rise of U.S. imperialism in the Caribbean—a factor propelled by security concerns—led to a deeper engagement by Washington with the region. This trend, however, was contradictory. Yes, Washington was seen as an improvement over London, and yes, this did lead to further U.S. investment in the region, notably in Jamaican bauxite and tourism generally. This was viewed by some on the island as compromising sovereignty, but it also led to a steadier influx of Negroes from the United States to the region (and West Indian migrants to the United States), and their influence was viewed widely as giving a boost to the struggle for independence.

Hence, when Bindley C. Cyrus of the prominent black newspaper the *Chicago Defender* arrived in Jamaica in 1945, the U.S. Consulate paid keen attention, giving him generally positive reviews in that he was "extremely critical of British Colonial Administration" and "indicated a distinct pro-American attitude," which was more than acceptable. But as they began to explore his ideas further, concern increased accordingly. He "appeared to be militantly pro-Negro"—which was not so good, as they saw it—"but not far to the left in his economic thinking," which was. Yet the elusive Cyrus "did not give any satisfactory explanation for the bitter stories which he has published in the 'Chicago Defender' concerning the treatment of Jamaican laborers in the Chicago area." Dismissing ideas concerning freedom of the press, Cyrus was "asked" bluntly "not to publish such stories in the future unless there was an honest description of the ameliorative measures taken by the United States government." Thus, despite his supposed "pro-American attitude," the shaken Cyrus "was grilled for [an] hour by Security officers," and he "impressed [Paul] Blanshard" of the U.S. legation "as a shallow, egotistic personality with political ambitions." Strikingly,

Cyrus had capacious hemispheric plans. In 1940 he proposed to President Roosevelt that the "Guianas" should be acquired by the United States and then colonized by African American migrants.[1]

Washington was coming to recognize that inheriting an Empire presented unique challenges, for even those who were "pro-American" had their own ambitions that were seen as potentially contrary to those of the United States. Cyrus was a "Barbadian by birth" and in 1942 ran for Congress. Although his ambitious colonization plan may have seemed at first glance to be pro-Washington, the very history of the United States demonstrated that colonists often rebelled against the nation that had dispatched them. Kingston's *Daily Gleaner* detected a developing pan-Caribbean and pan-African consciousness that transcended the provincial interests of disparate territories and peoples. "You see," said their writer, "not only West Indians but the coloured peoples of America, are greatly absorbed" with Jamaica.[2] This consciousness could potentially complicate the smooth execution of U.S. foreign policy.

Unsurprisingly, Washington was becoming increasingly concerned with the growing interest of West Indian exiles in North America in their homelands. Foremost among these was W. A. Domingo, born in Jamaica and widely suspected of being a member of the U.S. Communist Party. Kingston sought to detain him upon a visit to his homeland, a maneuver he countered by downplaying his previous activism.

A son of relative affluence, Domingo's father owned and operated a fleet of hansom cabs. His father passed away prematurely, and Domingo sought work as an apprentice tailor before arriving in the United States at the age of twenty-one.[3] "[I] lived in Boston and New York from 1910 to 1941," he maintained, "during which time I was engaged in the importing business." At this point Domingo was under severe scrutiny by the U.S. authorities and he no doubt felt that the better part of wisdom was to play down his radicalism and play up his business acumen. "I was a pioneer in importing minor tropical fruits and vegetables into New York," he contended. Moreover, said Domingo, "my American born son was in the U.S. Army." It was true that "from as early as 1918," Domingo asserted, "I was an exponent of self-government for Jamaica," but his concern now was that "there is a considerable amount of anti-American feelings [among] the middle classes and the upper classes of this country." The "ruling element of this country," he said, speaking of Jamaica, "shape the thought of the country in such a way as subtly to develop an excessive Briticism and unnecessary anti-Americanism." The "basic reason" for this attitude was their "fear of the race question" ("lynching" and the like). Still, the U.S. was not peculiar since in Jamaica "white men have wantonly killed black people, not once, not twice, but several times, but under forms of legality not a single white man has been hanged for such a crime within 40 years."

"I am primarily a Jamaican Nationalist," he maintained, nothing more. "I debated R. B. Moore, probably the most prominent coloured Communist orator, five times in which I affirmed that British Negroes should support Great Britain in this war. For this I was denounced by Communists in a pamphlet as a 'British supporter.'" Domingo even "bought $2000 worth of Defense Bonds in May 1941," yet despite all this he was interned upon arriving in Jamaica during the war,[4] and the United States was reluctant to take him back afterwards.

But after the war ended and the Cold War was erupting, Domingo's presence in Jamaica remained unsettling since he did have an idea of what actually occurred in the United States, propaganda about human rights virtues notwithstanding. Just after Winston Churchill's "Iron Curtain" peroration formally inaugurated a new global era, the U.S. consul, in a "restricted" message, informed the State Department sourly that "Domingo criticizes American journalists who cross-examine [People's National Party] leaders as if they were Communists, and thinks the journalists must have been primed by persons met at the hotels or 'some official of the country' they represent."[5]

Domingo was not altogether misleading. During his early years in Jamaica he "became friendly" with Marcus Garvey and, in fact, "served as first assistant secretary" in an organization there where the pre-eminent black nationalist was "second." Yet Domingo, who by all accounts possessed a "keen analytical mind," an "acerbic writing style and gregarious manner," also "loudly extolled 'Bolshevism.'" If the authorities had inquired, they would have been struck by the fact that his son was named "Karl Marx Domingo."[6]

Domingo was treading in sensitive territory. Jamaica was emerging as a potentially important Cold War ally, and a man like Domingo was capable of throwing sand into the gears. This was noticeably so in the realm of labor. At the crucially strategic Allis-Chalmers plant in Wisconsin, "of the plant's 603 black workers, 387 were Jamaican" as recently as the just concluded war.[7] But that was then, and now, with U.S. soldiers and sailors returning from various battlefronts, the need for Jamaican labor was dissipating. "The cancellation of further recruiting of Jamaica workers for labor in the United States has aggravated the difficulties of rehabilitating the returned servicemen," the secretary of state was told. Seeking to allay concern about his purported radicalism, Domingo sought stalwartly to "contrast the fair treatment of Jamaica workers in the United States, where color prejudice is acknowledged, with that given to Jamaica servicemen in England, where color prejudice is denied." As a result of such interventions, Washington was told, "the Jamaica press . . . seldom prints much criticism of the United States and the base at Fort Simonds is seldom if ever a subject of adverse comment." What was occurring was that Washington's felt need to retreat from the more egregious aspects of Jim Crow impelled the United States to move more aggressively against this toxin, unlike London, which felt little such domestic pressure to act similarly and, besides, had an Empire that rested firmly upon notions of being of "pure European descent." This situation could aid in eroding London's hegemony in the region, while facilitating the rise of Washington. Thus, when the African American William Hastie was appointed governor of the Virgin

Islands, some in Jamaica wondered why his contemporary, Norman Manley, was not appointed governor of Jamaica.[8]

Perhaps due to opportunism or pure dislike for the crimes that London had committed on the island over the centuries, Domingo—once viewed widely as a radical—became an articulate defender of the presence of the nation that was surely corroding British influence: the United States. "Any agitation," he argued, "against the [U.S.] bases is 'unnecessary, foolish and futile,'" and he added that "his three years of personal observation of the American personnel connected with the Jamaica Base Command had convinced him that no new form of race or color prejudice had been introduced into the island by the Americans." As he saw it, the "strong and growing American influence in Jamaican life," the "American radio, records, magazines and comics flow[ing] into the island and into the mentality of the people," was "far more than English material of similar nature while the returning Jamaican contract workers have brought back new ideas from their experiences in the United States."[9] Perhaps Domingo was so enthusiastic about this cultural flow from the United States and the potential impact it could have on literacy and anticolonialism that he underestimated its negative propagandizing import.

Thus, Domingo was not as sharp about the otherwise star-crossed presence of Jamaican laborers in the United States as he could have been. Of these "returned workers . . . very few have anything to show for their labor" and their "savings were not enough for a real start in life," he said. And, yes, they were "bitter and disillusioned for the most part," but their "present poverty [was] emphasized" most of all "by their memory of conditions in the United States."[10]

A reeling London, battered by the havoc of war, found it hard to compete with a United States whose mainland was largely untouched by the conflict and which entered the war well after Britain. Hence, part of Domingo's motivation may have become clear when this self-proclaimed "Jamaican nationalist" sought a visa to re-enter the United States. London's representative, perhaps not up to speed on the issues, dissented, blocking the effort to rid the Empire of one of its sterner critics "He is married to an American citizen," Clara Borjes informed the U.S. consul, "but he never became one himself. When we started constructing the bases he immediately left for Jamaica, presumably to urge the Jamaican construction workers to hold out for the American scale of wages. However, he was immediately placed in the internment camp upon his arrival and was only released after the construction was finished." Still, she argued, "I felt that Domingo would have less influence in a relatively small place like Jamaica than in a large city like New York," so, "from the standpoint of the Jamaican government, it would be better to leave him in Jamaica."[11]

A smarter Washington hesitated, realizing that an abrasive Domingo would be useful in dissolving the bonds of Empire in Jamaica. "I would consider a visa highly inadvisable," countered the U.S. consul in Jamaica. "He has consistently expressed a pro-American attitude in his writing," rather strange for a man considered radical, "and possibly holds no threat to our domestic interests." Yet he had been "violently anti-British"—so why not take him away from London's soil? "If Domingo remains in Jamaica he can do less harm than in Harlem. The British can handle him as a British subject on British territory more easily than we could on American territory."[12] So they were inclined to compel this self-proclaimed Jamaican nationalist to stew in Jamaica.

Domingo would not give up, which made sense since he had spent decades in the U.S. Northeast and had not lived in Jamaica in years. "My sympathies were with the wing of the Socialist Party which was led by Rev. Norman Thomas," he pleaded to the U.S. consul; "not once was I accused of being a Communist," he added somewhat disingenuously. He was now "nearing 58," well past the life expectancy of most men of African descent, and, understandably, his declining years could be cushioned more effectively in a developed nation.[13] Domingo did not realize that his profession of socialist beliefs was convincing Washington that his presence could be quite useful in a Jamaica that was radicalizing rapidly. "He was active in assisting NW Manley to smash the attempts of a dozen or so Communist Party members to push their way into the Peoples National Party," said U.S. diplomat George Kelly, speaking of Domingo. He was contrasted invidiously with Richard Hart and his ilk who were thought be the real reds. "Far from being a radical, Domingo has the rather anomalous position in Jamaica of not being a good socialist" in that he was termed derisively a "'Norman Thomas socialist' and is accused of being too nationalistic," as "illustrated by his opposition to West Indian Federation." But far from bringing him back to the United States, such views were rooting him more deeply in Jamaica, since he "believes in a relatively independent Jamaica with an economy directed towards the United States, as opposed to a close tie-up with the British Empire." Indeed, he was "considered pro-American almost to the point of chauvinism" given his "opposition to Marcus Garvey," while "reports of his having been to Moscow are totally unfounded."[14]

Besides his supposed value in stifling Communists, keeping Domingo in Jamaica may have had another purpose from Washington's viewpoint, for it appeared there was growing concern about the steady arrival of Jamaicans in the United States. Thus, concern about Domingo turned to concern about another Jamaican with a well-known surname: Amy Ashwood Garvey, the first wife of Marcus Garvey. The State Department "confidentially informed" London of her "efforts . . . to bring to the United States a number of Jamaicans ostensibly for employment as public servants," though it was felt it was a potentially profitable scam.[15] Supposedly she was involved in "obtaining jobs for 50,000 Jamaican women as workers" in the United States, which seemed beyond her capabilities and the nation's ability to absorb.[16] Turned away, Garvey turned on those she thought had rejected her. "I am surprised to find so many Uncle Toms in America today," she claimed. "[A]ll I can say about Toms now," she added militantly, "is to urge you to start preparing for a few funerals; that is how Toms in

Russia were taken care of." Something similarly stiff was required for Moscow's erstwhile transatlantic ally, she grumbled.[17] Not as tutored in the nuances of U.S. political discourse, which frowned upon such rhetorical broadsides, Amy Garvey was illustrating—as Domingo had earlier—how West Indians were bringing a new spice to political life in North America.

At the same time, West Indians who had sojourned in the United States and were now returning home were also attracting attention, suggesting how this migration process was transforming both sides of the equation. For example, Simeon A. Francis was born in Grenada in the late nineteenth century and migrated to New York City as a young man, where he lived for about two decades. About six feet tall, he was "rather slow and quiet" and "rather coarse with Negroid features," according to Washington. While in the United States, he was "connected with a numbers racket in New York City and . . . 'Dutch' Schultz and his associates 'moved in' on his organization and told him to get out whereupon he put a large quantity of U.S. currency notes in a number of trunks and sent them to Grenada as ordinary baggage." Though he was "very rarely seen" in Grenada, Washington was concerned about his presence nonetheless. He "raises race horses and lives with an almost white, sharp tongued woman," who was "apparently married but does not live with her husband." Francis had "more or less avoided me during the past 2 1/2 years," complained Washington's man, but his wealth represented a potential alternative power center to that of the United States and thus he merited scrutiny.[18]

Then there was Dr. Wilfred Rankin, a naturalized U.S. citizen born in British Guiana in 1907 but residing in Grenada in the postwar era. An Oxford University graduate, he taught sociology at Columbia and divinity at the Union Theological Seminary. He was five feet four inches tall with a "rugged build," "talkative," and prone to an "excellent choice of words" with a "flowery style." An "excellent" student of Latin, according to Washington, he was "closely connected with [the] Negro movement in the United States" and possessed a "liberal and progressive attitude." Deemed relevant was that he was "very dark"—a description that often cropped up in reports from a color-obsessed Washington.[19]

Hubert Julian, a West Indian adventurer who had circumnavigated the globe, including a stint in Ethiopia, also made his way to postwar Grenada.[20] He appeared on a platform with local hero and CLC leader T. A. Marryshow, with 500 assembled. Henry Taylor, the U.S. diplomat present, was dumbfounded when Julian, a skilled pilot in his own right, mentioned in passing that "black men have shot down white men from the skies." Taylor, whose mandate seemed to be detecting the slightest hint of supposed antiwhite sentiment, was mortified when "people in the crowd around me muttered, 'I like that'" in response to Julian's remarks. In Market Square in the island's administrative capital, Julian described the "Goering-Julian air challenge in which, it will be recalled when Colonel Julian challenged [Nazi leader Herman] Goering to an air duel over the English Channel, and Goering replied that he would accept it providing a baboon was painted on the outside of Colonel Julian's plane. The Colonel replied that he would do so providing that Goering identified himself by painting a pig on the outside of his plane." But it was not that simple exchange that concerned Taylor, for when Julian came to his "home for cocktails," the "Grenada Competent Authority who appears to be an extremely good friend of his interrupted to say it was a 'white pig,'" which Julian denied. As ever, Taylor seemed to have a particular concern over how whites were treated—even if they were Nazis.

"This is the second American citizen in less than two months who has appeared in Grenada on Mr. Marryshow's platform," Taylor advised, "addressing Grenadians concerning the color question and stressing a need for colored unity." Taylor "suspected funds from an outside source were coming into Grenada to stir up anti-white feeling," a sentiment Washington had difficulty distinguishing, perhaps understandably, from anticolonialism and anti-imperialism. Taylor and his government were in a quandary in that Jim Crow was gradually eroding due to wartime exigencies, Cold War pressures—Washington's desire to compete for hearts and minds in regions like the British West Indies—and postwar crusading by African Americans. This was providing this latter minority—and former West Indian exiles—with the wherewithal to travel to contested regions like the Caribbean, where the message they conveyed was not always pleasing to Washington. "There is a strong movement on the part of certain colored people in the United States," warned Taylor in his "confidential" report, "to press federation of the British West Indies for the prime purpose of seeing a colored independent entity composed of the [British West Indies] islands."[21] Now this could be an alternative power center—which if aligned with the global left which was its wont—could provide potent bolstering for African Americans.

In 1979, the coming to power of the leftist New Jewel Movement in Grenada was to incite mordant fears in Washington—though the entire adult population of this tiny island could fit comfortably in Yankee Stadium—but this concern did not magically materialize as the century was coming to a close. In 1947, Washington was worried about "arms . . . being smuggled into Grenada." The island was an armed camp in that "many of the common men" there "go about with revolvers concealed in their clothing."[22]

In the postwar era, Washington's diplomats were busily investigating all those who were thought to present a challenge to colonialism; foremost among them— ironically—seemed to be those who had spent time in the United States itself. Thus, a "confidential" dispatch spoke apprehensively of a visit to Grenada of Dr. Philip Savary, a "colored American citizen" born in British Guiana. Worryingly, he was "part proprietor of the 'Amsterdam News,'" the premier Negro journal in Manhattan, and "President of the Victory Life Insurance Company." He had just taken a leading part in collecting funds for the CLC and appeared to have the means and motive to press avidly for decolonization.[23] Somehow they were able to ascertain to the penny how much he and his wife held in accounts in the Corn Exchange Bank in New York and the Royal Bank of Canada in Grenada.[24]

The message that the relatively affluent Savary was delivering was not reassuring to the colonizer. While in Trinidad, he was the guest of Ralph Mentor, a leader of the influential oil workers. In an interview, he told a union journalist about his difficult journey to material comfort, punctuated with stories about his medical training at Canada's McGill University. "With pride," it was reported, he "attributes the successes he now enjoys to a strike that took place in British Guiana over thirty years ago. He relates that as a young man he was employed as a compositor" in Georgetown when a "general strike among the printing staff broke out. With the exception of the foreman all the printers had walked out of the plant. He was sent for by the boss and asked to return to act as a scab and assist in breaking the strike. He refused to do so. He knew that owing to his refusal to act as a scab when things returned to normal he would have had no job. This was the circumstance that induced him to make up his mind to leave British Guiana and go elsewhere in search of a living. He spent some time in Brazil and eventually he reached the United States in 1911 where he worked and studied"—and attained a level of influence routinely denied those in the British West Indies.[25]

The deleterious impact of white supremacy combined with a pervasive class-consciousness in a region where to be black was to be considered a fungible labor unit combined to create a situation where even the relatively affluent in the region were not necessarily susceptible to the overtures of Washington and London.

This increasing influence of those who had spent time in the United States illustrated the downside for colonialism when Washington began to supplant London as the major power in the region. For although the United States tolerated a fiercer system of Jim Crow internally, it also contained a larger population of African descent, which over the years had developed an infrastructure of opportunity involving colleges, markets—illicit and otherwise—and the like, that allowed for the flourishing of figures like Francis and Savary who could wield outsized influence in tiny islands like Grenada or even larger islands like Trinidad. That they were deemed to be race-conscious or otherwise bent on sovereignty suggested the nettlesome problem colonialism faced.

London recognized early on the potentially subversive influence that those from the United States could wield. During the war, writing from Downing Street, John Harrington reminded a colleague that "you may remember that some time ago I mentioned to you our possible interest in political movements amongst the Negroes in the U.S.A. . . . we must be prepared to meet a certain amount of disaffection in our West Indian Colonies after the war." Moreover, "even before the war there was a link-up between the more subversive elements in Jamaica and similarly minded organizations in New York." London was concerned about the spillover into the Caribbean of U.S. struggles. "It seems possible that America's Negro problem may become acute after the war," he confided. "If it does, it is certain to have troublesome repercussions in the West Indies."

He attached to this momentous memorandum an article adumbrating these themes penned by the recently elected communist councilman from Harlem, Ben Davis.[26]

This overall subject was deemed "top secret," and it was stressed that "*special care* should be taken to maintain the secrecy of the documents on this file. They should be locked in a steel press overnight and circulated *by hand at all stages*" (emphasis in original). Why the concern? It had to do with London's surveillance of the nationals of an ally, the United States—albeit third-class nationals: Negroes. "We have also taken up this question of obtaining information about American Negro movements," London conceded, "and have asked . . . to let us have [a] forthcoming FBI report on the Harlem Negroes," the group most influenced by West Indians. The focus was on the "Jamaica Progressive League in New York, which, if not actually Communist, at any rate had Communist affiliations." London's problem was that its Empire was far-flung and dependent on an impoverishment and degradation of the colonized that had become inconsistent with the high-flown promise and rhetoric of the war. That West Indians could also escape to the United States and accumulate what amounted to fortunes upon their return home also complicated the colonial mission.

It was not even clear if the FBI would cooperate. "Our representative," said one British official in a "secret" message, "says he will certainly apply to the FBI as suggested, but it has to be taken into consideration that on the Negro Question they may be particularly reticent as it is a political problem which appears to be rather 'hot' now," as it was "attracting considerably the interest of the Communists." Attached were copies of articles from the communist *Daily Worker* and the left-wing *New Masses*.[27]

Thus, from worrying about returning migrants, the United Kingdom then had to fret about West Indian Harlemites meddling in the Empire's African possessions. "It is obviously very undesirable that any of them should enter Nigeria," London said of "[Charles] Collins, [Moran] Weston or [Hope] Stevens," but the problem was "our Embassy does [not] find it easy to refuse them. Furthermore, refusal may cause a certain outcry among the West African students in New York." This presented a grave dilemma. "In the future," it was announced with resignation, "we shall find more and more Communist Negro politicians seeking to enter our Colonies and that sooner or later we shall have to start admitting them with the best grace we can muster. Refusing an application of this type is merely postponing the evil day."[28]

London was nervously concerned about the threat to their far-flung Empire purportedly posed by Harlem-based radicals. Intelligence reports were received regularly in London concerning meetings of the Council on African Affairs, headed by Paul Robeson, and "there was a great deal of ill-informed criticism of British administration in our African colonies," reported one irritated London agent of a particularly militant meeting.[29] Nonplussed, London was busily monitoring the activities of nationals of their ostensible ally. "Another document of considerable interest fell into my hands recently," said a British diplomat at the Manhattan consulate. It was "the minutes of a meeting of the NAACP" wherein "natives of India, of the West Indies, of the Gold Coast, Uganda, Burma and Puerto Rico met under the [Association's] umbrella to discuss their 'common problem' of *economic* exploitation by the white man and . . . they found themselves substantially in agreement." Attached were biographies of New Yorkers of West Indian origin, including Hope Stevens and Charles A. Petioni of Trinidad and Tobago, along with a note from John Harrington of the Colonial Office, who confirmed what was evident when he wrote, "I think it is clear that MI5 are taking an increased interest in [the] Negro political movement"[30] (emphasis in original).

It was not easy for the United States to acquiesce to this "increased interest," even if it targeted third-class citizens. For the United States was coming into increasing conflict with Great Britain over the fate of the West Indies, and any advantage gained by London was not seen as a plus in Washington. Jamaica's *Daily Gleaner* pooh-poohed the notion that grew during the war that the United States was intrigued with the idea of "acquisition . . . of certain of the Britain West [Indies] Islands." This was an outgrowth of the "silly season," it was said. "The people of these islands are strongly pro-British." Why? "Racially," it was stated with confidence, "they prefer the equality status that obtains throughout the British Empire to the discriminatory status that obtains in America."[31]

Jim Crow in the United States was to bedevil Washington's grand plan to increase influence in the Caribbean to the point where retreating from this policy became more than a pressing domestic concern, but a foreign policy mandate as well. This was so because this region contained strategic minerals in abundance, and gaining effective control of them would perpetually be problematic as long as Jamaicans and other West Indians could be convinced that a growth of U.S. influence could mean a great leap backwards.

"Since our only competitor in Jamaica is the Aluminum Company of Canada," said Walter Rice, vice president and general counsel of Reynolds Metals Company of Richmond, Virginia, "we are frankly fearful there may be some attempt to enact a mining law which would require processing of the bauxite either through the alumina stage or through the production of the metal itself, within the British Empire. Any such restriction would be ruinous to us since we are looking to Jamaica as a source of our ore in the near future." Frankly sharing his unease with the State Department's John Hickerson, he emphasized that "these deposits in our opinion are one of the most important ore bodies discovered in any part of the world in the past few years. They are particularly important to the United States because of their location," he stressed.[32] "We fear" that "there may be an attempt to frame the mining law in such a way that it will discriminate against an American company and in favor of a Canadian company," Rice told the segregationist U.S. secretary of state, James Byrnes of South Carolina.[33]

It was not just bauxite. Rollo G. Smith, acting chief of the American Republics Division of the U.S. Department of Commerce, stingingly referred to "complaints from exporters in the United States that the competent authorities in the various islands of the British West Indies have refused consistently to permit the importation of goods from the United States while at the same time permitting imports of similar goods from Canada." As a result, "anti-British sentiment has been growing among our manufacturers," he warned.[34]

The war had brought with it the specter of independence, but how would this majority black nation view a nation that enshrined white supremacy? Preliminary indications were not reassuring to Washington. Above all, the Jamaicans' own contacts with their northern neighbor were hardly comforting. Besides strategic minerals, the United States was filling labor deficits by dipping into the vast market of unemployed Jamaicans. Signaling the importance of this effort during the war was the fact that Samuel Zemurray, president of the powerful United Fruit Company—known for making and unmaking Central American governments—was "made responsible for recruiting labor in the Caribbean area other than Bahamas," while Secretary of State Byrnes "advised . . . of the extreme urgency to act immediately on the project."[35]

But by the time the war had wound down, Washington was wringing its hands about a "resolution of [the] Jamaican House of Representatives" directing that "two of its members investigate conditions among Jamaican laborers in the United States." At this juncture, Washington was not primarily concerned with the horrendous conditions endured by these workers, but instead what might befall the investigators. "As the officials sent" would "doubtless be members of the Jamaican Labor Party" of Bustamante and "colored, there might be" a "certain embarrassment if these officials were sent to the Southern States," according to this "strictly confidential" missive.[36]

Then, in a report whose circulation was "restricted" due to its sensitivity, John Lord of the U.S. Consulate in Jamaica observed that "at a meeting of the Kingston and St. Andrew Corporation on September 10, 1945, Councillor Willis O. Isaacs attacked the American nation as 'devoid of any decency, devoid of any culture, and devoid of that human feeling that makes for a respectful citizenry' because of the refusal of the Pan American airways in Miami to allow a colored journalist from Jamaica to eat in the airport's public restaurant."[37] This incident quickly captured headlines and incensed Jamaicans of various political persuasions.[38] As one furious Jamaican put it, "let us get it in our cranium that Jamaicans as a whole are colored people and in common with the big majority of coloured people all over the world it is time for us to talk out loud whenever acts of discrimination are practiced against us." Pointing to a particularly sensitive issue, he added, "they discriminate against us at the Canal Zone. You will find a policeman there saying anything he likes to a coloured man. He will say: 'Nigger, get off the sidewalk' and if you turn around to speak to him you get arrested." This was due, of course, to U.S. influence. "I have lived in America for about

32 years," said this Jamaican identified simply as "Mr. Fagan," and "I can tell you about discrimination especially in the South; they treat you like dogs." But now that the war was over, "we are in a new Jamaica" and voices must be raised, he insisted, against such rancid practices.[39]

Decades earlier, Washington made the decision to import West Indians to build the canal itself, then toil in the Canal Zone, but now, with the democratic promise of the war, it was becoming increasingly difficult to reconcile democracy with Jim Crow practices. U.S. diplomats were blunt about this. "West Indian Negroes in the Panama area are confronted with a type of racial discrimination by the American authorities which is similar to the discrimination practices in the Southern States and it is especially resented by them because the discrimination is obvious and more severe than the racial caste practices of the British colonies." The reality was that "nobody votes in the Canal Zone and its status as a territory is lower than that of Puerto Rico or the Virgin Islands." Again, there was a confluence between West Indian and African American sentiment as the "American Negro press" had "some direct influence in the West Indian community in Panama. On one little newsstand in a slum section" of the Canal Zone, said an unnamed U.S. emissary in a "confidential" dispatch, "I found large stacks of America's two leading Negro weeklies, the 'Chicago Defender' and the 'Pittsburgh Courier' and the proprietor assured me that he sold 75 of the former weekly and 125 of the latter."[40]

With every passing day it was evident that U.S.-style Jim Crow was incompatible with Washington's desire for growing influence in the British West Indies. The U.S. Consulate was upset by the penchant of Jamaican journals to focus on "recent lynchings in the United States," which were clearly of "interest to Jamaicans." Their compatriots were part of a larger "Negro community with thousands of Jamaicans living and working in the United States and thus exposed" to what one local publication acidly termed "the dangers of contact with the savage and bestial elements of the white North American population." The journal in question, *Public Opinion*, conceded candidly that "the emancipation of slaves in the southern states has remained a dead letter on the American statute books" and that there existed in the United States the "same level of brutality which brought the odium of the world upon the head of fascist Italy and Nazi Germany." With words dripping with sarcasm, reference was made to the "cosmic joke" that somehow the United States could "now pose as the liberator of mankind on two continents." Instead, it was stated, the "motto of the American Government and Legislature might well be 'freedom for whites and foreigners only.'" With his own sarcasm intact, the U.S. consul general in Jamaica, Edwin C. Kemp, asserted in his remarks, the circulation of which was "restricted," that "the effluvium of the Communist line seems to rise from the last paragraph," referring to the final racially tinged words of the journal.[41]

If this kind of inflamed sentiment were limited to Jamaica, it would be a problem that could be contained. The problem for Washington was that it was not so localized and could be found in the most remote outposts in the British West Indies. When a U.S. diplomat traveled during the war to tiny Dominica, a land marked by dense forestation, he found to his surprise that "the people of this island are more interested in political thought than the people of any other island in the Windward group. I talked with more people who were interested in political ideas in the five days in Dominica," he averred wondrously, "than I have done during three months of residence in Grenada." And, strikingly, "on several occasions I was taken to task on the subject of America's race problems," admitted Charles Whitaker in a "confidential" dispatch. Exacerbating this common concern was that "with the exception of two American planters," it was "difficult to imagine a more tumbled-down group of plantations and a more 'down in the heel' shabby and hopeless group of owners than one finds on some of the plantations in Dominica . . . almost all the buildings which I saw are approaching the last stages of dilapidation."[42] The problem for Washington was that for years these planters had played upon the mystique of white supremacy to bolster their class position, but now that the war had discredited this ideology—at least, officially—Washington ran the risk that its own state-sanctioned Jim Crow would merge in the public mind in places like Dominica with the odiously ineffectual policies of this plantocracy.

Similarly, in St. Lucia a "confidential" postwar report revealed that "many of the leading businessmen stated that they noticed quite an anti-white feeling throughout the island." Washington's man thought that "most of the anti-white feeling is being stirred up by labor leaders." Adding to the complexity was that "practically all the leading businessmen have colored blood but do not consider themselves as colored people." A conflation between color and class had developed—not an unusual trend in the region—but this did not augur well for the United States with its overwhelmingly white elite; diversifying the color of this elite could, at least, erode this troublesome conflation.[43]

For it was evident that St. Lucia was not unique. In Grenada, this same diplomat, Henry Taylor, found "increasing anti-white feeling." It was disheartening, he thought. "Everyone with the slightest tinge of colored blood literally 'goes around with a chip on his shoulder' expecting some insult from the pure whites and often misinterpreting perfectly well-meant remarks." Again, he blamed labor leaders, who found it easier to whip up color—as opposed to class—resentments. Still, he thought this was something new. In order to blunt Japan's race-based appeals, London and Washington had to up the ante in promising democracy, with considerable focus on the "Atlantic Charter" and the "Four Freedoms," while Britain was hardly enthusiastic about decolonization and the United States was not eager to retreat from white supremacy. As for Taylor, he saw a new development with this rising consciousness, a "manifestation of the unrest being felt by subject people throughout the world."[44]

Taylor harped on the idea that there was a "noticeable dislike of white people here, which for the most part does not show on the surface of the leading social class but is clearly evidenced by the working class." Taylor was fighting a two-front war, working overtime to reverse this trend while seeking simultaneously to influence his fellow Euro-Americans. "I am trying through the medium of social calls, discussions with businessmen and displays of . . . photographs showing colored people in the United States to ease the idea of anti-Negro aversion on the part of the Americans," he said wearily. Certainly, if this "anti-Negro aversion" in the United States could be curbed, this could simultaneously ease the "noticeable dislike of white people" that boded ill for Washington.[45]

Washington faced a policy dilemma in the British West Indies in the early postwar era, and it was not just the suspicion that "anti-white" feelings were growing. "A strongly federated West Indies might be to the detriment of American interests," stated U.S. diplomat Charles Whitaker. Why? His concern was the "American leased bases" in the region and that a "federated West Indies might make stronger demands for the return of the bases and these demands might carry more weight than the scattered demands of a few loosely organized labor groups as is the case at the present time"—a pointed reference to CLC.[46] After all, a federation would not only permit a common market, economies of scale, and a potentially profitable specialization of labor—it could also allow the disparate fingers of the British West Indies to coalesce in a mighty fist that could then be turned in a militant fashion against U.S. bases in the region. Whitaker was responding to a rising tide of concern in the United States itself about the supposed dangers emanating from Washington's backyard. A debate ensued as to whether the British West Indies would be a "liability if acquired by the United States,"[47] an effective demolition of federation. Whitaker was wary of the region's "deep-seated social and economic problems," a potential albatross for a postwar U.S. economy already reeling from pent-up labor demands. The problem was that the "British government" chose to "look with suspicion and jealousy upon American help in this area." Still, Whitaker advised Washington in "confidential" terms that the "United States should not yield one inch with reference to its base agreements," which were perceived as crucial to national security.[48]

The problem Washington encountered was that its immovable refusal to "yield one inch" was being met with an irresistible force emerging in the British West Indies. The U.S. vice consul in Antigua, Nicholas Fuller, forwarded to headquarters a news item reporting that a driver "stretched his hand to assist the Colonel's wife" at the local U.S. base, but "she recoiled with horror, and hissed, 'I have never touched a Negro's hand in my life!'" The clearly displeased Antiguan columnist responded angrily, "to the majority of Americans at this base we are just Negroes to be used, exploited, fooled and thrown aside."[49] The knotty question faced by Washington was whether these bases could be maintained while Jim Crow, with all of its detritus, reigned supreme. Clearly something had to give.

CHAPTER 7

Will Labor Rule?

T HE LATE 1940S WERE A TIME OF INTENSE LABOR turmoil in the British West Indies. The democratic promise of the war and the deplorable conditions endured by workers combined to produce a militant response. Hundreds of miles and numerous differences separated a necklace of islands stretching from Jamaica to British Guiana, but they all shared in common an upsurge of labor that was propelled in part by the common program agreed to at the founding of the Caribbean Labour Congress (CLC).

Tiny St. Kitts, whose entire contemporary population is smaller than the student body at the Ohio State University, provides a useful microcosm of the entire region. Despite the formidable barriers to travel and communication, shortly after the war ended, the major union federation there greeted a visiting Richard Hart, president of the Jamaica Government Railway Employees Union, and V. C. Bird, the chief leader in Antigua,[1] whose visit was reciprocated by the Basseterre leadership. Hart brought funds for the St. Kitts union to use to organize workers in neighboring Montserrat, which was added to funds received from Curacao and New York for various purposes—which may have been an outgrowth of an effort to establish contact with the controversial Harlem congressman Adam Clayton Powell, Jr.[2]

Hart, the leading Jamaican Marxist, received a rapturous reception, lecturing to a hall in Basseterre that was "packed to capacity" as a "large crowd filled the street outside," then made a triumphal tour of the small island.[3] His journey there was torturous and indicative of the formidable barriers to transisland organizing. He flew from Jamaica to St. Kitts—which took six hours including a layover in the Dominican Republic. Yet it seemed that the island's entire 18,000 strong population had turned out to hear him, starved as they were for change. Hart was struck by the fact that the island was "entirely taken up with the cultivation of sugar cane," with "no small cultivators"—"everyone works for wages on the 59 sugar estates, which are owned by 15 people." Housing was "tragic due to the fact" that these abodes were "in gully courses" and "the land on which they stand is owned by the estate. In case of strikes, the owners have in he past ejected tenants, depositing their houses on the road." There were "high property qualifications for the Legislature," which effectively barred the majority from political representation.[4]

St. Kitts—along with Antigua—was a bulwark for the Leeward Islands generally in that in most of these nations, "notably in Anguilla, Montserrat, Nevis and Barbuda," there were "no labor unions at all." However, in St. Kitts and Antigua, according to a U.S. report, there were "two fairly militant organizations, which have conducted a number of strikes in recent years." The "fact that 200 or 300 whites in St. Kitts and Antigua own nearly all the sugar plantations, factories, and stores, is a constant source of irritation to the black majority," it was added with refreshing candor. This suffocating white supremacy was also inefficient in ways large and small. Antigua had "two tennis courts on opposite sides of the same street, one for whites and one for all other persons." White supremacy was also flexible, as Antigua also witnessed "the rise to commercial power of a group of Syrians."[5]

Though it was said about Jamaica, what the acid-tongued U.S. emissary Paul Blanshard uttered actually had regional application. The "prevailing philosophy and practice of the dominant white community," he proclaimed in 1945, was "avoiding all manual labor under all circumstances. The whole civilization screams with the moral: hard work plus a black skin equals poverty nevertheless; soft work plus white skin equals comparative wealth. At the top of society there is [no] positive correlation between work and wealth. The laziest people on the island are the white women, and they live in the most luxury, the hardest working people on the island are the black field women"—and "they are the poorest."[6]

So, though cross-border organizing was difficult, it occurred—and was feared—particularly after the rise of the CLC facilitated it. Hence, T. A. Marryshow of Grenada received a "rousing welcome"[7] in St. Lucia, though when he visited Aruba seeking to forestall layoffs in the critically strategic oil sector, he was expelled—a development that was "keenly watched throughout the Caribbean."[8] In turn the St. Kitts-Nevis union was sending funds to their counterpart in British Guiana.[9] These crisscrossing visits and acts of solidarity suggested that a major barrier to labor advance in the region—the ability of populous Britain to isolate and dominate tiny islands—was being eroded by the adhesive of labor solidarity across the barrier that was the Caribbean Sea.

It was good that the union in St. Kitts was so active, for the crisis in the region demanded urgent action. In Grenada, CLC's Marryshow asserted that the "slum housing" was deplorable; "that such conditions should exist in a Christian community was unbelievable," he declared.[10] At the same time, one commentator was "coming down St. John Street," a major thoroughfare in St. George's, and wit-nessed "crowds surging (and many persons running) northward along Melville Street. I was told," he said, "they wanted bookings for Aruba. Yet many thousands of acres of Grenada soil are uncultivated or under-cultivated," he lamented.[11]

While the island was reeling, old practices, like hearty barnacles, continued to drag Grenada down. There was a "problem of American tourist traffic," thought one U.S. diplomat, as the "color problem has a bearing . . . in that any hotel accommodation which might be available in Grenada to cater to tourists would have to admit local brown and black peoples on the basis of equality"—and these tourists would rail against such. There was hardly a sector in Grenada that Washington could rely on. There was "as in most islands of the West Indies . . . a settlement of poor Scotch people who have become mentally and physically weak through generations of interbreeding," a reigning symbol of the perils of constructing whiteness in such an environment, though this was hardly the lesson being drawn by Washington's man, Henry Taylor. What concerned him was that "since the construction of the American bases in Trinidad, many laborers have gone abroad to work and have returned with new ideas."[12]

Laborers were going abroad due to the dearth of work at home—but that's not the way Washington saw it. Speaking of Grenada, St. Vincent, St. Lucia, and Dominica, U.S. diplomat Charles Whitaker remarked that "it is difficult for an employer to insist upon higher standards for he must in effect beg and cajole his laborers to work for him at all." As he saw it, "since the demand for work to be done is almost greater than the supply of laborers, any laborer reasonably skilled by local standards can pick and choose his job at almost any time and at present the simplest carpentry jobs usually involve 4 or 5 telephone calls and several weeks of delay before they are started." Whitaker's remarks elided the manifest difficulties faced by the unskilled in favor of an analysis that acted as if the total universe of labor consisted of the skilled. What concerned him above all was the perception that the balance of power might be shifting ever so slightly in the eternal battle between capital and labor, raising the nightmarish specta-cle that the latter would eventually rule. "In the past," he recalled, "the organ-ization of most labor unions has involved a political speech-making campaign, a rapid, enthusiastic growth of the union . . . to a membership of a few hundred members and then the activities of the union usually ended when the treasurer or the president absconded with funds." Unions, he thought, were "for the most part personal political machines under the leadership of the politicians," along the lines of what Bustamante had built in Jamaica. Though the CLC did "appear to be liberal but quite reasonable," there was concern that their model of unions, which was quite ample in its ambition, might supplant the older brand. Yet because of the backwardness that afflicted these islands, the old model's shelf life was assured, he thought; "superstition still plays an important role in the life of the country people. Many of these still believe in the evil spirits and the spell of the 'Evil Eye.'"

But ironically, the growth of U.S. influence might have been serving to under-mine the influence of U.S. capital. Since the war there had been a "definite growth of closer ties with the United States," a trend facilitated since it became "more dif-ficult for students to travel to England." Writing in early 1946, Whitaker observed that U.S. "movies until very recently have had a monopoly of the Windward Islands market" and the "dependence of the area upon the United States for food and other supplies during the war" had not abated. "Pan-American Airways has made Miami and New York only a few hours away," while the "presence of American soldiers and sailors" spread a certain kind of influence that was magnified when "many members of the American armed forces . . . married . . . local girls."[13]

But this formidable influence from the north was having a contradictory impact, as Jim Crow was greeted with hostility in the islands, just as the images and actualities from the United States were serving to undermine British colo-nialism. For example, when the union in St. Kitts needed to improve its then primitive method of communication, it simply approached its counterparts in Antigua and asked them to "secure on our behalf from the American base a used car costing not more [than] five hundred dollars and a used typewriter costing about sixty dollars."[14]

Still, whatever pleasantness Whitaker detected in Grenada and its vicinity was belied by the stark realities that gripped the entire region. By the summer of 1946 there was a severe famine in tiny Anguilla. "Most of the people seem to be under-fed," remarked the writer William Braithwaite. "Some have no money to buy food; and others who have a small sum of money can find little or no food to buy. . . . [D]uring the worst of the war years," it was lamented, "conditions were never as bad as they are today. Everyone is feeling the pinch . . . as I travel around the island I notice many gardens prepared for planting but empty for lack of seed. How will these people survive?" he asked worriedly. "How will they pay their taxes?"[15] There were "deaths in Nevis due to starvation," it was reported, while "the grim spectre of hunger [was] stalking through St. Kitts, Nevis and Anguilla."[16] Some were existing on "little more than sugar and water," while the colonial gov-ernment appeared "hopelessly wedded to the folly of feeding the masses on imported food for the most part."[17]

The colonizers should not have been surprised since "the question of ade-quate supplies of food seems almost always a problem" in Anguilla, said one observer. "Save for corn, peas and a few other items of diet grown during favourable weather, the island is not capable of producing vegetables in suffi-cient quantities." Primitive in the best of times, there was "little or no money circulating among the bulk of the people" there, while government fell back on the "old excuse that quality of soil and low rainfall are unsurmountable barriers to development of the land."[18] Things had deteriorated to the point where the normally somnolent dispossessed of Anguilla "were now realizing the value of organizing" and decided they "would welcome the benefits to be gained from the Workers League," which long had established a foothold in St. Kitts.[19]

St. Kitts should have been the economic locomotive that helped to pull even tinier Anguilla along, but it too was suffering. St. Kitts, for example, ranked "as one of the places where the number of deaths of infants to the thousand is the highest in the world."[20] In the British West Indies, the "death rates from tuberculosis . . . appeared to be higher than in England [and] Wales."[21] Returning military veterans were displeased to discover that they were returning to an island of misery they thought they had left behind after their shedding of blood to create a new world. Soon "ex-service men's demonstration[s]" were becoming common in the region, not least in St. Kitts, as there was "much dissatisfaction among returned veterans in that island over the inability to get suitable employment." It was a "source of spiritual distress," not to mention political and economic.[22] A "period of hardship has set in," moaned one journalist. "The amount of work available both on sugar estates and at the factory is very limited. The earnings of most of the workers are far from what is required to provide the necessities of life on a decent scale. A great many persons have no jobs at all." There was "less emigration" in 1947 than previously, as this safety valve was clogged, while the "prolonged drought" meant "hundreds of people are crying out for the want of work."[23]

There had been a "good deal of work" for Kittitians in the Virgin Islands, but by late 1946 those jobs were disappearing. "Scores of persons from St. Kitts and other neighboring British islands who held jobs for a long time in St. Thomas were suddenly discharged. . . . United States officials assisted by detectives" were "handling the matter of rounding up aliens and shipping them back home." Returning home was of little avail since typically "none of the two banks doing business" in St. Kitts chose to "employ Negroes on their clerical staffs" or otherwise.[24]

As so often happened when unemployment increased, the cry soon arose that there were too many people on the island—and some had to go. "Those who cry out 'too many babies,'" complained the *Workers' Weekly*, "are ducking the issue. The island once fed a larger population than the present number," but "today King Sugar dominates the island. In the dull season large numbers of agricultural workers only get a few days' work during some weeks. Many get no work at all. Town dwellers thus do not earn as much to cope with living cost"[25]—but the colonialists were not buying this line. *The Union Messenger* pressed the point that "the larger question of overpopulation can be properly taken care of by [a] federated West Indies which will need extra men to develop large areas like British Guiana" and British Honduras.[26]

It was not long before "the most striking demonstration ever witnessed" in St. Kitts occurred. It was an enlightening manifestation in every sense of the term. On 17 October 1947, "the streets were thronged with thousands of people," an estimated ten thousand to be precise, more than half of the island's population. They "stretched out in a long line marching through the entire town" of Basseterre "under the bright light of flaming torches. The march ended at Warner

Park," where a demand was put forth by the unions for the ouster of the colonial administrator. The throngs were led by "leaders of the Labour Movement."

The torches were not just a means for illuminating the darkness. They were also an ominous signal. Constructed of "pieces of bamboo about 3 to 5 feet in length," at the "top of some were bottles with kerosene oil and a wick burning at the mouth of each."[27] The "nearness of cane fields to villages" was a "sore point" in St. Kitts. "In the event of fires," it was a "source of danger," since "in some instances the cane field is hardly more than five feet from the village."[28] The threat of fire was a looming danger for colonial investments and a prevailing attraction for freelance saboteurs.[29] Thus, during the war "cane fires broke out on a number of estates in the island." The union issued a "circular urging" workers to "disassociate themselves [from] what is suspected to be a crude expression of dissatisfaction on the part of labour."[30] But the cane fires continued[31] and accelerated further after the war to the point where a "cane fire score board" was devised.[32] Cane fires in neighboring Barbados were monitored in St. Kitts, as if there were some sort of competition; "cane fires have been set every night in nearly all the parishes . . . there had been 176 fires which burnt nearly 1450 acres of canes."[33] This was understandable since fires in Barbados were frequent and devastating,[34] a condition exacerbated by repetitive droughts.[35] So when workers marched with torches in hand, their opponents quite rightly shrank in fear.

Besides starvation and unemployment, there were other reasons for St. Kitts labor to be upset. In the spring of 1947 a typical incident occurred when a domestic servant "was dismissed without notice and was insulted and beaten by her employer." This reflected a "steady undercurrent of hostility by employers of domestic servants," who were routinely and "grossly underpaid in St. Kitts" with "most of them receiving less than a shilling a day."[36]

Workers were less susceptible to accepting such maltreatment in the postwar era, one reason being their organizing across borders was increasing confidence in each island. Thus, the CLC found one of its more receptive audiences in St. Kitts, as early 1947 saw Norman Manley, T. A. Marryshow, Albert Gomes, Grantley Adams, and V. C. Bird descend on the island.[37] The vicinity of the courthouse in Basseterre "was filled to its capacity and crowds thronged the Pall Mall Square" at the "opening of the conference on closer union of the Windward Islands and Leeward Islands."[38] Though Washington thought that keeping these islands apart was a key to their being dominated, islanders were thinking the exact opposite—that closer union was the only way to stand up to the major powers.

At this juncture, leading the charge against the status quo was the founding father of an independent St. Kitts, Robert Bradshaw. Then maintaining close ties to the CLC, Bradshaw was renowned for his imposing physical appearance and authoritative manner. He had a "fighter's face" with a clipped officer's mustache which "sometimes gave him a forbidding look." He was to acquire "sophisticated tastes" and a penchant for "immaculately tailored suits, old-fashioned high wing collars and on occasions sported a flower in his buttonhole. At his most urbane he was dressed in a pin-stripe suit and knee-breeches." He lacked formal education, but he was a "veritable master in the history of the British Monarchy and the indigenous Caribbean peoples, fine wines, the culinary art and antiques," not to mention maintaining "an affinity for matters of heraldry" and "old ceremonial military swords." He "often boasted of his Ashanti origins," which was "undoubtedly part of his appeal."[39]

That was the postindependence Bradshaw, for during his rise as a union leader he developed a reputation for militancy that was at odds with his later image as an Epicurean. For under the leadership of Bradshaw and his comrade, Joseph France, their union ignited a major industrial dispute at least once every year between 1944 and 1949. When London contemplated placing a detachment of infantrymen near St. Kitts, this was perceived as a response more to union militancy than to Empire security. By the end of 1947, the union had 8,887 members out of "total sugar industry work force of 10,271." This blanket union coverage of workers was a product of their aggressive tactics. The houses of workers who continued to turn out for work during strikes and job actions were picketed, which could be quite intimidating on a small island and which inexorably forced most of them to capitulate. Ironically, unlike Jamaica, where the most advanced unions were led by Marxists like Richard Hart, in St. Kitts the union movement's philosophy was a combination of West Indian nationalism and Garveyism "suffused by the rhetoric of class." This was not unique to St. Kitts, as elements of this approach can be found in Trinidad's "Buzz" Butler, St. Vincent's Ebenezer Joshua, and Grenada's Eric Gairy.[40]

Bradshaw's militancy was evident during the war; it was then that he spoke out vigorously against some unnamed "persons on this island" that tended to "fabricate stories about the labouring classes" to "make [them] appear as a mass of 'Witless Nyagurs [sic].' "[41] His confrontational tactics embodied the disposition of the island itself, as the realization dawned that St. Kitts was being viewed as a pawn on a chessboard where London and Washington were the main players. There was stunned disbelief when, before lend-lease was negotiated, Senator John Miller of Arkansas advocated U.S. seizure of "Bermuda, Bahamas and all islands of the West Indies owned by England, France, Netherlands" and that "battleships" should be dispatched to "do the job."[42] Islanders recognized that some form of independence was the surest route to guarantee that this pawn-like status could be altered, so as early as 1940 a workers' organ was asking "what of a West Indian Federation?" The answer to this query was self-evident, it was thought, as already the advantages of "inter-island, inter-colonial communications by sea, air and wireless" were seen as both a result of and a motivation for federation.[43]

At this point Bradshaw embodied these currents, particularly the notion of British West Indies unity in the face of a rapacious U.S. imperialism. In St. Kitts, he proclaimed in early 1946 that "we have had no Yankees and we want none. Forward to federated British West Indies!" He wanted Washington to "know categorically and in terms too plain to be mistaken that we don't want him."[44] As he saw it then, it was Washington that was a "menace to the British West Indies; and stands as a direct stumbling block in the pathway of progress in which we are rapidly moving toward the goal of political federation." The United States, he thought, was "definitely set on taking these islands. She therefore falls ipso facto on the same basis . . . as Hitlerite Germany and imperialist Britain." Why was he so hostile to the United States? "The vast majority of the inhabitants of these islands are black," he argued, and whether the British West Indies should accede to U.S. domination "can be answered in the negative a thousand times by reference alone to the barbarous treatment of blacks within the borders of the United States itself." He was astonished by the "shameful atrocities committed against blacks in these islands by the same Yankees since we have been forced to share our island homes with them." He agreed with a comrade who asserted, " 'I am glad we have no American armed forces here; and even their presence in Antigua 60 miles away is too near for comfort.' As a colonial administrator," he declared, "Uncle Sam is definitely backward." Just look at Puerto Rico and the Virgin Islands, he asked, for "on these grounds alone the U.S. is disqualified to govern the West Indies. Another disqualification for the U.S. is the fact that her government is entirely capitalistic."[45] Bradshaw's comrades sought to bolster London so as to better resist Washington, asking "when will Negro Governors" be appointed in the British West Indies, a question posed after an African American was appointed governor of the Virgin Islands, a maneuver that was viewed as more cynical than sincere.[46]

When anti–racial bias laws were passed in New York, a similar tack was taken: "strangely the land of lynching parties and home of the Ku Klux Klan has gone one better than our great Empire with respect to curbing race prejudice."[47]

Veering from espousals of federation to odes to the Empire to protect the islands against U.S. imperialism, Bradshaw's line varied—but what did not was his unstinted hostility to Washington, which did not bode well for this power's future plans in the region. Worse, from Washington's viewpoint Bradshaw was taking his militancy to neighboring Antigua, site of an important U.S. base. In the spring of 1947, "before a large audience" of workers, Bradshaw spoke "for nearly two and a quarter hours; and when he intimated his intention to conclude, the enthusiastic audience, whose full attention had been held by the speaker loudly demanded that he should continue." With appropriate socialist-tinged joie de vivre, "the singing of the 'Red Flag' brought the meeting to a close."[48]

Washington felt it could not afford to remain indifferent as labor leaders in the British West Indies began to flaunt what were thought to be symbols of Soviet solidarity. This was particularly the case as the balminess of wartime détente morphed into the frostiness of Cold War. Much of this concern, unsurprisingly, focused on Jamaica, which contained some of the most militant unions and most resolute Marxists and had the added advantage of having one of their compatriots—Ferdinand Smith—serving as second in command of one of the most powerful U.S. unions, the National Maritime Union, which had true transcontinental reach. Malcolm Hooper of the U.S. mission in Kingston referred worriedly to this union and to the prospect of federation. A visiting Bermudan, Dr. E. F. Gordon, noted negatively how federation was being "thwarted by the white oligarchy," and thus the goal of his host, the CLC, was "far distant away." As for the CLC itself, somewhat unconvincingly, Hooper reassured his superiors in Washington that the organization "did not take on any outward show of Communistic grandeur."[49]

Those of Jamaican origin were abundant in the extraordinarily crucial Canal Zone, and in a "secret" dispatch, W. Lansing Collins, Jr., of the U.S. legation warned of the "possibility of Communist-inspired organization in Panama attempting to unify peoples of the Caribbean."[50] The United States shone a bright spotlight on one Eustace Alfred Davis, born in Jamaica in 1898, who had toiled in the Canal Zone since 1920 and had "been receiving shipments of printed matter by express from one A. Richard Hart" that included CLC material. He had also received "shipments of printed matter at the customs office in the company of Jose A. Brouwer, Socialist Deputy in the Panamanian Assembly."[51] Brouwer, "son of a Dutchman," was "reported to be a paid Soviet agent," according to Washington.[52] A "secret" message from the U.S. mission in Panama reported nervously that "plans were going forward [for] the organization of some kind of a conference of the peoples of the Caribbean and indicating a possible tie-up between the Communist Partido del Pueblo of Panama" and Manley's PNP.[53] Generally, there was an uncommonly large concern with the prospect of Panamanians becoming involved with CLC [54] and the idea it represented, that its tentacles should spread throughout the hemisphere.

But this was an extension of the growing hysteria about the "Red Communist issue" in Jamaica. Fingered were Richard Hart, the activist Kenneth Hill, the novelist Roger Mais, and the politician Willis O. Isaacs. Symptomatic of the desperation was the visit paid to Norman Manley by a well-placed U.S. diplomat in Kingston. Did he discuss subsidies from Moscow? No. His pressing concern was "how the word 'comrade' came to be used as a definite appellation for members" of Manley's political party. The tactically wise Manley gave credit to Sir Stafford Cripps of London, not Stalin. The "fact" that Manley was "not anti-Communistic leaves a big question mark in mind as to whether the lack of public, active anti-communism does arise from his pacific nature"—or something more devious and wicked. Warily, this diplomat added in a response deemed "secret," "whether Norman Manley will prove to be a Kerensky type or of a redder hue remains to be seen."[55]

At this time, radical flourishes did not separate the British West Indies unduly from Black America. After all, in the Harlem that both shared, the city councilman was a Communist—Ben Davis, elected in 1943 and re-elected in 1945. It was hardly by chance that a "Black Red" surged to office in this district, as he was propelled by a West Indian community that long since had established a reputation for not being adverse to radicalism. Figures like Richard Hart and Norman Manley in Jamaica, Cheddi Jagan and Forbes Burnham in British Guiana, and Robert Bradshaw in St. Kitts were both the leading figures in their homelands *and* leading radicals. The radicalism in Harlem and the British West Indies was mutually reinforcing, and it was Washington's task to disrupt if not quarantine this trend.

J. Edgar Hoover, the bulldog-like chief of the FBI, was wary of this radicalism. In a "confidential" message, he informed the State Department of extensive "West Indian Negro activities" in the "New York area" and singled out the Jamaican leader, Frank Hill, who had "made an approach" to the left-wing journal *PM* requesting they "make a survey of existing conditions in various Jamaican farm labor camps in the United States." Hill, said Hoover, also had "been in contact with Hope R. Stevens, a Negro Communist attorney" in Harlem.[56] Yet another Washington official spoke in "confidential" terms about the sizeable "extent of support in the United States for the establishment of a Negro-dominated Socialist Commonwealth in the British West Indies."[57]

But what really riled Washington was the visit of the Democratic Socialist Norman Manley to Harlem to raise funds for the CLC and other independence efforts. Hoover was not happy with the October 1945 "dinner" given "in honor of Manley by several Negro Communists," including the leader of the National Maritime Union, Ferdinand Smith, and the intellectual Max Yergan.[58]

The National Association for the Advancement of Colored People (NAACP) was riled too—and not only because Washington was riled. The NAACP, founded in 1909, was the oldest and largest civil rights organization in the United States. At this juncture, it was part of the left wing in the United States, and in 1944 had asked its venerable seventy-six-year-old founder and self-proclaimed socialist, W.E.B. Du Bois, to return as a kind of foreign minister to coordinate the group's activity in the realm of global affairs, notably leading a massive push for decolonization in places like the British West Indies.[59] Their leader at the time of the Manley dinner, Walter White, was a balding, bespectacled, unprepossessing man of less-than-imposing stature, who then was espousing the left-wing line then dominant in Harlem. He may have sensed a kindred spirit in Manley, who too was light-skinned and could have passed for white. Thus, in blunt terms White informed the FBI director, Hoover, "I was one of several speakers at dinner at the McAlpin Hotel" in honor of Manley and was told "that a record was made of every word that was spoken" by a "representative of either the FBI or the British intelligence.'" Perhaps more worrisome was that "house detectives acting under outside instructions were told to pick up every scrap of paper that might have any writing or printing on it that might have been left behind."[60] Washington, which had come during the war to realize the importance of the Caribbean to its own national security, had taken an increasing interest in Jamaica in particular. NAACP board member Alfred Baker Lewis was disturbed when informed by

W. A. Domingo that "Jamaican immigrants to the United States are frequently
questioned by immigration authorities at Miami and are warned not to have
any connection with [Manley's] People's National Party . . . immigrants from
other countries are not required to sever their political connections with their
homeland."[61]

Obviously the authorities were quite concerned about the kind of transnational racial solidarity represented by Manley's visit. If they had been able to
listen to Manley's remarks before the NAACP board, their concern may have
been magnified. "We in Jamaica, a very small part of the British Empire" said
Manley, a man with powerful oratorical range befitting a seasoned courtroom
lawyer, "nevertheless occupy today a position of strategic importance in the general colonial struggle." Manley was not engaging in puffery when he said that
"every West Indian is looking to Jamaica for leadership." Nor was he over-
reaching when he linked this struggle to the continental home of most of the
CLC's and the NAACP's constituency. "African advance is in the air," he
insisted, "but African colonial advance is going to be considerably affected by
the results of the West Indian experiment. The status of colored people the
world over must be affected by the achievements of the West Indian people
and by their success or failure as a people."[62]

Manley was not wrong. Figures like Du Bois and George Padmore long had
linked the struggles of West Indians, Africans, and African Americans. U.S.
Negroes were strategically positioned to influence the foreign policy of the leading power, and their general inability to vote would change to the extent that their
international lobbying brought the British West Indies and Africa to sovereignty—
which was an obvious incentive to embrace a visiting Manley. Manley could not
only raise funds in Manhattan and liaise with a growing overseas Caribbean community, but he could also give impetus to lobbying efforts that would bring him
closer to power. His journey to New York, in other words, was part of a righteous
circle.

This mutual love feast continued—for a while. 1946 found Manley back in
Harlem, addressing a mass rally at 124th Street and Seventh Avenue, where he
was joined by the NAACP's Roy Wilkins.[63] Then the coterie of CLC leaders
engaged by the NAACP was extended to include Albert Gomes of Trinidad.[64] The
association then began to introduce the wiser entrepreneurs—who sensed opportunities in getting in on the ground floor of decolonization—to British West Indies
leaders. White provided an introduction to Manley for Jerome Weinstein—"head
of . . . a large publishing and printing concern in the United States," who was visiting Jamaica; "I know you will enjoy meeting him," he assured his opposite number.[65] White took time to introduce Manley to stalwarts from the all-important
independence movement of India. J. J. Singh of the India League of America
found "the lunch with Norman Manley . . . not only very interesting but most
enlightening" and thanked White for "asking me to be present."[66]

White was also bringing Manley together with liberal members of the higher echelons of U.S. society. That was the import of an October 1946 luncheon at Manhattan's posh Biltmore Hotel. Among the elite who came to meet and greet the CLC leader were former State Department official Sumner Welles, novelist Pearl Buck, congressman Adam Clayton Powell, publisher C. B. Powell, and attorney Thurgood Marshall.[67] The energetic White also sought to bring Manley and Grantley Adams together with a "few others to discuss closer integration activities" of "West Indian Negroes and American Negroes." This was a "very important conference," he added without exaggeration.[68]

However, it was not easy for the NAACP to steer left when the nation in which it was contained turned sharply right with the dawning of a virulent red scare and a frigid Cold War targeting those thought to be agents of Moscow. Initially this was manifested in what appeared to be an old-fashioned bureaucratic snafu featuring an NAACP clash with the American Committee for West Indian Federation (ACWIF) that included such champions of sovereignty as Richard B. Moore, but it also was said to include NAACP leaders such as White and Channing Tobias and the conservative intellectual George Schuyler.[69] This was a vehicle not built to withstand the stiffer breezes brought by the abrupt change in the political temperature, though it did not appear that way initially. Indeed, as late as the summer of 1947 the ACWIF was distributing funds for the CLC's crusades, with White's apparent acquiescence.[70]

But things were changing rapidly in 1947, as was the mind of Walter White. Weeks after this disbursement, White upbraided Augustine Austin of the ACWIF after a story appeared in the Negro paper of record, the *Pittsburgh Courier*,[71] detailing this intervention. "Certainly I cannot afford to involve the Association," he huffed, "if Austin is going to act in this manner. He goes down there," speaking of Jamaica, "and announces that an American Committee for West Indian Freedom has been formed and hand a program to them which has never been submitted to any of us, including myself as Co-Chairman with Austin." White, who had circumnavigated the globe and was usually proud of his overall knowledge, now was taking an opposite tack. "I who know so little about the Caribbean," moaned White, was now being billed as an expert. Besides, there was "another West Indian faction led by Wendell Malliet which is bitterly opposed to Austin and his group," and he wanted no parts of this sticky wicket.[72] He expressed "considerable puzzlement" about this turn of events and told Austin that "several were annoyed" by what had occurred, accusing the West Indian activist of acting peremptorily without consultation.[73] What may have inflamed White's ire was the prominent press report in which Austin declared that federation "would have a psychological effect" on Negroes' own "status in the great republic," the United States. Many in Washington, particularly Dixiecrats, were not happy with the idea of confronting their eternal foe— the Negro—when he had the backing of nearby sovereign states.[74]

Within days of White's intervention, the U.S. consul in Trinidad and Tobago, Ellis Bonnet, sent a "restricted" message to Washington observing that "another development which may become important concerns the efforts being made to obtain active support for increased autonomy for the British West Indies or eventual federation, in the United States among British West Indian residents . . . and sympathetic American Negroes. Visitors from the United States to the West Indies and the West Indians returning from visits to the United States have reported an active interest among groups in the United States in the political aspirations of the inhabitants of the British West Indian colonies." Attached were a sheaf of articles from regional newspapers documenting this concern, including a story about the visit of Barbados's Grantley Adams to the United States and his attempt to form a pro-federation group that included White, Robeson, the contralto Marian Anderson, and others.[75]

If Washington had been able to intercept Richard Hart's mail, they would have received confirmation of their suppositions. For as Chicago's George Francis McCray told "Brother Hart" in early 1948, "for the first time in history American Negroes are really beginning to develop an interest in the West Indies. [I] am certain the number of persons visiting there will increase during the next few years." This was a turnabout from recent trends, he thought. "I don't know what the attraction is, but at the moment most Negroes at least from this area are vacationing in Cuba and Haiti rather than in the British West Indies."[76]

Austin, a prominent Harlem real estate agent, was also a major bankroller of the CLC, to the tune of thousands of dollars.[77] The backtracking Austin, who also was a principal in the Antillean Holding Company, which looked to do business in the region, told White directly, "I am sorry for any such misunderstanding," he said regretfully, but what was occurring soared far beyond a misapprehension.[78] What was happening was that a Cold War was descending that forced a split in both the CLC and the NAACP on a right-left axis, with the former pole—which was embodied by White and Grantley Adams of Barbados in the first place—moving at warp speed to place distance between themselves and those to their left, men such as Du Bois and Richard Hart. A Cold War had descended that ultimately was to weaken what had been a generally united movement for sovereignty, federation, and labor rights.

CHAPTER 8

Cold War in a Hot Zone

G RANTLEY ADAMS WAS WORRIED. He had given a fervently anti-communist speech at the United Nations that had won him plaudits in Washington, but his concern was how it would play in Barbados. But hours before his plane was to land at Seawell Airport, a large crowd in Bridgetown assembled to greet him. Three columns of trade unionists formed the guard of honor at the airport, and on the triumphal procession from the airport to Bridgetown some eleven miles away, the path was lined with cheering masses. Squads of bicycles led the way and more than fifty cars followed as the "cheers of thousands and tens of thousands" shouted hosannas. "They came from every village and hamlet" and "at the Garrison Savannah about one mile from the city, the crowds became so dense that the procession was brought to a halt," as "the streets at time became impassable."[1]

One Barbadian, Freddie Miller, recalled thirty years later, "I remember . . . while canvassing St. George in 1948, I went to a friend's house in South District to hear the radio broadcast of Grantley's speech at the Paris Conference." Some were not impressed. "Following his speech a member of the Russian delegation asked, 'who is that black man that is defending the British policy of bringing independence to the British colonies, especially in Africa?'" recalled Miller.[2] Certainly, Adams's words were even more effective since he came from a colonized land and was of African descent.

At his controversial 1948 speech in Paris, the man who was to be rewarded later by being knighted as Sir Grantley Adams, opposed a Soviet-Indian resolution on anticolonialism in stridently anticommunist terms—though during the war, like so many others, he was unstinting in his unalloyed admiration for Moscow. George Padmore of Trinidad was dumbfounded by Adams's strident defense of British colonialism. It was, he said with bafflement, "the first time in the history of British foreign policy that a politician outside the United Kingdom . . . has been invited by His Majesty's Government to serve upon a diplomatic mission representing the Cabinet of the day." The delegate of the Ukraine said that Adams was "simply the mouthpiece of the metropolitan power and a traitor to his own people." This was mild compared to the brickbats tossed at him by the Pan-African Federation in London and the anticolonial *West African Pilot*.[3] Adams's speech was widely—and correctly—perceived as auguring a split not only in a movement in the British West Indies crusading for sovereignty, federation, and labor rights, it also signaled that the path to decolonization globally and particularly in Africa would not be smooth. Thus, Adams's sympathetic biographer is not wrong in suggesting that "dissatisfaction with Grantley's speech spread from critical spirits in West Africa and from London to Harlem, New York City."[4]

Reaction in the West Indies was equally strong. It was recognized that a pivotal turning point had been reached. Strikingly, a decision in 1948 by the NAACP's W.E.B. Du Bois to push for a human rights agenda at the United Nations that would embrace the cause of embattled U.S. Negroes led to his being bounced from the organization he had founded, which kicked off a Cold War in Black America that likewise brought drastic consequences.[5] That same year Adams played a similar role—albeit in a diametrically opposed way—within the CLC and the British West Indies, with similarly dire results. Adams was responding to the gauntlet tossed down by British prime minister Winston Churchill, who in his infamous March 1946 peroration at Fulton, Missouri, spoke in foreboding terms about the "Iron Curtain" that supposedly had descended in Europe. The launching of a global anticommunist crusade was of a piece with a gathering Cold War that was to compel Social Democrats like Norman Manley to break with Marxists like the CLC leader Richard Hart, to the detriment of British West Indies sovereignty, federation, and labor rights.

The stakes were incredibly high—and, as a result, the rhetorical volleys tossed back and forth were likewise explosive. Richard Hart, the embodiment of the CLC left, sharply criticized the remarks of Adams, which he saw correctly as indicating a wounding split in the ranks. Reaching for authority to "Dr. Azikiwe's 'West African Pilot'" that attacked Adams as the "type of African leader that Britain loves to advertise to the world," Hart reprimanded his CLC colleague.[6] Adams and his supporters struck back vigorously. "Seldom have I seen such intellectual dishonesty in a critic," said Adams of Hart; "an attack on his beloved Russia temporarily unbalanced the state of his mind" and led him to a "despicably dishonest fabrication." With undisguised contempt, he added that "when the cabin boy persists in attempting to seize the control of and navigate the ship on his own, it is time the remainder of the crew got together in the interest of their passengers. How long must the CLC be at the mercy of the aberrations of this wretched, rash, intruding—Comrade?"[7]

In the midst of hailing the 1948 election of Harry S. Truman as U.S. president ("the results would indicate that the American worker has not veered to the left of center and unlike his counterpart in Great Britain has not yet been won over to the flag of socialism"), Adams's Barbados Workers Union took a jab at Hart too: "the course of action adopted by him can only be deemed completely unwise, precipitous, and irresponsible."[8]

"Adams, Yes, Vishinsky, No" was the headline in the journal of Barbados labor, as Hart was equated with the Soviet leader. The conflict reached Jamaica— the superpower of the British West Indies—when Hart's party, the People's National Party (PNP), on a motion of Willis O. Isaacs, passed a vote of censure "against the Editorial Board of the party organ" for reflecting Hart's viewpoint. In Trinidad, Albert Gomes lashed out at Hart—"you will observe that I do not address you as 'Comrade,'" he observed contemptuously before launching a tirade. "[Y]ou should cease behaving like a superintendent of an orphanage or a reformatory, or like some pathological spinster who had been made head-mistress of a girls' school. You are Secretary of a Labour Congress, not head of the Politburo or 'butcher' of a concentration camp." He assailed Hart, who simply had pointed out that heretofore decolonization had been foremost on the CLC agenda and Adams had departed sharply from this consensus on anti-communist grounds. Gomes would have none of this, however, as he berated Hart for "quoting from the American Committee of West Indian Federation," thereby joining his assault with that in the United States spearheaded by the NAACP's Walter White. "Certain of our so-called American supporters are per-suaded that providence has especially picked them out for the purpose of bring-ing freedom to the West Indies from British Imperialism," he spat out, while adding that these U.S. Negroes would be well-advised to stick to their domes-tic knitting; "we do not lynch Negroes in the West Indies nor do we ask that they should ride in separate coaching on our trains." Bludgeoning Hart and the left from all angles, he said that "it is a fact . . . that the impact of American great-ness upon the well-known inferiority complex of the West Indian often produces Yankee jingoism in a rather exaggerated and grotesque form," but somehow Hart had managed the rare feat of being both a dupe of Washington and Moscow, as Hart and his comrades were said to have "collected the views of a series of crackpot pro-Soviet organizations."

As for Gomes, he pronounced himself in "full agreement" with the "poli-cies" of London. "[W]e need the greatest possible solidarity," he pleaded, "between Britain, her Commonwealth and her colonies, together with her allies, in order to meet the Soviet threat of slavery disguised as salvation." Yes, "the CLC deserves to succeed," he added quickly, "but first we must find an effec-tive insecticide with which to deal with the verminous elements," for "there is no place for Communism in the West Indies."[9]

In turn, Grenada's T. A. Marryshow derisively called Gomes "Trinidad's problem child, politically speaking. Opinions to him are a matter of gear. He, or rather she," he observed with a gendered bias, "changes them as she does her gowns—low neck and high neck without warning. Young, fat and still far from forty, he is fluid molten material" with "no following whatsoever among the masses."[10] The CLC was cracking on an axis of anticommunism.

London was not displeased with Gomes's views. In an analysis of this man of Portuguese descent, born in 1911, it was noted that he "came into prominence in Trinidad shortly before the war as a trade union leader," but since 1946 "Mr. Gomes' outlook has undergone a marked transition," as his "present political philosophy is very much that of the reformed radical. There is no organized party system in Trinidad and he therefore commands no party or personal following. Mr. Gomes may be described as a moderate right wing politician with a firm belief in the value of private enterprise." He was "almost as much a West Indian as a Trinidadian figure." He has a "philosophic turn of mind enlivened by a keen sense of humour. His opinions are intelligent and well-balanced. In debate he has been described as 'ebullient and noisy.'" Despite this effusion, even this most enthusiastic recommendation felt compelled to note that he had a "tendency to contradiction between his public and private utterances."[11]

The CLC did not die with this right-left split, but it was harmed grievously. Hart and his comrades sought to push back, pointing out that Adams, Gomes, and their colleagues were diverting attention away from the intolerable socioeconomic conditions in the British West Indies, most notably Adams's own Barbados. For at the same time a call was made in Paris for a Caribbean focus on Moscow, ordinary Barbadians were languishing under the rule of London. At one high-level meeting. Adams underscored the "truth . . . of the statement that malnutrition and starvation throughout the island were widespread and that infant mortality, due to undernourishment on the part of mothers and infants was disgracefully high."[12] Things had gotten so bad there that "His Excellency" was discussing seriously "emigration to Brazil" for his subjects, but sadly "stated that it was unfortunate that there was no opening for Barbadians there." So he "proposed to send a Commission to British Guiana and British Honduras"—the region's reliable safety valves—to "examine conditions there with a view to the settlement of people of all races and the finding of homes for displaced persons." Desperation was so widespread that one leader suggested "that enquiries should be made . . . regarding the possibility of obtaining employment for Barbadians in the Argentine Republic."[13] Panicking, it seemed that the Barbadian authorities saw their fellow subjects as pawns on a chessboard, to be moved around at will. About fifty Barbadians were dispatched in 1948—as Adams was railing against the supposed threat of communism—to Surinam "accompanied by their families,"[14] yet there was no surcease since at the same time there was "repatriation of old and destitute Barbadians from Cuba," six hundred all told, who presented a "very difficult problem especially in regard to housing."[15]

Despite this abject misery, it was not altogether surprising that a man from Barbados would emerge as a major stumbling block to progressive advance. "Little England" had a relatively large resident European population of means and conservatism. Earlier the colonial authorities had been able—"through a clever manipulation of the internal politics"—to thwart the Barbados Progressive League with Adams's help, and he "consolidated his hold on the organization in the process." Historically, Adams had sided with the powerful "plantocracy" and, as a result, was seen as more pliable than Wynter Crawford, his prime opponent, who was "viewed with alarm" by these same forces.[16]

As the easternmost island in the Caribbean and a sentinel capable of providing an early warning for hemispheric incursions from Moscow, Barbados was taken quite seriously in Washington. The "most thickly populated of all Caribbean territories," with a "density six times that of Western Europe and higher than that of Japan," it possessed "nearly all the fundamental ingredients of social revolt except the physical means of revolt." Washington also knew that "racial distinctions between white and black are clearer in Barbados than in other West Indian islands. In several institutions on the island the color line actually exists, all citizens of color being excluded from the two leading social clubs on the island, the Barbados Aquatic Club and the Barbados Royal Yacht Club," an outgrowth of the fact that the "British white colony is proportionately larger than in other British islands of the Caribbean." The level of apartheid was sufficiently worrisome that even U.S. diplomats representing a nation that guaranteed Jim Crow were worried. "Identification of economic supremacy with racial discrimination makes the situation doubly dangerous," it was reported, "since there is large brown middle class to serve as a cushion between the master and the subject races."[17]

Barbados "even looks more English than West Indian," said one journalist. "Bridgetown, the capital, could be transplanted bodily to, say, Bristol, and match that ancient English port perfectly." The "first place in the [Empire] in which the sugar cane was planted,"[18] it was a "dark carbon-copy of Albion," where they "play more (and mostly better) cricket than any of the other islands. They speak a clipped English that would not be out of place in Sussex," and it was a "sort of outer shire England"[19]—it was proud of its conservatism, a conservatism that produced Grantley Adams's anticommunist tirade in Paris.

On the other hand, it would be one-sided to view the split in the region as wholly a product of the internal dynamics of Barbados, for that would hardly explain similar developments in Jamaica. The CLC had not been able to attract the wily Alexander Bustamante and his legions of organized workers to their banner, and after the proclamation of the Cold War, it became apparent that more and brisker winds would be added to his sails. Washington had reason to be skeptical of the tall, imposing Bustamante, who was not averse to imbibing alcoholic beverages in profusion before the lunch hour. U.S. diplomats knew, for example, that stories of his birth and parentage were exaggerated. "The whole Spanish story was manufactured by Busta," one report noted, calling him by his nickname and referring to stories about his alleged parentage. Such tales were designed "to help him masquerade as a pure white man of Spanish extraction in Cuba and the United States"—ironic in light of his being perceived as leader of the dark-skinned workers of Jamaica. At "19 [he] married a white, British woman of 40 here in Jamaica, then lived under the name of Clarke here until he went away to Cuba and there or in Panama adopted the name of Bustamante for the first time. This wife, his first, died many years ago." In Cuba he had gained renown as an "organizer of labor gangs . . . which had been used to break strikes" and also served a term as a member of the police force there. Apparently this was deft preparation for his return to Jamaica and his establishment of his eponymous trade union that one U.S. emissary termed "one of the most complete labor dictatorships in the world."[20]

Bustamante "cannot be dismissed as a bad joke because he represents genuine power," said Paul Blanshard of the United States. "He is unquestionably the most powerful labor leader in the British Caribbean today." This was due in part to his questionable business practices that bound members of the union to him personally. "I have met [men]," said Blanshard astonishingly, "who have borrowed money from him at the rate of 250 percent a year." But Blanshard, like the nation he represented, was in a quandary, since "this pro-American attitude of Busta's is quite genuine" which augured well for his prospects in Washington's backyard—something he well knew. By early 1945 Bustamante was sitting pretty "beside a modern, glass-covered desk in his small private office, in a tight fitting shoddy wool suit with vest which he keeps buttoned in the heat. His bearing is military and pontifical," added Blanshard. He claimed leadership of a union with 200 branches with 100,000 men. Repeatedly, at this juncture, the burning query was posed: "[T]o what extent is the political situation in Jamaica a fascist situation? Busta himself resembles the fascist stereotype in many particulars." Pointedly, Blanshard found that "the reaction of the upper classes of Jamaica to Bustamante is quite similar to the early reaction of European upper classes to Hitler and Mussolini." The "Bustamante incipient alliance with the upper classes could easily be transformed overnight into a fascist dictatorship," he warned.[21]

Repeatedly, Washington was considering the provocative question of "to what extent is the political situation in Jamaica a fascist situation." This was being asked in early 1946 just as the political climate was changing dramatically in the direction of Cold War. Bustamante, then at sword's point with labor forces backed by Manley and Hart, together and separately, declared that "'if I have got to be a dictator or a Hitler in Jamaica, I'm going to crush every Jew in Jamaica or compel them to leave the island.' . . . his excuse for this utterance was that the two leading newspapers are published by Jews and he was particularly angry at the moment with Michael de Cordova, Jewish chief owner of the 'Gleaner.'"[22]

Still, this burst of anti-Semitism was characteristic both of Bustamante's deep-seated conservatism and Washington's refusal to denounce him as a result. In a "confidential" message forwarded by the U.S. vice consul in Jamaica, George Kelly, this sober diplomat observed ominously that "on May 12, 1947 the endemic unemployment problem of this island, augmented by the recent return of some ten thousand ex-servicemen and thousands of ex-farm workers from the United States, serve as political fuel in a long-simmering 'show-down'" between Bustamante's Jamaica Labour Party and Manley's People's National Party.[23]

Subsequently, after Bustamante "stated that American troops might be useful to put down certain 'Communist' elements, a motion requesting the government to demand a review of the lease agreements" at the U.S. base "was thrown out by the Jamaica Labour Party majority" after one solon "opened the debate with a lengthy attack on American policies." This parliamentarian, Willis O. Isaacs, went on to assert that "certain American citizens living in Jamaica were taking an active interest in the politics of Jamaica. He feared that, should there be any major conflict, the American army would move into this country and take complete charge." His comments were directed principally at Roman Catholic priests who were "reported to be verbally advising members of their congregations not to vote for the PNP."[24] Naturally, Bustamante defended the base agreements and the U.S. military presence in Jamaica. Washington was willing to look the other way when the subject of Bustamante's transgressions arose because of a concern about labor, not only the radical variety, but labor generally. The "attitude of the Jamaican black labourer," said one U.S. emissary in July 1946, "is ascribed to his historical background, making any sense of compulsion to work associated with previous conditions of slavery." If "he is satisfied with three days' wages, he will not work four, and if wages are increased, he will only work two days."[25] Perhaps a strong hand would be needed if Jamaican labor were to ever conform to the diktat of capital.

Moreover, the presence of these bases assured a continuing interest by Washington. Though suffused with Jim Crow, U.S. diplomats were concerned that in Jamaica, "the racial attitudes of many British white planters and businessmen are quite similar to the attitudes of Southern white employers in the United States. This is particularly true when the question of Negro education is discussed. There is genuine fear in white conservative circles of educated Negroes inspired with 'the wrong ideas.'" Of course, Washington could justifiably be more concerned with white supremacy in the British West Indies as opposed to the United States itself given what it saw as unfavorable racial ratios in the region that could easily become tinder for rebellions spearheaded by the organized left. So special attention was accorded to the fact that "fear of racial violence is especially strong in the eastern parish of St. Thomas, which was the scene of the famous rebellion of 1865 under Governor Eyre. Mob demonstrations in that Parish in recent years have been quite frequent and some American-born planters have brought their families to Kingston for safety." The idea that Jamaica was an explosive keg waiting to detonate had dawned on Washington as they recalled a fabled incident when Learie Constantine, a well-known cricket player with brown skin, was asked with his wife to leave the Imperial Hotel in London. There was "so much indignation" afoot in Jamaica as a result "that the Secretary of State for the Colonies felt called upon to denounce any color discrimination in Great Britain." It was such explosiveness—along with its size—that solidified Jamaica's reputation as the bellwether of the region, or as Washington put it, "in almost every way the most important British colony in the West Indies."[26]

This clear importance was why the repeated visits to Jamaica of radicals like Paul Robeson were viewed with such concern. This concern skyrocketed as the Cold War was launched in the United States and within the Caribbean. As Adams was heaving rhetorical broadsides in Paris, November 1948 found the famous actor-activist in familiar haunts: Jamaica. There, as a "secret" report from the Jamaican authorities reported, he "gave a free open-air concert which was largely attended" where he "spoke freely on racial questions, with particular reference to the Negro's high opportunity of creating his own culture and social order in Jamaica." Kingston's commentator was not impressed, however, noting "there is no lack of self-consciousness among the Jamaican population, and that it is not to be expected that he would have expressed any sentiments on racial equality which had not already occurred to the great majority."[27]

This commentator may have been paying attention to the wave of labor unrest that had disrupted Kingston in the early postwar years. "Train service halted"[28] and "37 pickets herded into police van"[29] were typical headlines from 1946; "protracted 'Gleaner' strike" was a headline from December 1947 from the paper of the same name;[30] "bus strike enters fourth week"[31] and "bus conductors beaten up on way to work"[32] said other headlines from March 1948. During this latter strike, things got out of hand. A "time bomb" exploded on one bus, leading to massive injuries, and "public meetings" were "banned" as a result, giving rise to further fears of the fascism that Bustamante's ascendancy was said to augur. "Never in Jamaica's history," said the island's leading journal, "including even the most turbulent years of its uprising, has the country faced such a dangerous situation as the violence which has been let loose on Kingston by those brutes who are secreting bombs in passenger buses."[33]

Thus, the CLC split came at a particularly auspicious moment as a wave of labor disturbances rocked the region. Coordination at the highest level could have helped each respective island struggle while directing the tide of unrest toward sovereignty and federation, but the rift in the ranks made this difficult at best. For as in Jamaica, Trinidad was also hit with a tsunami of worker turbulence. By early 1947 there were riots being "suppressed with tear gas," along with the "alleged beating up of strikers, the arrests of 'agitators' and pickets, held in jail without being charged." Strikers had "set fire to oil-fields," which even then could grab the attention of the most blasé bureaucrat in London or Washington. They "armed themselves with a variety of weapons—hatpins, pitchforks, rifles."[34]

As in Jamaica, labor forces in Trinidad and Tobago were afflicted with divisiveness within the ranks; this too suggested that Adams's controversial remarks in Paris cannot be laid solely at his doorstep or that of Barbados. As so often happened, there were commonalities in the region that soared beyond the peculiarities of any particular nation. Trinidad, with its sizeable population of South Asian origin, was unique but it too had its version of the Adams flap—a controversy that scarred this otherwise beautiful nation.

George Padmore, one of the most illustrious sons of Trinidad and Tobago, described his homeland as an "exotically beautiful tropical maiden, the size of Delaware with pointed green mountains, flowing trees and fields of waving cane." By way of contrast, neighboring Curacao, "half the size of Rhode Island" was a "barren, dun-coloured crone, sterile and scrub-covered, unattractive save by the ornamentation." But what united these neighbors was precisely what attracted the major powers to their shores: oil. For "without oil Curacao would probably perish. Without oil Trinidad would see very lean and hungry times."[35]

But with oil, Trinidad and Tobago was a prize, which simultaneously gave labor leverage. By the late 1940s, the Oilfield Workers Trade Union (OWTU) had "7000 members," according to Padmore, which meant it was the "most stable and best organized" union there. "When it started twelve years ago," he said in 1949, "the oilfield workers (three-fourths Negroes, one-fourth Indian) were getting from 7 to 24 cents an hour, depending upon skill. Today they are getting from 30 to 50 1/2 cents an hour." It was the "only labour group on the island to own a printing plant, with press and linotype, as well as its own building costing $9000," and it also had "offices in strategic parts of the country." Led by "big, dour energetic John Rojas" and Ralph Mentor, a "plump, amiable shrewd man in his forties," the OWTU embodied the promise of the CLC. Rojas "seems to be rather far to the Left. So, for that matter," said Padmore, who was in the process of retreating to the safety of anticommunism, "are many of the native politicians and labour leaders in the Caribbean. They all seem enthusiastic about Paul Robeson," which suggested that "coloured fellow travelers and Stalinists have been journeying to this area off and on for the past fifteen years bringing 'The Message,' giving the local boys the benefit of their Kremlin training and then returning to Harlem to direct events safely from afar."[36]

In a "strictly private and confidential" message circulated among British trade unionists, it was acknowledged that the OWTU was "generally considered the best run and most powerful trade union in Trinidad." Hailing from a nation that tended to sanctify racial origins, intense focus was placed on this matter. Rojas was a "mixture, probably of Spanish or Venezuelan and Negro blood," while Quintin O'Connor was "Negro with white blood." As for Albert Gomes, he had failed to secure re-election to his post as head of the "Federated Workers Union," which was perceived as tied to his having "recently inherited a 'fortune.'" Besides, "by acting as Mediator over the waterfront strike, he had weakened the union in the eyes of the movement." As for "Buzz" Butler, who had risen to prominence during the labor unrest of the 1930s, "the power seekers and unscrupulous as well as the honest fanatics have been attracted to him like steel to the magnet."[37]

H. V. Tewson, the leader of British labor, was informed that a "good deal of the trouble in the Colony" was the "result of rivalry between some of the leaders of the unions," an assertion that was sadly true.[38]

For there was yet another cloud that blurred this rainbow of good news for the OWTU and the CLC, for, like Jamaica's Bustamante, Trinidad had its own labor leader who was unwilling to adhere to the consensus forged by the "coloured fellow travelers and Stalinists" and was seen by some as the most prominent of the "unscrupulous." In Trinidad and Tobago, Butler, who had come to symbolize the worker upsurge of the late 1930s, was viewed by many on the left as a kind of demagogue. Butler, said labor leader Ralph Mentor in the spring of 1946, "has at last broken the ice and come out in his true colors as an electioneering agent of Mr. Timothy Roodal," the leading "oil and theatre magnate." Yes, claimed Mentor, "empty drums make plenty noise."[39] "Butler stages a colossal fiasco" was a typical assault by his fellow unionists on the person of the eccentric and bearded leader.[40] Butler was "three hundred years behind the times," it was alleged.[41]

Reference was being made to the bitter 1947 contest in the strategically sited oilfields. As his opponents saw it, Butler "appeared in the oil-belt and commenced propagating hostile propaganda against" the OWTU. "Vulgar abuse of its leadership and ridicule and contempt of democratic procedures were the lines harped upon." Like Bustamante, Butler was said to lead a "fascist union," replete with "hooligan elements." Why such invective? "Crude oil was thrown in the public road with a view to capsizing buses conveying workmen to work; bottles and stones were thrown at passing vehicles, particularly at nights; and crowds at certain points would block vehicles and pull out workmen on their way to work, forcibly relieving them of their breakfast baskets and tool[s] and turning them back from work. In the early stage, the police forces were exceedingly tolerant," as Butler's men engaged in "queer activities," including "sabotage" and setting "fire . . . to a number of oil wells," which meant "water reservoirs in one district were emptied."[42] Butler, who had been ousted from the OWTU in 1939, was mounting a fierce counterattack.[43] The "situation in the South was deteriorating," said the colonizers, as "incidents of unrest and violence were on the increase."[44]

The OWTU, where left-wingers were hegemonic within the leadership, also had little liking for Grantley Adams.[45] He had performed a "shameful surrender" it was thought, an "unfortunate speech." At the same time, more than once[46] Robeson claimed the front page of labor's journal to espouse his ideas.[47]

This split in labor's ranks, which mirrored that in the CLC itself, was a boost for the colonizers. At the same time, Butler's visible role helped cast him as a staunch opponent of colonialism, the pole position in the race for sovereignty, federation, and labor rights. A "critical situation" had "arisen in the oilfields at Point Fortin," according to the colonizers, as "two wells had been fired." One was "brought under control but the other, a high pressure well, was still on fire and was likely to continue to burn for two to three weeks," it was said in early

1947. "It was felt by the management of the United British Oilfields of Trinidad that these were deliberate acts of sabotage by highly skilled ex-employees whose services had been dispensed with as a result of the apparently abortive strike which was still continuing in the oil industry."[48]

Butler's men were assaulting the citadel of power, as "shortly before" the Executive Council of the colony "sat . . . the Secretariat of the Legislative Council Chamber had been invaded by a mob of several hundreds of persons who were believed to belong to Butler's Party and that a clash had ensued with them and the police," with the latter carted away "hurt."[49] In response, the authorities "proposed expulsion from the island of Butlerites belonging to Grenada and St. Vincent,"[50] which may have been a cover for dealing with so-called "illicit recruitment of Grenadian labour" generally.[51] Upping the ante, "under threat of a general strike," the Council "advised that His Excellency should grant a desired interview" with Butler—tactfully it was decided to "overlook" this threat.[52] This decision may have been influenced by the "number of disastrous fires which had occurred recently."[53]

Butler remained on the offensive. "Certain unemployed followers" of his were "squatting on Crown lands and on lands belonging to United British Oilfields of Trinidad Ltd. The company was most anxious to have them removed from the lands," said the Executive Council with understatement, "since they constituted a potential danger to the safety of the Company's property." Gomes, who sat on the council and was a CLC leader as well (in addition to serving as president of the Federated Workers Trade Union) asked whether the ban on Butler, which had been imposed in response to his militancy, should be removed since it appeared that by making a martyr of him the authorities were actually strengthening his influence. Another member of the council noted that there would always be trouble in the oil fields since "the Oilfield Workers' Trade Union did not represent the majority of the oilfield workers who were mostly members of Butler's trade union," so he wanted Butler to be certified as the bargaining agent for the workers. Gomes objected "since he regarded Butler as mentally unstable and one who could not be relied on to respect any agreement to which he was a party," though he acknowledged that the "workers were fully suspicious" of the OWTU "ever since they had arranged to have the Companies deduct from their salaries their monthly dues to the Union."[54]

The "Butlerites" were not only strong in the oil fields, but they had some strength among sugar workers also. Just as 1947 was the year of strikes by oil workers, 1948 witnessed an eruption among sugar workers. "Intimidation of workers and sabotage had been reported." Again Butler was in a jurisdictional battle with another union, this time with the All Trinidad Sugar Estates and Factory Workers' Trade Union, and, again, a good deal of his ire was directed at workers who failed to follow him. As thousands of workers went on strike, reports proliferated about "stoning, arson"—and worse. Anticipating Adams's deviation later that year, Gomes—a union leader—demanded that the government "should take firm measures to deal with the strike." As the authorities saw it, Butler was seeking to "get control of the sugar workers so as to break another union which had already succeeded in establishing [a] sound industrial relationship with manufacturers." The colonizers' consensus was that Butler was "nothing more than a megalomaniac," though a dissenting opinion held that his union "represented a much larger body of workers in the sugar industry than any other organization." But "His Excellency's own view was that if Butler was given any recognition it would be to invite a state of anarchy in the colony."[55]

But it was not as if the authorities were in total control to the point where they could dictate results. They had sought the "banning" of the "blowing of horns, the carrying of lighted torches and the unlawful assembly of persons numbering more than ten armed with sticks," but this "had not had any influence on the situation which from recent reports . . . was growing worse. Approximately 11,000 tons of cane at Usine St. Madeleine and Esperanza Estate had been burnt; attempts had been made at the latter Estate to let loose the stock on the countryside." The feared cane fires "had . . . resulted wherever meetings by Butler's followers had been held," as he was busily "inciting the people."

"Drastic steps should be taken," advised the colonizers, including Gomes, who "pressed for immediate and drastic action." Actually, "stern action was required," argued another member of the Executive Council. This brave talk could not obscure another troubling concern: "pro-Butlerite" sentiment among the police, which would make harsh approaches difficult at best. Though Butler was a nationalist of a Garveyite hue, the authorities were seeing "Communist interference in the present strike and the source of Butler's financial support,"[56] as they desperately sought to link their campaign with the emerging dominant zeitgeist of anticommunism.

This proved to be unavailing. "Acts of sabotage continued" in the oil fields, it was reported in March 1948, as "gangs of masked men armed with cutlasses were intimidating the workers." The "situation was not good," it was said with icy reserve. Again, Gomes was leading the charge, as he "inveighed against the form of gangsterism which was being practiced by followers of Butler."[57] Gomes, who had played a pioneering role in the formation of the CLC and, thus, was seen as a tribune of labor rights, now had been transformed—as the chilling blasts of the Cold War coursed throughout the region—into a staunch opponent of labor militancy. But even Gomes acknowledged that the horrid working conditions in the British West Indies were enough to drive the most complacent laborer to fiery activism. He had visited Aruba in 1946, for example, and "had seen for himself the conditions of the labour camps," a ghastly sight that compelled him to advise the colonial authorities to be "very careful in sending Trinidad labour to Aruba since conditions were most primitive."

Moreover, there was a material basis for some British West Indies leaders to sign on to the latest policy directive from Washington. For it was evident early on that this power, which had emerged triumphant after World War II with its physical plant basically unscathed and with its rivals and allies reeling in agony, could dole out more benefits in the British West Indies than the previous hegemon—London—which was now overstretched and, in any case, had perfected a colonial model based on penury. This was driving not only events in Trinidad and Tobago but also the ascendancy of Adams and Bustamante and their equivalents. By September 1947, there were worries at the highest levels in Trinidad and Tobago about the "very serious position in which Great Britain now found itself as a result of the dollar shortage," which could mean "drastic measures" and a "grave situation. Inevitably the Colony's economy would be seriously affected since it was closely linked to the economy of the Mother Country." The secretary of state for the colonies "proposed that imports from all sources should be drastically curtailed and that steps should be taken to exercise rigid control over the spending of dollars in non-sterling areas." This could only mean a "period of austerity was before the Colony and that restrictions even more severe than in wartime would have to be imposed."[58] "Drastic import restrictions" were "to be imposed" that meant "further restrictions on the commerce of the Colony" that "would result in the laying off of a considerable number of shop clerks thus adding to the unemployment problems of the Colony."[59]

Soon George Padmore was capturing the sentiments of many when he observed in late 1949 as economic retrenchment was biting that "there is wide resentment against England for charging higher prices for cheaper goods than could be bought from the United States." London's "inflated prices for shoddy goods" was a "very sore point."[60] Soon there were dire reports of the "many who have been attempting to leave the country surreptitiously to make illegal entry into the neighboring Republic of Venezuela in the effort to secure jobs which they are denied in their homeland." "[P]eople are hungry, jobless, homeless and ill-clothed. In desperation many are being forced to commit crimes."[61]

The extreme degradation that existed in the region was bound to be made worse by this "austerity," and this made the rise of the dollar's home—Washington—seem like manna from heaven. In the spring of 1948 the colonizers were concerned since there were "quite a number of American cars . . . being purchased by natives of the Colony from personnel attached to the United States bases." These vehicles were being "being sold at fabulous prices" and amounted to a "racket since it was a flagrant evasion of the Customs and Foreign Exchange regulations."[62]

On the other hand, the proliferation of U.S. personnel in Trinidad and Tobago had brought to the fore issues besides a greater number of cars on the market. There was a "danger of local feeling being embittered against American personnel," warned the authorities, not least because of a particularly egregious "shooting incident at Pointe Gourde." The authorities "warned of possible worse incidents occurring in the future as a result of personal vendettas against American personnel. . . . His Excellency felt that the United States Naval Authorities were pursuing a very short-sighted policy in this connection."[63]

London was upset with gathering U.S. influence. The U.S. base operated a radio station that broadcast music and news. Now there were only "6000 civilian radios . . . in use in Trinidad," not enough, one would think, to make a palpable difference—but that's not what the colonials thought. "Certain British officials, including officials of the Colonial Government," said Washington's man on the scene, "wish to terminate broadcasting in Trinidad by the American army in an effort to increase British and reduce American influence and prestige." In its stead, "efforts [were] being made to establish a British broadcasting station."[64] No, said an influential local journal, the U.S. "armed forces radio station should remain" since "it has won the enthusiastic support of local owners of receiving sets."[65]

Despite their differences, Washington could have no fundamental quarrel with London's policies that promoted white supremacy. In a testament to the failures of colonialism, in early 1948 the colonizers were contemplating "employing Poles, Italians and other foreign candidates who possess technical and professional qualifications . . . as a result of the dearth of professional and technical candidates." The immediate question was why Trinidad and Tobago had to look abroad—more specifically to Europe—for personnel. A related reality was the attempt by the colonizer to ignore those few from the British West Indies who had managed to acquire skills that had traditionally been systematically denied. Thus, during the same meeting where interest was expressed in recruiting "Poles and Italians," "doubts were expressed about the practical knowledge and ability of Dr. Arthur Lewis," the future Nobel Laureate in Economics, who was seeking the "post of Economic Adviser." It was recognized that failing to hire this dark-skinned man from St. Lucia "would have most unpleasant repercussions in the British West Indies." Yet despite the potentially damaging ramifications, the authorities chose to offer this post to a competing candidate of melanin deficiency, illustrating once more how colonialism was stifling the development of the region.[66]

There was a "yacht and social club for whites only" in Trinidad and Tobago. "There are clubs which it is well nigh impossible for a black man to join," Padmore lamented, "and certainly not a black woman." This atmosphere of fractiousness also contributed to the reality that there were "extremely few marriages between Negroes and East Indians."[67]

This officially sanctioned apartheid was no minor matter. "While the specter of Communism in Europe and Asia is haunting the western powers," Padmore announced in mid-1949, "it is the danger of the revolt against the colour bar and racial segregation in Africa and other sections of the Colonial Empire which is causing British officials at Whitehall the greatest uneasiness."[68] This helps explain the vitriolic reaction to colonialism by Trinidad and Tobago labor leader John Rojas. "The history of British Imperialism in the West Indies," he charged, "is a history of murder, suicide, inadequate hospital facilities, wage slavery, bad housing and frustration." The "wealth and material resources of Trinidad have been taken to the United Kingdom," he said accusingly, while "the British Trade Union Federation has never opened its arms to us."[69]

The situation in oil- and gas-rich Trinidad and Tobago was even more complex because there were rifts between factions symbolized by Gomes, Butler, and the OWTU. Late in life, Gomes spoke in glowing terms about Butler, referring to his "arresting appearance" and "his head that recalls another Negro leader, Jomo Kenyatta—same beard, same intense eyes, same aura of majestic, brooding pugnacity. Bible in one hand, fan in the other," other than Bustamante he was "the most picturesque grass-roots politician in the West Indies. He is an immaculate dresser, black seemingly his favourite colour, and never moves out of doors without his black Homburg."[70] But in 1948, when Butler was viewed as a more fearsome character, Gomes was not opposed to his being barred from certain areas of Trinidad and Tobago. But he then relented, concluding that "the ban prohibiting Butler from the Counties of Caroni, Victoria and St. Patrick should be relaxed since its maintenance served only to make Butler a hero in the eyes of his followers."[71]

The shame of it was that, his flaws notwithstanding, Butler was a mass leader with followers in legions, and that he found himself at odds with the CLC and the OWTU was to the detriment of both—and to the advantage of those who sought to launch a regional version of the Cold War, which would only mean ill for militant labor of whatever stripe, with all tarred as "red." This became clear when Butler decided to visit Great Britain amidst the 1948 turmoil "with the declared object," said the Colonial Office, "of demanding from HM's Government 'freedom for the workers of Trinidad.'" Though he was under siege by the CLC and the OWTU left, while in London he echoed their concerns, as he "played a prominent part in the proceedings, which concluded with a resolution deploring South Africa's policy on this matter." This gathering was "attended by more than 100 people," and he was "enthusiastically welcomed" by those who apparently were not unaware of his "so-called 'hypnotic' powers as an orator." The fear of Butler was reflected in the fact that it was directed that "special care should be taken to maintain the secrecy of the [Butler] documents . . . they should be locked in a steel press overnight and circulated BY HAND at ALL STAGES"[72] (emphasis in original).

The authorities in Port-of-Spain wondered about the "suggestion" that was "made that the sugar companies, and perhaps some of the oil companies too, have been paying to keep Butler out of harm's way in England. I find this hard to believe," said Sir John Shaw, writing from Government House, "but in Trinidad all things are possible. Sugar has had a bumper year unhindered by strikes and labour troubles which is probably due to Butler's absence since September 1948." Whatever the case, Sir John did not hesitate in asking plaintively: "[W]ould it be possible for the Special Branch to watch him intensively for a week or two, and find out what he is really doing? I have heard that he is living in poor circumstances in the East End, in close touch with the Communists. I am also wondering whether he has married or is living with a European woman. If this were so, and it became known," he pondered devilishly, "it might do a lot to discredit him and impair his influence."[73]

Thus it was that in December 1948 a Colonial Office agent found himself at a London meeting "held by the Coloured Workers Association of Great Britain and Ireland." There were about "50 persons . . . present, a third of which were coloured, mostly Negroes." The main speaker, Butler, arrived late but proceeded to fire up the audience with tales of worker woe in Trinidad and Tobago, where one "either worked or starved," as "there was no dole for them to draw when they became unemployed." It was a "scandal," Butler asserted, "that they should be governed by a fascist representing a socialist government," referring to Sir John Shaw. A master of the dramatic, Butler unfurled a Union Jack, "which he claimed was stained with blood . . . men, women and even a few children had been fired upon by the order of Col. Walter Angus Miller, police chief, who was of German descent. 'Should not this man be hanged by his neck for this deed,'" asked Butler. Instead, "he had been promoted and sent to Tanganyika." Despite the inflamed rhetoric, the agent busily scribbling notes was heartened by the fact that "the 'Daily Worker' was not on sale neither [was] there any Communist literature."[74]

Butler, besieged on all sides, told the London authorities directly that "we know and appreciate that 'Whites' are ready and willing to meet with all their military might and Power any threat to *their* freedom and independence." Yet he could "neither understand nor appreciate why they (Whites) are just as ready and willing to deny Blacks under the Old Flag."[75] Soon the headline blared, Butler "disappears from London," as he was "short of money" and, besides, "London weather had not been kind to him."[76]

So Butler returned home to a region that was grappling, not always successfully, with a multilayered crisis compounded by colonialism, white supremacy, and serious fissures within the ranks of labor that spelled ill for the aspirations of the CLC. But as Adams's famous—or infamous—remarks in Paris suggested, this region had been transformed. Washington, the growing power in the Caribbean, had managed to impose its vision, which privileged the idea of targeting those perceived as the agents of Moscow. The problem for the region was that these presumed agents also happened to be the staunchest advocates of labor rights to rescue the common man and woman from the snares of poverty.

FIGURE 1   Demonstration against British colonialism in St. Kitts, early 1950s (from far right: C. A. Paul Southwell, holding placard; Joseph Nathaniel France, wearing light-colored suit with white hat; F. T. Williams, to France's left.
(Courtesy of the National Archives of St. Kitts-Nevis)

FIGURE 2   Operations at bauxite mine in British Guiana, 1948: London's Caribbean colonies produced untold wealth, including bauxite, petroleum, and numerous agricultural products.
(Courtesy of the Library of Congress)

FIGURE 3 These Jamaican women breaking and carrying rocks in early twentieth-century Jamaica symbolize the difficulties in surviving under the harsh conditions faced by Caribbean labor.
(*Courtesy of the Library of Congress*)

FIGURE 4 As these dwellings in early twentieth-century St. Kitts suggest, housing for the working class in the region was not commodious.
(*Courtesy Library of Congress*)

FIGURE 5 Soldiers from the United States engage in maneuvers during World War II in the British West Indies: This region was critical to the protection of U.S. national security, which led to increased U.S. influence there during the war.
(*Courtesy of the Library of Congress*)

FIGURE 6 A sign in a Harlem window in 1943 suggests the continuing influence of Marcus Garvey: There was an influx of laborers from the Caribbean to the United States during the war. Similarly, as Caribbean nations surged to independence after the war, their reluctance to accept the dictates of Jim Crow played an essential role in the crumbling of this system.
(*Courtesy of the Library of Congress*)

FIGURE 7   Robert Bradshaw, founding father of independent St. Kitts-Nevis. Like many other leaders in the region, he emerged from the labor movement. However, as the Caribbean left declined as the Cold War accelerated, like others he was not able to fulfill his initial progressive promise.
(Courtesy of the National Archives of St. Kitts-Nevis)

CHAPTER 9

The Left Retreats

I T IS APPARENT," Richard Hart concluded forlornly in early 1949, "that the cessation of publication of the 'CLC Bulletin' has left a terrible gap. I am far too broke to finance the publication of another issue. I have, however, received an unsolicited contribution collected by the Jagans in British Guiana of six pounds," he added, brightening, "and I am going to bring out another issue. Would you be able to print it for me for this sum?" he importuned his comrade, Frank Hill, of Montego Bay, Jamaica.[1] That same year Hart demanded from the CLC treasurer, H. W. Springer, "a balance due to me from the CLC" of more than seventy pounds.[2] "I don't like the idea of the CLC incurring such a large debt to me," he added.[3] M. Joseph-Mitchell of the League of Coloured Peoples of London informed Hart in April 1949 that "[l]ast year your 'Bulletin' was being received by the office regularly up to October," then "all communication from you ended."[4] Finally, in 1952, as the organization was rapidly expiring, Hart asserted with some exasperation that the CLC "is heavily indebted to me as I have had to carry a considerable excess of expenditure over receipts out of own pocket."[5]

The split in the ranks of the Caribbean Labour Congress (CLC) was a severe body blow to the group's fortunes. Grantley Adams's 1948 address to the United Nations also was a setback to the original vision of sovereignty, federation, and labor rights, and the rift was too profound to paper over. Though the CLC left was able to hang on bravely for a few years afterward, 1948 marked a turning point, a hinge year whereby the promise and militancy of the early postwar years cascaded downward rapidly. At a time when Adams was sounding the tocsin against communist advance, notably in Eastern Europe, Hart—on the other hand—was extending the hands of friendship to the embattled comrades there. "I am afraid that people in this part of the world are very ignorant of the progress being made in the USSR, Czechoslovakia and the other Eastern Republics," Hart lamented in addressing the Prague journalist Bedrich Roohan. Interestingly, he added that "for years before and during the late war the easiest station to pick up was the German station which was going at all hours. At one stage a commentator called 'Lord Haw Haw' had begun to exercise a mass influence in this city," he said, speaking of Kingston. Yet "for the past two months," he noted in the fall of 1948, "I have not been able to get Moscow at all and Prague only once, very indistinct."[6] Hart's lament spoke directly to the growing and gnawing concern that he—and the CLC generally—were becoming a Trojan Horse for Moscow in the region. If that was so, the USSR was noticeably derelict in establishing a distinct communications link with its presumed surrogates.

These political rifts and resultant sagging finances were also having an impact on the CLC's ability to expand its remit beyond the British West Indies. It was in 1948 that Hart felt compelled to reprimand Gabriel Henry of Martinique. Speaking as "a comrade," Hart sought to "express our dissatisfaction with the assistance which has been given us in our efforts to establish close relations between the workers of the French West Indies and the workers of . . . British and Dutch territories. I hope you will take this criticism in the spirit of comradeship in which it is meant and will not be offended by my frankness." What concerned Hart was that "no reply has yet been received to our invitation to your organization and the Confederation Generale du Travail (on whose behalf you wrote) to affiliate with the CLC." He also sought to reassure Henry that "language [would be] no barrier." But it was difficult for Henry to focus on an organization, the CLC, which was widely thought to be merely concerned with the British West Indies, when other issues impinged; even Hart felt constrained to offer "sincere condolences at the assassination of one of your candidates in the recent Municipal elections."[7] Henry, in any case, reminded Hart that his nation was "no longer a colony but a department, i.e. we are to benefit [from] all social progress won by the French workers in Europe."[8] Semantics could not obscure the fact that this Caribbean island was still being ruled from Paris, not Fort-de-France, and the reality remained that a French colony in the midst of a passel of British islands surging to independence was not only anomalous but also detrimental to the overall goal of sovereignty.

Hart persevered. "The coming together of the representatives of Labour in the Dutch, French, American and British possessions is long overdue," he told E. Henny Eman, president of the Aruba Labour Union, and, he added bravely, they were all "well on the road to the establishment of a common front."[9] The Arubans, less tied to their European colonizer than the Martinicans, chose to cooperate with the CLC.[10]

But that this tiny island chose to throw in its lot with the CLC was not an indicator of growing from strength to strength. A more telling indicator occurred in the spring of 1949 when Jamaican unions "appealed to their members to support the present strike of Canadian Seamen's Union [CSU] and to decline to unload a Canadian vessel in the port of Kingston. These appeals met with no success," according to one unnamed colonial official, "and the vessel was unloaded without incident. Later . . . Mr. C. W. McDonald, a representative of the Canadian union, arrived in the island and working closely with Mr. Richard Hart, the Secretary of the Caribbean Labour Congress, attempted to dissuade portworkers and merchant seamen from handling cargo carried by Canadian vessels and from accepting employment on these vessels." But this was a hard sale given the perception that "the Canadian union is widely reported to have opposed the employment of Jamaicans on [Canadian] ships"—a questionable assertion but yet another indicator of why the labor solidarity that had been propelling sovereignty was now flagging.[11]

Hart sought to make the sale nonetheless, devising a plan for the CLC to collaborate with Canadian sailors. "What Canadian ships have called at your ports to date since the strike commenced?" he asked CLC affiliates. Were they "manned by CSU men or strike-breakers?" he asked. "What action, if any, was taken by local unionists to support their strike?"[12] "One of the striking members of the Canadian Seamen's Union, who was shot in the head by a strike-breaker when Canadian National Steamships were boarded in Canada was a Jamaican named Terrence Steward," Hart said. "It is true," Hart added, "we are not satisfied with the CSU policy as regards displacement of West Indians on Canadian National Steamships," but he thought strict labor solidarity was the optimal vehicle through which this nettlesome matter could be addressed—a point that some in the CLC disputed.[13]

Despite the urgency of Hart's tone, F. L. Walcott of the Barbados Workers Union was decidedly unimpressed. "My dear comrade," he told Hart, "my union appreciates your attitude in the matter but feels the situation does not merit the CLC taking any more positive steps." As he saw, it there was a jurisdictional competitor to CSU, which made any external solidarity inappropriate.[14] This was not just a matter of the traditionally conservative Barbados weighing in, for Joseph France, a leader of St. Kitts workers, confided that "the position of my union with regard to work on the waterfront is weak. . . . We shall do our best in this matter," he added apologetically, "but we are sorry we do not view it as advisable for us to attempt to tie up boat[s] with such a wide chance of failure."[15] Others in Basseterre were not predisposed to aid Canada, for as one local journalist acknowledged, the "Deputy Minister of Labour in Canada has officially announced that there is an acute shortage of labour in that country, and labour will have to be imported to that country to fill the gap"—yet there was "absolutely no chance for Jamaican or other West Indian persons. Instead European 'Displaced Persons' will be called upon to fill the gap."[16]

Lionel Francis of the British Honduras National Labour Union was also unimpressed with CSU. Yes, they were "removing English, Greek, Norwegian," and other sailors of diverse nationalities from ships, but, unlike the British West Indies, these nations were not subsidizing Canadian shipping. Hence, he wanted to see a "Caribbean Seamen's Federation having as one of the objectives an INTERNATIONAL WAGE AGREEMENT"[17] (emphasis in original).

Hart had another agenda in mind when he was pressing for solidarity with Canadian workers. He recognized that these small islands had a vitally crucial lifeline, which was shipping, and influencing this industry was critical to the future of labor. Hart congratulated Joseph France for proposing "in the event of strikes against shipping agents in any port our affiliate organizations in other ports should prevent the loading and unloading of all cargoes destined to or coming from the port of the strike." Yet Hart had to concede that "we have by no means yet reached the position of unity and strength in all territories where we can say the word and be sure of success."[18]

Despite these setbacks, Hart had good news to report to the CSU leadership in Quebec. "I have been able to secure agreement between the two unions organizing longshoremen here to refuse to load the 'Canadian Challenger' when she docks here on Saturday morning," he asserted elatedly in April 1949. "This has been a very difficult task in view of the fact that the longshoremen are about equally divided between the Bustamante union and the United Port Workers Union and that the two unions are constantly at rivalry." As it turned out, this divisiveness was to prove decisive, for the battle between the CLC left and Bustamante's formidable forces and Adams's growing legions were to curb the militancy that had percolated to the surface in the war's aftermath. Indeed, Hart ended his salutations to his Canadian comrade by stating that it was "unwise to cable in view of the probability that the shipowners' spies would then have learnt of our plans and diverted the ship to another port."[19]

Yet another sign of the times also involved Canada and Jamaica in 1949. It was then that "a Dr. Endicott, who described himself as the Chairman of the Canadian Peace Congress, arrived in Jamaica" and, said a colonial official, "with more than its usual naivete the 'Daily Gleaner' gave good publicity to him and his views, quoting as saying in an interview 'there can be no peace while the colonial order exists,'" a statement viewed as highly inflammatory. "Meanwhile the Managing Director of the 'Gleaner' has undertaken to ensure that the paper will not again be used as a medium of Communist propaganda."[20] This undertaking would further restrict the boundaries of anticolonial discourse, to the CLC's detriment.

What had occurred in the early stages of the Cold War was a standoff between the CLC left and its detractors, with both able to mobilize thousands in support. But as time wore on, the proximity of the region to the power least devastated by war and able to communicate directly—in English—often with African Americans doing the talking as Jim Crow barriers melted, increasingly placed the CLC in a disadvantageous posture.

Thus, in late 1948, the journal of the Seamen and Waterfront Workers Trade Union of Port-of-Spain spoke effusively of "Paul the Memorable," referring to Robeson's performance before a "gathering of over 20,000 persons, free, gratis and for nothing." They were heartened by his "often repeated statement"—not to be fulfilled—"that he expects to be back here many times in the not distant future." There were "many children of the West Indies in various professions and high callings who have slighted and separated themselves from the people whose purse has nourished and educated them"—but, happily, Robeson was not among these.[21] Robeson was becoming a lodestar for the Caribbean left. Just before his visit to Trinidad he was present in Jamaica as 30,000 marched under the CLC banner. A "vast throng jam-packed the stand enclosure and occupied a large part of the open spaces including the race tracks" as sharp "attacks were made" on Bustamante, "who was accused of standing in the way of West Indian unity." Apparently inspired by Robeson's presence, Robert Bradshaw of St. Kitts exhorted, "we in the other Caribbean islands of the [British West Indies] shall not sit by" and "will not be satisfied until a socialist government is returned to the House of Representatives of Jamaica." Bradshaw was struck "from the time he landed in Jamaica" with the "similarity between the people of Jamaica and his own people in St. Kitts and Antigua."[22]

At the same time the soon-to-be persecuted Robeson was making his way southward to Trinidad, Albert Gomes was making his way eastward to London, a city rapidly absorbing a growing number of migrants from the British West Indies. But his message was not congruent with that propounded by Robeson in Port-of-Spain. In fact, that Gomes and Robeson were now at cross-purposes was suggestive of the dilemma confronted by the CLC. For David Lewis, the CLC leader in this British metropolis, had to reassure that "the left will not attack Gomes in any way," though it was guaranteed that "the Trinidad people . . . will put him on the spot with questions during the meeting. They feel very bitter against him." As he saw it, the portly Gomes was "primarily interested in Trinidad being able to use the dollars she owns in America & this is because he needs American equipment for certain industrial & commercial ventures."[23]

These bruising opinions notwithstanding, Gomes was received politely at this "inaugural meeting" of the London CLC. There were "125–150 present mainly West Indians." Forbes Burnham of British Guiana "was in the chair" as Gomes "spoke briefly . . . praising its officers including you," he told Hart.[24] This diplomatic offensive continued when Grantley Adams arrived in London in the late summer of 1948 to address a "public meeting under the joint auspices of the London Branch" of the "Pan-Africa Federation & League of Coloured People." The "audience was of West Indians, Africans, East Indians and English friends. The crowd" was "equally as large as that [which] heard Busta" in London "where he was heckled."[25]

But the wily Gomes, perhaps anticipating a similar welcome, tailored his remarks for the CLC left stronghold that was London, for "as soon as he returned to the West Indies his remarks were contrary to what he said here. In London he agreed that Bustamante was a veritable dictator," but he reversed this view upon returning home.[26]

Gomes's apparent reversal was a reflection of the fact that during the 1948–1949 era it was not easy to predict which side would prevail, the CLC left or its detractors. Certainly if responding to this potent query were to be gauged by monitoring the amount of labor strife in the region, it would be easy to conclude that those seen as the champion of the workers—Richard Hart and his comrades—would soon be coming to power throughout the region.

Certainly Hart and the CLC left had gained in prestige as the result of his July 1948 visit to Port-of-Spain. He journeyed there on behalf of the organization, and after he met with leaders of the various unions and all the political organizations, they agreed to reconcile their differences and cooperate. That the warring parties agreed to participate under the CLC's aegis served to burnish the group's reputation as an honest broker—though the lack of participation of "Buzz" Butler's forces suggested there was more work yet to be done. As Hart recalled later, "the pressure organized in Trinidad as a result of the intervention of the CLC was an important factor in causing the Secretary of State for the Colonies to decide that . . . the new Constitution for [Trinidad and Tobago] should provide for a majority of elected members on the Executive Council," which administered the colony. This was a concrete step toward sovereignty and independence. There were worrisome signs, however. Hart thought that "the return of the Conservatives to office in Britain in 1949" led to a "shift in public policy" that "seemed to be encouraging insular fears among the smaller units" or islands, encouraging them to fear that their interests would be submerged in a Jamaica-dominated federation. As it turned out, these fears materialized. "Unfortunately," concluded Hart later, "the delegates from the larger territories, Jamaica and Trinidad and Tobago, and the observers from British Guiana displayed no interest in combating the British government's approach. At that time, Mr. Bustamante's party was in office in Jamaica. The Trinidad delegation was dominated by Albert Gomes. Dr. Eric Williams and the People's National Movement were not yet on the scene. The People's Progressive Party" of the Jagans "had only recently been formed, and had not yet won office in BG." Thus, it was much easier for the Bustamante-Gomes tendency to prevail.[27]

Hart sought vainly to challenge their rising hegemony. Speaking to thousands in Port-of-Spain at an open-air meeting in Woodford Square Park, he insisted that "all this nonsense in Trinidad and Jamaica about small island[s]" was "very ridiculous." It was "up to Jamaica and Trinidad particularly to lead the way in view of the fact that they possessed the largest politically-minded population."[28]

As ever, tiny St. Kitts-Nevis was a useful barometer for the larger region. Paul Southwell of Basseterre, speaking of his homeland in the spring of 1948 as it was convulsed with disputes over wages for sugar workers, remarked that "this island is one of the most fertile" of all these "islands. It is not without reason that an old historian was caused to say, in those days when the nations were struggling for possession of these islands, that whoever owned this island could control the others."[29]

If this broad assertion was true, then certainly there were granite-like obstacles blocking the path of progress in St. Kitts. For one, as stagnant pools proliferated and animals of various sorts sashayed among humans, Basseterre found itself "under siege by mosquitoes," with some being of a "species much larger in size than the kind usually seen within the limits of the town."[30] When heavy rains arrived—which was not infrequently—the "mosquito nuisance" arrived alongside. "The dreaded malaria and typhoid fever" were "largely attributed to the mosquito." And both were duly expected.[31] There were the usual catastrophes looming besides, for example, "complaints for scarcity of bread" were "getting more numerous."[32] The year 1948 also witnessed a "shortage of meat," a condition brought on by an "outbreak of anthrax in the island of Nevis."[33]

With such a deteriorating environment, this was not a propitious moment to go on strike, but this is precisely what sugar workers did in 1948. Week piled upon week, hunger spiked upward, yet the workers hung on. Hart was pleased that by the spring the strike was "nine weeks old" and the "strike front" remained "solid," but he then began to fret that the "Sugar Producers [Association] may have decided to sacrifice the 1948 crop in order to break the union through starvation of the local population."[34]

This was "so far the most event[ful] period in the life of the Union," concluded the island's labor body during this pivotal year of 1948. "In no single span of twelve months have there been so many important happenings in the industrial sphere." In response, the "government increased the strength of the police force" while the unionists in turn escalated, for when "certain vessels arrive[ed] . . . during the strike [and] tried to unload cargo in Nevis . . . a deputation of union officers who were promptly dispatched to the island, secured support of Nevisians and prevented the landing of the goods."[35] This militancy demonstrated that the union was not without weapons, something that the strike itself should have confirmed since it "tied up both the sugar industry and the wharves" with 6,000 workers participating, which was about a third of the island's population, meaning it reached into virtually every household. When "an attempt was made to transfer a ship" from St. Kitts to Antigua, the union in the latter refused after hearing from its comrades in the former. This was a direct result of the labor unity brought by the CLC.[36]

This growing assertiveness was worrying the colonizers, who had good reason to believe this was a contagion that could spread. Perhaps not coincidentally, Grantley Adams was dispatched to Basseterre. Addressing a sizeable rally in Warner Park, his remarks were "conciliatory." He "told the workers that their demands must not be unreasonable."[37] It was not long before the Cold War intervened, with the major daily newspaper warning ominously that the strikers were "posing as a Trade and Labour Union," but "in reality" they were part of a "communistic political institution" that desired "nationalization of the sugar industry."[38] Their worst fears seemed to be realized when, concomitant with the strike, there was an eruption of the fearsome cane fires, a potent weapon of the not so weak. "The burning of what remains of the standing sugar cane continues," the major island daily said with disgust. "The very foundations of the island's economic stability has been sapped" as the "crypto-Communists who shouted throughout the island, that sugar cane should be eradicated and that from its ashes a new and better St. Kitts would rise have been taken even more literally than they could have hoped for."[39] This indicated that despite the harsh conditions, the strike was being resolved to the workers' advantage.

As it turned out, this strike was "probably the most decisive event in the struggle for dominance in St. Kitts," and it placed the island inevitably on the path to independence. But this came at a steep price. "Some died from extended periods without food," while "about 51,294 tons of cane were burned. Waterfront workers refused to work on certain merchant-planter related imports and exports." Ripples from this conflict flowed throughout the region, suggesting once again the crucial importance of otherwise tiny St. Kitts-Nevis. As a result of the strike, workers "received sympathy from waterfront workers on other Caribbean islands. They refused to work on ships taking certain cargo to St. Kitts," and they received a demonstration of their own strength. These workers received "thousands of dollars from friends and relatives in countries far and near. These included the U.S.A., Cuba," and others. All told, "about 10,000 workers were involved in the strike."[40]

Bradshaw, born in 1916, emerged from this struggle with an enhanced status. He was president of the island's major union in an unbroken skein from 1944 to 1978, though leading this thirteen-week strike was probably the highlight of his reign. In 1967 he became the first premier of St. Kitts-Nevis-Anguilla, and his leadership of the strike was a major reason why.[41] However, the disintegration of the CLC left removed from the scene a militant progressive pole that could pressure Bradshaw; absent that pressure, he was facing pressure overwhelmingly from domestic elites and local reactionaries to which he had to respond. Thus, by the end of his tenure, the early promise of Bradshaw's dominance had dimmed considerably. He was intolerant of opposition, which came mostly from his left, and retaliated harshly when Anguilla sought to separate in 1969. He developed a passion for the finer things in life, including antiquities and Mercedes-Benz automobiles. This abandonment of progressivism reached something of an apogee after he embarked on a long-term romantic liaison with Eugenia Charles, the long-time leader of Dominica, who was considered to be the Margaret Thatcher of the region.[42] His opponents deemed him despotic, "and sometimes he appeared to take the law into his own hands." But there was no one to challenge the plantation owners until trade unionism as symbolized by Bradshaw arrived, and the currency he earned then paid dividends at the polls thereafter. He was a class militant, but like some of the other comrades in the region, he relied heavily on the Bible and his charismatic leadership, which proved to be inadequate to the stiff challenge presented by the Cold War. When he passed away in 1978 as a result of cancer of the spine, that seemed to be a metaphor for his deteriorating dearth of backbone in confronting the challenge presented by the Cold War.[43]

Yet the force of the 1948 strike was a shock to the system of colonialism from which it never recovered. Desperately seeking scapegoats, the island's elite quickly settled on the colonial governor of the Leeward Islands, Earl Baldwin. There was "deep distress" among unionists when he was "relieved of his duties" in early 1949. On the other hand, the sugar producers were "rejoicing at his recall to London" and were "openly boasting" that he was "recalled because he . . . dared to take a stand against them in issues affecting labour."[44] Robert Bradshaw of St. Kitts and Vere Bird of Antigua were as upset as the sugar barons were overjoyed. The latter denied that they opposed Baldwin "because of his friendliness to the natives," though their protestations were not widely accepted among most islanders.[45]

What could not be denied was that Baldwin, the " 'naughty boy' son" of a "Tory pipe smoking" former premier, was not wildly popular among regional elites. Progressives argued that the barons "preferred the snobbish official cocktail parties that he refused to give." They also thought he was not sufficiently hostile to regional "schemes for the starting of new industries to relieve poverty and stop emigration," as they desired "only big dividends from investments already made."[46] "I put my foot wrong with the white population," said Baldwin, "when I told them that they were doing nothing for the natives." As he saw it, "the whites were very different from the English Tories. They were 'absolutely reactionary,' " though his assertion that "these people in the islands are children and they want a father" inferentially exposed the general backwardness among resident Europeans that swept within its ambit even those who thought they were on the side of the angels.[47]

But what befell Baldwin was a small scene from a larger drama. Though London may have desired accommodation with the masses of islanders, continuing a lengthy historical pattern, the domestic colonizers were not as prone to compromising. For example, Grantley Adams was clearly one of the best things that ever happened to the European elite in the region—but they did not necessarily see it that way. In a "personal and confidential" missive from Barbados, Sir Thomas Lloyd noted that "our friend Grantley Adams is in many ways the wisest politician in the area and a man of principle. Like Manley, he has an able wife," though she was "probably less embittered than Mrs. Manley. One has, however, to remember one or two things," he reminded. "The Barbadian Bourbons hold him in deadly enmity and would move heaven and earth through their allies in other Colonies to make things hot for them. They have never forgotten 1937 and do not see that as a moderate leader he is worth his weight in gold."[48] Ultimately what happened was that Washington's growing influence allowed London to assert its sway over the regional "Bourbons," which prevented the kind of political polarization that could have strengthened the CLC left to the benefit of sovereignty, independence, and labor rights.

For their part, the CLC protested Baldwin's recall. "It is difficult for Social-
ists in the Caribbean," it said, "to understand the mental processes of a Socialist
Secretary of State for the Colonies who recalls a Socialist Governor to gratify the
idiosyncrasies of reactionaries in the Leeward Islands."[49] So London bent to the
whims of local reactionaries who were incensed about what they saw as a growing red threat in the region.

But this bending did not break labor militancy. For in addition to St. Kitts
"there were simultaneous strikes in sugar factories owned by Henckell-Du Buis-
son in Antigua [and] Trinidad." Regional poverty rather than red conspiracy was
driving unrest in the Caribbean, though some chose to focus on Hart's "close
personal ties with Bradshaw" and his visit to St. Kitts during the 1948 strike.[50]

Though Paul Southwell had argued that control of St. Kitts was essential to
hegemony in the region, the U.S. military installation in neighboring Antigua
and the centuries-long jousting for control of this island among various European contenders suggested that it was, in fact, this island which was critical.
Located about 500 miles southeast of Puerto Rico and covering an area of 108
square miles, it was frequently subject to drought. There was a decided African
presence in Antigua in that "English fitted to the Twi sentence structure"—a
grouping of West Africa—characterized the patois, which was "interspersed
with a few Twi words." Just as Bradshaw's prominence in trade unionism led to
his dominance of politics in St. Kitts, something similar occurred in Antigua with
Vere Cornwall Bird, a former Salvation Army worker. There was "no room for
the development of a peasant class . . . instead Antiguan conditions favored the
development of a rural proletariat." Early on, almost "ninety percent of the
labor force had been unionized" and "since 1945 the Labour Party had captured
every elected seat in the local legislature." This organization formed in 1945 as
the "Political Committee of the Antigua Trades and Labour Union which itself
was organized in January 1939" during the midst of the regional labor upsurge.
At this juncture, union members routinely addressed one another as comrade,
carried red flags at demonstrations, and were vigorous in their denunciation of
"sugar barons" and colonialists. By 1962 the union "boasted a membership of
approximately 17,000 out of a total labor force of about 19,000." As in St. Kitts,
class struggles took on a racial dimension "because the labor force was Negro
and the employers [largely] Caucasian," so "political and economic struggles in
Antigua had not only been battles between 'haves' and 'have-nots' but also racial
contests between black and white.[51]

As in St. Kitts, the CLC left took a particular interest in Antigua. Like
Bradshaw, Bird was in constant communication with Hart. Born in 1908 and
quite tall, Bird's height was accentuated "by the ever-present felt hat with black
band," which may have been "his only affectation." Quite the ladies' man—Bird
was also quite sensitive about his age—he eventually fathered a number of sons
who followed him into politics. He became renowned as a Salvation Army
preacher, and the skill as an orator for which he became notorious was honed

during this time. His stentorian tones boomed "over the largest crowds as clear as a drum."[52] Blessed with a commanding presence, a fluent tongue, a surfeit of common sense, a "natural talent for flattery, persuasion and compromise," not to mention an "ability to never let the right hand know what the left was doing, and the talent to lie convincingly when necessary," Bird was a man to be reckoned with.[53] For a while, he represented the core of a working-class progressivism that characterized the CLC.

When a ship arrived in Antigua after the St. Kitts strike where she "could not get loaded," Bird reciprocated; "we refused to load for three days," he told Hart.[54] The existence of the CLC facilitated the relatively new development of interisland labor coordination, which in turn strengthened the efforts of each island. In late 1947, just before the sugar strike in St. Kitts erupted, Bradshaw "spent the . . . weekend up here," as Bird informed Hart. "We had a good time together," he said. They "had a torchlight demonstration"—and indicating the powerful example of the larger islands—it "ended as at Jamaica with a monster meeting." They "had some labour trouble" in Antigua, and such manifestations were seen as conducive to such disputes being settled favorably.[55] Beaming, Bird later informed Hart about a strike in Antigua where they had a contractor "under the vise. We have closed him down and have his jobs picketed. He is a very haughty fellow so it seems he prefers to go under than bow."[56]

Haughtiness was an apt term to describe the European elite that dominated the commanding heights of the Antiguan economy. They had their "own club to which men of colour, however eminent in their professions, are not admitted," and there was a "separate white people's tennis club" and residential segregation.[57]

At this juncture, like Bradshaw, Bird was viewed as part of the CLC left, cooperating closely with Hart. "Thank you very much for the assistance you gave me during our crop disputes," Bird told Hart in the spring of 1948. "As a result of your assistance our people were greatly strengthened and instead of reduction in wages every class of workers received increases. We are sending you copies of our agreements." A prime proponent of regional cooperation, Bird declared, "I feel that one of the greatest services that could be rendered to the organization is for copies of all agreements to be made available. A favorable agreement from one colony could be very helpful during negotiations in other colonies." As he then saw it, "American corporations by dealing with us separately are getting away with a lot," whereas he wanted to "put up a united front to the Americans. Now that the Mexican government is holding out for better terms, if this is done I am sure that it will result in much benefits for our workers."[58]

Unsurprisingly, Bird stood with Hart after Grantley Adams's controversial 1948 speech at the United Nations. But it was unclear to what extent the CLC left could assist his struggling island as it confronted the brutal aftermath of a three-year drought that was "real awful . . . work on the plantations and the people could not work in the plots. It meant relief work on a large scale." It also meant the union was "hit for income." A "Mr. Bell" of Jamaica "spent a month" in Antigua, at Hart's behest, "in search of underground streams" but in the long run it was unclear if the CLC left wielded enough heft to keep leaders like Bird—who were not the most advanced ideologically in any case—in lockstep with progressive forces.[59]

For a while it seemed that Bird and Hart would remain on course as a dynamic duo of the CLC left. The Antiguans cooperated with Hart's attempt to aid the Canadian Seamen's Union and the protest against the removal of Earl Baldwin. Bird requested a "copy of the PNP Statement of Policy" from "Comrade Hart" in order to guide his party's deliberations.[60] But it was not just the Antiguan responding to the Jamaican's entreaties. "I hope you are taking note of what is happening in Africa," Bird told Hart in the spring of 1949. "I hope you will speak out against any Central African Federation that is not built on the vast majority of the population who are Africans," he said with rising ire. "I know stooges will not want us to put our necks out too much—but the job is there to be done."[61]

Antigua endured a sugar strike in 1948 at the same time St. Kitts did, but that tumultuous event hardly prepared the island for the uproar brought by labor unrest in 1951. The CLC left and Hart in particular rose to the challenge and performed admirably, but it was evident even then that regional labor was being forced to compromise. A powerful colonial metropole in London ultimately was compelled to back an emerging and even more potent Washington, and in the face of such formidable forces, unions could hardly resist.

Recalling these enervating days years later, Bird noted that after the strike was launched, labor "did not work again for the whole of 1951." Starved into submission, workers "'went into pastures and they would cut bush and boil the bush to make a soup: they went to the seaside, to the beach and they would pick up some cockles and that is how they lived in the whole year 1951. First three months and then nine months more. It lasted the whole year of 1951.' That broke Moody-Stuart and the planters,'" but almost killed labor. "Those were the days,'" recalled Bird, then in the twilight of his life, "when you couldn't get lawyers to represent the workers and our officers. . . . I couldn't get a lawyer to represent me."[62] Suffering a convenient lapse of memory and eliding the ineradicable fact that actually the lawyer, Richard Hart, had rushed to his side, Bird exposed the point that the existence of the CLC left no longer fit the narrative he chose to construct.

It was harder to forget, however, the turbulence that arrived when within ten days of each other, two powerful hurricanes destroyed between them "over 1300 houses around the island, seriously damaged another 2300 and rendered more than 6500 people homeless." It was then that a battered employer class organized a federation, which was seen by Bird and his union as no less than a "declaration of war against Antiguan workers," designed to provide a knockout blow against an even more battered working class. Soon there were "wildcat strikes among stevedores, peasant farmers, factory workers, cane-cutters and cotton-pickers," followed in the spring of 1951 by a "general strike," which—congruent with Bird's ties to the CLC left—had as a major demand the marking of May Day as a holiday. The importance of this strike is symbolized by the fact that the "first elections under full adult suffrage took place on 20 December 1951," as labor unrest was winding down.[63]

This strike, along with a companion action in Grenada, were among the convulsions generated by the CLC left that led directly to suffrage, elections, and, ultimately, sovereignty and independence. However, the price to be paid for this advance was distancing labor from the force which had helped to drive it to the precipice of victory, the CLC left, which also guaranteed that the kind of solidarity and sacrifice required for effective federation was jeopardized.

This was hard to envision clearly when after being summoned by Bird, Richard Hart arrived in Antigua in the summer of 1951. "I spent half of July and three days of August in Antigua," Hart informed his PNP comrades, "where I was busy doing a job for our sister organization, the Antigua Trades and Labour Union. The union there is the equivalent of our PNP and TUC combined." It was "very strong, thoroughly democratic, and ably and intelligently led." The colonial governor "appealed for a truce to end a general strike in the sugar industry and at the waterfront," and Hart's job was to "marshal the evidence and present the union's case." The commission "actually started its sessions in June when suddenly on the morning of the fourth day the Governor brought in troops by air from Jamaica. It seems the big boys had whispered in his ear that the revolution was at hand." There was a "smouldering resentment of a class which has been unable to reconcile itself to the loss of privilege and power which its ancestors enjoyed in the days of slavery." Symbolizing the importance of the kind of regional labor cooperation represented by the CLC, the Trinidad and Tobago union leader, Quintin O'Connor, accompanied Hart.[64]

They found a tense atmosphere in Antigua. British troops had "never been landed in Antigua before," according to Hart, and the union "viewed [their arrival] as an attempt to create an atmosphere of fear among the people."[65] But if the CLC left was intimidated, they did not reveal it at the time. At the inquiry into this hubbub, Hart bluntly asked Bird, "On this nationalization question, your views are socialist?"

"Yes," Bird replied simply.

Pouncing, Hart's opposite number asked Bird, "Do you know of any difference between what you believe in and what they practice in the USSR?"

At this point Bird could not be made to flinch in the face of Soviet-baiting. "I don't know," he said. "I have never gone into it. . . . I am a democratic socialist." Bird was asked, "When I was here last, I observed there were quite a few people wearing red ties; was there any significance attached to it?" Again, Bird did not retreat. "It is a socialist significance," he admitted. "[W]e are among those who are trying to find a new order for the people."[66]

That this inquiry and strike was resolved to the union's advantage was due in no small part to the role of the CLC, but its resolution also revealed fault lines that had arisen at the time of Adams's 1948 UN speech. F. J. Carasco, president of the Seamen and Waterfront Workers Union of St. Lucia, had sought to cooperate with his Antiguan counterparts at the CLC's behest. He had been informed that "Antigua cargo should not be handled at this port" of Castries "in order to support the Antigua workers" in their waterfront strike. Yet this cargo was "unloaded at Barbados and further that Mr. [Grantley] Adams had rushed to Antigua in an effort to settle the dispute." Carasco was perplexed. "[W]e were bitterly criticized," he informed Bird, "for our refusal to handle this cargo here especially as we did not know the reasons for the strike and you can imagine our feelings now that we are told of its being discharged in Barbados."[67] As long as Bridgetown was allowed to play the role of conservative outlier and gadfly, the survival of the kind of class solidarity that the CLC left demanded would be in jeopardy.

This incident also unveiled the larger point that the colonizers were coming to recognize that anticolonial concessions had to be made lest the situation get out of hand and the kind of socialist solidarity which Bird so eloquently symbolized would expand and, thereby, jeopardize the emerging Cold War consensus Washington was seeking to forge. It was precisely at this point that Bird began his slow but steady retreat from his previous commitments. This is revealed in his contact with Richard Hart. As early as February 1950, Hart was "very disappointed" with "Comrade Bird," since he had not "heard from you concerning the indebtedness," the fifty pounds owed for legal services rendered to the Antiguan union. "You promised to attend to the matter immediately," Hart reminded him vainly, referring to a debt that stretched back to 1947.[68] "As you know I make no charge for my services," Hart reminded Bird again in the midst of the 1951 strike, "but the funds of the CLC have long since been a minus quality and I have to carry all the expenses out of my pocket, which I cannot afford to do. I do not have a penny to pay airmail passage or send cables" and the "'Bulletin' has long since ceased publication but I am still paying the printer's installment on their bill out of my pocket. I even have to pay personally for the stationeries on which to write letters."[69]

But Bird was hardly listening. Though independence did not arrive until 1981, he was well on his way to a form of public corruption, nepotism, and cronyism that made his ruling Antigua Labour Party a regional scandal and a laughingstock. Antigua and neighboring Barbuda were run like a family estate.[70] In full-scale flight from his previously articulated socialism, Bird converted his nation into a "jet-age Cannes of the Caribbean," that by 1971 had "33 hotels, drawing 65,000 tourists annually, a casino, [and] an oil refinery." Yet the opposition charged that the "hotels and refinery hired Antiguans for menial work but reserved the best jobs for whites."[71] All traces of the CLC left's ideology had been erased as Antigua became the epitome of a neocolony. Neighboring Grenada also had embarked on a militant path in 1951 but—unlike Antigua—it sought to carry forward this legacy after independence.

CHAPTER 10

Small Islands/Huge Impact

E VERYONE IS SO SCARED because of recent events in Grenada," observed Sir Thomas Lloyd nervously, speaking from the conservative citadel that was Barbados in the spring of 1951.[1] He was referring to massive strikes that convulsed the spice island that was Grenada as he wrote. The acting governor argued that what was at play was not a wage dispute but a "communistic uprising organized" by Eric Gairy,[2] a former primary school teacher who, like many of his compatriots, had been forced to seek work beyond the confines of the island before returning in 1949.[3]

This invocation of Cold War rhetoric and the highlighting of Gairy—an analogue of Bustamante and Butler in that he was a charismatic labor leader who came into sharp conflict with those to his left—were symbolic of the era. The colonizers came to realize that Gairy, like Bustamante, could be accommodated in a way that the CLC left could not, though this recognition was not immediately obvious to them.

Gairy's moment in the spotlight came in 1951 when Grenada was rocked by an exceedingly turbulent strike. But even as this historic event was developing and strict solidarity with the strikers was the order of the day, E. A. Mitchell, president of the Grenada Workers Union, assailed Gairy's "distortions, fantastic promises and lies and above all" his appeal to "an illiterate mass swayed by the promise of a millennium." Gairy, he thought, was an "unscrupulous popinjay on a mission of foul abuse and constant threats." His "party and union" were "primarily, if not solely a business proposition and a swindle," not unlike what Bustamante had engineered in his eponymous union. This was no real union, said Mitchell, since "all but two or three" of the "executive" were "small shop proprietors," thus, his "former first lieutenant" was a "business man of some reputed cunning." Conveniently, "no records" were "kept by this party and union," there were "no books and no money" and a surplus of "class jealousy and hatred." As he saw it, "democracy is running amuck in Grenada," as "decent citizens of the community are publicly named, denounced and defamed and then pinpointed for 'action' against them."[4]

Eventually Gairy became known as a flamboyant dresser and the biggest spender on the island. Like Bradshaw and Bird, he ultimately developed an appreciation for the more refined things of life and was routinely chauffeured in a well-appointed automobile, which enhanced his growing reputation, like Bird of Antigua, as the island's leading ladies' man. Like Bird, he was a remarkable orator, perhaps more so in that he was as "good as most Hollywood actors" in his ability to imitate any accent, had a repertoire of jokes, and kept a pet monkey and calypso singers on hand to entertain crowds. He was also an intense spiritualist who believed in reincarnation. It was said that the movie "Island in the Sun" was filmed on Grenada intentionally because the "closest real-life approximation in the West Indies to Harry Belafonte's role as a mystical island leader of underprivileged Negroes" was the man known as "Uncle."[5] Gairy came to develop a predilection for white suits, white shirts, and white shoes, which he owned in profusion, along with an array of cuff links and spectacles. He also came to possess an assortment of walking sticks, cosmetics, and sashes of all descriptions.[6]

Like Bird in Antigua, Gairy eventually claimed "virtual ownership" of his nation and became increasingly involved in "private finance," with control of a "bar, a restaurant and hair dressing salon . . . a guest house," and countless investments.[7] When he traveled to the United Nations in the spring of 1979 to urge the investigation of UFOs, a group of left-wingers led by attorney Maurice Bishop dislodged him from power and embarked on a progressive course— aided by the then aging Richard Hart—before their experiment was squashed by an October 1983 invasion by the U.S. military.[8]

Though the entire population of Grenada barely crept above five figures, the U.S. authorities had long kept a close eye on Grenada, perhaps anticipating the unrest of 1951 and the invasion of 1983. Certainly Grenada, which produced a number of men that became influential in neighboring oil-rich Trinidad, seemed to have a penchant for developing a corps of crowd-pleasing leaders. For example, there was Charles Grant, born in 1895, who became a leader of the Grenada Labour Party. In 1919, while in Trinidad, he was involved with a dock strike and "saw the effectiveness of group action." It is unclear if this is where one of his more distinctive traits emerged: he had "only teeth in his upper denture and [was] missing many teeth in his lower jaw." He conferred with Captain Cipriani in 1929 in Grenada, which inspired his organizing. He administered a small store on the island, which provided support for his spouse and eight children. He went on to play a role in the CLC.[9]

More than Grant, it was T. A. Marryshow who was the Grenadian who played the most prominent role in the CLC and regionally. When the U.S. diplomat Charles Whitaker met him in July 1946 he could not tell if the wily Grenadian was slightly deaf since "when spoken to" he "asks the person addressing him to repeat what has been said"—or, alternatively, whether this was "done to gain time and prestige." He was "very well read" and was "particularly interested in matters of political interest and others which pertain to the West Indies," suggesting that unlike many leaders in the region he had a true pan-Caribbean vision. He was a student of political theory who was able to weave these notions into his frequent public declamations. He was an "excellent public speaker," had a "dramatic delivery and knows how to hold an audience." A modest man of small pretensions, he lived in a "medium sized rather run down house in the poorer residential section of St. George's." Like many of his fellow Grenadians, the "color question" was a "delicate one with him." Unlike some in the region, he felt that "West Indians should go to Tuskegee Institute and Howard University" for higher education, reflective of his pan-African bent. "The matter of family should be avoided," Whitaker advised, "as Mr. Marryshow is not married, although he has five or six children with different women, who bear his name." An imposing man, more than six feet tall, he had an "excellent bearing," which perhaps sheds light on why his opponents intimated that he was "partially supported by his various girl friends." No friend of Washington, "he takes the part of Great Britain in any argument in any discussion concerning Great Britain and the United States," though he maintained a "considerable correspondence with leaders of Negro groups in Harlem." Yet because of his modest means, it was felt that a "job with a title or a few dollars in the right place might make a difference to the tone of his speeches."[10] Marryshow was also a prolific writer and journalist and a singer who held delegates at the 1921 Pan-African Congress "spellbound by oratory after which he sang Negro spirituals."[11]

Washington's close attention to events in tiny Grenada seemed to be justified when tumult erupted there. A "general strike" lasted for four weeks in 1951 "and involved all agricultural and road workers throughout Grenada. It resulted in the loss of 124,226 man days," as "damage was done to 80 estates," much of it due to "widespread arson." Gairy "emerged victorious" and "became the arbiter of political fortunes of Grenada at least for the next thirty years." All this occurred amid repeated accusations that the leaders were unreconstructed Bolsheviks, though the causes of the unrest were much closer to home. For example, as the strike was erupting, 87 percent of the homes in Grenada were of "wood, wattle and mud."[12] "An average working labourer" in Grenada, said one unnamed CLC militant, "must work six hours of a nine hour day in order to purchase a bar of soap, for a week's use; or alternatively a domestic servant must do half a day's work to buy one pound of sugar."[13] Grenada had long been a poor backwater of the region. In 1940, E. Marese Donovan, president of the Grenada Trades Union, confided to the colonial governor, Sir Henry Bradshaw Popham, that the "spirit of the people is dejected and broken." "Only today," he continued with regret, "a most pitiable sight was to be seen outside the walls of the labour office, no less than one thousand people went there in search of

employment, with the net result that only twenty individuals were chosen
(or two gangs). The rest walked away crestfallen. This condition cannot continue," he warned ominously, "something must be done."[14]

Yet, as these momentous events were unfolding in 1951, the CLC—which
had come into being precisely to assist and coordinate solidarity on such
occasions—was missing in action, wounded by the divisiveness unleashed by
Grantley Adams's 1948 UN speech and the concomitant precipitous drop in its
budget. "It is quite a while since we heard from the Congress," Richard Hart
was told in late 1951 by Clarence Ferguson, secretary general of the Grenada
Workers Union. By then water mains had been "cut," a "Roman Catholic school
in St. Andrew's Parish with an average attendance of one hundred and eight was
destroyed," while "clashes developed between strikers and others willing to
work." London had dispatched "naval launches," which "took police parties up
the coast to deal with disturbance," and "all scavenging services in St. George's"
were "suspended," which gave this capital a unique aroma. As Ferguson viewed
the uproar, he placed it in wider context. "Grenada in this century always has
shown a strongly progressive mood in comparison with her bigger neighbours
of the British Caribbean. Much of the self-government spirit of the West Indies
found early birth in St. George's. Grenada's politicians were the only West Indians who successfully withstood attempts to have introduced the sedition laws
common to this region." He was concerned about the rise of the "mob leader,"
that is, those "under the sway of the unusual Mr. Gairy," but he was more concerned about the unrest. "[T]housands of all categories of unskilled workers
and several artisans are idle," while "small steel helmeted, truncheoned police
parties" hovered. At one juncture, "police opened fire" as "5 buildings burned"
and "private cars" were "stopped and passengers accosted at several points."[15]

The situation was "very grave," said the journal of the Barbados Labour
Party and the Barbados Workers Union, suggesting the reach of these events.
Police had been dispatched from other islands, including St. Lucia, which was
bound to inflame passions among the strikers against their fellow islanders. A
state of emergency was declared and Gairy and his chief lieutenants were
arrested and detained for a while. More buildings were going up in flames, and
"hooliganism prevailed." As in St. Kitts, arson erupted as "crops on many estates"
were "destroyed wantonly" with an "estimated damage and loss to the island"
of a "quarter million dollars." Roads were blocked and trenches dug, as if an
actual war had exploded, as opposed to a metaphorical one. "Racial prejudice"
was "evident," this journal concluded, "for two English ladies were dragged
from a car, the car destroyed and robbed."[16]

"Conditions in Grenada continue to be tense," one journalist declared in
late February 1951. "[F]our more buildings have been burnt down, including
a Government agricultural station and an estate overseer's quarters . . . transportation remains difficult as the strikers are constantly erecting roadblocks."
Physical attacks on the authorities were escalating. "Colonel Keith Stewart,

acting aide-de-camp and private secretary to the Governor of this island, received a severe head wound when his vehicle was ambushed and stoned in a suburban area."[17]

George Padmore was moved to "voice . . . indignations" at developments in Grenada, notably the "shooting down of unarmed Negro workers . . . by police dispatched to that island by the Governor of Trinidad." He was incensed. "[N]ot without reason," he said, "Trinidadians are being accused by their Caribbean compatriots in this country as 'colonial mercenaries and gendarmes of vested interests.'" Padmore thought this did not augur well for pan-Caribbean unity and found it worrisome that increasingly, for example, Antiguan police would be sent to repress St. Kitts—and vice versa.[18]

These riotous and disorderly events were unfolding as a restless crowd gathered in Market Square in St. George's, Grenada, at approximately 8 P.M. on 8 March 1951. They had come to listen to Eric Gairy, their leader, as he explained the latest stage in an extended confrontation with the colonizers. The pious Gairy began with a recitation of the "Lord's Prayer," a deft touch illustrating his religious piety before a crowd of mostly believers. Then, turning to his left, he addressed "comrades and friends" as he castigated the colonial government for their "mistake in declaring a state of emergency and ordering the detention of the two leaders of the Grenada Manual and Mental Workers Union" after their job action. Speaking of himself as "Uncle Gairy," he then appealed to those assembled on the basis of color, a basis for their own degradation. "In Grenada," he said, "we talk about white people and they are not white people. As soon as a little nigger has a less pigmentation . . . they say they are white people," but this would never happen with "Uncle Gairy," who would never cross the color line and desert the mostly darker masses. Then the agile orator turned to class, noting that "in some places in this our lovely little island our people are so poor that father, mother and children sleep almost together. Children under the bed, children under the table—and when I say bed, I mean straw. As a result of these deplorable conditions, the children must have sin; some of the little boys are so mannish . . . our little boys and girls become men and women before their times."

Then, after touching upon the universal parental concern about the fate of their children, the nimble speaker turned to negative suggestion, a specialty of his, imploring the crowd repeatedly not to resort to violence to attain their noble aims. At once this immunized him against the charge that he was responsible for any violence that might erupt, while planting the seed of disruption firmly in the minds of the assembled. Subsequently, his oratory took a turn that clashes with modern sensibilities when he announced boldly that "Uncle Gairy has more girl friends than any man in Grenada. I am talking about old women and so on. Even the children in the cradle try to say 'Uncle Gairy' as their first words. A chap told me that even the cock is crowing 'Uncle Gairy.'" Presumably, his boasting about his powers of attraction suggested a seductiveness and ramrod-firm political virility that could allow him to stand strong against the authorities.[19]

By then Gairy was "head of two largest organizations," the union and the party, and thus was akin to Bird in Antigua and Bradshaw in St. Kitts—the latter a not infrequent visitor to Grenada. At one meeting, Bradshaw referred to the "1935–1937 riots and disturbances in the West Indies," where, he said, the "shooting started first in my island," suggesting that if the authorities were not careful, something of similar regional consequence could recur in 1951. He expressed confidence in the leadership of Grenada. "[T]he island is fortunate in having the youngest labour leader in the West Indies"—Gairy—and the "eldest statesman," Marryshow. "[W]hat one lacks in experience the other one has in a storehouse. I wish I had somebody like Marryshow with whom I could join forces," he said wistfully.[20]

Bradshaw had become a kind of Johnny Appleseed of protest in the region, moving from island to island planting kernels of dissent. Before his arrival in Grenada, he had visited Bermuda, though his message was similar and thus illuminative of developments on the spice island. He "urged" the "coloured Bermudians . . . to wake up and free themselves from political disabilities." His voice rising with insistence as he addressed hundreds, Bradshaw proclaimed, "those of us who are coloured and are conscious of that fact, feel that the fate of the coloured man in one part of the world is the concern of all of us." Yes, he continued, "we are endeavouring in the West Indies to develop a spirit of oneness first as West Indians and then as coloured people," which explained his journeys to St. Kitts's neighbors. "Toward that end," he added, "before I left home I instructed the Local Chamber of Commerce that after December 31st [1950], black hands of black stevedores would not be touching cargo originating from South Africa," as "merchants [were] bringing in wines & cheap salt fish from there." Bradshaw was resolute, stressing, "we are endeavouring to break down these silly barriers of class and endeavouring to sweep away the superficial restriction which are placed upon us by the barriers of water." The authorities might deem this subversion, but Bradshaw saw commonalities between St. Kitts, Bermuda, and Grenada that mandated united action. "[O]ur people are still barefooted," he lamented, and "still without electricity" and "unable to eat three squares a day."[21]

So moved, Bradshaw saluted his fellow workers in Grenada during his sojourn there. He was outraged by the double standards he espied, observing that the "imperialist powers"—meaning London and Washington—were too keen to deploy aggressive police to confront strikers as opposed to their actions at home. "They were too quick to shoot out here," he declared, "whereas in their own countries police used tear gas and batons in almost every case."[22]

Certainly the turmoil then gripping Grenada was suggestive of a militancy that made surrounding islands seem tame by comparison. By late February 1951, George Green, the acting governor of the Windward Islands, was declaring that

"civil power is unable to control the situation and . . . military assistance is necessary." This was an understandable response to the flexing of muscles by the
union. Registered in 1941, by September 1950 the Grenada Labour Party had a
membership of 593. Following the regional model, it was tied to the union federation, which by then had 2,500 members. "Membership has undoubtedly
increased" as a result of the early 1951 unrest, said the secretary of state for the
colonies, to the point where Gairy claimed a membership of 9,000.[23]

Hence, the island was in the grips of a massive wave of class-based turbulence with decided racial overtones. Harold Shannon, the estate manager of
Tuilleries in the parish of St. Andrew's, was feeling the heat. He had noticed that
some of Gairy's comrades "were passing in their official car carrying a red flag.
My mother and brother were in the field nearby," he said, "and heard shouts of
'Stalin for King' emanating from the car." Later, after Gairy had been detained,
he noticed "one of the union cars, flying the usual flag, passed shouting to the
crowd as they went by 'tonight we burn St. George's.' I was told personally," he
noted chillingly, "in the presence of a reliable witness, by one Joseph Baptiste
[a Butlerite recently returned from Trinidad] that he would kill me and my kind
and that furthermore there could be no peace until all Priests were killed and
the churches burned."[24]

Reaction of the besieged planters "ranged from the stoical to the hysterical.
They had obviously been through a most trying time," said the acting governor,
"and were still sitting up nights guarding house and outbuildings. One said he
was even afraid to go around his plantation." When these jumpy and anxious
planters met in March 1951, they remained skittish. "[F]eelings ran extremely
high and several of those present appeared on the verge of hysterical boasting,
incidentally that they went about armed and were, in fact, armed at meeting with
me," remarked the acting governor, perhaps betraying his own unease. As this
official saw it, Gairy was an "egoist ambitious for power and with an inferiority
complex apparently because of his dark colour." Thus, Gairy "had aroused class
jealousy and hatred and even racial feelings which," he claimed astonishingly,
"were almost non-existent in Grenada where there is no colour discrimination."
Hence, he added, "depending on your informant, Gairy is a Heaven-sent leader
or a representative of the forces of Evil. He has, I am reliably informed, been
hailed as a reincarnation of Fedon"—the legendary antislavery rebel—"and has
been heard to say that Grenada needs a blood purge." As he saw it, "intimidation" was rife, and the authorities were "sitting on an active volcano" and had
been "for some time."[25]

As some saw it, the protesters were not only race-baiters but race-baiting
Bolsheviks. Noble Smith concluded that "one of the leading members of the
Legislative Council" of Grenada, who represented the "employer's point of
view,"[26] said that "Grenada was suffering from Communist inspired disturbances
from which it would take a long time to recover." The depressed Smith "regarded
the future so pessimistically that he proposed to sell out his own estates." Gairy,

he thought, "had now succeeded by methods of intimidation in overcoming all opposition" to the point where "many people were paying [him] large sums of protection money."[27]

London found "some justification of the planters" and their fears. "[A]lthough there is as yet nothing to indicate that recent events were Communist-inspired," it was announced in the spring of 1951 that "it is now known that some Communist literature was sent to Mr. Gairy's followers and Mr. Barltrop has reported that the cry was sometimes raised 'Stalin for King.'"[28] This was much too mild for Noble Smith. "A fire has been kindled in the West Indies," he announced portentously, "which will require the united efforts of all right think-ing persons to extinguish." As he viewed things, "our social and economic struc-ture is in danger of becoming a pitiable ruin in the horrible conflagration which a diabolical brain"—Gairy—"has conceived."[29]

Nerves were rubbed so raw that Walter Knight, a retired civil servant resid-ing on the island, was spooked by an artistic depiction. "I am attaching a paint-ing," he said to an unnamed interlocutor, "entitled 'It's the Time.' It is marked at the bottom left hand corner, 'F. Benjamin' . . . the drawing depicts a crowned black man enthroned and holding in one hand a sword or scepter, and in the other, a lantern and a flag emblazoned with a delineation of Africa encircling a star, and on his person are numerous medals and the replica of the map with the star decorating the region over his heart. Each of this enthroned person's feet is placed on the head of a white man; on the right side of the painting is a black man hurling a white man from the height of the platform on which the ruler is sitting, and on the left side another black man has a foot placed on the left side of a white man's head." As Knight saw it, this was more than the flowering of one imagination. "It may be worthy of mention," he observed, "that there have been cases of three white persons who have been beaten or injured, among them two women, without apparent or reasonable cause. In St. Andrew's, I am informed that there is usage of an expression 'the liquidation of the white minded persons in the community.'" That was not all. "[O]f myself personally," he added forebodingly, "I have been warned by various persons that my residence, among several others, is listed to be destroyed by fire and that I am liable to be kid-napped for ransom. Presumably I am classified among 'white minded' persons."[30] Meanwhile strikers by the hundreds were routinely rallying, ostentatiously dis-playing their brawn to the authorities. On one memorable occasion, "shouts went up when Mr. Gairy arrived on the scene, dressed in a mixture of sports and evening wear, bare-headed and carrying his walking stick."[31]

Perhaps Knight should have consoled himself with the notion that at least the protesters were not simply targeting "white" persons. What this did suggest was that the old colonial model based on mass deprivation of suffrage and dem-ocratic rights was increasingly becoming untenable, particularly since the Cold War discourse was targeting real and imagined deprivation of rights in Eastern Europe—but how could these charges be credibly maintained when the mighty

British Empire was languishing under a suffocating tyranny? Ultimately this dilemma was resolved with concrete steps toward suffrage, then independence and sovereignty.

Bradshaw of St. Kitts had expressed solidarity with his laboring counterparts in Grenada and, apparently, had imbibed inspiring lessons from what had transpired there. For it was in July 1951 that a whopping 20,000 demonstrators—a figure larger than the entire population of St. Kitts, perhaps signifying the participation of other islanders—demonstrated in Basseterre. "[M]oving like a gigantic army," they marched resolutely through the streets, demanding "adult suffrage." At one point, "the lines of swift moving buses shuttling to and from the capital appeared as though it would never end." Marchers were aligned four abreast, "two males to the right and two females to the left," both united in favor of simple democratic rights.[32] As the noon hour passed, "the sun shone down with a brilliance which [provides] the enchantment that causes poets to break into song. The Mother Colony of the West Indies was to open yet another illustrious page of history" with this stirring remonstration. Later in this pivotal year of 1951, the uproarious events of St. Kitts and Grenada reached fruition when elections—finally—were held in Grenada, St. Lucia, Barbados, and St. Vincent.[33] Again, Grenada was a bellwether, with labor's candidates receiving 12,238 valid votes or about 64 percent of the total, which placed Gairy on a glide path to become the first prime minister of an independent Grenada in 1974.[34]

But, in a sense, Grenada had been preceded by developments in even tinier St. Vincent, for months before this momentous election, Ebenezer Joshua and George Charles had returned to their homeland from Trinidad to found a veritable army of liberation, a "political grouping which won all eight seats to the Legislature in the first elections held under universal adult suffrage. The basis for the electoral mobilization" was the union movement. Joshua led a strike during this same year, 1950, then from "1951 to 1956 he called yearly strikes in the sugar belt" as he confronted "the planters, the colonialists" and "sell-out union leaders."[35] Just as Bustamante, Bradshaw, Butler, and Gairy had spent considerable time abroad, Joshua returned to St. Vincent from Trinidad, "where he had gained practical experience in the practical school of Butler's mass politics."

The strategically sited St. Vincent—about a hundred miles west of Barbados, sixty-eight miles north by northeast of Grenada and twenty-one miles south of St. Lucia—was also similar to its neighbors in another key respect: it was a "'skinocracy'—power being related to colour—the black masses remaining at the bottom of the social ladder." These masses were also concentrated in agricultural labor, which was "tainted with the sense of social inferiority." Thus, labor unrest was not only an outlet for the release of class tension, it also provided an "opening for the aggression that had built up" among the laboring class that could be unleashed "against the white planters." These tendencies were apparent in the "two important organizations" that "were born out of the 1935 struggle: . . . the St. Vincent Workingmen's Association and the St. Vincent Labour Party."

The compounding of this class and race tension contributed to particularly bitter confrontations between labor and capital, as the colonial regime "used every possible lever—rival labour leaders, the police, the legal system, the planters, the planters' press and the colonial bureaucracy." But also like its neighbors, St. Vincent developed a kind of political unionism that was not as prevalent elsewhere in the hemisphere.[36]

A S SUGGESTED BY THE PERIPATETIC BRADSHAW, traveling from St. Kitts to Bermuda to Grenada as he made a rousing call for solidarity with the victims of apartheid South Africa, the leaders and organizations of the British West Indies were hardly opposed to the notion of addressing issues that stretched beyond the confines of their homeland. This concern also stretched to their towering neighbor, the United States, which also happened to have a sizeable population of African descent and was increasingly being grouped with apartheid South Africa as a target of concern.

This was occurring as West Indians were obtaining suffrage rights and surging toward sovereignty, which added heft to their concern, particularly as Washington became sensitive to Moscow's charge that the United States was engaged in cynical hypocrisy in crusading for human rights globally while tolerating profound abuses at home. Sovereignty would also mean these Caribbean territories wielding votes and influence within the UN—as Grantley Adams had demonstrated—the Organization of American States, and other hemispheric and global bodies.

Washington had work to do, for many of the leaders of the British West Indies were not keen on the United States, not only because some were keener still on London, which had clashed over the decades with the Colossus of the North, but also because of their own unfortunate experiences in the land of Jim Crow.

This lengthy list included Wynter Crawford of Barbados, Grantley Adams's leading foil. Because of the proliferation of migrant laborers from his homeland in the United States, he frequently found himself in postwar Florida. At Camp Murphy, he found "conditions there" to be "deplorable" and "great dissatisfaction existed among the Barbadians." No doubt this, along with the rampant Jim Crow he experienced, colored his opinion of the United States. Thus, he traveled to Tennessee "and was the guest there of Attorney Z. A. Looby," who was to play a leading role in knocking down the walls of Jim Crow, and he "went to Chicago where he visited Attorney B. C. Cyrus," who was active in the CLC. Crawford, to his pleasant surprise, was "amazed" at the "active interest by the liberal forces in America in West Indian affairs"—an interest that was reciprocated to the benefit of both.[37] Later Cyrus set a goal of $25,000 to raise for the CLC, "urged financial and moral support of the efforts and programme" of the group, and sought to involve NAACP leaders in the initiative.[38]

However, when Crawford traveled from New York City southward in the early postwar era, things did not proceed smoothly. "I knew about the racial prejudice in the South," he recalled later, "but I really was not aware of its extent." While in South Carolina, he noted with irritation, "I followed the white passengers to the restaurant. A chap inside the restaurant came flying out and grabbed me by the waist and pushed me outside. So I put my other bag down to knock him down and he held my two hands and said, 'Man, you want to get killed? If you make another step in there, that man has a gun to put a shot in you. You cannot come in here.'"

The dumbfounded Crawford replied, "What nonsense are you talking!" But he accepted his fate, though he added bitterly that "it was terrible in those days down in the South."

Things did not improve appreciably when he arrived in Florida. He could not even get a meal at the airport, so this influential leader picked up the phone and called Juan Trippe of Pan-American Airways and informed him that Barbados would not let his airline land there unless he could get something to eat. Ultimately, this airline had to yield.[39]

But Crawford was not alone in his disenchantment with Washington. Albert Gomes, a CLC founder from Trinidad, had become one of the more conservative leaders of the region. Yet looking back in life, he too was furious about his experiences in the United States. "As a student in 1929," he recalled, "I had discovered to my horror that West Indians who were white or sufficiently clear-skinned, often claimed to be 'South Americans,' thereby invoking, in the defence against racial discrimination, a geographical complexion that West Indians as a rule preferred to forget." That experience left an indelible impression upon him. "[I]t was, however, some twenty-six years later, in 1955, that the awful reality of racial segregation hit me," he recalled with asperity. Again, "the United States provided the experience," and, like Crawford, it was Florida—this time Gainesville—that provided the startling racial rudeness.[40]

Surely it would not be simple for Washington to secure allies in its backyard as long as nationals from there were being treated so atrociously. Definitely this dilemma provided further impetus for Washington to put its racial house in order.

Washington had its own complaints—but they only revealed that its Jim Crow was fomenting regional repercussions that could be upsetting. In the early postwar era, Washington's man in Kingston, Jamaica, was gravely concerned about the "trial of a United States Navy sailor who was nearly cut in two a few months ago by a Negro sailor from an American merchant vessel in port at the same time. [Norman] Manley was retained by an American Negro group to defend the assailant, who was acquitted by the jury." The assailant, James Hunter, a Negro whose roots were in British Honduras, may have faced a decidedly different fate if he had committed such a crime in the United States. His acquittal might encourage others to wreak racial revenge upon Euro-Americans once they arrived in the Caribbean, which could not be good for either U.S. national security nor its developing competition with Moscow. The U.S. consul was dismayed by Manley's "reticence" in response to this controversy, as the tactful Jamaican leader had "refrained from anything more than slight general conversation" about this charged matter. The diplomat was left to wonder if Manley felt the "knifing" was "done by a disembodied spirit." If so, this was an ill omen for the future.[41]

Yet Jamaicans had reason to be wrathful about U.S. policies. In 1948, an agency in New Orleans was seeking from the Kingston consulate "confidential information regarding the racial background of Lester Ebanks" which was "vital . . . in planning for a young baby born in an out-of-wedlock relationship between a white American girl and Mr. Ebanks." They wanted to know whether he was "of Latin origin or whether he is part Negroid. The point is, of course, in great importance in planning either for adoption or foster home care of the baby." The elusive Ebanks was a "seaman" born in "Spanish Honduras," though his "last known address" was in the Bahamas.[42] The answer to this inquiry would determine the fate of this child with, of course, any hint of "Negroid" background dooming the infant to a third-class existence. The gumshoes in the region ascertained that his "parents are both of very dark complexion and there is no doubt that Lester Ebanks is part Negroid," which sealed the fate of his progeny.[43]

Such roiling events were complicating U.S.-Jamaica relations tremendously. Visiting Jamaica for three long weeks in late 1948, the African American congressman from Harlem, Adam Clayton Powell, Jr., expressed concern that U.S. efforts to discourage tourism to Jamaica was spurred more by racism than interest in the well-being of visitors. This was of a piece, thought Powell, with overall Jim Crow policies that had been exported southward. "[R]acial segregation was virtually unknown on Jamaican soil," he claimed, "until it was introduced in the American base area during the war." As for the U.S. consul, Nelson Park, he had a different issue he was pursuing. "[T]here has been no indication," he told his superiors in Washington with relief in a "confidential" message, "that American tourists might have been particularly offended by the relative lack of a 'color line' in Jamaica."[44]

Jamaicans were hardly prepared for the raw crudity of the color line they encountered in the United States. After a Jamaican pastor refused to sit in the back of a bus in Chattanooga, he was beaten. Kingston's *Daily Gleaner* editorialized against the "brutal manifestations of race prejudice which occur in the Southern States of the United States" and denounced the fact that "some American citizens conduct themselves in a manner typical of the thugs of the Gestapo."[45]

On the other hand, it was not as if the Empire was devoid of this kind of bias. Robert Bradshaw of St. Kitts was mortified in 1949 when he went to dine in a London restaurant. Why? "I sat at a table," he said, "that was set for two. I was told by a waiter that the table was occupied." He was told to wait, for "not less than fifteen minutes." But waiters refused to seat him. It was "useless to argue," so he complained to Whitehall that he had been "discriminated against and treated in this fashion because of my colour."[46] This was a "complete disregard for my position," he argued. It "offended my dignity and greatly offended my status."[47]

Jamaican Americans particularly and West Indians in the United States generally were in a unique position to mobilize their compatriots—north and south—against Jim Crow, which could only redound to the detriment of white supremacy in the hemisphere. The CLC long had survived on the basis of largesse from these North American expatriates. These migrants thought they were subjected to all manner of discrimination in their new homeland and believed that a strong and independent British West Indies or at least a vibrant CLC would be useful in their own struggles against bias.

This was the backdrop for a campaign spearheaded by the United Caribbean American Council and the American West Indian Council, assisted by friends of the CLC such as Richard B. Moore of Barbadian heritage, against immigration restrictions. "The Caribbean peoples," it was proclaimed in July 1949, "are the only peoples in the Western Hemisphere who would be subjected to the destructive and discriminatory restriction upon immigration which this provision would impose. All of the other peoples of this American hemisphere are permitted to enter the United States without any such restrictions." Was this just another form of Jim Crow since the British West Indies was, perhaps, the darkest region in the hemisphere? This "restrictive provision," it was declared, "is aimed also at discouraging and deterring people of African descent from entering the United States. This reflects adversely upon the fifteen millions Americans of African descent who constitute the largest single minority in this nation of minorities." It was "all the more hurtful in view of the specific measures recently adopted by the Congress of the United States to increase and facilitate the entry of Europeans into this country." Whatever the case, these groups argued passionately that "any further limitation of immigration is a matter of life and death. For many years immigration has afforded the means of relieving conditions of poverty, malnutrition and high mortality in the Caribbean colonies." Suggestive of the importance, "the legislatures of Barbados and Trinidad have passed resolutions urging the removal of this provision," though it was striking that "the objectionable provision was not in the bill as originally drafted but was introduced at the special [insistence] of the State Department." This bureaucracy, "acting through its Visa Division, already maintains a policy strictly interpreted by United States consuls in the Caribbean area, whereby persons of African descent, seeking permanent entry into the United States, are required to present extraordinary and unreasonable guarantees of support from their relatives or friends in the United States sponsoring their applications for admission."[48] A St. Kitts journal termed it a "cruel and inhuman blow struck against West Indian Negro Americans when the House passed HR 199 limiting the immigration of West Indians to 100 persons per year." It was speculated that this was related to the fact that "West Indians are to be found among the most

militant and staunch trade unionists" in the United States, pointing to Ferdinand Smith of Jamaica, leader of the National Maritime Union.[49]

Richard B. Moore, who was the moving force behind this initiative on West
Indian migration, also happened to be a key U.S. contact for the CLC. In the
spring of 1950 he decided to "forward a substantial sum to aid the organization"
and was "hopeful that we will be able to raise at least $5000 within the next two
months." This was good news for Richard Hart, who had been holding the
organization together almost wholly based on his Kingston law practice. It was
unclear, however, if Moore could continue this level of support since the United
States was gearing up for a war in Korea that would exact a mighty toll on those
of his ideological persuasion. Already, Moore conceded, "we have been compelled to turn almost wholly to the Caribbean and fraternal organizations, to the
progressive labor organizations and to the plain people"—and the resources of
all three were stretched thin. Thus, "the business and professional group which
furnished the main financial support in 1947 has not responded now," he admitted with regret. Sensing which way the wind was blowing, they had turned in a
different direction. "Failure to give such support has emanated chiefly from
[Alexander] Austin who has objected strenuously to any association with progressive persons and groups," as he had bowed to the growing distaste of the
NAACP for those thought to be within the orbit of communists.[50] The CLC and
its closely linked goals of labor rights, sovereignty, and federation were buoyed
principally because of its ability to raise funds in the United States. When that
ability began to wither, so did the CLC—and its goals.

Moore thought he knew why and the reason was imbedded in Adams's 1948
UN peroration. "A small group of professionals here who feted Adams following his surrender to imperialism at the United Nations Assembly in Paris have
withheld support from our Council because of my stand in upholding the interests of the African and other colonial peoples," he informed Hart in the spring
of 1950. Now they were seeking to "associate [Norman] Manley with Adams in
these ventures," and the prospects for this were far from dim.[51] Desperately
seeking to stanch the bleeding, Moore reached out to Ferdinand Smith, the
Jamaican trade union leader, but he had just been chased from his leadership
post in the National Maritime Union as a direct result of Cold War pressures
and was hardly in a position to respond favorably. Still, Moore, in "raising the
$10,000 fund" for the CLC that was "urgently needed," contacted Smith; "only
yesterday we received letters of resignation from two members of the business
and professional group which had furnished the main financial support in 1947,"
he acknowledged.[52]

At this moment Moore had fallen under the intense gaze of the FBI, and
they were not pleased with what they saw. He was "very much engaged in the
New West Indian Movement," said one bureau report in 1947, "and claims he
is now interested in the Vital Question of West Indian Independence." With evident disgust, it was added that the "Communist clique runs thru out all of the

West Indian groups" and "more and more [they were] following the international tactics of Russia as a means of developing their concept of the Colonial Question thru-out the West Indies."[53] Described as five feet eight inches tall with "light skin" and "kinky hair graying slightly," Moore was pointedly deemed a "member of the Communist Party since 1928."[54] He was not hirsute, keeping his "hair cut short," and he was "clean shaven" with "small eyes." An intellectual of some note, Moore was able to disseminate knowledge by running a popular bookstore—which an agent of the FBI chose to visit in late 1949. The "Frederick Douglass Bookshop" was "located at 141 West 125th" Street, in Harlem's heart. Special note was taken of the "magazine article in the window which was titled 'Second Caribbean Labour Congress.'"[55]

Writing from Antigua, Helen McDonald invited the Colonial Office in 1949 to "investigate (in cooperation with U.S. Anti-American activities if possible) the activities of the 'United Caribbean American Council,'" particularly Moore. His group "poses as an innocent and benevolent society," she sniffed, but "among those responsible for its formation was Du Bois, the well-known Negro Communist writer and agitator." This "Council" had "affiliations and agents in every W.I. island," she charged, and its "Communist sympathies" were evident "by the persistent use of the Communist term 'comrade.'"[56] The council found it difficult to withstand the pressure unleashed on it.

Because of the influence of figures like Moore, West Indian leaders were frequent visitors in Harlem. Thus, in the spring of 1949, Robert Bradshaw "addressed a mass meeting at the Renaissance Casino" and "attended a banquet in his honour on the same night."[57] And while Bradshaw was sojourning in Harlem, Harlem's influential intellectual, George Schuyler, was visiting St. Kitts.[58] Similarly, Grenada's T. A. Marryshow, a confidante of W.E.B. Du Bois, was likewise a frequent visitor to Harlem. On one memorable visit in early 1950, he was introduced by attorney Hope Stevens—a West Indian migrant who was a frequent liaison for delegations from the region—who presented him with a hefty $10,000 check for the CLC. Giving thanks, he pointedly informed African Americans that "your destiny is one with your brothers in the Caribbean and a free nation there will redound to your prestige and advancement."[59]

A British agent said of this visit that Marryshow "was given a big hand recently by the Grenada Mutual Association at the Elks Auditorium, 160 West 129th Street, New York City." He was said to be "without doubt the No. 1 statesman of the West Indies" and "is for Dominion status that a Federated West Indies may take her rightful place in the British Commonwealth." Marryshow said "that the West Indies were [the] oldest colonies of the British Empire and there was a hidden history that should be read as regards their basic, building value to the pyramid of Britain's greatness. Negro slavery did it." Yet the British West Indies was "first to serve—last to deserve!" said the Grenadian leader. He contrasted Ceylon, now with Dominion status, with the British West Indies and asked pointedly, "[I]s it because the West Indies are preponderantly

peopled by blacks?" The wily Marryshow answered "yes and no" when asked if
it was "the aim of the [CLC] or of the West Indies for that matter, to be rid of
British rule." Concluded the CLC leader, "it all depends on what you mean. . . .
Colonial Office rule or the severing of all ties with Britain?"[60]

These were brave words, and Marryshow, whose own Grenada was a model
of militancy, had good reason for his optimism. But at that precise moment,
the CLC, on whose shoulders so much hope rested, was in the process of
unraveling—a process which reached its apogee in British Guiana.

CHAPTER 11

Militant British Guiana

T HE DISLODGING OF THE CHEDDI JAGAN REGIME in 1953 in
British Guiana was the formal acknowledgment of the bitter reality that
the CLC left-labor model would not be allowed to attain hegemony in
the region. This paved the way for the rise of an alternative—authoritarian labor
politicians such as Bradshaw in St. Kitts, Gairy in Grenada, and Bird in Antigua,
whose lust for power and limited vision also ensured that federation would not
reach fruition. This momentous and portentous development that indelibly
marked the early Cold War in the region also guaranteed that hundreds of thousands would not be able to escape the snares of poverty.

Moreover, a portion of British Guiana's substantial population of South Asian
origin was reluctant to enter a federation where it would be outnumbered
by Africans. This was particularly so after the events of 1953 made clear that
London—and Washington—would not allow the left to come to power in
Georgetown, an ascension that could have comforted this population with the
reassurance that whatever the racial and ethnic configurations, democracy would
reign. Instead, the events of 1953 encouraged a split in Jagan's party on "racial"
lines. Hence, Forbes Burnham, once a stalwart of the CLC in London during
his stellar years as a student there, formed a heavily African party that was not
hostile to baiting this population of South Asian origin, which convinced them
that federation was not the proper route to pursue.

Still, in many ways, British Guiana was the key nation of the region. It was
the largest territorial unit in the region that flew the Union Jack and was an
absorber of "surplus" population from islands such as Barbados, and it was also
a nation that was geopolitically strategic as the only English-speaking nation in
South America and a neighbor of the continent's giant, Brazil.

Though London was the ostensible ruler, as Jagan saw it, "the main cause . . . for the suspension of our Constitution was pressure from the government of the United States." On the other hand, he thought London saw a kind of federation as a way to contain the radicalism that characterized British Guiana. But both London and Washington "deliberately fomented racial disturbances in order to prevent the transfer of full powers" to Jagan's party. As this unfolded, Burnham struck "alliances with conservative and racist elements," which "resulted in the class struggle appearing as Indians against Africans and Mixed and not as Coloured (Indians, Africans, Mixed) against white, as it had in the 1920s."[1]

Befitting colonial territories, it was London and Washington who were to shape the destinies of the British West Indies—and British Guiana—and that meant a circumscribing of labor rights, sovereignty, and federation.

GUYANA IS TWICE THE SIZE OF CUBA and even dwarfs the combined size of all the formerly British Caribbean islands, even including the Bahamas and British Honduras. It has the "highest annual temperatures in the world."

It also has some of the highest and most developed radical traditions on the planet. The radicalism of British Guiana inhered in a South Asian population that felt doubly victimized; their ancestral homeland was colonized by London, then they were transported thousands of miles to toil for a pittance on plantations in South America in the wake of the abolition of African slavery. When Singapore fell, it was reported "that the East Indians held anti-British celebrations on several estates. Both Negroes and East Indians who frequently fail to stand up in local motion-picture theaters when the King's picture is thrown on the screen," said the U.S. State Department wondrously, "were reported as hissing and jeering the royal picture during the playing of 'God Save the King.'" The influx of U.S. troops during the war was not calming either, as "persons of color have shown that they are very sensitive to any color discrimination practiced by American white troops in the colony."[2] Actually, the distaste may have extended beyond the troops. When seeking to visit the United States, one Guianese was informed that "when you apply do not give your race as anything but West Indian regardless of what. You may be urged to use Negro but by all means refrain from it." But what about use of your "birth certificate"? Well, "if it has the word 'black' or 'Negro' or coloured on it . . . apply at once . . . to have it changed," since "the word 'mixed' will be sufficient."[3]

On the other hand, there was so much disgust with the abject failings of British colonialism that even the advent of U.S. imperialism was viewed by some as something of a breather. When one U.S. operative spoke in the summer of 1944 with Jeranarine Singh, president of the East Indian Association, about the "possible acquisition by the United States of the British Caribbean possessions and British Guiana, a topic which has been widely discussed," he "stated that a majority would favor such a move." Still, he added significantly that "many Negroes resent the Americans because generally [they] do not accept the society of Negroes." Thus "in the early days of the American base, considerable antagonism was created by a tough group of American soldiers." Besides, "the Indians [were] very disappointed that the United States has not supported India's fight for freedom."[4]

Its sizeable population of South Asian origin notwithstanding, British Guiana was in many ways typical of the region. "The housing situation was really bad," said Jagan. A 1952 survey "found that the average number of persons per room was 2.6 and in some instances as many as 12 people lived in a single tenement room," while "illiteracy in 1931 was 74.04 percent among Indians and 64 percent among Amerindians." Children "were employed from the age of twelve upwards except in Buxton and Georgetown where they could be employed only from the age of fourteen. There was no social insurance scheme providing for sickness, unemployment or retirement benefits."[5] "Mules [were] being treated better than workers," during the colonial era, recalled Jagan. "Managers and overseers could have sex relations with non-white women," while "rum-drinking, gambling, dancing horse and mule-racing, and cricket were the principal pastimes of the whites." Of course, "none other than a white man could hold the post of overseers. This was a cause of frustration and bitterness" on the part of the nation's majority. Jagan himself "didn't wear shoes" until the "age of twelve"—and that too was not unique.

Jagan grew to become a handsome and charismatic leader. Of medium height with tawny brown skin, he had a shock of wavy hair, increasingly white as time passed, that complemented his dazzling smile. Somehow he was able to make his way out of British Guiana and wound up as a student at Howard University in Washington, D.C., and Northwestern University in Illinois, where he trained as a dentist—and encountered a virulent form of Jim Crow that transformed his existence and informed his political trajectory. "The first thing I became very conscious of was the question of colour," he recalled later; "somehow, in the U.S. a non-white is always reminded of the colour of his skin." As he saw it, "on the question of colour, the British [were] more subtle than the Americans," who approached the matter of race with a sledgehammer and a hangman's noose. "Many Indians," he observed, "because of their darker colour, were not treated as I was. In the 'south' of segregated cinemas, theatres and schools, they had no choice but to travel in the rear of streetcars and buses or in special railway carriages." Yet, with all that, it was the darkest of all, those of African origin, who were treated worst. In Chicago, "they allowed me to have a room and later took in some of my Hawaiian-Japanese fellow students. But this was as far as they were prepared to go; they drew the line when it came to Blacks, who were treated as beyond the pale, as outcasts."[6] Experiencing Jim Crow opened Jagan's eyes to the "plight of the American Blacks," which in turn increased his sympathy for his fellow Afro-Guyanese.[7]

As with so many others who sojourned in North America, Jagan's experience was transformative. Months after the fall of Singapore in 1942, when the fate of the war remained unclear, he affirmed that "the South and its prejudices will have to go. Now is the time for the Negro population to demand equality and to see that the Atlantic Charter materialize and bear fruit at home." He felt that the iron had to be struck soon since, he acknowledged, "after the war I'm afraid, when there is no more international quarrel and common enemy, all nations will drift back to internal social and economic conflicts." London was "fighting to liberate Poles, Czechs, Greeks and what not but liberation of countries under its own clutches is out of the question." Yes, "war is murderous and bloody, but at the same time it initiates change—change which is necessary for us." Thankfully, "there has been an awakening—the status quo that was is gone."[8]

It was that thought that animated Jagan's return to his problem-filled homeland, where he quickly began to stir things up. In December 1945 he posited that if British Guiana "had been independent and further had it been federated to Dutch Guiana, we could easily have become [a] productive center for finished aluminum and its products," yet the colonial "government is merely content in allowing the Canadians to scratch the surface of the earth with a handful of Guianese labour." But a "free and independent Guiana," he insisted, "can easily cooperate and eventually federate with her Latin neighbors, especially Brazil"—an indication that British Guiana had other options beyond the British West Indies.[9] Wages for workers were "only one-third to one-quarter of comparative wages in bauxite and smelting operations in the United States and Canada," and Reynolds Metal "did not pay any income tax for nearly ten years after it began operations." This was no small matter since nations of the Caribbean basin—Jamaica, the Dominican Republic, Surinam and British Guiana— "which supplied about 86 percent of the bauxite requirements of the North American aluminum smelters received only about 4 percent of the net income of the highly integrated bauxite-aluminum industry."[10] Early in 1948, with hardly any debate, the colony provided Reynolds with "an Exclusive Permission over an area of approximately 206,000 acres of Crown Land."[11]

The beauty of the Cold War from Washington's viewpoint was that it was useful in convincing London to give ground in its closely held Empire in the interest of anticommunist unity. It was in 1948 that a Colonial Office bureaucrat acknowledged that "we know from our recent discussions with the American stockpiling team that they are very much interested in getting increased quantities of bauxite for the USA and that they are looking to the Caribbean territories for such supplies." So London had a "general policy of welcoming American investment in projects in the Colonial territories." Thus, when it was ascertained that "the Reynolds Company of the USA and also the Aluminum Company of Canada" had "rights over bauxite deposits" in the region, it was decided that "an American company would presumably be treated exactly the same as a British company in connection with the grant of licenses for working bauxite deposits."[12] This was no minor matter for Washington, which required ever larger amounts of bauxite to fuel a boom in aircraft construction necessary not only for military purposes on the Korean peninsula and elsewhere but for civilian purposes as well to knit together a sprawling nation that stretched from sea to shining sea.

Months later another colonial bureaucrat conceded, "I don't know very much about the Reynolds Company but the information we have does not suggest that they would be likely to be the ideal operator of an industry," while its Canadian rival "has proved itself to be a very good and progressive employer. . . . I need hardly add that of the two, I should much prefer to see the Canadian company established."[13]

But where were Guianese while the fate of their resources was being determined? Early on, Jagan established himself as a fierce critic of this colonial order and a defender of labor. "As long as we are forced to continue buying at high prices whether imported trained personnel or imported goods manufactured by labour working for 4 to 5 times local wages," he argued in August 1946, "and to sell at cheap prices local agricultural products, so long will the standard of living of the inhabitants of this country remain low." He was a keen critic of the maldistribution of wealth and power that was a hallmark of colonialism. Thus, he denounced the "high property qualification" that tended to "debar the majority of the working people from holding responsible positions in the Village, Municipal and Legislative Councils . . . how can we expect any decent housing scheme to be carried out by the State dominated by land-owners and property-owners and real estate businessmen when any such scheme will tend to lessen the demand for housing thereby introducing the risk or reduction in the value for land and property?"[14] As Jagan then saw it, the "Legislative Council at that time was simply a debating society," as "laws were made not [there] but over rum swizzles at the exclusive Georgetown Club which the sugar planters and senior government officials frequented." The colonial government was "sugar coated," that is, dominated by "Booker Brothers, McConnell and Company Ltd.," and the sugar barons who "not only accounted for nearly three-quarters of the total sugar production but also monopolized commerce and trade and held commanding positions in the timber industry and in shipping." This "sugar-coated government used every device to serve big business," said Jagan.[15]

Even the staid economist W. Arthur Lewis asserted during the colonial era that the "impression is now widespread among the people that the Governor and officials are little more than tools of the white oligarchy of planters, merchants and bankers."[16]

As in other colonies, an emerging conflict between London and Washington was the presence of the military bases leased by the latter.[17] London did not improve its image in British Guiana when "contractors and officials of the U.S. air and naval bases," recalled Jagan sourly, "were persuaded not to pay the higher rates of wages (US 40 cents an hour) laid down by the minimum wages section of the United States Fair Labour Standards Act."[18] But bases were not the only roiling issue. "Export of wild birds" to the United States to the point where their "extinction" was at issue was a matter of some contention.[19] The colonial authorities even imposed a strict "prohibition of left-hand drive motor cars" in the country—and no "exception" would be made in the case of a desperately needed medic who "recently imported" such a vehicle from the United States.[20] A repeated issue of debate was an attempt by various U.S. personnel to obtain an "exemption from customs duty,"[21] just as repeated concern was expressed about "imports from American bases" and "purchases" from there, which were seen as distorting the local economy.[22]

But with all the London-Washington conflict, they were generally able to submerge their differences, not least since British Guiana contained one of the most radical labor movements in the region. As early as the World War I era, there was "strike fever" in British Guiana; there were three major strikes in the late 1940s that had a profound significance on the development of trade unionism and on conditions of work, not to mention various militant job actions by mental hospital workers, cinema operators, postal workers, and bus operators.[23] A high point was reached in early 1947 when labor leader Hubert Critchlow, "accepting the recommendation of the . . . Caribbean Labour Congress . . . resolved to secure a 40 hr. week." He was particularly concerned since "already the machines have displaced quite a number of workers," especially in the fields. "[S]urplus labour here has no avenue for employment. The local military force is being disbanded and with service men returning here a serious employment and economic crisis is going to arise."[24] Hence, labor had no choice but to organize.

Despite this militancy, a crushing setback was inflicted on labor in British Guiana in 1947. "Our offices and meeting hall were completely destroyed by fire which razed one and a half blocks of our city and caused damage estimated at a little over 1/4 of a million dollars. All our furniture, office equipment and stock," moaned labor's leader, Hubert Critchlow, "all our invaluable records dating back from 1905, documents, agreements, a wide assortment of labour literature, and Conference Reports have been reduced to ashes. We lost everything."[25]

Their memory may have been punctured but not their will. It was the sugar workers, predominantly of South Asian origin, who set the pace for labor in the nation and, increasingly, in the region. Writing in 1948, Jagan noted that sugar was the "only major industry until the relatively recent advent of the timber and mining industries and is still making the greatest contributions to the national income. It is responsible for the employment of about 30,000 persons per year, a large percentage of the adult population of the colony. With recent times, however, and particularly during the last 15 years, there has been a growing discontent." A "paradox" in British Guiana, as Jagan saw it, was "that in such a large country of 83,000 square miles, there is a definite land hunger. This is due to the fact land is either not properly drained and irrigated or not easily accessible.

86% of the area land is forest, 10.5% savannah, and the remainder lies on the coastal belt." A good deal of the land was taken up by sugar plantations "owned by companies . . . and individuals . . . abroad. A large percentage of profits earned are presumably sent abroad," though in British Guiana the "sugar estates" were a "Government within a Government" that countenanced a "more or less rigid Jim Crow system." Meanwhile, "housing for sugar estate workers" was "perhaps the most depressing of all their privations. For the most part they are low-lying, dilapidated ranges built without much plan, usually on an uneven compound. These compounds are usually badly drained."[26]

The "history of BG," said Jagan, "can truly be said to be a history of sugar. The history abounds with many instances of looting, bloodshed and murder." Thus, it was "Bookers" that was the "symbol of British Imperialism" in the country; "they are and indeed always have been the real rulers of our country."[27] Unsurprisingly, a turning point in the history of the struggle for sovereignty and labor rights came in 1948 when "all the sugar estates on the East Coast of Demerara went on a strike, the longest in the history of British Guiana." Then "five striking workers at Plantation Enmore were killed by police bullets on June 16, 1948," which was followed by a mass march led by Jagan, where he pledged to heighten the struggle for justice in their honor.[28]

The ruling Executive Council blandly noted that "police opened fire on a crowd" and that "recent events might well have the effect of intensifying the strike, and that the method of healing the breach most likely to achieve success would be to secure additional representation of the strikers' grievances."[29] But the local elite was not without weapons of its own. "Recent shootings had aroused considerable feeling amongst East Indians," said the council, so it suggested bolstering the "Manpower Citizens' Association," viewed as a sellout configuration by Jagan.[30] These elites had to do something, as the situation was rapidly spinning out of control. There was "definite evidence of intimidation amongst the workers, many of whom were afraid to return to work," said the council. They chose to "seriously consider issuing eviction notices against the strikers who were tenants on their lands," but then, sobering quickly, "members expressed doubt as to the wisdom [of] this."[31]

At the center of these events was Jagan, the trained dentist who quickly adapted to the evolving situation. "In 1949 I became the President of the Sawmill Workers Union," while the "BG Labour Union, working particularly among waterfront workers, was later headed by L.F.S. [Forbes] Burnham,"[32] Jagan observed. Burnham met Jagan in 1949. "Jagan had heard about me, I think, through Richard Hart of Jamaica," said Burnham years later, while "Critchlow was my father's friend. I had met Critchlow again when he went to the World Federation of Trade Unions conference in '45." Burnham's father was the "schoolmaster of a place named Kitty. He was of Barbadian origin," as was Burnham's mother. They "found it hard to make ends meet," but that did not prevent them from raising a son who became a beefy man of "six-foot two . . . at 215 lbs." The intellectual Burnham observed, "I had read 'Das Kapital' about twice. Indeed, I had read 'Das Kapital' when I was about sixteen." Subsequently, he came under the influence of Padmore in London—"he was our political mentor. And so, to a lesser extent was C.L.R. James. We learned our politics almost at the feet of Padmore," he stressed.[33]

Therein one detects the fissures that eventually disrupted politics in British Guiana, for Jagan evolved toward becoming an orthodox communist, while Burnham evolved toward socialist eclecticism, then authoritarianism.

But that eventuality was hardly envisioned on 1 January 1950, when the People's Progressive Party (PPP) was formed with Jagan at the helm. The name—tellingly—was an amalgam of the left-leaning Progressive Party of the United States (endorsed by W.E.B. Du Bois) and the People's National Party of Jamaica, to which Richard Hart belonged. A precursor was the "Political Affairs Committee" (PAC) that was spearheaded by Jagan, his wife Janet—an émigré from the United States who was to become a national leader in her own right—Ashton Chase, and Jocelyn Hubbard.[34]

The CLC worked closely with the PAC. For example, Richard Hart traveled to British Guiana in the period immediately preceding the PPP's formation seeking to heal partisan rifts. He brought together the leaders of various unions, the PAC, the League of Coloured Peoples, the East Indian Association, and others. All agreed to sponsor jointly a public meeting in the Town Hall in Georgetown, to be addressed by Hart, on the desirability of self-government for British Guiana.[35] An editorial writer "promptly denounced him and his mission"—which, given the radicalism then animating British Guiana, "proved the best piece of publicity Hart could hope for. For the next three days his hotel was swamped with phone calls and visits from Guianese," and "thereafter standing room was hard to get whenever he spoke."[36] So it was easy for Hart in early 1950 to heartily endorse the application of the PPP to affiliate with the CLC.[37]

This was part of a gathering unity that culminated in the PPP's formation, a development in which the person of Forbes Burnham was essential. Earlier he had played a pivotal role in the CLC branch in London. The branch also worked closely with the Communist Party of Great Britain, which counseled avidly against intimate ties with the United States—or the "Jim Crow International," which it was said to head.[38] Instead, the CLC collected signatures on a massive petition demanding "independence to the British West Indies" with "dominion status,"[39] a development which London noticed.[40] By 1949 the CLC in London had seventy-seven members, "56 fully paid"—and Burnham was a well-respected vice president.[41]

Perhaps because of Burnham's prominent presence, the branch often took up issues of moment to British Guiana. Thus in early 1951 the branch demanded that London not pass "legislation whatsoever on a racial basis" that could divide African from South Asian. "Our discussion was led by four British Guianese, two of whom were of East Indian extraction and two Negro. Each one is a trade unionist or student of political economy."[42] When the branch held its "fourth annual general meeting" in mid-1951, it had reason to be pleased. "[T]here are many organizations in London which boast full-time staff and spacious premises that never do one quarter of the work that has been done" by the CLC "on a purely voluntary basis."[43] London thought it had reason to be displeased, as it began a "secret" effort to finger communists within the branch,[44] a process it thought justified when the branch announced portentously in August 1950 that "any attempt to involve any West Indian or colonial people directly or indirectly in the Korean struggle must be resisted."[45]

This was not only a testament to the growing Caribbean population in London but also an indication of Burnham's talents. This seemed to augur well for his return to British Guiana, for there, since the tumultuous 1948 strike, labor was on the march, and "lawlessness"[46]—or a disregard of colonial norms—and unemployment[47] were both growing. The months following the birth of the PPP—which was to become a communist party, the only one in the British West Indies for years—witnessed a proliferation of labor unrest. By the fall of 1950 there were "strikes of workers on three sugar estates on the East Coast, and one on the East Bank, Demerara," along with other strikes at other estates, not to mention "unrest among other workers, including unclassified employees of the Government."[48]

Now British Guiana was no prize, with homelessness, shoelessness, and poverty as essential part of the landscape. Yet, stunningly, in early 1951, after reviewing a "confidential dispatch" from the acting governor of Jamaica, the Executive Council "agreed that difficult as the local economic and social problems might be, it was evident that conditions in British Guiana were better than in some of the other Caribbean colonies."[49] In part this was due to the natural resources of British Guiana that transnational corporations desired. The U.S. firm "Willems Industries" successfully applied, for example, for "concessions to mine columbite-tantalite in the Mazaruin area."[50]

Meanwhile, the London authorities were worrying nervously that British Guiana was not only reviving the fortunes of the CLC left-labor model but was becoming a beachhead for the dreaded communist foe in a sensitively strategic region. In early 1951, the colonial secretary was informed that the authorities should "keep in mind the existence of the [CLC] (or whatever [the] name is) and the possibility that trouble may spread from one Colony to another through this agency."[51] Soon the authorities recognized all too well the tie between the PPP and the CLC. It was in 1951 that a British liaison "attended the press conference" in London "called by Dr. Cheddi Jagan" at the "Indian Students Bureau, Exeter Street." His party was said to have "4000 members out of a population of 400,000. It was allied with the Caribbean Labour Congress but had no affiliations with any other party or [group]."[52]

In the key British West Indies territories, the CLC had encountered difficulties of various sorts. For example, in Jamaica there was Bustamante; in

Trinidad, Butler; in Barbados, Adams. But in British Guiana, the largest territory with the most sophisticated radicals, Jagan and Burnham were united—at least in the early stages—which meant that British Guiana exerted outsized influence within the regional left.

This was not minor, as London always had to be concerned about regional contagions. Thus, during this same time, the colonial governor reflected on the "fairly strong liaison between the labour groups in the different colonies and they are quick to express sympathy with strikers elsewhere in the area and even to attempt to raise funds to assist them, as was the case during the recent troubles in Grenada." The mordant concern was that "unrest in one place is infectious and very often spreads to others."[53] The fear was that British Guiana would be the locomotive for this tendency. The "disturbances in Grenada and stoppage of work in [the] sugar industry in Antigua" were marked by "local labour leaders [who] have recently visited Trinidad." Besides, "other instances of cooperation among labour leaders in West Indies, e.g. proposed visits of Jagan and his wife and Bradshaw to Jamaica" were of similar concern.[54] When "Buzz" Butler sought to visit British Guiana in the midst of a rancorous strike, the governor declared, "I am strongly opposed to any such visit in view of his reputation in Trinidad."[55] Grenadians, who were thought to carry some sort of militant virus, were deported in droves from Trinidad in 1951.[56]

As the Cold War became ever hotter, it seemed that the concerns became ever more hysterical. It was in 1949 that British intelligence received an unsolicited message from an unnamed correspondent who confessed to having "been an active member of the [Communist Party] from the age of 16." He had come "to London from Liverpool specifically to see Lord Baldwin, Governor of the Leeward Islands, regarding the subtle Communist influence shortly to be introduced into the islands by a number of trouble-makers." As he saw it, "some of those holding influential positions" in his firm, "Holland, Hannen & Cubitts," were reds and they were to be sent to the British West Indies to "bully the blacks and treat them as dirt (their wives [are] also to adopt the same course with their servants) thus making the natives hate the British administration." He must have thought there might be doubt about his panic-stricken warning, as he added with bold emphasis: "I SWEAR TO YOU ON THE BIBLE AS IN A COURT OF LAW THAT EVER [sic] WORD HERE IS THE ABSOLUTE TRUTH."[57]

From subversive persons, attention shifted to subversive literature. Though "His Excellency's view" was that "statements contained in public speeches constituted a greater menace," the portability of the written word meant that it packed more punch. Yet books, pamphlets, and journals were hard to "ban" since "the majority of those distributed locally were printed in the United Kingdom and were not prohibited there. Issues such as local publication such as [the PPP's] 'Thunder' would continue to be scrutinized with a view to prosecution should they overstep the existing law." The particular target was "dissemination of Communist literature."[58]

Of course, "subversive" persons could distribute "subversive" literature—which was one reason the colonial authorities began seeking to restrict the travels of the Jagans and other PPP leaders. "Janet and I were banned by the Trinidad Government in February 1952," said Cheddi Jagan. "Janet was declared a prohibited immigrant by Grenada in 1952 and [the] St. Vincent government in 1948—she could stay 14 days only in the latter on condition she addressed no public meetings." There, "nine crates of books imported from England" by Jagan were "seized and burnt on the flimsy excuse that I had no import license previously—[including] 'Nigeria, Why We Fight for Freedom.'" The Jagans were both peripatetic and charismatic, which was reason enough—as the authorities saw it—to clip their wings.[59]

A civil libertarian impulse initially curbed the enthusiasm of the colonials for such draconian measures. "Is the Government aware of the fact that a member of his Council, Doctor Cheddi Jagan, suffered humiliation at the hands of the immigration authorities in St. Vincent," the British Guiana governor asked in early 1949.[60] The CLC, sensing instinctively that barriers to travel were antithetical to its mission—if not generated by it—raised stringent objections,[61] though Grantley Adams had his doubts. Richard Hart gently remonstrated his "Dear Comrade" about his stated objection, noting "as your draft now stands we would be putting Mrs. Jagan in a position which she might not wish. The draft appears to confirm that Mrs. Jagan is a Communist. In fact, there is [no] Communist Party in British Guiana . . . the present trend of events in the colonial world," added Hart presciently in 1949, "makes it clear to me that the day is not far distant when certain governments are going to begin prosecution of the more militant leaders of our various movements whom they will label 'Communist' in the hope that this accusation will be sufficient to give them a carte blanche to imprison or victimize without trial or to discriminate against such persons by specially oppressive laws."[62] Norman Manley, soon to become a harsh critic of the PPP and Jagan, then objected to the "insults offered" to the Jagans and the "disgraceful conduct of the government of . . . St. Vincent."[63] The CLC requested that its affiliates "join the protest against the movement of Comr[ade] Dr. Cheddi B. Jagan . . . and his wife Janet" while traveling to St. Vincent.[64] Though the thinking was that these travel bans were intended to ensnare those suspected of being reds—or well on their way to being so—such as the Jagans, in fact Eric Gairy was barred from St. Lucia in 1952, Hubert Critchlow was barred from Trinidad as early as 1946, just as T. A. Marryshow was ordered to leave Aruba in February 1947. Such travel prohibitions were a concrete response to the CLC's efforts to federate small islands. For example, if there had been barriers to traveling from Massachusetts to Virginia, it would have been difficult for a United States of America to develop.[65] But soon such concern was to evaporate as the larger concerns of the Cold War took precedence.

The problem for the region as a whole—and notably British Guiana—was that the developing Cold War, which accentuated relentlessly the threat said to be represented by communists, swept within its ambit Jagan and his PPP, who had become the hope of the CLC and the labor-left. This meant that the most progressive and organized force in the British West Indies was under assault as hundreds of thousands were yearning for sovereignty and labor rights. Inexorably, as the Cold War took hold, the idea of sovereignty and labor rights weakened.

Soon the barriers to communication installed by the Empire were having a devastating effect. "There seems to have been a suppression of news" about the "St. Lucia strike and a deliberate confusion of reports in order to paralyze any action on a Caribbean basis as developed around the Grenada General Strike"— so complained Trinidadian activist John La Rose in early 1952. "We must develop the procedure for the future," he advised. "At any time that a strike develops in any of our islands information and the widest possible details will be supplied" to the CLC.[66] But the problem he did not quite grasp was that it was hardly by chance that news of this strike was generally unavailable. From Trinidad came a staunch resolution—"we the workers gathered in Woodford Square protest against the presence of HMS Sparrow which intimidates the St. Lucian workers"[67]—but by this point the CLC, the force that was designed to mobilize labor in such instances, was on the defensive and hardly able to respond effectively.

Then there were the bureaucratic hurdles. The colonizers objected to Richard Hart's communicating directly with London on behalf of the CLC and wanted him to speak only on behalf of Jamaica—which he resisted adamantly.[68] London recognized that acquiescing to the CLC demand represented an implicit subversion of the imperial order.

In January 1950, George Padmore was struck by the coincidence that "in the very same hall" in London where a few years before labor had united globally in the World Federation of Trade Unions, another message was being transmitted. There Critchlow of British Guiana, Adams of Barbados, and Bradshaw of St. Kitts had gathered, but the kind of red-friendly attitude that characterized the WFTU confab was not in evidence; in fact, denunciation of communists was much in evidence. Still, those assembled could not avoid mentioning the deteriorating conditions back home. Just as the moderate U.S. Negroes repeatedly stated during the Cold War that the best way to reduce red influence was to erode Jim Crow, Grantley Adams—who according to Padmore was "nobody's stooge"—"told the British delegates that the best way to combat communism in the colonies was by granting the colonial peoples more democracy and helping them build a better standard of life." Echoing Padmore, Critchlow remarked that in his homeland, "the working week was still 64 hours and . . . labour got as little as one dollar and 52 cents local currency per day."[69] Easing labor exploitation, it was thought, would erode red influence, but since labor degradation was essential to the colonial model of Britain—a nation still reeling from the ravishing of world war and hardly keen about redistributing wealth and power—realistically Critchlow should not have expected concessions. Of course, a diminishing of London's sway and the rise of Washington made it more likely—perhaps—that Critchlow's musing would emerge from the realm of dreams.

"Divide and Conquer" helped to explain how relatively small Great Britain could control an Empire that included such behemoths as India, perhaps twenty times larger in population. It did not take long for the colonials to focus on the extant differences between the African and the Indian as a point of relevance. In a secret dispatch from the colonial authorities, close attention was paid to the "police force" in British Guiana, which was "not disaffected. The lower ranks are predominantly African which may be a factor of importance if, as seems possible, disturbances are caused by East Indians. It is not recommended," contrary to past practice and indicative of the salience of this rift, "that Police Forces should be brought in from other colonial territories . . . there is a small strategic reserve available in the United Kingdom for use anywhere in the world, but with military commitments in being or anticipated in Malaya, in East Africa, Central Africa and Egypt, the possibility of a unit from this reserve being released for use in the West Indies is so remote as not to merit entertainment."[70]

Strikingly, as the colonizers were perceiving strains in the Empire from multipronged challenges across the globe, the CLC and the labor-left generally began to extend their bonds of solidarity globally, particularly to Africa. As is evident, the barriers to communication strewn in their path, limiting the movement of individuals and the dissemination of literature, was designed to decisively block this maneuver. Still, in mid-1951, Richard Hart—on behalf of the CLC and at the behest of the unions of British Guiana—instructed his affiliates that "we should undertake the organization of co-ordinated protests and demonstrations on August 1st, 1951, throughout the Caribbean colonies in connection with the Mixed Race Franchise Bill recently promulgated in the Union of South Africa." Actually, "action already taken by our various affiliate organizations include: the imposition of bans in some territories by the Trade Unions concerned against the unloading of any cargoes of South African goods; the passage of resolutions in the legislatures of some territories calling for the prohibition of trade with South Africa; protest meetings, resolutions, etc. in all territories."[71]

Stung as they were by the brutal lash of white supremacy, labor in the British West Indies approached the question of apartheid South Africa like it was a holy crusade. Even before Hart's démarche, St. Kitts-Nevis had sprung into action. In August 1948, the People's National Party of Jamaica requested that their St. Kitts counterpart "join the PNP in making representations to the Secretary of State for the colonies" concerning newly minted apartheid in South Africa and demanded an "embargo on imports" from that nation.[72] Subsequently, Joseph France of St. Kitts insisted that "on account of [the] deliberate and systematic application of its dreadful policy of apartheid . . . my union finds itself unable to advise its members of [the] Basseterre waterfront to handle any cargo originating in the Union of South Africa after 31st December 1950."[73]

Responding formally to Hart's démarche, the St. Kitts-Nevis Trades and Labour Union made it clear that the "union was at all times prepared to handle food-stuffs and drugs but not goods of any kind originating in the Union of South Africa."[74] This was quite worrisome to London and Washington, as apartheid South Africa was an anticommunist anchor of support at the tip of a mineral-rich continent and thought to be a bulwark against the prospect of insurgencies thought to be pro-communist. But it was not just South Africa that received scrutiny. Bradshaw of St. Kitts met with Frank Osborne, "representative for a Barbados firm which handles South African products, who inquired whether the union could not reconsider its decision" on apartheid, suggestive of the concern that was developing.[75]

The CLC also balked when objections were raised in London to the marriage of "Prince Seretse Khama" of Botswana to a European woman. This was a "complete repudiation of the socialist principles of racial equality for which the British Labour Party is supposed to stand," complained Richard Hart.[76] More worrying for Washington was that the CLC was increasingly training its sights on the United States itself. When W.E.B. Du Bois was put on trial in 1951 for being the agent of an unnamed foreign power—thought to be Moscow—the CLC declared that "all organizations and leaders throughout the Caribbean are urged to record their most vigorous protests against this latest outrage of the American reactionary forces."[77]

These "American reactionary forces" were increasingly being targeted by the CLC and its affiliates as Washington moved to fill the regional vacuum brought by the retreat of the Empire. This was due in part to the continuing migration of workers from the British West Indies to the United States. When V. C. Bird of Antigua and Robert Bradshaw of St. Kitts-Nevis visited labor camps made up largely of their compatriots in Florida in mid-1948, they were stunned. As Bradshaw observed, they found "shocking sanitary conveniences" and expressed "surprise that outbreaks of disease had not yet occurred." There were "awful living conditions" and "inhuman working conditions." The men were involved in "immense amounts of weeding—some of the weeds are nearly as tall as some men." Their "straw bosses" were "the worst types of 'poor white' and 'white trash,'" who never failed to "insist that the men are not to talk to each other while working and must now not answer back" despite the "vilest" language directed at them. "One Jamaican worker at Miami Locke camp when I told him who we were said, 'when we write home about the bad conditions under which we have to live and work here nobody believes us.'" Thus, "on the invitation of Hope Stevens" of Harlem, he came to New York City to address "Leeward Islanders there," and "$650.00 was collected to defray" their expenses, a sign of concrete solidarity.[78] Then Bradshaw's concerns were raised directly in his union's councils[79] and reached the local press as headlines screamed "workers dislike Florida jobs," "white foremen have the attitude of slave drivers."[80] A frightened "Kittian" writing from Florida complained bitterly, charging that "our lives are at stake" as they are "forcing us to work for less and they want to treat us like slaves." Now they were "threatening to send us home" and the workers were "told by natives that we may lose our lives if we come here to break down their price" for picking fruit.[81] Though the press also reported that a "large number of West Indian workers will be wanted for employment in the United States,"[82] the stories emerging from Florida were hardly reassuring.

The Empire, which had been weakened irrevocably by the war, was hardly in a position to address the horrendous economic inequalities that gripped the British West Indies. Thus, dispatching workers to the United States was one way to confront this problem. Barbados, historically, was the focal point of this problem, and an official there told the governor of the Leeward Islands in late 1950 that he was "aware of the need of outlets for the surplus population of the West Indian islands," but the traditional "outlets" were hardly capable of absorbing the numbers he had in mind. "I hardly believe," he proclaimed, "that British Guiana and British Honduras can offer appreciable relief, when the rate of increase of population is borne in mind."[83] He was so desperate that he did not rule out repatriation to Africa for some, which shines new light on the perhaps not coincidental revival of such ideas. Thus, months after this correspondence from Barbados, the Universal African Nationalist Movement, which had a branch in Jamaica, contacted London about the possibility of a mass repatriation to Liberia,[84] where an official indicated "acceptance of the said Plan as the basis upon which immigration" could occur.[85] In the summer of 1950, the Jamaican governor noted that "recently there has been renewed local interest in the 'Back to Africa movement.'"[86]

Ironically, as barriers were being erected to keep, say, Guianese out of St. Vincent, the path was lubricated for Caribbean migrants to flee to New York, Toronto,[87] and London. In a sense, grave apprehension about the presence of inter-Caribbean travel and the supposed militancy it brought facilitated migration to the more affluent regions of North America and Western Europe, which delivered a certain progressivism in the metropole instead, along with heftier remittances to the homeland. It also facilitated heftier donations to the CLC. In the spring of 1950, "American friends and West Indians in New York, Boston, Chicago, Detroit, Washington, D.C. and other cities" contributed $10,000 to the CLC,[88] a remarkable vote of confidence given their opposition to Cold War maneuvers.

These donors may have been responding to the extraordinary upsurge in British Guiana, where the CLC model of a militant labor-left leading the march to independence and sovereignty had reached its zenith. In late 1951, a British report on the PPP noted that it was "allied to the [CLC]" and "was a socialist party." Jagan was cited for the proposition that his homeland "did not want to exchange one imperialism for another (USA),"[89] which could not have pleased Washington—or London for that matter. Jagan was said to be "unfortunately under Communist influence which we are hoping may be reduced somewhat as the results of our talks with him,"[90] while "his wife is thought to be more big-oted and anti-British in her attitude."[91]

These were not encouraging words for those who viewed the PPP as a CLC model for the region. But soon both of these much-assailed organizations were to be subjected to an all-sided assault.

CHAPTER 12

Barbados vs. British Guiana

A S THE SECOND HALF of the twentieth century unfolded, the British West Indies was on the cusp of immense change. Riveting struggles had compelled the commencement of adult suffrage throughout a good deal of the region, which slowly was bringing to power forces that embodied the labor-left ideal of the Caribbean Labour Congress (CLC)—namely the Jagans—though London would retain ultimate power for some years to come. Yet since Grantley Adams had cast down the anticommunist gauntlet in Paris, the CLC itself had been under siege. These contrasting trends found it hard to coexist, and ultimately Adams of Barbados was to prevail over Jagan of British Guiana as a regional force, not least since Washington placed its weighty thumb on the scales of history. The onset of the war in Korea polarized politics decisively to the benefit of the prevailing ethos in the United States, as throughout the region forces that had been aligned with the CLC were compelled to either remain lined up behind Jagan and Hart or, alternatively, to line up behind Adams.

An ominous signal arrived in early 1952, appropriately enough in Jamaica—the lodestar of the region. It was then that Norman Manley's People's National Party (PNP), which had seemed to be a bulwark of the CLC, capitulated and expelled Richard Hart, along with three of his left-wing colleagues, on spurious grounds fueled by anticommunism. London's man on the scene, Sir Hugh Foot, observed at the time that "the debate at the Party Conference was long and acrimonious, and when the result of the voting was announced, there was some disorder, caused by supporters of the [Hart] faction, who threw bottles and chairs from the gallery of the Ward Theatre." The vote was roughly 128-75, suggesting that those who were defeated retained a modicum of support.[1]

Looking back years later, Hart adjudged that "Norman Manley made a serious mistake in pursuing that line," meaning aligning with Adams's anticommunism.

"What had happened," he said, "was that in 1951 local government elections, it was perfectly obvious that the Bustamante movement was in steep decline and that the PNP was going to win the next elections. This led to fears in the right-wing of the party about the influence of the left-wing," which was "all part of the post-war neo-colonialist phenomena." That was not all. "We wanted to have industries in Jamaica," said Hart, "but the policy of British imperialism was to prohibit or prevent or discourage the appearance of such industries." Thus, by weakening the left, Jamaica was also left to languish further in the death grip of neocolonialism.[2]

Similar developments were unwinding in Barbados. A little more than 165 square miles with a population in 1950 hovering around 200,000, this eastern-most island in the Caribbean had an astonishing density of 1,200 persons per square mile (compare Jamaica's figure of 294). There were a "larger number of whites than to be found in any other BWI colony," which sheds light on the island's notorious conservatism—the antipode of British Guiana. A report retained by Richard Hart in 1945 noted that "for many years the whites reigned supreme and the coloured population was completely acquiescent." Then Adams, a barrister, stepped forward and by 1941 workers had begun to orga-nize. Yet by 1945 unions only enrolled 5,587 members and "so far [had] failed to organize the thousands of sugar workers."[3]

Five years later, this opinion of Barbados had barely improved. By then[4] the "most important union in Barbados," the "Barbados Workers Union," had "about 12,000 members." Unlike other islands, there were "no appreciable number of peasants in Barbados," yet there was a "more rigid colour division in Barbadian society by reason of the existence of a proportionately larger number of white settlers originally here than in other British Caribbean territories. But the Bar-badian whites [largely] fall within the employing class or the upper brackets of the urban middle class and the division is therefore not one which cuts across the working class as, for instance, in the Southern States of the USA." In this island, "the badge of entrance to the socially elite circles in Barbados is money and a white skin," which facilitated Barbados's becoming the headquarters for London and Washington to beat back the labor-left upsurge.[5]

As elsewhere in the region, the turning point came in the early 1950s; 1951 was the year of the first elections under full adult suffrage—and, to that extent, a concrete step toward sovereignty and independence. But it was during this time that the Barbados Labour Party (BLP), under Adams's tutelage, "aban-doned its commitment to wholesale nationalization and set the Barbadian econ-omy on a course of controlled capitalism in the private sector." Moreover, unlike St. Kitts, which initially sought to boycott apartheid South Africa, the BLP backed the investment of the government's "surplus" in this polecat economy.

The Clerks' Union in Barbados was emblematic of labor in the nation in that it reflected an "essential conservatism." Thus when its fiery leader, T. T. Lewis, was sacked in 1949, "the union took no action. Its members themselves proved unwilling to come out and visibly support their President." There were "union members who would run back to their boss the next day and reveal what was said the previous evening at the Clerks' Union meeting." This "stopped people from speaking their minds," concludes Lewis's biographer. "[F]or example, someone who would be in line for a position as a senior clerk would jeopardize his future by making critical comments about big business. The laws of dismissal at that time were very easy. You didn't have to serve a lot of notice on employees." The nettlesome issue of "race" operated in Barbados in a manner not unlike that which operated in the United States in that "considerations of race are an integral part of the Barbadian psyche. They are, indeed, a persistent causal factor in West Indian history," not least because of the unique role of Barbados itself. "The sense of entitlement that skin colour has traditionally given white Barbadians would have led even the poorest of whites in Lewis' day to see equally poor blacks as the 'others' with whom they would have deemed they had little in common." As in the United States, this racial divide propelled an obdurate conservatism that reached fruition in the wake of Adams's UN speech. For Adams gained in popularity "buoyed up by the wave of popularity which followed his performance at the United Nations and the speech he made on his return to Barbados which tended to overshadow all other issues in the 1948 election."

As the CLC was splitting along a left-right axis, Adams's Barbados Labour Party was doing the same. Strikingly, opposing Adams was the Euro-Barbadian trade union leader T. T. Lewis, whom Adams denounced fiercely. The British leader, Sir J. Cameron Tudor, recalled a public tirade by Adams in Queen's Park in Bridgetown that he termed "the most appalling example of a platform performance by any politician that I have known . . . he launched into T. T. with a personal excoriation of the man. . . . [I]t was a very bitter personal attack and I regret to say," he said with lingering angst, "that there were racial overtones. The whole tenor of the speech was this: 'here is a man who looks different from us, who we have nurtured and taken [under] our wing and now look [at] how he has betrayed his party.' The crowd, which was composed mainly of agricultural workers and waterfront men was very much with Adams." Inevitably a party in opposition to the BLP developed—the Democratic Labour Party—but Adams "developed the tactic of labeling [it] as a subversive organization supported by Moscow"—"even as the BLP had been similarly categorized by the conservatives a few years earlier."[6] For it had not been so long ago that Adams himself was seen as Moscow's dupe by the planters, just as his "status" was "enhanced regionally by his 1947 election to the Presidency of the [CLC]."[7]

In a sense, the left-right split in Barbados was exported to the region, with British Guiana as the primary victim and Adams the avenging angel. Like a film dissolve, it only dawned slowly on the CLC left that Adams would move from the bombshell of his UN speech to the devastation of splitting the CLC itself.

As things were falling apart in Barbados, something similar was occurring in London, theretofore home of one of the CLC's stronger affiliates. "There would be no witch-hunt in the CLC," it was said bravely in mid-1951, and "there was no political test in the CLC." The branch's chairman, Dr. David Pitt, "said he thought it necessary to state that he was no Communist and never would be," but there were those who remained dissatisfied with this dearth of equivocation.[8]

So it was in March 1950 that Richard Hart contacted "Dear Grantley," informing him that there was "no possibility of holding the CLC Congress in April in Trinidad" since, despite the strength of the Oil Field Workers' Trade Union, he was "unable to get the necessary organizational assistance in Trinidad."[9] But Trinidad had its own problems. "My Union is in an awful financial state through supporting an unsuccessful strike which absorbed all its funds," complained the left-wing leader of the Public Works and Public Service Workers Trade Union in Port-of-Spain.[10] Besides, Albert Gomes, formerly a CLC stalwart, was now adapting to a rapidly changing environment. "Communism had found its way into the ranks of the workers of Trinidad," he posited, while adding, "I do not really believe that many individuals in this colony know what communism is."[11]

A CLC conference was slated for April 1950 in Trinidad, but a number of supporters—particularly those in a besieged New York City who sought to raise $10,000 to fund it—had "experienced the political pressure of the McCarthy era. . . . Hart's urgent appeals for funds were in vain and the conference was cancelled."[12]

Then the war in Korea erupted in June 1950, which was a turning point in the Cold War and a signal that Washington was stepping up its pressure globally and regionally. It seemed that the CLC was devolving into an organization funded out of Hart's wallet. The organization was "heavily indebted to me," he moaned in the spring of 1952, "as I have had to carry a considerable excess of expenditure over receipts out of my own pocket. This is quite apart from the fact that when it became apparent that the CLC could no longer afford to provide the clerical assistance which was needed."[13]

A telltale sign was the evident lack of contact between the Jagans and Hart, which, if the idea of monolithic conspiratorial "communists" held true, would be the opposite of what it was. "Dear Dick," said Janet Jagan in 1950, "how about some BWI news for 'Thunder,'" referring to her party's organ.[14] Then late in 1951 she noted that "your letters get rarer." However, things were perking up since she added that "your letter was read to the Executive last night and members are offering you a return ticket from Trinidad to BG." Forbes Burnham was still aligned with the CLC left, as he had informed Janet Jagan "to tell you"— referring to Hart—that "if you need accommodations in Trinidad, he can arrange to have you stay with his wife's family."[15]

Militant Grenada was also not that excited about a CLC confab, which too was telling. "My organization has always felt great concern over the moribund state into which the [CLC] had declined," said D. M. Patterson of the Grenada Workers Union, though he did "look forward with interest to the new life of the

Congress." Speaking frankly, he added, "I doubt our ability to face the heavy expenses that would be involved in sending a delegate."[16]

The turning point arrived in 1952. In April of that year, Francisco Aguirre, a leader of a pro-Washington labor federation in the region, presided over a meeting in Barbados with Frank Walcott of Barbados, who was one of Adams's closest comrades, and others in the British West Indies of like mind. They agreed to hold a conference in Bridgetown of regional unions that were already affiliated with the pro-U.S. International Confederation of Free Trade Unions (ICFTU), perceived widely as a rival to the left-leaning World Federation of Trade Unions (WFTU), seen as being in the corner of the CLC left and Moscow. By this juncture, the "campaign against the CLC's association with the WFTU had become a united front of colonial governments, newspapers, churches and all the major political parties"—except the People's Progressive Party of British Guiana, of course—"as well as several trade unions."[17]

So in August 1952 Adams, in his capacity as CLC president, told affiliates and branches of the "inevitability of a final cleavage in the Caribbean area between unions affiliated to the ICFTU and the WFTU, the activities of an unauthorized body in London calling itself 'The London branch of the CLC' and acting as an apparent Communist front organization." According to Adams, this served to "create a situation of extreme embarrassment and to raise issues of the gravest nature relating to the future of the CLC." This could not continue, he insisted.[18]

But the CLC left was moving in an opposing direction. Billy Strachan was a CLC leader in London, and that branch was rapidly becoming the focus of tension within the organization. So when he called for a meeting of the CLC leadership, it was hard to ignore; it was harder still when he sought to place only two items on the agenda—the fate of the London chapter and the question of the WFTU vs. the ICFTU. He told his "dear comrades" that the "dismemberment of our branch can only be a prelude to the destruction of the organization which originally came into existence to unify the many isolated struggles that West Indian peoples were waging." As he saw it, "the first attack on the work and character of the London branch was launched" by Albert Gomes of Trinidad, well on his way to moving away from the labor-left, and "an exposed opportunist." As he saw it, the London branch was "dangerous because of the opportunity we had of exposing British colonial slave-conditions at home in the United Kingdom, at the heart of the Empire."[19]

Then in September 1952, Adams moved to dissolve the CLC. Hart was beyond anger, telling his erstwhile colleague bluntly that "it is now quite clear that you have not got the support of the affiliate organizations of the CLC for your proposal to hold a Council meeting instead of the Full Congress," where a dissolution motion would encounter rough sledding. Briskly, Hart told Adams the facts, which also revealed the ideological lineup of forces at a turning point in Caribbean history. "[T]he following organizations have replied to my letter expressing support for a Full Congress only: Antigua Trades and Labour Union, TUC of British Guiana (including the BG Labour Union), People's Progressive Party of Guiana, TUC of Trinidad and Tobago, Peoples Political Party of St. Vincent." Then there was the TUC of Jamaica, which desired a "Full Congress and a Council meeting," and the PNP of Jamaica, which wanted only the latter.[20]

Hart did not stop there in berating Adams. "[Y]ou have decided on a policy of bringing about a split in the trade union and national movements in the Caribbean in line with the policy of the ICFTU. This will of course involve a reversal of the settled policy of the CLC that the matter of the international affiliations of each member organization of the CLC was its own concern." But Adams, undeterred, had decided with finality to "seek to 'dissolve' the London branch of the CLC" as a prelude to an overall liquidation. Forcefully, Hart sought to remind him of the "gravity" and "far reaching effects of the course you wish the CLC to adopt."[21]

Adams's agenda had congealed in June 1952 when he, along with Serafino Romualdi, assistant secretary of the ICFTU's regional body, convened a conference of the Barbados Workers' Union at Bridgetown's Hastings House. "It was attended by representatives of 17 trade unions from Barbados, [British Guiana], Grenada, British Honduras, and Suriname. The opening session was chaired" by ICFTU's delegate in the region, Serafino Romualdi. As Hart observed later, "the conference obviously had the blessing of the British government as Sir George Steel, Assistant Secretary of State in the Colonial Office, was thanked by Adams for having 'not only graced the opening of the Conference with his presence but had also put at their disposal that room and other facilities of the Colonial Development and Welfare Organization.' "[22]

Adams's allies were determined. An editorial in *The Torch* of Barbados referred derisively to the CLC as a "mix-up of several labour and trade union organizations" that "has been all but dead for some years," so Adams was right to prepare the last rites. Instead this group's troubles had "overflowed into this peaceful island."[23] A "secret" report from Jamaica as this controversy was rushing to a climax noted nervously that the "increased activity led by Ferdinand Smith and Richard Hart continues and there is growing evidence that these activities are meeting with success." It was conceded that a "confused situation exists in regard to the [CLC]" and it was "expected that Grantley Adams would lead a move to purge the [CLC] of Communist supporters, or to create a new organization to replace" it. Yet "the extremists in the [CLC] are active and determined and it is doubtful," it was added pessimistically, "if Grantley Adams will be able to expel them. It may be therefore that the [CLC] will be captured by the Communists. The activities of the Communists under the leadership of Ferdinand Smith, both in Jamaica and in the larger sphere of the British West Indies, must give rise to grave anxiety."[24]

Arriving in Bridgetown to discuss this controversial matter were Hart, Jagan, John La Rose of Trinidad, Ebenezer Joshua of St. Vincent, Wynter Crawford of

Barbados, Eric Gairy of Grenada, Vere Bird of Antigua, Alexander Bustamante of Jamaica, W. Arthur Lewis of St. Lucia, and others—though Ferdinand Smith of Jamaica, recently ousted from the United States, was denied entry. For those who sought to maintain unity, their journey was to no avail. The CLC split in the fall of 1952 and disappeared shortly thereafter.[25]

This occurred though Smith, now an official of the WFTU, proposed that his group would fund the CLC—or an equivalent body—with no strings attached, if the ICFTU would do the same. This body would not be affiliated to either, in other words.

It was on Monday, 3 November 1952, at Bridgetown's House of Assembly that this and other matters were discussed. Adams declared that "even if such a proposal was in the best interest of the Caribbean, [he] was sure that ICFTU would not agree to it and he admitted that their policy was to create a division of the workers on ideological grounds."[26] With that the CLC effectively fizzled.

Later the labor-left held a huge rally in Barbados as they sought to explain their viewpoint. Hart "held his audience entranced," said a local newspaper, "as he made an impassioned appeal for the unity and independence of the West Indies—an appeal so moving as to lead the vast Barbadian crowd to conclude that the CLC President [Adams] did not see things quite that way. But [what] Mr. Hart left undone was remedied by the Hon. E. T. Joshua of St. Vincent." Thus, "the CLC has impeached its President"—but Adams, on the fast track to knighthood, thought it was his adversaries who stood exposed.[27]

Jagan was distraught about the split in the ranks of the CLC. "We pleaded in the interests of West Indian unity," he recalled later, "that everything should be done to prevent the disbanding of the CLC. The CLC, we argued, had been the repository of all progressive thought in the Caribbean," and disbanding the CLC, he insisted, was "catastrophic for the whole West Indian labour movement," which "had some bearing on the break-up of the West Indies federation."[28]

THE RAPIDLY ERODING INFLUENCE OF THE CLC, along with the hawkish posture exuded by Washington in the wake of the war in Korea, did not augur well for the future of the People's Progressive Party (PPP) of British Guiana. Summing up the experience years later, Cheddi Jagan declared that "as a result of the rightist turn taken by the W.I. leaders, the PPP was attacked in 1953 and consequently, isolated after 1953. The West Indian leadership, in assuming Cold War positions . . . which was a departure from the stand taken in 1947, had sold out the interests of the people." Thus, he concluded, "federation was doomed to failure."[29]

Yet it was not preordained that the weakening of the CLC would automatically weaken the PPP—though that is precisely how things evolved. It did appear that the left's talons were so deeply entrenched in British Guiana that little could halt its forward march. This was partially due to the left's response to the all-sided crisis that gripped this South American nation. "There was no appreciable increase in production in British Guiana during 1950, in comparison with the previous year," it was announced officially in 1952. The "principal products of the colony" included "sugar, rum, rice, timber, bauxite, gold [and] diamonds." Despite these riches ripe for exploitation, "the total volume of employment was approximately the same in 1950 as in 1940," while "the average number of workers employed in connection with sugar factories in 1950 was somewhat lower than the corresponding average for 1949. During the grinding season an average of 5928 workers [were] employed directly by the factories," while "employment in the bauxite industry declined from 2300 at the beginning of the year to 2200 at the end of the first quarter." As a partial result, there was "definite migratory movement of workers from the colony or into the colony," thereby hampering British Guiana's historic role as a site for refuge of economic migrants from other parts of the British West Indies.[30]

Meanwhile, Cheddi Jagan, who had ascended to the colony's domestic ruling authority, the Executive Council, was engaged in parliamentary guerrilla warfare seeking to expand the bounds of democracy. Early in 1952 he introduced a "motion recommending enactment of legislation to provide for election to . . . Village Councils on the basis of universal adult suffrage"—but "after discussion" it was "agreed that the motion should be opposed when it came before the Legislative Council."[31] This was just an inkling of the contention that came to characterize politics in British Guiana. Symptomatic was the decision to "take adequate security measures against undesirable immigrants." This referred to an incident involving a "recent disturbance at the Chinese Association Hall in which a Chinese young man alleged to be a Communist had smashed a photograph of Generalissimo Chiang Kai-shek," which was deemed to be a major offense.[32]

No doubt a defiant foe of the Jagans, the Manpower Citizens Association (MPCA)—a union of sorts—was supportive of any measures taken against opponents of anticommunism, since this ideology was emblazoned on its escutcheon. Serafino Romualdi, who had helped to engineer the split in the CLC, "was an old friend of the union." In 1952 "he paid us a welcome visit," said the MPCA, "and expressed in no uncertain terms his belief and faith in the MPCA and in the work which the MPCA was doing in fighting communism." Romualdi, well-funded by U.S. sources, generously presented to the MPCA an "expensive projector and screen," in addition to films in profusion.[33]

Consequently, as elections approached in the spring of 1953, the atmosphere was not conducive for a balanced, measured response to a surging left which propelled Jagan into office. The PPP got "18 out of the 24 seats at the elections in April," said one Londoner sourly, "although it had a margin of only 2600 votes in a total poll of 147,600."[34] Already the thought had occurred that electoral legerdemain would be needed if the PPP were to be kept from power. This sedition was brewing despite the unavoidable fact that ultimate power rested in

London. However, that was apparently not reassuring to the colonizers, who a few months into his administration dispatched troops to overthrow Jagan.

There were a number of reasons why London and Washington were upset with Jagan's brief reign, besides the allegation that he was a communist. For he objected strenuously when in a typical maneuver a colonial bureaucrat sought to build a new house at taxpayers' expense,[35] just as he railed at the "extraordinarily high costs of erection of government buildings."[36] Jagan zealously objected to the routine corruption and looting that characterized colonial administration. "One Department has now been subdivided into five heads," he fumed in February 1953, even before assuming office, and "we are overburdening the taxpayers of this colony by adding to the expenditure on administration. The cost of administration is adding up to too great a percentage of our revenue."[37] Then he objected again when the government sought to provide a hefty subsidy to the "[British Guiana] Broadcasting Company," though this entity "refused to accept the [paid] advertisement" of his party.[38]

Shortly thereafter at his behest there was a move to "repeal . . . the Undesirable Publications Ordinance." At that same meeting there was "appointment of a Committee to investigate conditions of employment and wages of domestic servants and washers," an initiative not designed to curry favor with those who felt that shameless exploitation of such laborers was part of their birthright.[39] Jagan was no doubt responding to previous confiscations of literature intended for him, such as copies of "Soviet Woman" and "Soviet Literature"—both brought from London, where they were freely available—but were "destroyed . . . burnt" upon arrival in Georgetown.[40] Worried about what might happen when Jagan assumed power in April 1953, weeks before this the colonials began trying to put in place measures that would tie his hands on the vexed matter of banning literature. They saw no contradiction in the fact that this literature was freely available in London since, after all, British Guiana was a colony, with all that suggested in terms of antidemocracy. Jagan would have none of this. "Why the mad rush at this moment to pass this legislation," he asked plaintively, "when but two months from now we are going to have a new House of Assembly? Why?" And why was it that this bill "not only refers to literature but to recordings of the human voice."[41] Jagan filibustered for six hours seeking to stop passage of this bill. His comrades picketed for "two days." Jagan offered an amendment declaring that anything published or recorded or filmed in Britain should be allowed; this was defeated.[42]

These clashes escalated after Jagan assumed office. "Dr. Jagan informed His Excellency that the Elected Ministers were considering their attitude to the question of capital punishment but had not reached final conclusions. . . . His Excellency said he hoped that as elsewhere the question would not be made a political matter,"[43] which was a typical exchange of the time.

What was happening was that Jagan and the PPP were presenting an indication of what a government influenced by the CLC—albeit with London still retaining ultimate power—might do upon taking office. London and Washington had to wonder if Georgetown might become a vector for the transmission of radicalism, not only throughout the Caribbean, but, as well, into South America, historically a continent of no small concern to the United States. That thought had occurred to colonial authorities in London. In a "Top Secret" message, days before Jagan's overthrow, the secretary of state for the colonies was irate that "they have withdrawn the ban on the entry of West Indian Communists, with the sole object, I am satisfied, of making [British Guiana] a centre of Communist conspiracy in South America."[44]

This concern was not allayed when the "Elected Ministers" led by Jagan argued "that the ban from entering British Guiana imposed on Ferdinand Smith, William Strachan, John La Rose, Quintin O'Connor, John Rojas and Richard Hart"—the CLC left—"should be removed." London's man, Sir Alfred Savage, dissented vigorously. "His Excellency . . . considered that for a number of reasons the present credit of British Guiana was under suspicion and that while this continued foreign investors would be discouraged and development would be restricted in consequence." Jagan and the other "Elected Ministers," which included Forbes Burnham, "stated that they adhered to their view as they felt that the ban was not in keeping with the principles laid down in the U.N. Declaration of Human Rights in regard to the free movement of individuals. They pointed out that the persons named were free to enter the United Kingdom and they considered that there should be freedom of movement for all West Indians in the West Indian territories."[45] Sir Alfred backed down and the ban was lifted, but bruised feelings ensued, as this issue—debated vigorously in July 1953 as fears about radicalism rose dramatically in the hemisphere—was the most contentious debated during Jagan's brief tenure. This victory was an early indication of what Jagan's electoral success meant, for before his spring 1953 victory it had been adjudged that "in view of the . . . Communist activities of Mr. Richard Hart, Mr. John Rojas, Mr. [Quintin] O'Connor and Mr. John La Rose, these four persons should be deemed undesirable as visitors to British Guiana."[46]

Malignant concern was metastasizing that the PPP was determined to establish Georgetown as a regional center for the left in a way congruent with the dearest dreams of those who had founded the CLC. London was unhappy when Jagan and his allies "asked for the matter to be taken up officially," referring to the sensitively explosive matter of "racial discrimination," this time in Bermuda, "as it was considered intolerable for racial discrimination to be practiced in any British territory and in particular that members of the governments of British territories . . . should be subjected to personal affronts of this nature." But what would this mean for Barbados, not to mention the officially sanctioned policy of apartheid that reigned in the Colossus of the North?[47]

Still, if there was anything more rancorous than the idea of Georgetown becoming a way station for visiting radicals, it was the idea of empowering labor through decrees and laws. Even before Jagan came to power in 1953 he had pressed for a measure that would allow—in a manner akin to that of the National Labor Relations Board in the United States—for "unions with majority membership" in a workplace to have "sole jurisdiction for purposes of collective bargaining."[48] This was rejected.

But British Guiana labor knew it had one of its own in power once Jagan ascended to the throne, and it acted accordingly. In August 1953—weeks before he was overthrown—discussions at the highest level in Georgetown reflected "considerable dissatisfaction amongst sugar workers regarding the methods employed by the estates' authorities in weighing canes." The workers wanted "independent checkers to watch the scales," which management perceived as a threat to their hegemony.[49]

This was the prelude to a raucous strike that erupted days later. Work ceased at thirteen estates. The Guiana Industrial Workers' Union had been pressing for recognition by the Sugar Producers' Association for a long time. After all, the "Union represented a high proportion of the sugar workers," which had prompted Jagan's NLRB-style measure in the first place. "His Excellency" was quite displeased and "stated that it appeared that the union had shown complete disregard for normal trade union practice in calling this strike," and "he expressed strong disapproval of the fact that two Ministers of the Crown had given active encouragement to the strike; he added that the strike appeared to have the tacit approval of the Elected Ministers"—which was no revelation given Jagan's and Burnham's previous pro-worker disposition—"and in consequence people believed that it was a 'Government' strike. He did not believe the strike would have succeeded without the support of members of the Government. Finally His Excellency stated that Government must be the final arbiter in disputes of this kind but if the Elected Ministers continued to take sides it would be impossible for them to give the Government unbiased advice."

Actually, His Excellency was being somewhat disingenuous. Certainly the colonial government had hardly been neutral in previous strikes, least of all the Enmore conflict of 1948, where strikers were slain by the authorities and which impelled Jagan to commit himself to politics. Jagan's electoral victory had exposed baldly the seams of that ultimate oxymoron—colonial democracy. In pushing for a NLRB-style measure in British Guiana, Jagan had revealed the often hidden fact that the kind of democracy allowed in London and Washington was not appropriate for a colony—that's why it was a colony and not independent. But some in the United States and the United Kingdom came to recognize eventually that if such measures were disallowed in the colonies, how long would it be before similar rationales would lead to their being disallowed in the North Atlantic?

Jagan was a legislative lion, familiar with details and rhetorically ferocious. He and the PPP were pushing for the kinds of practices, for example receipt of controversial literature, that were boringly common in London. But if this were

to occur, this could undermine colonialism and the Empire itself, since the voters of British Guiana might begin to wonder why they should be ruled by a once
obscure family from northwest Europe. Recognition of this absurdity, perhaps,
drove Jagan and his allies to express reluctance about sending representatives
to Jamaica when "Her Majesty the Queen" visited; "in view of its other financial commitments, it cannot afford to accept the kind invitation," it was stated.[50]
As it turned out, this supposed brush-off of "Her Majesty" was interpreted by
"His Excellency" and others so inclined as a veritable casus belli justifying intervention. As it turned out, in a direct slap at lèse majesté, the coup was denoted
officially as "Operation Windsor."[51]

The "Elected Ministers" were not bending. In backing the strikers, one said
that "it was only possible to bargain successfully with the Sugar Producers at crop
time and the strike had therefore been called and he supported it." Another
member of the ruling Executive Council asserted that "if the employers continued to transport strikebreakers from one estate to another as they had recently
done, clashes would be inevitable."[52]

Just as British troops were about to put boots on the ground in Georgetown,
it was "feared that the [sugar] strike might spread to other categories of workers. His Excellency stated that he had just heard that employees in the Public
Works Department and Forestry Department had come out on strike."[53] Then
His Excellency acknowledged that "since the last meeting . . . other unions had
called strikes in sympathy with the sugar workers; he had also been informed
that Dr. Jagan . . . was President of one of the unions concerned," which made
him wonder about his neutrality.[54] Hours before the intervention, Jagan's "labour
relations bill" was debated, and "a large crowd of spectators again turned up in
the House" as this edifice "swelled to large proportions." There was "hysteria
over the bill," accompanied by the "most ignoble imputations" of "certain Ministers."[55] Just as the intervention was about to commence, the local press
reported that Janet Jagan acknowledged that a "constitutional crisis" was "rapidly developing" in British Guiana. Yet, tellingly accompanying this bit of news
on the front page of the local newspaper was an advertisement for a PPP course
on "Marxism-Leninism," another one of their courses on "socialism," and yet
another on "land reform." In London this would not have raised concern but in
Georgetown it was taken as a signal that the revolution was nigh. But actually
it was not revolution per se that was feared, but something else—something
strategic—was desired, for this same newspaper also reported that "an American news commentator said last night that U.S. forces will re-occupy the base
in British Guiana if the British Government fails to take steps to stop the Communist advance in British Guiana."[56]

British Guiana seemed to be spinning out of control—or from another
perspective, headed toward a revolutionary climax where the PPP, backed by
militant unions, would oust the colonial power decisively, seize power, and expro-
priate the economic royalists. Yet on the day before the October 1953 military

intervention, Jagan came before the Executive Council and reported that he "had received complaints that the Police Force had been asked to stand by for 24 hours a day. He considered that this order should be rescinded as the sugar strike was now finished and conditions had returned to normal." Cannily evading the real reason underlying this curious police maneuver, His Excellency observed airily that the "police had been ordered to stand-by generally as soon as the sugar strike started and they would continue to do so until the strike" was ended officially, which in his opinion had not occurred. "Dr. Jagan enquired whether the strike was not now over. His Excellency replied in the negative"—which led to yet another clash that was to erupt decisively the very next day.[57]

His Excellency did not reveal what he had told London a few days before, which was that the "security situation in the police and volunteers" had "deteriorated much more than previously believed. It is possible that at least 50 percent of both forces would refuse to accept full duty and such situation will worsen daily." Thus, he added ominously, "the proposed operation should commence without delay." It was "essential . . . that our D Day should be as early as possible next week."[58] In other words, despite the braying about the alleged communist threat posed by Jagan's government, actually it was the "threat" posed by militant labor that had motivated the brutal British intervention.

Finally, London had had enough. The PPP was "fomenting racial hatred," London asserted, and they were "prepared to use violence" to implement their devilish aims. Thus, said the secretary of state for the colonies, "I have therefore decided to . . . take away Ministers' portfolios and to take over full control of the government." He would also "declare a state of emergency" and "suspend the Constitution" in order to foil "this Communist plot."[59]

The Executive Council of British Guiana had a special session on 7 October 1953. "Dr. Jagan opened the proceedings by referring to a news broadcast by the BBC at 7:15 P.M. the day before in which it was stated officially that troops and naval forces were proceeding to British Guiana . . . he had been greatly surprised to hear this news." He wondered why "His Excellency had not consulted" the Council and warned that "the presence of the armed forces would act as a provocation." Sternly, His Excellency "replied that in recent weeks it had become clear to him that the [PPP] intended to provoke a constitutional crisis." There had been "inflammatory speeches . . . delivered both in the House of Assembly and at street corners and threats of violence had been made." A stunned Jagan "asked for details regarding the specific threats of violence and other matters mentioned," but his interlocutor stated that "he was not prepared to go into details at that stage." He pointed to cane fires, but Burnham responded by stating that "the illegal burning of cane fields had occurred from time to time in the sugar industry and this was not a particular act confined to strikes," as His Excellency had maintained. Burnham, an astute lawyer, demanded a definition of the term "constitutional crisis," but His Excellency evaded the query. So Burnham answered his own question by asserting that "the definition of a constitutional crisis was when one section of the Legislature defied the unanimous wishes of the majority of the Legislature which represented the majority of the people and impeded the progress of the measures which the majority wished to adopt." Burnham added triumphantly that "that had already happened and nothing had taken place," referring to blocking of various PPP measures. Jagan "stated that he considered the presence of armed forces in British Guiana would have an intimidating effect on the people and would prejudice the forthcoming bye-elections which could not then be called free elections"— but from the viewpoint of a growing number in London, it was "free elections" which brought the PPP to power in the first place and, thus, this was precisely the problem, not the solution.[60]

And that is how Cheddi Jagan found himself in his pajamas and bathrobe watching quizzically as his home was ransacked. British warships and troops descended on a typically sleepy Georgetown, while Harry Pollitt, leader of Britain's communists, denounced the "sugar bosses" for fomenting this crisis.[61] J. M. Campbell, chairman of the all-powerful Bookers corporation, countered by saying that the "government was dominated by bad men and women," while Washington found a "source of satisfaction" in London's intervention. In its statement, London said it acted to "prevent Communist subversion," since the Jagan regime was "completely under the control of a Communist clique."[62] Yet some of London's own soldiers, according to Jagan, were not sure what they were doing in the northern tip of South America. The PPP leader "said that he understood some of the soldiers had expressed surprise at having been brought to [British Guiana] and had asked where the war was. He said he and his colleagues were asking the same question."[63]

But what about the voters who put Jagan in power? Charlotte Drayton of Georgetown replied by saying they were little more than rabble, "purse-snatchers, robbers with violence, men who live off the prostitution of their women-folk and other ne'er do-wells." Actually, she argued, voting was the problem, since "this state of affairs could only have come about by Adult Suffrage when every 'jail-bird' could exercise his vote." She "sincerely" hoped that "Adult Suffrage be abandoned."[64] Norman Manley of Jamaica echoed the developing consensus from erstwhile CLC comrades, who now had received a message about what was permissible behavior. The PPP, he said, "betrayed [the] cause of colonial people."[65] Grantley Adams issued a "warning" to the British Labour Party "against fighting Dr. Jagan's battles when he and his party were a menace to democratic socialism in the West Indies." He endorsed what a British leader had said: "[H]owever much we regret the suspension of the Constitution, we should deplore far more the continuance of a Government that puts Communist ideology before the good of the people."[66]

On the other hand, South Africa's African National Congress, repaying the solidarity which it had been shown, protested, as did the regime in Guatemala— which fell victim to a similar intervention in 1954.[67] Meanwhile, "riot squads" disrupted the "first attempted mass meeting since a state of emergency was declared,"[68] but when "36 acres of canes" were "set ablaze—as sugar strike spread," the idea spread along with it that all were not pleased—least of all the workers—with London's coup.[69]

An indelible meaning of the coup against Jagan was exposed at the first meeting of the Executive Council after he had been dislodged. There was an "application by the Barima Gold Mining Company" of Canada "for exclusive permission to explore for manganese [in] a further area of 459,000 acres of Crown Land," and in response their "rental" was "reduced" by more than 600 percent.[70] Another meaning was the message sent to the now shredded CLC and denizens of the British West Indies—the ideas of the labor-left, as exemplified by the PPP, were now off-limits, verboten, and should not be pursued. Least of all should reasonable ideas include the idea of federation and sovereignty originally envisioned by the Caribbean Labour Congress.

CONCLUSION

THE BATTERING OF THE CARIBBEAN Labour Congress (CLC) and the overthrow of Jagan were vicious body blows to the once realistic dreams in the region of labor rights, sovereignty, and federation. Arguably, the region has yet to recover from this setback.

This is not how the matter was viewed in conservative circles. "Among most of the Europeans, including the well-to-do Portuguese" in the colony, "there were expressions of jubilation," Jagan recalled, speaking of his displacement. He wished to visit London to rally support, but neighboring islands refused his right to transit, as did the United States, French Guiana, and Suriname. "The British and American air lines refused to carry us. Finally we got out by chartering a plane," he remarked.[1] London was stung by the Jagan's government refusal to send a representative to greet the queen during her visit to Jamaica and admitted as early as 1954 that the People's Progressive Party's (PPP) demand for rapid decolonization was the real issue motivating his overthrow.[2]

Jagan was being demonized in the United States. As one journal typically put it, there had been a "militarized Soviet Zone in the Americas" that was "heavily laden with money and weapons, it has been kept from overthrowing the British Governor there only by the arrival of the Royal Marines." Unalloyed joy was expressed over the coup against the elected government. "Since the pro-Communist Progressive Party [sic] won 18 of the 24 seats in the Assembly and took over all the ministries last April 27, Jagan, the ousted Prime Minister and his aides were able to use government money to fly all over the colony agitating workers to strike and terrorizing those who refused." This "entire pro-Soviet Latin American-Caribbean labor network is run out of Jamaica by a Communist labor federation directed by none other than Ferdinand Smith, whom we helped drive out [of] the CIO's National Maritime Union." These devious radicals were seeking to provoke London and Washington, it was said; they wanted to "cripple harbor facilities and to prove to the Orient"—no small matter given the crisis in Korea and Malaya—that "we big bad white imperialists shoot down colored natives." There was a "danger of Soviet Revolution in Guiana" that was averted— barely. But the threat had yet to disappear since "what is happening in BG is exactly what happened in Guatemala."[3] London was displeased when Jagan's regime, during its brief 133 days in office, "started an 'African and Colonial Affairs Committee', which declared support for the Mau Mau in Kenya and the Com- munist terrorists in Malaya and specialized in vicious anti-British, anti-white propaganda"—the latter even more surprising in light of the fact that the alleged evil genius behind the regime happened to be "white," the U.S.-born Janet Jagan.[4]

Since Washington had the largest megaphone, the themes sounded there quickly became dominant in the hemisphere. When Jagan held a press confer- ence shortly after he was overthrown, he was asked repeatedly if his party was "Communist." He replied that "it was made into an issue. Two weeks, two Sun- days, before the election—which was held on the Monday," the notion was floated that the "PPP was a Communist organization and that PPP Communists were working against the interest of British Guiana." Actually the tipping point for London was the attempted passage of the "Trade Union Labour Relations Bill," while the communist issue was an ex post facto rationalization. But what about the "White Paper" that avowed that the PPP wanted to "establish a state in British Guiana similar to the Soviet state." Jagan replied, "[W]e would nation- alize public utilities—that doesn't seem to us totalitarian," since France and other European nations had substantial public sectors. Seeking to reassure, he went on to say that "there is no need to nationalize sugar." Veritably choking on his words, Jagan then remarked accurately that "we didn't pass any laws pre- venting anyone from exercising the franchise. There would still be free elections, you can vote for any party. . . . Mind you," he noted pointedly, "the Governor controls the police and the volunteers and, incidentally, the Fusileers." He was asked if his party was anticommunist. "Definitely not," was his swift riposte, and then he added, "I am a Marxist. I believe in the Marxist philosophy." Standing by his side, Burnham declared, "I have called myself a socialist," then said that "they would like to engineer a split between us. They have attempted to do it [by] searching his house," speaking of Jagan, "and not mine!"[5]

Jagan had a point. His colleague, Ashton Chase, later observed that the "Labour Relations Bill" was the factor leading to the coup. This legislation "aimed not only at guaranteeing to workers the right to join trade unions of their choice," but it "also attempted to prohibit unfair labour practices," in a manner congruent with Washington's own National Labor Relations Board.[6] But British Guiana was a colony and could not be allowed to enjoy the basic rights accorded in developed nations.

The PPP, in an official statement, derided the ostensible basis for the coup. "It is absolutely untrue that Dr. Jagan, Mr. Burnham . . . and Mrs. Jagan had planned to set fire to business property and residences of prominent persons and government officials." Why would a party controlling eighteen of twenty-four seats launch provocative actions against itself? "It is surprising that the government, in possession of proof, has not taken legal action against these individuals." The "PPP is not a Communist Party," which was a red herring in any case, it was suggested. "It is significant that while the PPP is accused of close ties to the WFTU, the ICFTU has done nothing to help the people struggling for self-government in British Guiana, rather . . . they backed fully the company dominated union, the MPCA." Crying for justice, the PPP insisted that a "plot has been invented where there is none. The issue of British Guiana today is not Communism. What is challenged is the very right to vote—the basis of democracy." But colonialism meant that British Guiana—and the British West Indies—could not enjoy the rights enjoyed in London. "The people were quite conscious of the issues—in fact Communism was one of the issues. The people voted and now force and the threat of bullets has taken away their democratic rights." Thus, "in the name of democracy, democracy is being destroyed by force."[7]

"My colleagues and I were relieved of our ministerial portfolios," Jagan said, while the "Governor was a virtual dictator"—all in the name of democracy. "[J]ust to be on the safe side," His Excellency "took away the guns of the local police!" Naturally, "all meetings were banned"—a diktat that was challenged immediately—and "raids on the offices of the [PPP] and the homes of Party leaders were immediately made."[8]

There were "several protest meetings" held in British Guiana, "with thousands of working people attending," all standing beside their deposed government. But Bustamante, Manley, and Adams—the leading personalities of the region—all backed the intervention. Jagan observed cogently that the CLC—and its uncertain fate—was linked to the tumult in Georgetown. "A few months back," he said in November 1953, "Richard Hart, Quintin O'Connor, John La Rose, Ferdinand Smith, [Ebenezer] Joshua and I met in Barbados. Richard Hart was not allowed to pass through Trinidad and another comrade was told that he would not be allowed to land in Barbados. They said that we met in order to conspire" against the region, but actually it was to meet with Adams about the destiny of the CLC. But now the unwary were being led to believe that they met "for a Communist plot to destroy the democratic government in the West Indies," as a myth was rapidly constructed to fit the prevailing zeitgeist.[9]

Richard Hart's coda was overly modest, though subsequently ignored, for it remains true that "during the period 1947–1951 the CLC with very slender resources and no paid staff did some useful work in providing exchanges of information on wages and conditions" and bolstering strikers.[10] This is much too modest a description of the scope of the CLC's efforts, even taken on its own terms. Certainly workers in Dominica were assisted considerably when the CLC was able to provide them with a "copy of the existing law governing small tenancies in Jamaica" when they were "considering the drafting of an agricultural small holding law" for their nation.[11]

Yet Hart was on to something. In a vicious one-two blow, the CLC went into a steep decline in 1952 and Jagan was toppled in 1953, and the region has hardly recovered since, though the Caribbean Congress of Labour, a far less ambitious entity, was founded in 1952 after its predecessor fell.[12]

The travails of British Guiana did not end there. Burnham was enticed to split from Jagan—a development facilitated by the inability of Africans and South Asians to unite on the basis of class, as the CLC had projected. These two top leaders were divided by a plethora of other issues which plunged the country into violent strife (a tragedy of Shakespearean proportions, stage managed, as it were, by the British and the Americans who profited in different ways from a scripted policy of 'divide and rule.')"[13]

The prime victim of this policy was the PPP. By the spring of 1954, Janet Jagan was forlornly informing a similarly beleaguered Richard Hart, "I haven't heard from you for some time." Seeking to bolster what she thought might be his flagging morale in the face of formidable obstacles, she reminded him not to "let their attacks get you down." For attacks were something she was coming to know all too well. "I feel like an old-timer who has been 'through the mill'. Police raids, arrest and all that goes with it is about as natural as blinking your eyes." "[H]ardly a day goes by when a comrade isn't raided. We had three today so far—and Party HQ yesterday." What was at issue? "Our dear 'masters,'" she said with irony flowing, "must be trying to smash the entire progressive movement in the Caribbean. Their failure is clear," however, since, she insisted, "our movement is definitely broadening during this period and is becoming more of a peoples movement than a party movement. Thousands who are not members identify themselves completely with us in this struggle." But a cautionary note was telling—"I haven't wholly converted my son. He seems to object to some of our activities"—for if her family was not altogether convinced, unsurprisingly there were others too.[14]

Janet Jagan herself, being born in the United States and Jewish besides—not to mention supposedly being from a Communist background—was increasingly fingered as the power behind the throne. (Interestingly, in the United States Shirley Graham Du Bois was said to play a similar role in moving, her spouse, W.E.B. Du Bois, to the left.[15]) "Her light eyes, small and impressive," and her hair, which was "unfashionably long," were deemed to be of relevance in explicating why her spouse refused to bend.[16]

For British Guiana—like the broader British West Indies—was a colony, and it was not easy for London and Washington to treat them in any other way, even as independence loomed, just as it was hard for the colonizers to fathom why any would choose to rebel. Still, it is harder to understand why the U.S. labor movement would seek to intervene in the region in league with their government when this resulted in a weakened labor movement in the Caribbean, which meant, inter alia, that U.S. employers could exploit cheaper labor there, thus undermining U.S. workers. Thus, over the coming years, the AFL-CIO often collaborated with the CIA in blocking Jagan's path to power.[17] Actually the die was cast in British Guiana in November 1952—just as the CLC was about to dissolve—when the International Confederation of Free Trade Unions (ICFTU) "announced the establishment of a fully equipped office in British Guiana. A projector and films were to be supplied" to Jagan's opponents.[18]

Strikingly, African Americans—who historically had taken positions at odds with that of their government—began to intervene in the region on the side of Washington. Of course, this was an outgrowth of the fact that the Cold War had split Black America as decisively as it had split the British West Indies, with those on the left either under siege or in compelled exile, as in the case of Ferdinand Smith. This provided an opening for those like A. Philip Randolph of the Brotherhood of Sleeping Car Porters, who had had frequent conflict with U.S. communists since the late 1930s and, consequently, saw no conflict in extending this struggle abroad.

Thus, it was no surprise when Martin J. Baptiste of the St. Lucia Workers Cooperative Union told Randolph that "my executive wishes to express its deepest appreciation for the courtesies extended to you and the AF of L during my stay in Milan." Naturally, given the emoluments that Randolph and U.S. labor could provide, he wanted to continue "our conversation as to your propose[d] conference with certain leaders in the West Indies."[19] The ambitious and expansive Randolph was looking further; after this festive gathering in Italy he told a colleague in Grenada that he was "giving some thought to the idea of developing some kind of relationship between the Negroes of Africa, the West Indies and the United States."[20]

These trends accelerated after the CLC fell on hard times and Jagan was overthrown. R. E. Basden, leader of labor on the Turks Islands, was enthusiastic about Randolph's idea of "the question of financial assistance to our Union." That was not all. "[A]s if our troubles were not enough," he noted with disgust days after Jagan's dislodging, "Communists in Jamaica have been trying to sow seeds of dissension in our ranks. So far they have not made much headway," though "help from your organization at this time would be very opportune," he added.[21]

It seemed that the most reliable way for unionists in the islands to obtain assistance was to raise the specter of a communist onslaught. Baptiste was "getting some sort of assistance" via Randolph, but, he added nervously, he was "confronted with many problems at the moment due to lack of certain materials needed desperately at the moment to combat the Communists, whose aims are to infiltrate into several organization[s] in the Western Hemisphere."[22] "I am very glad to know that you are set to combat infiltration of Communists into your Union," Randolph responded with verve. "[I]t is my plan around the first of next year to visit all of the South and Central American countries and West Indian islands for the purpose of meeting with the labor union leaders and workers"[23]—this was being proposed as Ferdinand Smith, his radical counterpart, was being barred systematically from this area. For at this same time Randolph was pouring funds into Smith's Jamaica, directing funds to Manley's People's National Party.[24] He was not alone, for organized labor in Cuba also helped to fund British West Indies labor, as a conduit for ICFTU.[25]

Unionists in Dominica were wondering how their lives would improve now that they had enlisted in the anticommunist army. "On behalf of six thousand people whom I represent," Emmanuel Christopher Loblack, president of the Dominica Trade Union, complained that "our market is closed," while "due to thousands of notices served to tenants by their landlords to give up possession," many families faced homelessness. Yet while "the meat market" was "closed the landlords are slaughtering animals secretly on their estates and this meat is shared [with] their friends" while "the masses are left with none."[26] Thus, he pondered, "as my organization is affiliated with ICFTU after receiving the circular" validating this membership, "I went out from door to door feeling the pores of the people by pointing out to them the necessity for defending the democracy, but I was reproached by many who said to me that they do not [know] what to do for they are living in a Democratic Country and cannot enjoy the peace and blessing of Democracy, through the oppression of the upper classes." He seemed genuinely perplexed by the dearth of benefits brought by this instantaneous proclamation of democracy and added that his constituents were not "Communist but they are becoming disloyal to the Empire."[27] Montserrat had likewise resisted stoutly the blandishments of communists, but its postwar history was nevertheless marked by a "sordid milieu" of "tyrannic regimes of landlords and their attorneys—starvation wages"—and worse.[28]

Loblack had discovered something that was becoming evident throughout the region: signing on to the anticommunist crusade was not bringing expected benefits. The "majority of the inhabitants of Dominica are unemployed," it was reported as the Cold War was being launched, and it was recommended that the authorities aid laborers as they sought to "take steps in seeking employment abroad for the unemployed in the form of emigration."[29] Similarly, an official Commission of Enquiry was dispatched to scrutinize the massive "labour unrest and strikes" that rocked St. Lucia in 1952 and, unsurprisingly, "found industrial relations on estates very unsatisfactory," marred by "deep-rooted mutual distrust."[30] Yet, continuing to hone "divide and conquer" tactics, London dispatched "police forces from St. Lucia" to Grenada whose "brutality . . . in mercilessly beating up the workers demonstrating" stoked mass outrage. London also outlawed "demonstrations for four months or more" in Eric Gairy's homeland in 1954.[31]

But with the routing of the CLC, the labor movement regionally had been disastrously wounded, and what had arisen in its wake was comparatively weaker. "As in many of the smaller territories in the Caribbean," Britain's Trades Union Congress was informed in 1954, "the trade unions of St. Vincent are organized on a mass appeal, and mass movement rather than on industrial lines, with the result that when the political supporters of the party are defeated the union suffers a setback." Moreover, as elsewhere, the "trade union movement . . . operated too much on the friendly society basis, paying out benefits without any relation to the number of years' standing of its members," thereby depleting the treasury.[32] With the decline of the militant model of unionism provided by the CLC, filling the vacuum was the model provided by Jamaica's Bustamante. In 1955 an otherwise friendly Washington still felt forced to assert that his political arm was "ostensibly a labor party drawing major support from the Bustamante Industrial Trade Union, the largest in Jamaica," but "in reality it has been a conservative party representing the point of view and supported by the business and propertied interests"—and it had "attracted more than its share of unprincipled persons."[33] "I am very sorry to hear of the attitude of the new labour movement in Jamaica," said Antigua's V. C. Bird, who soon was to be similarly accused.[34]

Likewise in Trinidad, the bludgeoning of the left created space for the resurgence of the messianic "Buzz" Butler, who by "methods of violence, intimidation and threats" was able to secure a foothold. London was pleased that he was "at pains to denounce Communism" and happy that he "has become more moderate in his public utterances," yet, as they saw it, no unionism was better than any kind of unionism. For it was an "open secret that for some time the Government had been concerned at the spread of Communist ideas and methods. The Trade Union Council (which included two of the principal unions) still remained affiliated to the Communist-run World Federation of Trade Unions." London was displeased when "the President General of the [Oilfield Workers' and Federated Workers' Union] had returned from behind the 'Iron Curtain' and was publicly expressing the greatest admiration for the Soviet system, and added to this, the events in British Guiana had greatly intensified the apprehension that, if not checked, Communist propaganda, overt and covert, would result in a very dangerous situation." "[W]hat has given more concern to the Government has been the association of trade union leaders—notably of the Oilfield Workers' and Federated Workers' Union—with the WIIP [West Indian Independence Party]," a "party, which it is alleged, not without evidence, is Communist inspired and to a large extent directed. The WIIP was inaugurated in 1952 after the return of several Trinidadians from visits to Communist countries and conferences."[35] This lean to the left was seen as a trend to be blocked, with little attention paid to either the impact on the living standards of workers or the trends that might arise to replace the one to be halted.

But as the examples of Dominica and St. Lucia suggested, the harsh conditions workers had to endure compelled deeper thought—and action—irrespective of the absence of militant models. Thus, despite the setbacks, labor in St. Vincent was able to mount one offensive after another. For it was in 1950, as recalled later by the island's contemporary leader, Ralph Gonsalves, that

Ebenezer Joshua and George Charles "returned from Trinidad to found the Eighth Army of Liberation—a political grouping which won all eight seats to the Legislature in the first elections under universal adult suffrage. The basis for the electoral mobilization was Charles' union," and "in two successive elections (1951 and 1954) Joshua won in that constituency," victories propelled by his leadership of a strike "at Mt. Bentick in 1950." From 1951 to 1956 "he called yearly strikes in the sugar belt" and "in the political and trade union fields Joshua and his working class supporters were on one side. On the other were the planters, the colonialists, sell-out union leaders . . . and sections of the middle class."[36] Joshua was accused of being a communist, though his Peoples Political Party was widely influential on the island and had a membership of about 3,000, no small number on such a small island.[37] Joshua incited passions to the point that in 1953 one Vincent Sardine issued a "sworn statement" to the effect that he had received "instructions of assassinating" him.[38] "Since this threat on my life was made," said the besieged leader, "my house is guarded night and day by faithful comrades."[39]

Joshua had also worked in Aruba with "Buzz" Butler and, marked by that experience, "began his meetings with a hymn and a prayer and because of this practice he was accepted by peasants and workers," and his charisma was such that "it became customary for him to address the public alone for more than three hours." Ultimately he became chief minister of the nation that became St. Vincent and the Grenadines, but he "died alone in relative obscurity,"[40] unable to fulfill the promise he had exhibited. This was not least because militant redistributive policies were hard to execute in such a small country, particularly when many of its neighbors—particularly Barbados, British Guiana, Jamaica, and Trinidad—were not moving in that direction, as advocated by the CLC.

Simultaneously, London was becoming gravely concerned with the activities of African Americans in the region, and not just the likes of Ferdinand Smith, for even Randolph was hardly opposed to independence. This apprehension sheds light on why a British agent was to be found in early 1951 at Lincoln University in Pennsylvania, a historically black institution, which like many of its counterparts had "students from British West Africa." His "confidential" report betrayed concern about the "considerable interest in African affairs amongst sections of Negro opinion in the United States." This was "quite apart from Communist organizations such as the Council on African Affairs," for London's man, Arthur Galsworthy, was "struck in New York by the amount of interest in African affairs and, indeed, colonial affairs generally shown by the 'Amsterdam News,'" the weekly that targeted African American readers. This interest was spilling over into the halls and rostrums of this journal's neighbor: the United Nations. London "strongly opposed" an anticolonial resolution there, while Washington's delegate—Edith Sampson, an African American—did not, though her government abstained. A fellow member of her delegation, John Sherman Cooper, "was horrified when told he could not vote in favour of the resolution. His desire to do so stemmed apparently from what he considered would be the consequences on Negro opinion in his own state" of Kentucky. Galsworthy found it "rather amusing to see how, when the vote was taken, Senator Cooper solemnly left the [U.S.] seat" and "put in it instead, to go through the motions of abstaining, one of his official advisers behind whom he took his seat. After the vote had been taken, Senator Cooper resumed the [U.S.] seat."

Yet one point was deadly serious. "One thing is very clear," said Galsworthy, "that the trend could have the makings of another Israel situation. There are already the beginnings of a move to instill into the minds of United States Negroes the idea that Africa is their motherland and her fight is their fight. I do feel that this trend will require very careful watching." He was correct. For as African Americans began to gain full suffrage, they expressed at the ballot box as much contempt for colonialism as the voters of British Guiana had when they finally received the opportunity to vote. This did not bode well for the future of the British Empire, which theretofore had ruled over a good deal of the British West Indies and Africa.[41]

London had to worry over the continuing encroachment in the region of its erstwhile partner in Washington, which considered the Caribbean jealously as part of its precious backyard. "U.S. capitalists control extraction of bauxite, gypsum, copper, iron ore, oil (except in Trinidad) and other rare minerals" in the region, asserted the British Communist Party, "ousting even British capital."[42] "Americans have purchased a number of plantations," said V. C. Bird of Antigua as the war in Korea was being launched. "They employ between 400 and 500 workers," a considerable number on such a small island, but "these workers are all members of the Antigua Trades and Labour Union but the Americans refuse to recognize the Union."[43]

Simultaneously, as the second half of the twentieth century unfolded, the United States was considering importing "some 400,000 farm workers" from the region, mostly for the fields of Florida.[44] They were being dispatched to an uncertain fate, for in the critical year of 1953, U.S. investigative journalist Stetson Kennedy reported that in the Sunshine State "not only has forced labour increased tremendously, but the violence employed to enforce it has been intensified. The forced labourer who has not been beaten with a pistol, club or lash is a rarity."[45] U.S. agents continued to recruit Jamaicans, particularly to work in their nearby colonial appendage, the Panama Canal Zone. Many of these workers were "well trained and some of them [were] highly skilled," including "quite a few engineers, pharmacists, doctors trained in England." But the all-out assault of white supremacy did not cease in Central America. In a typical scene, "three girls were sitting in a row typing. One was white, the other two colored. The white girl was classified as a clerk, at $200 a month, the other two were 'office help' at $50 a month. In a silver roll commissary, colored men worked as butchers. They were classified as 'meat cutters' at $60 a month, while the white butchers, doing exactly the same work, earned $250 and $300 a month." The

"story [was] the same . . . on every job, on every level." The pestilence of white
supremacy was so severe that one analyst concluded that "the fight in the Canal
Zone . . . is a fight of people of the non-white races against a legally authorized
policy of ruthless exploitation and suppression on the basis of color alone"—and
"not basically between workers and employers."[46] It was in such a hothouse
environment that Marcus Garvey's movement had flourished.[47]

But the workers of the region did not have that many choices, for the decisive factor in the political economy of the British West Indies in the postwar era
was the decline of that which had been essential: the sugar industry. Mecha-
nization "and the consequent redundancy of labour on sugar plantations" was
the hallmark and, therefore, the "labour force was greatly reduced." This
occurred as labor became more concerned with anticommunist purges than the
fate of theretofore indispensable industries, a direct result of the assault on the
CLC. This was no minor matter. In Trinidad and Tobago, for example, "apart
from government, the sugar industry [was] the largest single employer in the
country." As late as 1977 "some 15,000 people" were "directly employed in the
industry while some 10,000 cane farmers derive[d] a livelihood from sugar cultivation. When one adds to that the number of persons employed in spin off
industries such as bagasse, molasses, rum distilleries, confectionery, soft drinks,
etc., the total employment resulting directly from sugar [was] estimated to be
well over 30,000 people," in a nation whose labor force was about 400,000.[48]

But as the sugar industry declined, the number of workers declined correspondingly. Thus, after the induced collapse of the Jagan regime, the Communist Party of Great Britain noted that "in fact, during the last war and to an even
greater extent since, the exploitation of the colonial peoples has been great[ly]
intensified. Their living standards have been further depressed and Britain's
indebtedness to the colonies has mounted." In Jamaica, "out of a population of
1,340,000 no less than 200,000 were estimated unemployed in 1951. Hunger
stalks the land. There are no Unemployment Insurance schemes. Wages are low.
Mothers rarely have milk to give their children."[49]

Administratively and economically, the region was treated as a unit and this
fact was never more clear than at times of labor unrest, when employers realized that if, say, sugar production declined in Trinidad, it could be escalated in
St. Lucia. When the CLC declined, these maneuvers became more prevalent.[50]

So workers from the British West Indies continued to disperse, and in 1956
Norman Manley asked his ideological soul mate, A. Philip Randolph, to assist
in increasing the number of Jamaicans allowed to migrate to the United States
to toil as exploited farm laborers. Randolph then observed that there was a
"drastic reduction in the number of Jamaican workers employed on farms in the
United States, while at the same time the number of Mexican workers has been
increased to a peak of 400,000 during the period British West Indian workers
were cut back 87$\frac{1}{2}$%." Thus, he wanted the U.S. Labor Department to
deploy "British West Indian workers . . . instead of Mexican labor in all states

east of the Mississippi River." This was a "capital suggestion," he thought, since "unemployment" was "growing in Jamaica." Neither Randolph nor Manley contemplated if the benefit received for hopping on the Cold War bandwagon was worth it.[51]

Randolph had more authority in the U.S. Virgin Islands than in Jamaica but, apparently, had little clout there either. The leader of labor there, Earle B. Ottley, complained to Randolph about the "almost hopeless situation in St. Croix. The AFL-CIO island union on that island, although in existence for 13 years, has a paid up membership of only 11 as of last week," he announced mournfully in late 1958. "In St. John where the Rockefeller interests are the principal employers, there is no union at all." He requested "financial help," even a "competent organizer," but Randolph was hardly able to comply, which meant— a fortiori—that he was at a similar loss when it came to assisting Jamaica.[52]

Fleeing in various directions from the penury that gripped the British West Indies, laborers were also migrating in greater numbers to the United Kingdom after the war. This influx was not embraced by all in London, as one influential voice suggested instead that so-called "over-population in the West Indian islands" should be solved by "transfer of people from those islands to the two continental colonies, British Guiana and British Honduras."[53] The influx arrived in Europe nonetheless; this had accelerated in the early 1940s when "over 8000 service men and women from the Caribbean and many skilled technicians who had come to work in the munitions factories" arrived. Predictably, "in 1948 in Liverpool there were attacks on the Black community. Many people were injured or arrested after the Seamen's Union tried to bar Black seamen from working in British ports." All told "between 1948 and 1958 over 125,000 people from the Caribbean came to settle in Britain."[54] An "Information Booklet for Intending Emigrants to Britain," prepared in Barbados, sought to prepare these sojourners for what awaited them, observing "you may, for instance, be asked to do work which in Barbados you would think was beneath you." And, yes, "you will find that the people in the United Kingdom are less inclined to join you in conversation than your own people in Barbados."[55] The remittances of these workers were helping to keep their homelands afloat financially but, inexorably, many of these shamelessly exploited laborers in Florida, the Canal Zone, and London were hardly predisposed to accept the self-descriptions of the United States and Britain as the exemplars of human rights and virtue given their own degraded status.

Caribbean laborers were also fleeing to the United States itself, to the point that by 1955 a "Congressional committee . . . advised . . . not to admit more immigrants from the over-populated British West Indies, from which more than 10,000 Negroes left for Britain last year . . . the United States admits 800 migrants from the West Indies yearly."[56] London was understanding as to why Washington might not want to admit more of its "subjects." "The fact is," said a "confidential letter" from Whitehall, "would-be immigrants are all in practice

Negroes. It seems to us very understandable that Americans would want to limit the flow of Negro immigrants where practicable." The "subject is especially touchy at the moment," it was said in September 1955, "because the Negro problem in the United States has been brought more into the limelight by the efforts to desegregate the schools. Nor does it make much sense to argue that West Indians should continue to be admitted under the U.K. quota, since in fact their race raises a problem which immigration from the British isles does not." This question of immigration "should not be confused with bringing in West Indian labour under contract to work for a period of years and then returning to their own countries."[57]

Echoing this outlook, one U.K. newspaper noted that the "American Negro population is growing, and while it is evidently not growing fast enough to make the farming and agricultural states independent of imported seasonal labour, a substantial increase in the annual number of coloured permanent immigrants could only too easily raise an outcry which might arrest the liberalizing influences at work for the Negro population as a whole. It has to be remembered that the U.S.'s experience with immigrant coloured people has not been entirely satisfactory." But what of migration to the United Kingdom itself? This was "causing difficulties in many parts of the country" and the "disquiet shows no signs of abating."[58] So West Indian labor simply had to stew at home, blocked as they were from pursuing radical CLC/PPP-style remedies and blocked from migrating.

Reciprocally, the British West Indies kept a close eye on Black America, which—by the same token—did not augur well for Washington's empire of Jim Crow. In St. Kitts, Washington was "warned" that "injustice to Negroes may lead to communism."[59] Kittitians were aghast when "Municipal Judge Frank Myers ruled . . . that Washington restaurants are within their legal right when they refuse to serve Negroes."[60] Like others in the region, those of St. Kitts had high hopes for Black America and its potential political impact. Though they were "fourth class citizens in their own country, they are of first class importance in the world-wide movement to halt that march toward war," and they were "the key to the country's economy." As one journal in Basseterre saw it, "if Negroes stopped work the whole American nation would be at a standstill." Thus, following the path blazed by Paul Robeson, the question was posed that many in the United States would have preferred to avoid: "[W]ould the Negroes fight in a war against the Soviet Union? It is a question which Negroes are asking themselves. And more and more of them are answering with an emphatic 'NO.'"[61]

It was not easy for those predisposed to Washington's policies to be in total sympathy with the United States. An example arose when Norman Washington Manley of Jamaica received a "U.S. apology" after the Department of Justice "detained him at Ellis Island for 'security reasons' for nine hours on his arrival from England." Why such maltreatment for one who was willing to back U.S. policies that were not universally supported in the region? "A letter had been sent to U.S. Immigration officials from Jamaica 'suggesting that he was a Communist and a bad person to allow in the country.'" This infelicitous incident occurred after the eminent Manley had "represented the Vicks Vapour Company in a case before the Privy Council, the highest court in the British Empire."[62] Even Grantley Adams, who eventually was to be knighted for his service to the Empire, was compelled to endure "racial discrimination . . . whilst in Canada." He too was in transit, arriving in Montreal en route from London to Barbados. He was booked at the Windsor Hotel, "the hotel to which distinguished visitors are usually sent." But "on arrival at the hotel he was refused admission on racial grounds and spent the night elsewhere."[63]

This was the thanks accorded Manley and Adams after they had done so much for the Empire. After all, Adams had become a key man in the attempt to blunt the labor-left offensive in the region. "I did have some talk with him about the growing Communist threat in the Caribbean," said one British official in a "secret and personal" report, who found his interlocutor to be "sensible and thoughtful." "I am hopeful, however, that I have been able to reinforce Adams' own anxieties about the trend of events in the West Indies generally."[64] Thus, this Canadian incident provided "excellent feeding grounds for Communist propaganda," complained one newspaper in Barbados.[65]

Similarly it did not augur well for the Empire when one of the more conservative U.S. senators—George Malone, a Republican from Nevada and the "extreme right wing of the Republican Party"—"said that he would probably choose Communism in preference to 'bondage' if he live[d] in one of the colonial empires." It was a "repulsive slavery system," he thought.[66]

Yet with all of this mushrooming opposition to its colonial misrule, London did have some advantages, not least being squabbling among those of the British West Indies themselves. This was not only on the ideological level, as represented by the contrasting figures of Grantley Adams and Cheddi Jagan. It reached down to the grassroots. One of the problems that ensued when West Indian workers began migrating to the United States was the fracases that at times erupted between them. One incident "arose when a plate of soup was spilled accidentally by a Barbadian on a Jamaican. This caused the usual hot words, grew like a snowball and approximately 250 were involved. There was a lot of stone throwing and revolver shots allegedly fired by the Jamaicans and the fracas lasted approximately two hours when the police came in and quelled it." This was "the result of an old time feud between Barbadian and Jamaican workers," and there was "nationwide press and radio publicity given to the disturbance. It was in practically every newspaper and over every radio station in the country." Now it was acknowledged that the workers were "restless" and "idle and everyone is anxious to leave for home immediately" and were a "keg of dynamite," but the "divide and conquer" tactic that was alluded to with regard to the internal politics of British Guiana was also an interisland phenomenon[67]— though, fortunately, "the Bahamians were not involved in this fracas."[68] "I know well the difficulties which exist perennially between Jamaicans and Barbadians," said the African American publisher, Claude Barnett, but even he was taken aback by the ferocity of some of their quarrels.[69]

Thus, in the pivotal year of 1953 the government of Trinidad "prohibited non-Trinidadians from entering or remaining in the colony to engage in any of 147 occupations." This had a particularly noxious impact on Jamaica, which had "almost half the British Caribbean's population" and "in the best of times has a fourth to a fifth of its workers unemployed." The "situation in Barbados particularly disturbs nearby Trinidad," according to a U.S. intelligence report, since the former "has one of the densest agricultural populations in the world, over 1500 per square mile." These islands "badly need some external outlets." Federation would have facilitated this, just as unemployed workers in Michigan could move to Texas, but an equivalent was not easy to attain in the British West Indies. "Cuba and Central America are no longer outlets and most South American countries prefer Europeans." There was British Guiana and British Honduras, but the former was in turmoil and the latter "distrust the islanders." There was "no prospect of British Honduras joining a West Indian federation [soon]," as "half of the population" were of "Spanish, Caribbean and Mayan derivation" and had "no interest in British West Indian affairs." A "much graver threat" to the region, it was said, "is the increasing group consciousness of the East Indians in Trinidad," which was heightened after one of their own—Jagan—was treated so shabbily. On the other hand, "East Indians in British Guiana have presented a much less united front than those in Trinidad."

Thus, the "influential 'Daily Gleaner' of Kingston, Jamaica claimed that East Indians in Trinidad and British Guiana envisaged an Asian West Indies of Trinidad and British Guiana and an African West Indies of the remainder, a partition like that which took place in India." Meanwhile, "for years the white group, which has dominated business and politics, opposed federation and talked grandiloquently of British Guiana's 'continental destiny.'" They were "mostly of Portuguese origin" and, perhaps naturally, longed for closer association with British Guiana's powerful southern neighbor, Brazil.[70] Kingston had a "large well-to-do Jewish population" that also was not necessarily enthusiastic about alterations of a colonial order that had not disadvantaged them.[71]

The colonialists looked longingly to British Guiana and British Honduras as their all-purpose remedy to decline in the British West Indies, moving "redundant" workers to South and Central America as if they were crops to be marketed. But the nation that was to become Belize was hardly welcoming to this idea—or the proposed migrants. The *Daily Gleaner* of Kingston cited one Jamaican as wondering, "I wonder why there is a prejudice against Jamaicans" in British Honduras. "[T]he opposition in British Honduras to federation is really an extravagant expression of suspicion of Jamaica immigration. It is mixed up too with Latin American influence."[72] "One of their main objections to federation," it was said of British Honduras, "is the prospect of BWI Negroes (particularly

Jamaicans)" moving there. "[T]hey are not keen on having Negroes from anywhere; if they could overnight rinse themselves white they would do it." Of
course, British Honduras rolled out the red carpet for Mennonites of European
extraction.[73] It could have been added that the colonized had learned well from
the colonizer in imbibing biases against the darker-skinned. But this Central
American colony should have been welcoming virtually any that chose to move
there, for it faced a serious long-term threat to its territorial integrity from neighboring Guatemala.[74] Besides, steamily hot and terribly underdeveloped, it "has
always been the Cinderella colony," as the *Gleaner* put it. "[F]ifty or sixty years
ago a man who was offered the post of Governor there, simply declined on the
ground that [British Honduras] would be 'the end of everything.'"[75]

   Obviously, to ascribe some of the retrograde attitudes of British Honduras
solely to the denizens there would be an error, given the suffocating reach of
colonialism. Months after the overthrow of Jagan, the colonizers were seeking
to "secure election of the National Party and Independents" over a contending
force, assuming that the former would be friendly to colonialism.[76] London was
pleased when a group of workers backed the ICFTU and, "like . . . the rest of
the free world," decided "to condemn Communism, red or white, with all our
hearts." But the problem faced by London was reflected in their accompanying
statement that "because of our bitter experience, we condemn colonialism in
almost the same breath as communism."[77]

EPILOGUE

B Y THE CRUCIAL YEAR of 1953 the British West Indies by one definition had a total population of 2.8 million, with Jamaica—the largest
island—containing about 1.5 million inhabitants, whereas Montserrat
had only 13,000; the thirteen islands comprised approximately 8,000 square
miles, of which 4,700 were in Jamaica, 2,000 in Trinidad, and 1,300 divided
among the other eight territories. (Of course, British Guiana, with a land mass
of 83,000 square miles, was only slightly smaller than Great Britain.) Their gross
national product amounted to about 230 million pounds, perhaps $500 million,
with Jamaica comprising about half of this total. The average per capita income
of the islands was about 69 pounds, with Trinidad—the richest—having a per
capita income of 121 pounds, Barbados about 79, and Jamaica 73. In contrast
the United Kingdom had a per capita income of 312 and the United States
about 846—suggesting once more that the colonizers were more adept at fighting communism than bringing a better life to the colonized. The colonies of the
British West Indies lurched toward independence in the postwar era, Jamaica
arriving at this exalted status in 1962, St. Kitts-Nevis in 1967, Antigua-Barbuda
in 1981, etc. A form of federation had arrived finally in 1958 but quickly disappeared by 1961, as Jamaica voted to secede, affirming the idea—as Trinidad's
Eric Williams put it—that "one from ten leaves nought."[1]

It was hard for a farsighted notion like anticolonial federation with labor in
the driver's seat to take flight when the region had been crippled ideologically
by the compelled purge of the left, as symbolized by the Caribbean Labour
Congress (CLC), which had been in the vanguard of advocating this now abandoned ideal.

It had been an ignominious end to an idea, federation, that as "early as
1856 . . . became a subject of discussion in the West Indies"[2] and that had been

"in the air since 1867" in various forms, such as a "loose grouping of the Leeward Islands" in 1871 and an attempt to forge a Windward group in 1885. The other blow to the labor-left—the deposing of Cheddi Jagan—had been as detrimental to the fate of federation, if not more so, than the decline of the CLC. It did appear that many among the South Asian majority in British Guiana interpreted the toppling of their favorite son as an ethnic as much as a political blow, and the apostasy of the African, Forbes Burnham, who broke with the People's Progressive Party (PPP) and rose to power on a wave of violence and authoritarianism that targeted this majority, added credence to their supposition. Thus, federation was interpreted negatively by some South Asians. As a study commissioned by the Communist Party of Great Britain in 1956 put it, "those of Indian descent fear they would be but a tiny minority in a federation." A similar sentiment arose in Trinidad. Yet even in Barbados, there were "mixed feelings" about federation, though it was viewed as an "avenue for its surplus population." But some among the potent European minority were leery, seeing their power possibly dissolve as more Africans became part of the same political unit they occupied. In Dominica there was opposition as even trade union leaders felt that the current configuration of federation would benefit the larger units at the expense of the smaller.

Bravely, Janet Jagan responded that "our stand of federation has been the same [as] the Caribbean Labour Congress stand for many years," though she acknowledged frankly that "feeling is unusually high against federation amongst the masses."[3] Years after this complex chapter in Caribbean history had concluded, Cheddi Jagan restated the PPP viewpoint which backed federation northward, as well as federation with "other countries surrounding us." "I have heard arguments both for and against federation," he conceded, with "some championing the cause of continental destiny and pointing out that we are as far from Jamaica as Africa is [sic] and so on; others emphasizing that we are on the South American continent and have nothing to do with the West Indies from a geographical point of view." However, he acknowledged—albeit obliquely—the apprehension concerning federation harbored by some South Asians.[4]

The split in British Guiana that took on ethnic overtones—personalized in the outsized figures of Jagan and Forbes Burnham—had a tremendously negative impact on the region, hampering the forging of working-class unity. Burnham "would subsequently receive British and U.S. assistance in his struggle against Jagan"—which tipped the balance decisively against the PPP. The "effort to discredit and undermine Jagan reached another plane when prominent West Indian nationalist leaders, including [Grantley] Adams, [Norman] Manley and Albert Gomes of Trinidad and Tobago, visited British Guiana in mid-1955 and publicly criticized the PPP leadership for leaning toward communism," according to the scholar Gordon Oliver Daniels.[5] British Guiana was the largest unit territorially in the region and Trinidad and Tobago was the richest, with ample oil and gas reserves, and both had substantial South Asian populations—and similar problems. For in the latter nation, "the scenario of an African-dominated and urban-based grouping in political power and an East Indian rural-based grouping in political opposition characterized Trinidadian politics from 1956 to 1986 with obvious implications for race relations." The "elections of 1961 had brought the country to the brink of racial war," while the rise of "Black Power"— which flourished in soil where class-based alliances had been weakened—further complicated this complex ethnic picture. "[T]he irony was," says the writer D. V. Trotman, "that demands for African cultural revival [were made] against a government hitherto seemingly enjoying the benefit of undisputed racial allegiance." As he saw it, this disturbing picture was reflected in a popular cultural export—calypso—wherein South Asians were routinely painted as clannish or reactionaries, or ignored. Similarly, the other popular export—steel-band music—"painted out" the South Asian, as artists often sang of "black and white" as if they were in Mississippi.[6]

Trinidad and Tobago was a nation (unlike the other major nations: Barbados, British Guiana, and Jamaica) where a party rose to power—headed by the academic, Eric Williams—that did not grow out of the labor movement. Ironically, Albert Gomes, who had done so much to sideline CLC and labor forces generally, was a primary victim of this process. According to his sister, Isabella Goddard, "Bertie"—as he was known—"was hounded down by fanatical supporters of the then government after the 1956 victory. He could not even visit his mother in Belmont. His car would be pelted, we had feces thrown at our house. He was tormented. He was jeered and called 'Big Belly Gomes'. Bertie was hunted to the point of having to flee his native country to save his sanity."[7] This occurred though the 300-pound politico "was a defender of and identified readily with the black grass-root art forms of steelband music." His "political spectrum was as broad as his massive girth. It encompassed espousing Marxist and Socialist ideas through Liberalism and ended up in ultra-Conservative [ideas] and a rabid anti-communis[m]." Perversely, the latter "no doubt helped in diminishing his popularity with the masses," and, thus "tormented," he "fled his homeland."[8] Eric Williams—who in another irony pioneered the uncovering of black history then was later hounded himself by Black Power advocates— was Gomes's chief tormenter.[9] Also, ironically, Gomes, who attended City College of New York, wrote movingly about the persecution of African Americans, as he was repulsed and shocked by their treatment in the United States.[10] Gomes, a former Greek-style wrestler of some merit who went on to smoke cigars and pipes in profusion,[11] eventually went into exile in England,[12] but he retained a lingering bitterness of what had befallen him,[13] perhaps not realizing that the decline of the labor-left, which he once boosted, may have had something to do with his unfortunate plight.

For Gomes, the fall had been precipitous. He was one of Trinidad and Tobago's top leaders from 1950 to 1956—known then for his pugnacity and feared as a debater and political wrestler, not to mention his fourteen children—before the rise of Williams. His fall and Williams's rise also accompanied the dissolution of federation, which left him angry. "No single West Indian territory," he cried, "possesses the human or material resources to maintain independence as a distinct and separate entity." During the debate prior to dissolution, he vowed that he "would leave the West Indies" if federation were dissolved. Gomes, who entered the trade union movement in 1937, kept his promise.[14]

Climbing over a politically prostrate Gomes, Eric Williams—a "small man with heavy dark glasses and a hearing aid"—became the embodiment of independent Trinidad and Tobago. Born in 1911, the son of a civil servant, he was seen as "logical, receptive, discursive" and had spent a considerable amount of time in the United States in the epicenter of racial segregation: Washington, D.C. He was said to have a "deeply emotional anti-Americanism" that was "generally attributed to some traumatic experience involving [the] colour bar" in that superpower. He "suffered humiliation in Britain too," said one of his nation's major organs, "but does not feel the same measure of antipathy towards the British."[15]

Washington did not agree. Williams "does not impress me as a radical," said one unnamed U.S. diplomat in a "confidential" 1947 report. "[H]e informed me he found less color discrimination in the United States (Washington, D.C.) than in Trinidad or England, despite the fact that he is not able to enter the Mayflower Hotel and certain other places in the United States."[16]

Whatever the case, Williams was a brilliant scholar, though "in his later years he was clearly suffering from a touch of paranoia and seemed to trust few, if any, people." He "seldom entertained," but was a "poker player"—a skill that may have been helpful when he engaged in high-stakes negotiations with Washington over the fate of their military base.[17] Yet a founding member of Williams's Peoples National Movement—Ferdi Ferreira—felt that his "number one weakness" was his "over-sensitivity and suspicious nature." He was "always on his guard" and "always on the look-out for motives," and, "like J. Edgar Hoover, he would wave 'the file' which he had on everybody."[18] His nervousness assumed new heights when he "banned his own books."[19]

The taciturn Williams "spoke as little as possible to the press. At cocktail parties it was even worse. He would go into the corner and stay there the whole evening until it was time to go home." Not only did Williams "not suffer fools gladly. He does not suffer equals gladly," for "when you talk with him, you are on his wavelength alone; talk becomes a monologue because, quite simply, he knows that he knows all. His hearing-aid is just an alibi for that habit. He talks at you, not with you. He is the world's worst conversationalist. He lacks completely the gift of small talk."[20]

For his part, Williams had a well-honed sense of mission. "West Indians had traditionally deserted the West Indies—Padmore for Africa, [C.L.R.] James for the absurdities of world revolution"—while Williams chose to fight the good fight against colonialism at home.[21] Yet Robert Bradshaw of St. Kitts was unsparing in declaring that "despite the fact that the majority of people here and abroad blamed" Jamaica "for the collapse of the Federation, I have said and will ever maintain that Dr. [Eric] Williams did more to break up the Federation than did anybody else."[22]

Thus, to his credit, it was Williams who spearheaded the profoundly important struggle to oust the United States from its base of "8000 scenic acres on Trinidad's northeast peninsula,"[23] which Washington viewed as the "Gibraltar of the Caribbean" and critical to the nation's security.[24] The momentum created by this Trinidad and Tobago struggle no doubt positively influenced St. Lucia's successful attempt in 1960 to compel the United States to return "1700 acres" it had obtained from the colonial power in 1941,[25] which in turn had an impact on the effort by Antigua to oust Washington from its soil.[26]

Though Washington was being pushed out of its vast array of military bases, it remained an ominous and forceful presence in the Caribbean. Simultaneously, London was engaged in a headlong retreat. "One of the consequences of the decision to decolonize," said Richard Hart, who felt it necessary to go into exile in London, "was that the British government had to inform British manufacturers that the market for their products in the former colonies could no longer be preserved for them . . . one way or another the traditional imperialist policy of restricting industrialization of the former colonies would have to be abandoned"[27]—and one way or another the United States would seek to fill the vacuum. For tiny territories in the absence of federation were susceptible to being masticated and swallowed by the United States. They remained caught between the Scylla of London and the Charybdis of Washington, even as independence loomed. As early as 1949 a St. Kitts writer peering across the Caribbean Sea noticed that "devaluation of [the pound] must produce inflation in an island like Antigua that is so dependent on North America for such very essential supplies as food, lumber for shelter, clothing. When inflation is coupled with mass unemployment, discontent must rear its head and be manifest everywhere."[28]

Bustamante, the big winner when the CLC was battered and Jagan dislodged, wielded his newly enhanced authority by opposing federation, feeling that the smaller islands would be parasites on the host that was Jamaica. He had never been a fan of federation, stressing the palpable differences between the territories. "Jamaica can walk," he emphasized, but "Trinidad is creeping. Barbados and British Guiana are right behind Trinidad or almost the same. St. Kitts and St. Vincent are attempting to creep and only attempting. Antigua is creeping, and of all the other small islands, some can barely creep on the palm of their hands, and others on hands and feet, and others not at all, yet you say to us, 'we want to federate.' How can the walking and creeping and the babe who has not begun to creep yet, how can they walk on the same avenue."[29] Bustamante's anticommunism wore well in London and Washington, and he may have been the biggest regional victor when the CLC was destroyed and Jagan overthrown.

So, consistent with past regional patterns, Jamaica set the pace that others followed, and when the Social Democrat, Manley, felt compelled to sign on to the anticommunist crusade, in a real sense that spelled disaster for both Jagan and the CLC.[30] Yet it was hard to see what material benefits Jamaica derived from this decision—unless one counts perversely the resultant Dickensian conditions in Kingston's ghettoes that produced two of its principal global exports: reggae protest music and Rastafarianism. But even here there was a connection to Washington, for as the Constabulary in Kingston noted in 1967 when these linked phenomena of music and religion were about to take off, "the Rastafari cult [sic] in Jamaica was started in 1933 by a man named Leonard Percival Howell," who "went to the United States of America (USA) in 1916 and was a member of the United States Army Transport Service until 1923. Subsequently he traveled to South America, France and Abyssinia." At that juncture, "as far as can be determined," there were "some nineteen hundred Rastafarites [sic] throughout the island." But even here there was a link to the left, as Richard Hart had "defended" one of their members in Montego Bay and "won the case, no doubt gathering considerable prestige."[31]

Yet neither the left that Hart represented nor the rising Rastas were the dominant factors in the British West Indies' most populous nation. Increasingly, that honorific was accorded to Washington and its local allies. Thus, from the deposing of Jagan in 1953 to 1956, the United Steelworkers of America—which like most U.S. unions had resourcefully and systematically purged communists— "subsidized" the trade union arm of Manley's party "by paying the salary of Ken Sterling, its bauxite-alumina workers organizer," but that did not halt the steady decline in the standard of living of Jamaican workers.[32]

Certainly when Manley's son—Michael Manley—came to power in the 1970s, he faced some of the same dilemmas (and endured some of the same modes of destabilization) that had faced Jagan in 1953. For Michael Manley too had to endure bitterly contentious relations with the powerful, in his case the potent transnational corporation, Kaiser Aluminum,[33] which also operated in Yugoslavia, Venezuela, Colombia, Mexico, and Peru[34]—thus underlining that the CLC's idea of worker solidarity across geographic boundaries was simple common sense when management did the same as a rudimentary matter of conducting business. Kaiser also mined bauxite in British Guiana and kept a close eye on developments there. "[O]ur sources report that Burnham has no Communist leanings as does Jagan," the company was told in 1964, and "Africans are more aggressive and show a willingness to cooperate with the opposition party." Thus "it is anticipated"—as it turns out, correctly—"that in the next five to ten years Jagan will be completely out of the picture in British Guiana."[35] Kaiser, based in California, was able to draw upon confidential briefings from then Central Intelligence Agency chief John McCone in figuring out events in the region. "[I] enjoyed lunching with you and appreciated the opportunity of visiting," remarked Edgar Kaiser after an intimate tête-à-tête in 1964 "at the

McCone residence."[36] The "briefing session on British and French Guiana, Surinam and Jamaica which you so kindly arranged . . . presented a most informative picture of the political and economic situations in each of the countries," McCone was told. This intelligence would prove "helpful to [Kaiser] in forming a judgment of the supply of bauxite in the world market, with particular reference to the situation in this area."[37] With such formidable foes, Jamaica was outnumbered and outgunned, but it could have moved to redress the imbalance somewhat if it had stayed the course with the CLC.

The decline of labor-left forces also had a detrimental impact on Antigua, where V. C. Bird had been deemed part of this progressive bloc. But this soon was to change as he could merely look southward to British Guiana and espy what befell those who bucked the Cold War consensus. Most famously, with the staunch aid of Richard Hart and the CLC, Bird and his followers "broke Moody-Stuart and the planters" in a tempestuous 1951 strike.[38] Born in one of his nation's "worst slums"[39]—"abominable living conditions" with "bad and congested housing, dirt track roads, no pipe-borne water, no electricity"[40]— consistent with the times, he rapidly moved to the right. Though he had once been close to Hart, often demonized as a communist, in Bird's Antigua, "opposition parties" were "never mentioned except to denounce them and to say that they are Communists and they have received money from Fidel Castro."[41]

The freckled Bird, whose face had numerous liver spots, gave birth to a political dynasty—or aviary—that featured his sons Vere, Jr. and Lester. Eventually Bird's face "appeared on the label of beer bottles and casino chips, his name on [the] international airport and his hands in everything." Antigua, once in tune with the region's boycott of apartheid South Africa, became notorious as a transshipment point for arms to this outlaw state. Antigua became a "place where, for the right price, one can buy everything from a diplomatic passport to a government minister." Perhaps not unrelated was the point that "no other English-speaking island in the eastern Caribbean has had a greater U.S. presence or received more U.S. dollars than Antigua." The nation had "virtually abandoned its sovereignty where the giant of the north is concerned . . . any aircraft belonging to the U.S. government can land on Antigua at any time of the day or night, without prior notice and without anyone on board having to go through Customs or Immigration." When Grenada moved in a revolutionary direction during the 1979–1983 era, it was Antigua that became the point of the spear aimed at the spice island. Yet many Antiguans remained grateful that Washington did "what Great Britain had never done: trained Antiguans in semi-technical and technical jobs [and] paid them fair salaries."[42]

Of course, the massive U.S. presence came with a price. "Since to the Americans any woman who was phenotypically white in Antigua was assumed to be socially suitable, they were immediately taken with the Portuguese women who, lacking the Antiguans' knowledge of their own history, they 'saw' as white. Much to the surprise of nonwhite middle-class Antiguans, a group they had considered their inferiors was suddenly being treated as superior. Thus the Americans bypassed the group that saw itself as appropriate on a class basis and chose instead a group that they saw as appropriate because of its color. To the dismay of the nonwhite middle class, the definition of 'white' suddenly shifted around them."[43]

Robert Bradshaw of St. Kitts may only have been marginally better than Bird. He had a fighter's face and a "clipped officer's moustache which gave him a grim, forbidding look."[44] Surely the political opposition in this Lilliputian territory found Bradshaw to be ill-omened, since "the Leader of the Opposition had been thrown into prison for opposing and [then] fled the country. Others, for no greater crime than writing a letter criticizing the government, have also been imprisoned." Fifteen years after Jagan's overthrow, Bradshaw was "not only Premier, but President of the Sugar Workers Union and at the same time control[led] the police." There were "two Mr. Bradshaws"—not in the sense that he found the time to occupy more than one full-time post, but in that he was at once an "elegant and urbane" bureaucrat and an "alarming . . . Mr. Hyde" comparable to the hideous Duvalier in Haiti.[45] Still, the champion in the tyrant of the Caribbean sweepstakes was most likely Grenada's Eric Gairy, with his penchant for UFOs and his ability to consume gargantuan amounts of champagne: "I never have less than four bottles in all on a Saturday night," he confessed.[46] He was dislodged by Maurice Bishop and his comrades in 1979, who would have had a better chance of remaining on course if Jagan had not been overthrown in 1953.

Eugenia Charles, the leader of independent Dominica, stood famously by the side of President Ronald Reagan as he launched an invasion of Grenada in 1983. This invasion was "often cited as a precedent for the Panama and Persian Gulf Wars of the 1990s" and "has been described as a turning point for American foreign policy, a shift from post-Vietnam restraint," induced by that staggering defeat in Southeast Asia in 1975. Her homeland was—and is—an enchanting land of mist-covered mountains, tumbling waterfalls and lush rainforests that abound with wildlife and rare orchids, while its socioeconomic makeup was far less pretty, given the "lingering preoccupation with skin color" and incomes dependent upon the vagaries of the banana market. Charles was unmarried and childless and, sadly, had "taken—and returned—more sex-related verbal abuse than any of the world's other female heads of government." Her father, who died in 1983 at the age of 107, was "influenced by the ideas" of George Washington Carver and Booker T. Washington and "for a time signed his name 'John-Baptiste George Washington Carver Charles.'" His pervasive influence on her hardly prepared her for Jim Crow when she visited Miami, but this did not sour her opinion of the United States—though later she said "she never wanted to set foot in the United States again." Unusually, the towering leader (she was five feet nine inches tall) had a long-term intimate liaison with a fellow political leader—Bradshaw—whose political trajectory resembled hers.[47]

This intimate tie between Charles and Bradshaw was emblematic of the increasingly closer relationships between and among the former colonies of the British West Indies. This was symbolized by CARICOM, or the Caribbean Community, which was moving toward a single market as the twenty-first century dawned. This was a belated recognition of the perception signaled by the CLC when decades earlier it trumpeted the virtues of labor rights, sovereignty, and federation of tiny islands and nations that were often overshadowed, if not dominated, by their powerful neighbor to the north. But CARICOM was enduring hard times with its signature crops of sugar and bananas. "Replace sugar and bananas with money from reggae and soca," blared one headline. "Sean Paul," a popular performer, "makes more money in sales than revenue from bananas,"[48] it was claimed—which, if true, was more of a comment on the parlous state of agricultural producers in a globalized economy where big capital—not small nations—reigned supreme.

Though sugar had been planted on the island for centuries, by 2006 St. Kitts had "stopped producing sugar" as the prices for it were falling, "while Trinidad and Barbados are planning eventually to get out of the sector as well, leaving Guyana, Jamaica and Belize as the only ones still producing in a region where sugar has been the king crop for 400 years."[49]

Guyana in particular could hardly abandon sugar, since today it is one of the poorest nations on the planet, an outgrowth of the punishment it had received for its temerity in electing a Marxist to high office in 1953. After the collapse of the Soviet Union, Cheddi Jagan returned to power, then his widow became that nation's first woman president in 1997, not long after her husband's death. Yet during my research visit there in 2005, I was able to witness that the ouster of Jagan in 1953 had done little to arrest Guyana's sad and tragic underdevelopment—and probably accelerated it.

What will befall the sugar and banana workers in the region, particularly given the anti-immigrant walls being thrown up in the United States and worldwide and the inability of Guyana or Belize to play their historic roles as safety valves, absorbing economic refugees? What Richard Hart and Cheddi Jagan pointed out decades ago as the region's central problem—the prices of commodities produced in the British West Indies were controlled largely in foreign capitals and tended to decline relative to the cost of finished goods (tractors, stoves, air-conditioners, etc.) that mostly had to be imported—has yet to be overcome. The fate of these workers is unclear, but what is evident is that it is hard to see how they benefited from the Cold War that afflicted the Hot Zone that is the former British West Indies.

REFERENCES

Introduction

1. Cheddi Jagan, *Forbidden Freedom: The Story of British Guiana* (London: Hansib Publications, Ltd., 1954).

2. *Daily Chronicle* (Georgetown), 14 October 1953.

3. Jagan, *Forbidden Freedom*, iii.

4. Gerald Horne, *Red Seas: Ferdinand Smith and Radical Black Sailors in the United States and Jamaica* (New York: New York University Press, 2005).

5. Minutes of Executive Council Meeting, 7 July 1953, National Archives of Guyana, Georgetown.

6. Minutes of Executive Council Meeting, 9 September 1953, National Archives of Guyana, Georgetown.

7. *TIME*, 1 June 1953.

8. Gordon Oliver Daniels, "A Great Injustice to Cheddi Jagan: The Kennedy Administration and British Guiana: 1961–1963" (Ph.D. dissertation, University of Mississippi, 2000), 88. See also Stephen G. Rabe, *U.S. Intervention in British Guiana: A Cold War Story* (Chapel Hill: University of North Carolina Press, 2005).

9. Cheddi Jagan, *A West Indian State: Pro-Imperialist or Anti-Imperialist?* (Georgetown: New Guyana, 1972), 6.

10. See e.g. Charles Mills, "Red Peril to the Green Island: The 'Communist Threat' to Jamaica in Genre Fiction, 1955–1969," *Caribbean Studies* 23 (Nos. 1 and 2, 1988): 141–165.

11. *New York Times*, 23 March 2006.

12. Daniels, "A Great Injustice to Cheddi Jagan," 36.

13. Gaylord T. M. Kelshall, *The U-Boat War in the Caribbean* (Annapolis, Md.: Naval Institute Press, 1994), xiii, xi.

14. "West Indies Conference," St. Thomas, U.S. Virgin Islands, 21 February 1946, Doc. 204 G/133, Hoover Institute, Stanford University. See also "American Foreign Service Journal," April 1952, Reel 7, No. 107, William Hastie Papers, University of North Carolina, Chapel Hill.

15. Frank McDonald, "The Commonwealth Caribbean," in *The United States and the Caribbean*, ed. Tad Szulc, 126–156, 127, 128 (Englewood Cliffs, N.J.: Prentice Hall, 1971).

See also Richard Hart to David Lewis, 27 February 1948, Richard Hart Papers–University of the West Indies, Jamaica. The British West Indies, said Hart, contained "111,000 square miles and the total population" was "just under 3 million." (Note: this collection of Hart materials is to be designated hereinafter as "Richard Hart Papers–UWI" and are to be distinguished from Hart materials at the Schomburg Center, the University of London, and elsewhere.)

16. W. Burghardt Turner and Joyce Moore Turner, eds., *Richard B. Moore: Caribbean Militant in Harlem* (Bloomington: Indiana University Press, 1988), 84; For a useful account of the CLC, see O. Nigel Bolland, "Democracy and Authoritarianism in the Struggle for National Liberation: The Caribbean Labour Congress and the Cold War, 1945–1952," *Comparative Studies of South Asia, Africa and the Middle East* 17 (No. 1, 1997): 99–117.

17. Tony Martin, "Eric Williams: His Radical Side in the Early 1940s," *Journal of Caribbean Studies* 17 (Nos. 1 and 2, Summer and Fall 2002): 107–119, 111.

18 *Crisis*, 34 (No. 8, October 1927): 264.

19. Nelson R. Park to U.S. Secretary of State, 7 December 1948, Record Group 84, Foreign Service Posts of the Department of State, Jamaica, Kingston Consulate, Confidential File, Box 8, National Archives and Records Administration, College Park, Maryland.

20. *Daily Gleaner* (Jamaica), 10 September 1947.

21. Lloyd W. Brown, "The American Image in British West Indian Literature," *Caribbean Studies* 11 (No. 1, April 1971): 30–45; Winston James, *Holding Aloft the Banner of Ethiopia: Caribbean Radicalism in Early Twentieth Century America* (New York: Verso, 1998).

22. Joyce Moore Turner, *Caribbean Crusaders and the Harlem Renaissance* (Champaign-Urbana: University of Illinois Press, 2005), 39, 121, 122, 81.

23. *Trinidad Guardian*, 2 November 1948.

24. Robert Alexander, ed., *Presidents, Prime Ministers and Governors of the English-Speaking Caribbean and Puerto Rico: Conversations and Correspondence* (Westport, Conn.: Praeger, 1997), 47. See also David Lowenthal, *The West Indies Federation: Perspectives on a New Nation* (New York: Columbia University Press, 1961).

25. Lennox Pierre and John La Rose, "For More and Better Democracy for a Democratic Constitution for Trinidad and Tobago," published by the West Indian Independence Party of Trinidad & Tobago, 1955, British Library, London.

26. George Padmore, "Hitler Makes British Drop Color Bar," *Crisis* 48 (No. 3, March 1941): 72–75, 82.

27. *Daily Gleaner*, 11 October 1960.

28. Sir Hesketh Bell, G.C.M.G., *Glimpses of a Governor's Life: From Diaries, Letters, and Memoranda* (London: Sampson Low & Marston, circa 1946), 27: "The influence which France is able to create in any territory in which she has established her authority, even for a few years is extraordinary."

29. Charles Whitaker to Ralph Moloney, 23 May 1946, RG 84, Box 3, Foreign Service Posts of the Department of State, British West Indies, Grenada Consulate, Security—Segregated General Records, 1944–1948, 1946–1948, National Archives and Records Administration, College Park, Maryland.

30. Alfie Roberts, *A View for Freedom: Alfie Roberts Speaks on the Caribbean, Cricket, Montreal and C.L.R. James* (Montreal: Alfie Roberts Institute, 2005), 43.

31. *Sunday Guardian* (St. Kitts), 29 September 1957.

32. Margaret Locket, *Antigua Then: Scenes from a West Indian Childhood* (Washington, D.C.: Antigua Press, n.d.), 53, 92.

33. *The Union Messenger* (St. Kitts), 31 May 1947.

34. Alec Waugh, article, 18 October 1952, Box 23, Marjorie Nicholson Papers, London Metropolitan University, North Campus.

35. Annette Palmer and Clement London, "Migratory Labor in the English Caribbean (1940–1945)," *Journal of Caribbean Studies* 5 (No. 3, Fall 1986): 199–215, 204, 206, 207.

36. "Confidential" Report from Henry Taylor, 28 November 1944, RG 84, Box 3, Foreign Service Posts of the Department of State, British West Indies, Grenada Consulate, Security—Segregated General Records, 1944–1948, 1946–1948, National Archives and Records Administration, College Park, Maryland.

37. William Dixon, *From Riots to Responsibility: History of the Barbados Workers' Union* (Barbados: BWU, 1991), 5, Barbados Public Library, Bridgetown.

38. Linda Basch, "Transnational Social Relations and the Politics of National Identity," in *Islands in the City: West Indian Migration to New York*, ed. Nancy Foner, 117–141, 124, 125, 134, 138 (Berkeley: University of California Press, 2001).

39. Minutes of Council and Assembly, 1942–1944, 25 April 1944, Barbados Department of Archives, Bridgetown.

40. Executive Committee Minutes, 15 May 1947, Barbados Department of Archives, Bridgetown.

41. Report, January 1938, Labour Party Archives, Manchester, U.K.

42. Newsletter of People's National Party, 12 December 1942, Labour Party Archives, Manchester, U.K.

43. Vilna F. Bashi Bobb and Averil Y. Clarke, "Experiencing Success: Structuring the Perception of Opportunities for West Indians," in Foner, *Islands in the City*, 216–236, 223.

44. *The Union Messenger*, 20 November 1947.

45. *Barbados Daily Nation*, 6 July 1989.

46. George Padmore, *The Life and Struggle of Negro Toilers* (London: Red International of Labor Unions for the International Trade Union Committee of Negro Workers, 1931), 57, British Library, London.

47. *Daily Gleaner*, 5 January 1970.

48. Quoted in Horne, *Red Seas*, 244.

49. James Walvin, "Sugar and the Shaping of Western Culture," in *White and Deadly: Sugar and Colonialism*, by Pal Ahluwalia et al., 21–31, 22 (Commack, N.Y.: Nova, 1999).

50. Robert Morris, "The Effects of the Great Depression," in *Emancipation: Aspects of the Post-Slavery Experience of Barbados*, ed. Woodville Marshall, 39–55, 46 (Bridgetown: National Cultural Foundation, 1988).

51. Ibid.; Horne, *Red Seas*, 244.

52. Karla Slocum, "Globalization, the Nation and Labour Struggles within St. Lucia's Banana Industry," in *Revisiting Caribbean Labour*, ed. Constance Sutton, 98–117, 102 (Kingston: Ian Randle, 2005).

53. Tough and complicated negotiations regularly occurred between the transnational corporations that controlled the bauxite industry and their Jamaican interlocutors. See Files 4/60/2a11; 12; and 13, Norman Manley Papers, National Archives of Jamaica, Spanishtown. On oil in Trinidad and the general question of resources in the region, see e.g. Jason Parker, "Ripples in the 'American Lake': The United States, Race and Empire in the British Caribbean, 1937–1962" (Ph.D. dissertation, University of Florida, 2002), 190, 192.

54. Odida T. Quamina, *Mineworkers of Guyana: The Making of a Working Class* (London: Zed, 1987), 17–18.

55. C. E. Davis, *Jamaica in the World Aluminum Industry, 1938–1973* (Kingston: Jamaica Bauxite Institute, 1989), 74.

56. C. Loblack to H. V. Tewson, 11 December 1951, 972.22/2, Trade Union Congress Papers, University of Warwick, U.K.

57. Susan Lowes, "The Peculiar Class: The Formation, Collapse and Reformation of the Middle Class in Antigua, West Indies, 1834–1940" (Ph.D. dissertation, Columbia University, 1994), 324, 327, 331. See also Harvey Neptune, *Caliban and the Yankee: Trinidad and the U.S. Occupation* (Chapel Hill: University of North Carolina Press, 2007).

58. Roberts, *A View for Freedom*, 29.

59. Richard Hart, "Trade Unionism in the English Speaking Caribbean: The Formative Years and the Caribbean Labour Congress," in *Contemporary Caribbean: A Sociological Reader*, ed. Susan Craig, 59–96, 84, 85, 86, 88 (Maracas, Trinidad and Tobago: College Press, 1981).

60. Sutton, *Revisiting Caribbean Labour*, ix.

61. Daniels, "A Great Injustice to Cheddi Jagan," 83.

Chapter 1

1. Paul Nehru Tennassee, "Emergence of the Caribbean Labour Movement," Caribbean Labour Series, No. 3, 1987, 17, West Indies Collection, University of the West Indies, Jamaica. "[T]he first formal efforts to organize unions began in Jamaica, Trinidad, Barbados and Guyana during 1892–1919. Mutual aid societies were formed."

2. O. Nigel Bolland, *Struggles for Freedom: Essays on Slavery, Colonialism and Culture in the Caribbean and Central America* (Belize City: Angelus Press, 1997), 196.

3. Hazel M. Woolford, "Hubert Nathaniel Critchlow: The Crusader," *History Gazette* (No. 43, April 1992), British Library, London.

4. Carlyle Harry, *Hubert Nathaniel Critchlow: His Main Tasks and Achievements* (Georgetown: Guyana National Servicing Publishing Centre, 1977), British Library, London.

5. "Critchlow: A Legend that Is," unclear provenance, Hd6635.3.z55c74, West Indies Collections, University of West Indies, Jamaica. See also Winston F. McGowan, James G. Rose, and David A. Granger, eds., *Themes in African-Guyanese History* (Georgetown: Free Press, 1998).

6. Vertical File on Hubert Critchlow, n.d., National Library of Guyana, Georgetown.

7. Remarks by Hubert Critchlow, "The Voice of Coloured Labour: Speeches and Reports of Colonial Delegates to the World Trade Union Conference—1945," British Library, London.

8. *Daily Gleaner* (Jamaica), 3 September 1947.

9. "Report of First Commonwealth Labour Conference Held at The House of Commons, London," 27 July to 1 August 1925, British Library, London.

10. Walter Rodney, *A History of the Guyanese Working People, 1881–1905* (Baltimore: Johns Hopkins University Press, 1981), 174, 181.

11. William Patterson to J. R. Clynes, 17 April 1930, CO323/1096/10, Public Records Office, London.

12. Handwritten note from Colonial Office, May 1930, CO323/1096/10, Public Records Office, London.

13. Note, February 1930, CO323/1096/10, Public Records Office, London.

14. Wendy Charles, "Early Labour Organization in Trinidad and the Colonial Context of the Butler Riots" (Paper, University of the West Indies–St. Augustine, Trinidad, 1978), West Indies Collection, University of the West Indies, Jamaica.

15. Rodney Worrell, "Pan Africanism in Barbados," in *The Empowering Impulse: The Nationalist Tradition of Barbados*, ed. Glenford D. Howe and Don D. Marshall, 196–220, 202, 205 (Kingston: Canoe Press, 2001).

16. W. K. Elkins, "Black Power in the British West Indies: The Trinidad Longshoremen's Strike of 1919," *Science and Society* 33 (No. 1, Winter 1969): 71–75.

17. Governor of British Honduras to the Secretary of State for the Colonies, 10 May 1920, GH3/5/4, Barbados Department of Archives.

18. From WIPSA to Secretary of State for the Colonies, 8 January 1920, GH3/5/1, Barbados Department of Archives.

19. Minutes of the Directors' Meetings and of General Meetings of the St. Kitts Workers League, 12 October 1932, J. E. Fidel O'Flaherty Collection, National Archives of St. Kitts and Nevis, Basseterre.

20. Minutes, 7 December 1932, J. E. Fidel O'Flaherty Collection.

21. Minutes, 19 February 1933, J. E. Fidel O'Flaherty Collection.

22. Minutes, 8 August 1933, J. E. Fidel O'Flaherty Collection.

23. "Private and Confidential" Report, January 1935, William Gillies Papers, Labour Party Archives, Manchester, U.K.

24. Memorandum, circa 1936–1937, William Gillies Papers, Labour Party Archives, Manchester, U.K.

25. Governor of the Windward Islands to the Secretary of State for the Colonies, 5 November 1935, CO321/362/8, Public Records Office, London.

26. "Commander in Chief, America & West Indies" to London, 8 November 1935, CO321/362/8, Public Records Office, London.

27. "Extracted from the 'Voice of St. Lucia', Issue Dated 31 October 1935," CO321/362/8, Public Records Office, London.

28. Letter from Government House, Grenada, 12 November 1935, CO321/362/8, Public Records Office, London.

29. Sir Cosmo Parkinson to London, 5 November 1935, CO321/362/8, Public Records Office, London.

30. Ibid.

31. Letter from Government House, 12 November 1935, CO321/362/8, Public Records Office, London.

32. S. M. Grier to Sir Cosmo Parkinson, 17 November 1935, CO321/362/8, Public Records Office, London.

33. Letter, 25 November 1935, CO321/362/8, Public Records Office, London.

34. Letter, 7 December 1935, CO321/362/8, Public Records Office, London.

35. Sir S. Grier to Sir Cosmo Parkinson, 18 December 1935, CO321/362/10, Public Records Office, London.

36. Report from TUC—London, 25 September 1930, 972.9/1, Trades Union Congress Papers, University of Warwick, U.K.

37. Nyahuma Obika, *An Introduction to the Life and Times of T.U.B. Butler: The Father of the Nation* (Point Fortin, Trinidad and Tobago: Caribbean Historical Society, 1983), 91.

38. *Daily Gleaner*, 3 April 1977.

39. *Daily Gleaner*, 5 February 1947.

40. *Trinidad & Tobago Illustrated*, 17 May 1947, National Library of Jamaica, Kingston.

41. John Milton Hackshaw, *One Hundred Years of Trade Unionism* (Diego Martin, Trinidad and Tobago: JMH, 1997), 3.

42. *Trinidad Guardian*, 23 July 1972.

43. Woodville K. Marshall, ed., *I Speak for the People: The Memoirs of Wynter Crawford* (Kingston: Ian Randle, 2003), 105.

44. Brinsley Samaroo, "The Contribution of Adrian Cola Rienzi to the National Labour Movement," in "A Tribute to Rienzi: Speeches Delivered at the Opening of the Rienzi Complex," 24–34, 26–27, National Library of Trinidad and Tobago, Port-of-Spain.

45. Marshall, *I Speak for the People*, 105.

46. *Trinidad Guardian*, 1 August 1996.

47. C. L. R. James, *The Life of Captain Cipriani: An Account of British Government in the West Indies*, 1932, Trade Unions Congress Collection, London Metropolitan University North Campus, U.K.

48. Clipping, 3 December 1961, File on Cipriani, National Library of Trinidad and Tobago, Port-of-Spain.

49. Report, 1 June 1937, CO295/600/1, Public Records Office, London.

50. "Private and Confidential" Report, February 1932, Labour Party—International Department, William Gillies Papers, Labour Party Archives, Manchester, U.K.

51. Report, March 1932, Labour Party—International Department, Labour Party Archives, Manchester, U.K.

52. Report from Government House, Port-of-Spain, 10 August 1937, CO295/600/1, Public Records Office, London.

53. Neville Richards, *Socialism in the West Indies: Its Origins and Aims* (Port-of-Spain: West Indian Federal Party, 1959), 6.

54. Officer in Charge to Inspector Southern Division, Constabulary Station, Fyzabad, 14 June 1937, Part I, Uriah Butler Correspondence—National Archives of Trinidad and Tobago, Port-of-Spain.

55. Transcript of Uriah Butler Case, 13 September 1938, CO295/608/5, Public Records Office, London.

56. No. 2626 to Inspector of Southern Division, 5 May 1937, Part II, Uriah Butler Correspondence.

57. No. 1937 to Inspector of Southern Division, 17 May 1937, Part II, Uriah Butler Correspondence.

58. Officer to Inspector of Southern Division, 8 February 1937, Part II, Uriah Butler Correspondence.

59. Report, 1 June 1937, CO295/600/1, Public Records Office, London.

60. Officer in Charge to Inspector of Southern Division, 8 March 1937, Part II, Uriah Butler Correspondence.

61. Kelvin Singh, "The June 1937 Disturbances in Trinidad," in *The Trinidad Labour Riots of 1937: Perspectives 50 Years Later*, ed. Roy Thomas, 57–80, 59–60 (St. Augustine, Trinidad: University of the West Indies 1987).

62. Report, July 1948, CO537/3812, Public Records Office, London. See also Appeal of Uriah Butler, 14 June 1938, CO295/608/4, Public Records Office, London.

63. Security Investigator, County of St. Patrick to Security Officer, 11 November 1939, Part I, Uriah Butler Correspondence.

Chapter 2

1. Report, 7 July 1938, Trade Unions Congress Papers—International Department, Labour Party Archives, Manchester, U.K.

2. See in particular Ken Post, *Arise Ye Starvelings: The Jamaica Labour Rebellion of 1938 and its Aftermath* (The Hague: Nijhoff, 1978).

3. Marcus Garvey to Malcolm McDonald, 26 May 1938, CO137/827/1, Public Records Office, London. See also Amy Jacques Garvey, *Black Power in America: Marcus Garvey's Impact on Jamaica and Africa* (Kingston: AJG, 1968).

4. *Negro Worker*, March 1937, CO323/1518/9, Public Records Office, London.

5. Francis Mark, *The History of the Barbados Workers Union* (Bridgetown: BWU, n.d.), 33, West Indies Collection—University of the West Indies, Jamaica.

6. Report from Hugh Watson, 5 January 1939, Box 1, RG 84, Foreign Service Posts of the Department of State, Jamaica, Kingston Consulate, Confidential File.

7. Albert Gomes, *Through a Maze of Colour* (Port-of-Spain, Trinidad and Tobago: Key Caribbean, 1974), 195.

8. Resolution from Jamaica Workers and Tradesmen Union, 3 May 1938, CO137/827/1, Public Records Office, London. See also Lawrence A. Nurse, *Trade Unionism and Industrial Relations in the Commonwealth Caribbean: History, Contemporary Practice and Prospect* (Westport, Conn.: Greenwood, 2002).

9. George Padmore, "Labor Trouble in Jamaica," *Crisis* 45 (No. 9, September 1938): 287–288, 308.

10. Governor Edward Denham to "My Lord," 14 May 1938, CO137/827/1, Public Records Office, London.

11. Report, 26 May 1938, CO137/827/1, Public Records Office, London.

12. R. S. Peat to Colonial Secretary, 6 June 1938, CO137/827/1, Public Records Office, London.

13. R. S. Peat to Malcolm McDonald, 13 June 1938, CO137/827/1, Public Records Office, London.

14. State Department to U.S. Consul in Kingston, Jamaica, 13 March 1936, Box 1, RG 84, Foreign Service Posts of the Department of State, Jamaica, Kingston Consulate, Confidential File, National Archives and Records Administration, College Park, Maryland.

15. Report from Hugh H. Watson, Consul General, 14 January 1938, Box 1, RG 84, Foreign Service Posts of the Department of State, Jamaica, Kingston Consulate, Confidential File.

16. Report from Hugh Watson, Consul General, 3 July 1939, Box 1, RG 84, Foreign Service Posts of the Department of State, Jamaica, Kingston Consulate, Confidential File.

17. Letter from Brimberg Textile Corporation, 11 April 1939, Box 1, RG 84, Foreign Service Posts of the Department of State, Jamaica, Kingston Consulate, Confidential File.

18. Harold Mitchell to Malcolm McDonald, 10 June 1938, CO137/827/1, Public Records Office, London.

19. Jamaica Kincaid, *A Very Small Place* (New York: Farrar Straus, 1988), 23–24.

20. Report from Hugh Watson, 12 May 1938, Box 1, RG 84, Foreign Service Posts of the Department of State, Jamaica, Kingston Consulate, Confidential File.

21. Report from Hugh Watson, 22 July 1938, Box 1, RG 84, Foreign Service Posts of the Department of State, Jamaica, Kingston Consulate, Confidential File.

22. Report, 16 June 1938, CO137/827/1, Public Records Office, London.

23. Report, 15 June 1938, CO137/827/1, Public Records Office, London.

24. Helen P. Hyatt-Short to Neville Chamberlain, 15 June 1938, CO137/827/1, Public Records Office, London.

25. Maria Gertrudis van Enckevort, "The Life and Work of Otto Huiswood: Professional Revolutionary and Internationalist (1893–1961)" (Ph.D. dissertation, University of West Indies–Jamaica, 2000), 3. See also A. M. Jones, *The West Indian Socialist Tradition* (Trinidad: Educo Press, 1987), West Indies Collection, University of West Indies, Jamaica.

26. Roy Thomas, ed., *The Trinidadian Labour Riots of 1937: Perspectives 50 Years Later* (St. Augustine, Trinidad: University of the West Indies, 1987), 10, British Library, London.

27. James R. Hooker, *Black Revolutionary: George Padmore's Path from Communism to Pan-Africanism* (London: Pall Mall Press, 1967), 5.

28. J. R. Hooker, *Henry Sylvester Williams: Imperial Pan-Africanist* (London: Rex Collings, 1975).

29. Gerald Horne, *Red Seas: Ferdinand Smith and Radical Black Sailors in the United States and Jamaica* (New York: New York University Press, 2005), passim.

30. Winston James, *Holding Aloft the Banner of Ethiopia: Caribbean Radicalism in Early Twentieth Century America* (New York: Verso, 1998).

31. Michael A. Gomez, *Reversing Sail: A History of the African Diaspora*, (Cambridge, U.K.: Cambridge University Press, 2005), 132.

32. John Milton Hackshaw, *The Company Villages: A Brief History* (Diego Martin, Trinidad and Tobago: Pan-Caribbean Research Bulletin, 1999), 1, 2, British Library, London.

33. Report, 26 July 1937, CO137/821/16, Public Records Office, London.

34. "The Ambassador" 2 (No. 2, 1952–53), Box 4, Folder 7, Ethelred Brown Papers, Schomburg Center, New York Public Library.

35. Report, 22 March 1938, CO137/821/16, Public Records Office, London.

36. Report, 30 July 1939, CO137/838/10, Public Records Office, London.

37. Report, 31 October 1937, Box 7, File 7, Richard B. Moore Papers, Schomburg Center of the New York Public Library.

38. Article by W. A. Domingo, *Jamaica Tomorrow* 1 (No. 3, January 1938), CO137/827/1, Public Records Office, London.

39. From No. 2910, ag: Lcpl. Alcindor to Superintendent–Southern Division, 8 May 1939, Part I, Uriah Butler Correspondence.

40. From NCO La Brea to Superintendent Southern Division, 10 May 1939, Part I, Uriah Butler Correspondence.

41. Tilbert St. Louis, Corpl 2464 to Detective Superintendent, 27 September 1939, Part I, Uriah Butler Correspondence.

42. From NC Officer i/c, La Brea to Superintendent, Southern Division, 4 April 1939, Part I, Uriah Butler Correspondence.

43. *Trinidad Express*, 17 September 1995.

44. From Industrial Adviser to Honourable Colonial Secretary, 30 October 1939, Part I, Uriah Butler Correspondence.

45. Sahadeo Basdeo, "History of the Trinidad Labour Movement," in *A Tribute to Rienzi: A Collection of Speeches Delivered at the Opening of the Rienzi Complex*, 16–23, 22 (San Fernando, Trinidad and Tobago: Battlefront Publications, 1982), National Library of Trinidad and Tobago, Port-of-Spain.

46. Eric Williams, "Federation: Two Public Lectures," no date, no provenance, National Library of Trinidad and Tobago, Port-of-Spain.

47. G. Addinton Forde, "The 1937 Disturbances of Barbados: A Summary of the Report of the Dean Commission of Enquiry," 1999, Barbados Department of Archives, Bridgetown.

48. Mark, *The History of the Barbados Workers' Union*, 4, 30, 31.

49. David Browne, "'Go Bravely Big England; Little England is Behind You': Barbadian Society and Polity during World War II," History Forum, University of the West Indies–Cave Hill, Department of History, 1997, 18, Barbados Department of Archives, Bridgetown.

Chapter 3

1. Gerald Horne, *Race War! White Supremacy and the Japanese Attack on the British Empire* (New York: New York University, 2004), passim.

2. Brian Dyde, *A History of Antigua: The Unsuspected Isle* (London: Macmillan, 2000), 232.

3. Hugh Watson to "Mr. Mayer," 8 July 1940, RG 84, Box 1, *Foreign Service Posts of the Department of State, Jamaica, Kingston Consulate, Confidential File*.

4. Gaylord T. M. Kelshall, *The U-Boat War in the Caribbean* (Annapolis, Md.: Naval Institute Press, 1994), 290, 240, 366.

5. "Report of the United States Commission to Study Social and Economic Conditions in the British West Indies, Appointed by the President of the United States on November 13, 1940," Reel 21, No. 546, Part 3, Departmental Correspondence File, President Franklin D. Roosevelt's Office Files, 1933–1945, Library of Congress, Washington, D.C.

6. Juni Liburd and Fitzroy Bryant, *The Politics of St. Kitts & Nevis: The Road to Independence, 1930–1980* (n.p., n.d.), National Archives of St. Kitts and Nevis.

7. Glen Richards, "Masters and Servants: The Growth of the Labour Movement in St. Christopher-Nevis, 1896 to 1956" (Ph.D. dissertation, University of Cambridge, 1989), 269, 296–297.

8. Minutes of the Directors' Meeting and of General Meetings of the St. Kitts Workers League, 30 March 1935, J. E. Fidel O'Flaherty Collection, National Archives of St. Kitts and Nevis.

9. Minutes, 21 November 1935, J. E. Fidel O'Flaherty Collection.

10. Minutes, 14 August 1935, J. E. Fidel O'Flaherty Collection.

11. Minutes, 22 October 1935, J. E. Fidel O'Flaherty Collection.

12. Victoria Borg-O'Flaherty, *Pioneers of the St. Kitts-Nevis Labour Movement* (Basseterre: St. Kitts Trades and Labour Union, 1989), 1.

13. Minutes, 7 October 1935, J. E. Fidel O'Flaherty Collection. "Marryshow landed here on his passing through on his way home and placing himself at our service delivered a very interesting address to a large audience at the Apollo . . . a promise was made by him that he would in the not very far future visit us and spend a couple of weeks with us."

14. Minutes, 6 January 1936, J. E. Fidel O'Flaherty Collection. "Mr. Thomas Brookes an Attorney at Law in America, now on a visit to his homeland was present as a visitor."

15. Minutes, 4 March 1936, J. E. Fidel O'Flaherty Collection. "The President informed the meeting that the hall used by the Sandy Point Branch has been kindly placed at the use of the Branch by the owner Mr. Jack who resides in New York . . . vote of thanks and appreciation of Mr. Jack's kindness this was carried with unanimous applause."

16. Minutes, 29 September 1935, J. E. Fidel O'Flaherty Collection. "Mr. V. E. John reported having come across some young men at St. Pauls who were endeavouring to improve themselves intellectually, they hired a room where they held meetings but had very little to read, he had promised to see what could be done to help them along, he suggested that an effort be made by the League to get in touch with them."

17. Washington Archibald, *Reflections on an Epic Journey* (St. Kitts: Washington Archibald, 1993).

18. Joseph E. Fidel O'Flaherty, "The Industrial Politics of the Sugar Industry in St. Kitts" (Diploma, Ruskin College–Oxford, 1978), National Archives of St. Kitts and Nevis. See also Mary Turner, ed., *From Chattel Slaves to Wage Slaves: The Dynamics of Labour Bargaining in the Americas* (Bloomington: Indiana University Press, 1995).

19. Minutes of the Executive Committee of the St. Kitts-Nevis Trades and Labour Union, 30 March 1940, National Archives of St. Kitts and Nevis.

20. Minutes of the Executive Committee of the St. Kitts-Nevis Trades and Labour Union, 12 April 1940, National Archives of St. Kitts and Nevis.

21. Minutes of the Executive Committee of the St. Kitts-Nevis Trades and Labour Union, 28 July 1941, National Archives of St. Kitts and Nevis.

22. *Workers' Weekly* (Basseterre), 18 July 1942.

23. *Workers' Weekly*, 3 April 1943.

24. *Workers' Weekly*, 19 June 1943.

25. *Workers' Weekly*, 10 February 1945.

26. *Workers' Weekly*, 27 February 1943.

27. *Workers' Weekly*, 21 February 1942.

28. *Workers' Weekly*, 4 April 1942.

29. Richard Hart to Spouse, 11 March 1942, Reel 6, Richard Hart Collected Papers, Schomburg Center of New York Public Library.

30. Report from Government of Jamaica, 10 November 1942, Richard Hart Collections, National Library of Jamaica, Kingston.

31. Report from John Lord, U.S. Consul, 28 May 1943, RG 84, Box 3, Foreign Service Posts of the Department of State, Jamaica, Kingston Consulate, Confidential File.

32. Report from John Lord, 27 August 1943, RG 84, Box 2, Foreign Services Posts of the Department of State, Jamaica, Kingston Consulate, Confidential File.

33. Minutes of Assembly, 30 March 1943, Barbados Department of Archives.

34. "Executive Committee Minutes," 3 May 1945, Barbados Department of Archives.

35. Report, 1 July 1944, FO371/38536, Public Records Office, London.

36. Sherman Briscoe to Claude Barnett, Part III, Series A, Reel 3, No. 057, Claude Barnett Papers, Columbia University, New York City.

37. Report from Office of War Information, Department of Agriculture, 21 October 1943, Part III, Series A, Reel 3, No. 079, Claude Barnett Papers.

38. Frank Pinder to Col. Philip G. Bruton, 7 October 1943, Part III, Series A, Reel 3, No. 095, Claude Barnett Papers.

39. Frank Pinder to Claude Barnett, 12 January 1944, Part III, Series A, Reel 3, No. 290, Claude Barnett Papers.

40. Claude Barnett to Colonel Philip G. Bruton, 12 February 1944, Part III, Series A, Reel 3, No. 0318, Claude Barnett Papers.

41. Press Release from Associated Negro Press, February 1944, Part III, Series A, No. 367, Claude Barnett Papers.

42. *Antigua Trades and Labour Union, Commemorative Brochure, 1939–1989*, (St. John's, Antigua: Hansib Publishing Company, 1989), West Indies Collection, University of the West Indies, Jamaica.

43. Nyahuma Obika, *An Introduction to the Life and Times of T.U.B. Butler: The Father of the Nation* (Point Fortin, Trinidad and Tobago: Caribbean Historical Society, 1983), 91.

44. Quintin O'Connor to Acting Colonial Secretary, 14 April 1942, RG 84, Box 1, Foreign Service Posts of the Department of State, Port-of-Spain (Trinidad, British West Indies), Consulate, Confidential File, 1939–1942, National Archives and Records Administration, College Park, Maryland.

45. See e.g. *Trinidad Guardian*, 29 April 1944; *Union Messenger* (St. Kitts), 4 October 1944; *Daily Bulletin* (St. Kitts), 16 May 1945; *Daily Chronicle* (British Guiana), 18 August 1945; *West Indian* (Grenada), 11 October 1945; *New York Amsterdam News*, 2 September 1944 and 27 January 1945.

46. Report from Charles Whitaker, 7 June 1944, RG 84, Box 1, Foreign Service Posts of the Department of State, Grenada Consulate, British West Indies, Security—Segregated General Records, 1944–1948, National Archives and Records Administration, College Park, Maryland.

47. *The Labour Advocate* (British Guiana), 16 January 1944.

48. J. W. Cowling, *Forced Labour in the Colonies* (London: Peace News Ltd., 1943), 3.

49. *Workers' Weekly*, 8 January 1944.

50. Report from John Lord, 20 December 1943, RG 84, Box 3, Foreign Service Posts of the Department of State, Jamaica, Kingston Consulate, Confidential File.

51. Report, 4 January 1940, RG 84, Box 1, Foreign Service Posts of the Department of State, Jamaica, Kingston Consulate, Confidential File.

52. Report, 20 September 1944, RG 84, Box 4, Foreign Service Posts of the Department of State, Jamaica, Kingston Consulate, Confidential File.

53. Report, 20 August 1942, RG 84, Box 2, Foreign Service Posts of the Department of State, Jamaica, Kingston Consulate, Confidential File.

54. Albert Gomes, *Through a Maze of Colour* (Port-of-Spain, Trinidad and Tobago: Key Caribbean, 1974), 57.

55. F. A. Hoyos, *Grantley Adams and the Social Revolution: The Story of the Movement that Changed the Pattern of West Indian Society* (London: Macmillan, 1974), 131.

56. Ibid.; Browne, "'Go Bravely Big England'".

57. Kelshall, *The U-Boat War in the Caribbean*, 240.

58. Report by Captain Peter E. L. Russell, 2 June 1942, RG 84, Box 4, Foreign Service Posts of the Department of State, Jamaica, Kingston Consulate, Confidential.

Chapter 4

1. Remarks by Delegate, in George Padmore, ed., *History of the Pan-African Congress* (London: Hammersmith, 1947), 27. See also Anthony Shepherd, *The Postal Censorship in Barbados During the First and Second World Wars* (British West Indies Study Circle, 1984), British Library, London.

2. George Padmore, "The Voice of Coloured Labour: Speeches and Reports of Colonial Delegates to the World Trade Union Conference—1945," British Library, London.

3. *Barbados Advocate*, 31 March 1944.

4. "BG & WI Conference," 28 February–1 March 1944, Grantley Adams Papers, Barbados Department of Archives, Bridgetown.

5. Clipping, 27 September 1945, No. 23, Richard Hart Papers, University of the West Indies, Jamaica. On the CLC meeting, see *Barbados Advocate*, 20 September 1945; *Port of Spain Gazette*, 4 October 1945; *The West Indian* (Grenada), 27 September 1945; *Trinidad Guardian*, 2 October 1945.

6. "Official Report of Caribbean Labour Congress Conference held at Barbados from 17th to 27th September 1945," Richard Hart Papers, University of London.

7. *Workers' Weekly* (Basseterre), 2 January 1943; 28 November 1942.

8. See W. A. Domingo to Rayford Logan, 9 November 1940; Leopold Melo to W. A. Domingo, 28 September 1940; and Leopold Melo to Ethelred Brown, 28 September 1940; all in Box 166–23, Rayford Logan Papers, Howard University, Washington, D.C.

9. Memorandum from Hubert Young, 27 July 1940, CO318/442/1, Public Records Office, London.

10. Report from Sir G. Ogilvie Forbes, 25 July 1940, CO137/846/10, Public Records Office, London.

11. Report, "Secret," 28 July 1940, CO137/846/10, Public Records Office, London.

12. Report from Sir G. Ogilvie Forbes, 27 July 1940, CO137/846/10, Public Records Office, London.

13. Report from Sir G. Ogilvie Forbes, 29 July 1940, CO137/846/10, Public Records Office, London.

14. *New York Amsterdam News*, 3 October 1942.

15. See "Provisional World Council of Dominated Nations," 1945, Box 7, Folder 6, Richard B. Moore Papers, Schomburg Center of New York Public Library.

16. Charles Petioni to E. R. Stettinius, 20 April 1945, Box 8, Folder 1, Richard B. Moore Papers.

17. Report, 23 May 1942, 100–2542, Richard B. Moore File, Federal Bureau of Investigation Headquarters, Washington, D.C.

18. Report, 26 June 1941, 100–11857, Richard B. Moore File.

19. Report, 22 September 1941, 100–11857, Richard B. Moore File.

20. Richard B. Moore to "Dear Lowe," 7 June 1945, Box 8, Folder 1, Richard B. Moore Papers.

21. Report from Gilbert Holliday, 9 May 1945, CO968/121/4, Public Records Office, London.

22. British Consulate to British Embassy in Washington, D.C., 29 March 1945, CO968/164/5, Public Records Office, London.

23. Colonial Office to "Dear Pembleton," 17 December 1945, CO968/164/5, Public Records Office, London.

24. Presidential Memorandum for the Secretary of War, 19 March 1941, President's Official File, 2469, Franklin D. Roosevelt Library, Hyde Park, New York.

25. Memorandum for the Secretary of State, 19 April 1940, OF 48p, President's Official File.

26. *West Indian Crusader* (St. Lucia), 17 April 1943.

27. *Barbados Advocate*, 6 April 1943.

28. *The West Indian*, 10 July 1945.

29. *Daily Chronicle*, 26 September 1945. (This newspaper account and those immediately preceding can all be found in Box 108 of the Charles Taussig Papers located at the Franklin D. Roosevelt Library, Hyde Park, New York.)

30. FBI, "Survey of Racial Conditions in the United States, 1943," 10b, Box 21, President's Official File, FDR Library.

31. Report, 12 June 1944, LAB26/55, Public Records Office, London.

32. Report from Sir George Gater of the Colonial Office, 2 August 1944, LAB26/55, Public Records Office, London.

33. Hilary McD. Beckles, *Corporate Power in Barbados; The Mutual Affair: Economic Injustice in a Political Democracy* (Bridgetown: Lighthouse, 1989), xii.

34. *The Economist*, 8 July 1989.

35. *Barbados Daily Nation*, 6 July 1989. See also Howard Johnson and Karl Watson, eds., *The White Minority in the Caribbean* (Kingston: Ian Randle, 1998).

36. Woodville K. Marshall, ed., *I Speak for the People: The Memoirs of Wynter Crawford*, (Kingston: Ian Randle, 2003), ix, 32, 34, 73, 57. See also Tom Barry et al., *The Other Side of Paradise: Foreign Control in the Caribbean*, (New York: Grove Press, 1984). See Sam Davies et al., eds., *Dock Workers: International Explorations in Comparative Labour History, 1790–1970*, (Aldershot, U.K.: Ashgate, 2000).

37. Hilary Beckles, *A History of Barbados: From Amerindian Settlement to Nation-State* (Cambridge, U.K.: Cambridge University Press, 1990), 170–171. See also Glenford D. Howe and Don D. Marshall, eds., *The Empowering Impulse: The Nationalist Tradition of Barbados* (Kingston: Canoe Press, 2001).

38. Marshall, *I Speak for the People*, 111.

39. Anthony De V. Phillips, "Grantley Herbert Adams, Asquithian Liberalism and Socialism," in Howe and Marshall, *The Empowering Impulse*, 165, 185, 166.

40. Ibid.; Karl Watson, "Sir Grantley Adams as Seen by Others," in Howe and Marshall, *The Empowering Impulse*, 186–195, 192.

41. Francis Mark, *The History of the Barbados Workers Union* (Bridgetown: BWU, n.d.), 86, West Indies Collection—University of the West Indies, Jamaica.

42. F. A. Hoyos, *The Rise of West Indian Democracy: The Life and Times of Sir Grantley Adams* (No city: Advocate Press, 1963), 11, 25.

43. *Nassau Daily Tribune*, October–November 1942.

44. *Workers' Weekly*, 20 June 1942.

45. See "Private and Confidential" Report from the International Department of the Labour Party, April 1943, Labour Party Archives, Manchester, U.K.

46. Creech Jones to "My Dear Willie," 28 May 1943, Labour Party Archives, Manchester, U.K.

47. Memorandum from Alan Dudley, 23 December 1943, FO371/38536, Public Records Office, London.

48. Memorandum, 16 January 1944, FO371/38536, Public Records Office, London.

49. *Workers' Weekly*, 27 June 1942.

50. *Workers' Weekly*, 22 May 1943.

51. Albert Gomes, *Through a Maze of Colour* (Port-of-Spain, Trinidad and Tobago: Key Caribbean, 1974), 57.

52. *Vanguard* (Trinidad and Tobago), 7 July 1945.

53. *Vanguard*, 14 July 1945.

54. *Workers' Weekly*, 20 October 1945.

55. *Workers' Weekly*, 9 June 1945.

56. *Workers' Weekly*, 27 March 1943.

Chapter 5

1. Circular, June 1947, No. 33, Richard Hart Papers, University of West Indies, Jamaica.

2. Richard Hart to Claude Gordon, Executive Secretary of Jamaica Associates in Boston, 1 April 1947, Richard Hart Papers, University of the West Indies, Jamaica.

3. Richard Hart to David Lewis, 27 February 1948, No. 20, Richard Hart Papers, University of the West Indies, Jamaica.

4. H. V. Wiseman, *The West Indies: Toward a New Dominion?* (London: Fabian Publications, 1948), Richard Hart Papers, University of the West Indies, Jamaica.

5. V. C. Bird to Richard Hart, 26 October 1946, No. 3, Richard Hart Papers, University of the West Indies, Jamaica.

6. Richard Hart to T. A. Marryshow, 22 January 1946, No. 3, Richard Hart Papers, University of the West Indies, Jamaica.

7. Vivian Henry to Richard Hart, 29 November 1947, Richard Hart Papers, University of the West Indies, Jamaica.

8. Richard Hart to Vivian Henry, 16 February 1947, Richard Hart Papers, University of the West Indies, Jamaica.

9. *The Masses* (Kingston), 22 September 1945. See also Hart article on federation in *The Masses*, 29 September 1945.

10. "Official Report of CLC Conference held at Barbados, from 17th to 27th September 1945," Richard Hart Papers, University of London.

11. Report, 1947, No. 34, Richard Hart Papers, University of the West Indies, Jamaica.

12. Minutes of 12 January 1947 Meeting, No. 3, Richard Hart Papers, University of the West Indies, Jamaica.

13. Richard Hart to T. A. Marryshow, No. 4, Richard Hart Papers, University of the West Indies, Jamaica.

14. Richard Hart to Albert Gomes, 23 February 1947, No. 7, Richard Hart Papers, University of the West Indies, Jamaica.

15. George Padmore to Richard Hart, 26 February 1947, No. 7, Richard Hart Papers, University of the West Indies, Jamaica.

16. George Padmore on behalf of the Pan-African Federation to Richard Hart, 4 September 1947, No. 18, Richard Hart Papers, University of the West Indies, Jamaica.

17. W. E. B. Du Bois to "Dear Mr. Hart," 18 September 1946, No. 7, Richard Hart Papers, University of the West Indies, Jamaica.

18. Florence Nichol on behalf of T. R. Makonnen, 16 April 1948, No. 7, Richard Hart Papers, University of the West Indies, Jamaica.

19. CLC Secretariat's Report to 1947 Congress, Richard Hart Papers, University of London.

20. George Padmore to "My Dear Richard," 23 October 1947, Richard Hart Papers, University of the West Indies, Jamaica.

21. "Report—Popular Edition, Second Caribbean Labour Congress, Coke Memorial Hall, Kingston, Jamaica, September 2–9 1947," hd 6571.c3 1947, West Indies Collection, University of the West Indies, Jamaica.

22. Report, 8 May 1947, CO537/2259, Public Records Office, London.

23. Ernest W. T. Robinson to Richard Hart, 25 August 1948, No. 33, Richard Hart Papers, University of West Indies, Jamaica.

24. E. F. Gordon to Richard Hart, 17 April 1947, No. 33, Richard Hart Papers, University of West Indies, Jamaica.

25. *Bermuda National Review*, October 1947, National Library of Jamaica, Kingston.

26. Report, circa 1947, CO537/2259, Public Records Office, London.

27. Gerald Horne, *Black and Red: W.E.B. Du Bois and the Afro-American Response to the Cold War, 1944–1963* (Albany: State University of New York Press, 1986).

28. Gerald Horne, *Red Seas: Ferdinand Smith and Radical Black Sailors in the United States and Jamaica* (New York City: New York University Press, 2005).

29. Richard Hart, *Time for a Change: Constitutional, Political and Labour Developments in Jamaica and Other Colonies in the Caribbean Region, 1944–1955* (Kingston: Arawak, 2004), 14, 16, 17, 22, 26, 39.

30. *Daily Gleaner* (Jamaica), 17 February 1946.

31. Richard Hart to T. A. Marryshow, 20 March 1946, No. 4, Richard Hart Papers, University of West Indies, Jamaica.

32. *TIME*, 4 March 1946.

33. *Daily Gleaner*, 13 May 1947.

34. Alexander Bustamante to Richard Hart, 1 September 1947, No. 19, Richard Hart Papers, University of West Indies, Jamaica.

35. *Daily Gleaner*, 3 September 1947.

36. *Daily Gleaner*, 3 September 1947; 8 September 1947.

37. *Vanguard* (Trinidad and Tobago), 6 October 1945.

38. *Daily Gleaner*, 10 September 1947.

39. *Daily Gleaner*, 11 September 1947.

40. F. A. Hoyos, *The Rise of West Indian Democracy: The Life and Times of Sir Grantley Adams* (No city: Advocate Press, 1963), 117.

41. I. G. Fonseca to Richard Hart, 24 October 1947, No. 39, Richard Hart Papers, University of the West Indies, Jamaica.

42. Richard Hart to David Lewis, 27 February 1948, No. 20, Richard Hart Papers, University of the West Indies, Jamaica.

43. Richard Hart to A. Creech Jones, 13 November 1947, Richard Hart Papers, University of the West Indies, Jamaica.

44. *Daily Gleaner*, 14 September 1948.

45. Clipping, December 1946, Richard Hart Papers, University of the West Indies, Jamaica.

46. Clipping, 29 November 1947, Richard Hart Papers, University of the West Indies, Jamaica.

47. Circular, circa 1948, Richard Hart Papers, University of the West Indies, Jamaica.

48. Arthur John Riley to Richard Hart, 28 March 1947, Richard Hart Papers, University of the West Indies, Jamaica.

49. Report from Progressive Seamen's Union—Jamaica, 1 September 1947, Richard Hart Papers, University of the West Indies, Jamaica.

Chapter 6

1. Report, 1 May 1945, RG 84, Box 5, Foreign Service Posts of the Department of State, Jamaica, Kingston Consulate, Confidential File. On Cyrus's capacious proposal, see Jason Parker, "Ripples in the 'American Lake': The United States, Race and Empire in the British Caribbean, 1937–1962" (Ph.D. dissertation, University of Florida, 2002), 43.

2. *Daily Gleaner* (Jamaica), 27 April 1945.

3. Joyce Moore Turner, *Caribbean Crusaders and the Harlem Renaissance* (Champaign-Urbana: University of Illinois Press, 2005), 34.

4. W. A. Domingo to Joseph M. Jones, 19 November 1943, RG 84, Box 3, Foreign Service Posts of the Department of State, Jamaica, Kingston Consulate, Confidential File.

5. U.S. Consul to Secretary of State, 25 May 1946, RG 84, Box 6, Foreign Service Posts of the Department of State, Jamaica, Kingston Consulate, Confidential File.

6. Turner, *Caribbean Crusaders and the Harlem Renaissance*, 35, 74.

7. Judith Stepan-Norris and Maurice Zeitlin, *Left Out: Reds and America's Industrial Unions* (Cambridge, U.K.: Cambridge University Press, 2003), 230.

8. Edwin C. Kemp, Consul General, to Secretary of State, 25 June 1946, RG 84, Box 6, Foreign Service Posts of the Department of State, Jamaica, Kingston Consulate, Confidential File.

9. Edwin C. Kemp, Consul General to Secretary of State, 8 July 1946, RG 48, Box 6, Foreign Service Posts of the Department of State, Jamaica, Kingston Consulate, Confidential File.

10. Edwin C. Kemp to Secretary of State, 14 November 1946, RG 84, Box 6, Foreign Service Posts of the Department of State, Jamaica, Kingston Consulate, Confidential File.

11. Clara Borjes to Edwin C. Kemp, 8 November 1946, RG 84, Box 6, Foreign Service Posts of the Department of State, Jamaica, Kingston Consulate, Confidential File.

12. U.S. Consul to Clara L. Borjes, 12 November 1946, RG 84, Box 6, Foreign Service Posts of the Department of State, Jamaica, Kingston Consulate, Confidential File.

13. W. A. Domingo to "Mr. Wahlstrom," U.S. Consul, 27 April 1927, RG 84, Box 8, Foreign Service Posts of the Department of State, Jamaica, Kingston Consulate, Confidential File.

14. George Kelly to Secretary of State, 2 May 1947, Record Group 84, Box 7, Foreign Service Posts of the Department of State, Jamaica, Kingston Consulate, Confidential File.

15. State Department to London, 11 April 1944, Record Group 84, Box 4, Foreign Service Posts of the Department of State, Jamaica, Kingston Consulate, Confidential File. See also *Daily Gleaner*, 25 April 1944, 26 April 1944.

16. "Secret" Report from State Department to U.S. Consul in Jamaica, 27 April 1944, Record Group 84, Box 4, Foreign Service Posts of the Department of State, Jamaica, Kingston Consulate, Confidential File. See also *People's Voice*, 4 March 1944.

17. *People's Voice*, 2 April 1944.

18. See Report by Henry Taylor, 19 June 1947, "Political Activities of Colored American Citizens in Grenada," RG 84, Box 3, Foreign Service Posts of the Department of State, British West Indies, Grenada Consulate, Security-Segregated General Records, 1944–1948, National Archives and Records Administration, College Park, Maryland.

19. "Confidential" Report, 19 June 1947, RG 84, Box 3, Foreign Service Posts of the Department of State, British West Indies, Grenada Consulate, Security-Segregated General Records, 1944–1948, National Archives and Records Administration, College Park, Maryland.

20. On Julian's visit to Grenada, see *The West Indian* (Grenada), 2 October 1947.

21. Report from Henry Taylor, 2 October 1947, RG 84, Box 3, Foreign Service Posts of the Department of State, British West Indies, Grenada Consulate, Security-Segregated General Records, 1944–1948, 1946–1948. See also Report from Henry Taylor, 2 October 1947, RG 84, Box 3, Foreign Service Posts of the Department of State, British West Indies, Port-of-Spain (Trinidad, British West Indies) Consulate, Confidential File, 1944–1947.

22. Henry Taylor to Secretary of State, 19 June 1947, RG 84, Box 3, Foreign Service Posts of the Department of State, British West Indies, Grenada Consulate, Security-Segregated General Records, 1944–1948, 1946–1948.

23. Henry Taylor to Secretary of State, 25 August 1947, RG 84, Box 3, Foreign Service Posts of the Department of State, British West Indies, Grenada Consulate, Security-Segregated General Records, 1944–1948, 1946–1948.

24. Henry Taylor to Secretary of State, 25 August 1947, RG 84, Box 5, Foreign Service Posts of the Department of State, British West Indies, British Guiana Consulate, Confidential Records.

25. *Vanguard* (Trinidad and Tobago), 20 January 1945.

26. John Harrington to "Dear Vivian," 14 August 1944, CO968/121/4, Public Records Office, London. See also Gerald Horne, *Black Liberation/Red Scare: Ben Davis and the Communist Party* (Newark: University of Delaware Press, 1994).

27. "Colonel Vivian" to "My Dear Harrington," 4 October 1944, CO968/121/4, Public Records Office, London.

28. See Report, circa 1944, CO968/121/4, Public Records Office, London.

29. John Harrington to "Dear Cayzer," September 1944, CO968/121/4, Public Records Office, London.

30. L. G. Holliday to "Dear Middleton," 18 April 1945, and note from John Harrington, along with biographies, CO968/121/4, Public Records Office, London.

31. *Daily Gleaner*, 22 August 1944.

32. Walter Rice to John Hickerson, 7 September 1945, RG 84, Box 5, Foreign Service Posts of the Department of State, Jamaica, Kingston Consulate, Confidential File.

33. Walter Rice to James Byrnes, 16 October 1945, RG 84, Box 5, Foreign Service Posts of the Department of State, Jamaica, Kingston Consulate, Confidential File.

34. Memorandum from Rollo G. Smith, 7 February 1946, RG 84, Box 5, Foreign Service Posts of the Department of State, Jamaica Consulate, Confidential File.

35. "Strictly Confidential" memorandum from Charles Taussig, 20 March 1943, RG 84, Box 3, Foreign Service Posts of the Department of State, Jamaica, Kingston Consulate, Confidential File.

36. Memorandum from John Lord, 25 July 1945, RG 84, Box 5, Foreign Service Posts of the Department of State, Jamaica, Kingston Consulate, Confidential File.

37. Memorandum from John Lord, 12 September 1945, RG 84, Box 5, Foreign Service Posts of the Department of State, Jamaica, Kingston Consulate, Confidential File.

38. *Daily Gleaner*, 11 September 1945.

39. *Daily Gleaner*, 12 September 1945; 9 October 1945; 11 October 1945.

40. Report, 6 March 1945, RG 84, Box 1, Foreign Service Posts of the Department of State, Jamaica, Kingston Consulate General, Reports and Related Records of Paul Blanshard, National Archives and Records Administration, College Park, Maryland.

41. Memorandum from Edwin C. Kemp (quoted remarks from the journal are included in this memo), 27 August 1946, RG 84, Box 6, Foreign Service Posts of the Department of State, Jamaica, Kingston Consulate, Confidential File.

42. Report, 1 August 1944, RG 84, Box 3, Foreign Service Posts of the Department of State, British West Indies, Grenada Consulate, Security-Segregated General Records, 1944–1948, 1946–1948, National Archives and Records Administration, College Park, Maryland.

43. Henry Taylor to Secretary of State, 15 May 1947, RG 84, Box 3, Foreign Service Posts of the Department of State, British West Indies, Grenada Consulate, Security-Segregated General Records, 1944–1948, 1946–1948.

44. Report from Henry Taylor, 19 June 1947, RG 84, Box 3, Foreign Service Posts of the Department of State, British West Indies, Grenada Consulate, Security-Segregated General Records, 1944–1948, 1946–1948.

45. Henry Taylor to Secretary of State, 17 December 1946, RG 84, Box 3, Foreign Service Posts of the Department of State, British West Indies, Grenada Consulate, Security-Segregated General Records, 1944–1948, 1946–1948.

46. Report from Charles Whitaker, RG 84, Box 3, Foreign Service Posts of the Department of State, British West Indies, Grenada Consulate, Security-Segregated General Records, 1944–1948, 1946–1948.

47. See the *Saturday Evening Post*, 21 April 1946; 28 April 1946; 5 May 1946.

48. Report from Charles Whitaker, 5 June 1946, RG 84, Box 3, Foreign Service Posts of the Department of State, British West Indies, Grenada Consulate, Security-Segregated General Records, 1944–1948, 1946–1948.

49. *The Worker's Voice* (Antigua), 31 July 1947, RG 59, Decimal File, 844k.4016/7-3147, Box 6059, National Archives and Records Administration, College Park, Maryland.

Chapter 7

1. Minutes of Executive Committee of St. Kitts-Nevis Trades and Labour Union, 16 October 1945, National Archives of St. Kitts and Nevis.

2. Minutes of Executive Committee of St. Kitts-Nevis Trades and Labour Union, 16 May 1946, National Archives of St. Kitts and Nevis.

3. *Worker's Weekly* (Basseterre), 22 September 1945.

4. *Public Opinion* (Jamaica), 27 September 1945.

5. Report on "Social and Political Forces in Dependent Areas of the Caribbean," December 1944, RG 84, Foreign Service Posts of the Department of State, Jamaica, Kingston Consulate.

6. Paul Blanshard, "Personal and Published Comments on the Benham Report," 20 March 1945, RG 84, Box 1, Foreign Service Posts of the Department of State, Jamaica, Kingston Consulate General, Reports and Related Records of Paul Blanshard.

7. *The Union Messenger* (St. Kitts), 21 March 1947.

8. *The Union Messenger*, 16 April 1947. See also Bonham C. Richardson, *Caribbean Migrants: Environment and Human Survival on St. Kitts and Nevis* (Knoxville: University of Tennessee Press, 1983), 149; Sir Probyn Inniss, *Whither Bound St. Kitts-Nevis?* (St. John's, Antigua: Antigua Printing and Publishing, Ltd., 1983); Elisabeth Wallace, *The British Caribbean: From the Decline of Colonialism to the End of Federation* (Toronto: University of Toronto Press, 1977).

9. Minutes of Executive Committee of St. Kitts-Nevis Trades and Labour Union, 22 May 1947, National Archives of St. Kitts and Nevis.

10. *Vanguard* (Trinidad and Tobago), 14 April 1945; *The West Indian* (Grenada), 3 March 1945.

11. *Vanguard*, 24 February 1945.

12. "Confidential" Report from Henry Taylor, RG 84, Box 3, Foreign Service Posts of the Department of State, British West Indies, Grenada Consulate, Security-Segregated Genera Records, 1944–1948, 1946–1948.

13. Report by Charles Whitaker, 20 February 1946, RG 84, Box 3, Foreign Service Posts of the Department of State, British West Indies, Grenada Consulate, Security-Segregated General Records, 1944–1948, 1946–1948.

14. Minutes of the Executive Committee of the St. Kitts-Nevis Trades and Labour Union, 27 April 1944, *National Archives of St. Kitts and Nevis*.

15. *The Union Messenger*, 31 August 1946.

16. *The Union Messenger*, 29 September 1947.

17. *The Union Messenger*, 29 September 1947.

18. *The Union Messenger*, 29 August 1947.

19. Minutes of the Directors' Meetings and of General Meetings of the St. Kitts Workers' League, 28 November 1946, J. J. Fidel O'Flaherty Collection, National Archives of St. Kitts and Nevis.

20. *The Union Messenger*, 15 February 1945.

21. *St. Kitts-Nevis Daily Bulletin*, 1 March 1948.

22. *The Union Messenger*, 28 September 1946.

23. *The Union Messenger*, 24 August 1947.

24. *Workers' Weekly*, 23 November 1946.

25. *Workers' Weekly*, 9 November 1946.

26. *The Union Messenger*, 19 May 1946.

27. *The Union Messenger*, 18 October 1947.

28. *The Union Messenger*, 14 March 1947.

29. See e.g. Gerald Horne, *Fire This Time: The Watts Uprising and the 1960s* (Charlottesville: University Press of Virginia, 1995); Bonham C. Richardson, *Igniting the Caribbean's Past: Fire in British West Indian History* (Chapel Hill: University of North Carolina Press, 2004).

30. *Workers' Weekly*, 15 May 1943.

31. *Workers' Weekly*, 28 March 1942.

32. *The Union Messenger*, 26 June 1946.

33. *The Union Messenger,* 31 March 1945.

34. *Barbados Sunday Advocate*, 30 June 1974: "During its early history the city of Bridgetown . . . suffered from not less than six devastating fires"; *Barbados Advocate-News*, 19 June 1969: "Golden Square fire was one of the city's worst." The 1910 fire was "believed to be the work of an incendery [*sic*]." There was also a "fire disaster in 1860"; *Barbados Advocate-News*, 1 February 1970. See also R. G. Coz, "Scheme for Fire Prevention and Protection," "FI Fire Supt., Fire Brigades.", 16 September 1948, Barbados Department of Archives: "The Fire Protection of Bridgetown is at a dangerously low level. Until protection is raised to a requisite standard a widespread conflagration is a certainty—time is the only unknown factor. Additionally, average fire losses are at least three times normal the size for a city of Bridgetown's size" and there were "inadequate fresh water supplies."

35. *Barbados Sunday Advocate*, 12 June 1977: "1858—a year of drought." *Barbados Sunday Advocate*, 19 June 1977: "1863 was another dry year."

36. *The Union Messenger*, 10 April 1947.

37. *The Union Messenger,* 27 January 1947.

38. *The Union Messenger*, 29 January 1947.

39. Carlene Payne, "The Heroic Construction of St. Kitts: 'Papa Bradshaw'." Paper Presented at St. Kitts-Nevis Conference, University of the West Indies, UWI Continuing School of Studies, 30 April–3 May 2000," National Archives of St. Kitts and Nevis. See also Mary Turner, ed., *From Chattel Slaves to Wage Slaves: The Dynamics of Labour Bargaining in the Americas* (Bloomington: Indiana University Press, 1995).

40. Glen Richards, "Masters and Servants: The Growth of the Labour Movement in St. Christopher-Nevis, 1896 to 1956" (Ph.D. dissertation, University of Cambridge, 1989), 365, 370, 371, 373–374, 387.

41. *Workers' Weekly*, 25 July 1942.

42. *The Union Messenger*, 23 May 1940.

43. *The Union Messenger*, 28 March 1940.

44. *The Union Messenger,* 8 February 1946.

45. *The Union Messenger*, 16 February 1946.

46. *The Union Messenger*, 8 January 1946.

47. *The Union Messenger*, 11 October 1946.

48. *The Union Messenger*, 28 March 1947.

49. Dispatch from Malcolm Hooper, 30 September 1947, RG 84, Box 7, Foreign Service Posts of the Department of State, Jamaica, Kingston Consulate, Confidential File.

50. Dispatch from W. Lansing Collins, Jr., 18 January 1947, RG 84, Box 7, Foreign Service Posts of the Department of State, Jamaica, Kingston Consulate, Confidential File.

51. Carlos C. Hall, Charges d'Affaires, U.S. Embassy–Panama, to Edwin Carl Kemp, Consul General of U.S. in Kingston, Jamaica, 31 March 1948, RG 84, Box 3, Foreign Service Posts of the Department of State, Jamaica, Kingston Consulate, Confidential File.

52. Dispatch from U.S. Embassy–Panama to Secretary of State, 20 September 1947, RG 84, Box 7, Foreign Service Posts of the Department of State, Jamaica, Kingston Consulate, Confidential File.

53. Dispatch from Reginald Bragonier, 5 March 1947, RG 84, Box 7, Foreign Service Posts of the Department of State, Jamaica, Kingston Consulate, Confidential File.

54. See Dispatch from Reginald Bragonier, Second Secretary of U.S. Embassy, 8 October 1947, RG 84, Box 7, Foreign Service Posts of the Department of State, Jamaica, Kingston Consulate, Confidential File.

55. Malcolm Hooper to Secretary of State, 22 January 1948, RG 84, Box 8, Foreign Service Posts of the Department of State, Jamaica, Kingston Consulate, Confidential File.

56. J. Edgar Hoover to F. B. Lyon, 13 August 1945, 844D.00/8-1345, RG 59, Box 6052, Decimal File, National Archives and Records Administration, College Park, Maryland.

57. Report from "Mr. Mackay," 5 June 1947, 844C.5043/6-547, RG 59, Box 6060, Decimal File.

58. J. Edgar Hoover to FBI, 16 October 1945, 844d.01/10-1645, CS, LE, RG 59, Box 6052, Decimal File.

59. See e.g. Gerald Horne, *Black and Red: W.E.B. Du Bois and the Afro-American Response to the Cold War, 1944–1963* (Albany: State University of New York Press, 1986).

60. Walter White to J. Edgar Hoover, 24 October 1945, Part 14, Reel 10, No. 758, NAACP Papers, University of Texas, Austin.

61. Alfred Baker Lewis to NAACP, 23 January 1945, Part 16, Reel 9, No. 468, NAACP Papers.

62. Remarks by Norman Manley, 8 October 1945, Part 14, Reel 10, No. 774, NAACP Papers.

63. Circular, 15 January 1946, Part 14, Reel 10, No. 788, NAACP Papers.

64. Walter White to Dr. Cecil Marquez, 16 May 1946, Part 14, Reel 10, No. 792, NAACP Papers.

65. Walter White to Norman Manley, 14 February 1947, Part 14, Reel 10, No. 794, NAACP Papers.

66. J. J. Singh to Walter White, 22 October 1945, Part 14, Reel 11, No. 558, NAACP Papers.

67. List for 20 October 1946 luncheon, 11 October 1946, Part 14, Reel 10, No. 736, NAACP Papers.

68. Walter White to Norman Manley, et al., 9 June 1947, Part 14, Reel 10, No. 797, NAACP Papers.

69. See List, September 1947, Part 14, Reel 10, No. 812, NAACP Papers.

70. Augustine Austin to Walter White, 19 July 1947, Part 14, Reel 10, No. 811, NAACP Papers.

71. *Pittsburgh Courier*, 15 September 1947.

72. Walter White to Channing Tobias, 15 September 1947, Part 14, Reel 10, No. 835, NAACP Papers.

73. Walter White to Augustine Austin, circa 1947, Part 14, Reel 10, No. 837, NAACP Papers.

74. *Daily Gleaner*, 2 September 1947.

75. Ellis Bonnet to Secretary of State, 26 September 1947, RG 84, Box 7, Foreign Service Posts of the Department of State, Jamaica, Kingston Consulate, Confidential File. See *Trinidad Guardian*, 9 July 1948; *Evening News* (Trinidad), 19 June 1947.

76. George Francis McCray to Richard Hart, 22 March 1948, Richard Hart Papers, University of the West Indies.

77. W. Burghardt Turner and Joyce Moore Turner, eds., *Richard B. Moore: Caribbean Militant in Harlem* (Bloomington: Indiana University Press, 1988), 81.

78. Augustine Austin to Walter White, 31 October 1947, Part 14, Reel 10, No. 839, NAACP Papers.

Chapter 8

1. F. A. Hoyos, *The Rise of West Indian Democracy: The Life and Times of Sir Grantley Adams* (No city: Advocate Press, 1963), 141.

2. "Barbados Labour Party, 40th Anniversary," 31 March 1978, Commemorative Booklet, Barbados Department of Archives.

3. F. A. Hoyos, *Grantley Adams and the Social Revolution: The Story of the Movement that Changed the Pattern of West Indian Society* (London: Macmillan, 1974), 131, 137, 139, 140, 141.

4. Hoyos, *The Rise of West Indian Democracy,* 135.

5. Gerald Horne, *Black and Red: W.E.B. Du Bois and the Afro-American Response to the Cold War, 1944–1963* (Albany: State University of New York Press, 1986), passim.

6. *Trinidad Guardian,* 16 November 1948.

7. *The Beacon* (Barbados), 11 December 1948 (This is "the paper of the Barbados Labour Party and of the Barbados Workers Union.")

8. *The Beacon,* 6 November 1948.

9. *The Beacon,* 6 November 1948.

10. *CLC Bulletin,* September–October 1948, National Library of Jamaica.

11. "Secret" Report, 15 January 1952, CO1031/962, Public Records Office, London.

12. Executive Committee Minutes, 26 May 1948, Barbados Department of Archives.

13. Executive Committee Minutes, 9 January 1947, Barbados Department of Archives.

14. Executive Committee Minutes, 26 May 1948, Barbados Department of Archives.

15. Executive Committee Minutes, 18 March 1948, Barbados Department of Archives.

16. David Browne, "'Go Bravely Big England; Little England is Behind You': Barbadian Society and Polity during World War II," History Forum, University of the West Indies–Cave Hill, Department of History, 1997, Barbados Department of Archives.

17. Report on "Social and Political Forces in Dependent Areas of the Caribbean," December 1944, RG 84, Box 1, Foreign Service Posts of the Department of State, Jamaica, Kingston Consulate.

18. Clipping, *Sunday Guardian* (St. Kitts), 2 February 1958, Barbados File, National Library of Jamaica.

19. Clipping, *Newday,* October 1957, Barbados File, National Library of Jamaica.

20. "New Facts about Alexander Bustamante," 20 February 1945, RG 84, Box 1, Foreign Service Posts of the Department of State, Jamaica, Kingston, Consulate General and Related Records of Paul Blanshard.

21. "Confidential" Dispatch from Paul Blanshard, 23 January 1945, RG 84, Box 1, Foreign Service Posts of the Department of State, Jamaica, Kingston Consulate, General Reports and Related Records of Paul Blanshard.

22. Memorandum, uncertain provenance, 26 January 1946, RG 84, Box 6, Foreign Service Posts of the Department of State, Jamaica, Kingston Consulate, Confidential File.

23. Dispatch by George Kelly, 2 June 1947, RG 84, Box 7, Foreign Service Posts of the Department of State, Jamaica, Kingston Consulate, Confidential File.

24. Dispatch from Nelson R. Park, 17 September 1948, RG 84, Box 8, Foreign Service Posts of the Department of State, Jamaica, Kingston Consulate, Confidential File.

25. Edwin C. Kemp to Secretary of State, 8 July 1946, RG 84, Box 6, Foreign Service Posts of the Department of State, Jamaica, Kingston Consulate, Confidential File.

26. Report on "Social and Political Forces in Dependent Areas of the Caribbean," RG 84, Box 1, Foreign Service Posts of the Department of State, Jamaica, Kingston Consulate.

27. "Airmail Secret Jamaica Report of the Month of November 1948," National Library of Jamaica, Kingston.

28. *Daily Gleaner,* 17 February 1946.

29. *Daily Gleaner,* 26 February 1946.

30. *Daily Gleaner,* 27 December 1947.

31. *Daily Gleaner,* 13 March 1948.

32. *Daily Gleaner,* 9 March 1948.

33. *Daily Gleaner,* 6 March 1948.

34. *Trinidad & Tobago Illustrated,* 17 May 1947.

35. *Vanguard* (Trinidad and Tobago), 12 November 1949.

36. *Vanguard*, 19 November 1949.

37. Undated Memorandum, circa 1940s, 972.9/3, Trades Union Congress Papers, University of Warwick, U.K.

38. Colonial Office to H. V. Tewson, 23 May 1947, 972.9/3, Trades Union Congress Papers.

39. *Vanguard*, 13 April 1946.

40. *Vanguard*, 21 December 1946.

41. *Vanguard*, 29 November 1947.

42. *Vanguard*, 15 February 1947.

43. *Vanguard*, 9 February 1946, 14 February 1946.

44. Minutes of Executive Council, 23 May 1947, National Archives of Trinidad and Tobago.

45. *Vanguard*, 13 November 1948.

46. *Vanguard*, 14 June 1947.

47. *Vanguard*, 16 October 1948.

48. Minutes of the Executive Council meeting, 17 January 1947, National Archives of Trinidad and Tobago.

49. Minutes of Executive Council Meeting, 21 January 1947, National Archives of Trinidad and Tobago.

50. Minutes of Executive Council Meeting, 22 April 1947, National Archives of Trinidad and Tobago.

51. Minutes of Executive Council Meeting, 10 December 1947, National Archives of Trinidad and Tobago.

52. Minutes of Executive Council Meeting, 16 May 1947, National Archives of Trinidad and Tobago.

53. Minutes of Executive Council Meeting, 10 February 1948, National Archives of Trinidad and Tobago.

54. Minutes of the Executive Council Meeting, 25 November 1947, National Archives of Trinidad and Tobago.

55. Minutes of the Executive Council Meeting, 2 March 1948, National Archives of Trinidad and Tobago.

56. Minutes of the Executive Council Meeting, 10 March 1948, National Archives of Trinidad and Tobago.

57. Minutes of the Executive Council Meeting, 16 March 1948, National Archives of Trinidad and Tobago.

58. Minutes of Executive Council Meeting, 9 September 1947, National Archives of Trinidad and Tobago.

59. Minutes of Executive Council Meeting, 10 December 1947, National Archives of Trinidad and Tobago.

60. *Vanguard*, 12 November 1949.

61. *Vanguard*, 20 August 1949.

62. Minutes of the Executive Council Meeting, 23 March 1948, National Archives of Trinidad and Tobago.

63. Minutes of Executive Council Meeting, 16 March 1948, National Archives of Trinidad and Tobago.

64. Ellis A. Bonnet to U.S. Secretary of State, 27 June 1946, RG 84, Box 60, Foreign Service Posts of the Department of State, Port-of-Spain (Trinidad, British West Indies) Consulate, General Records, National Archives and Records Administration, College Park, Maryland.

65. *Trinidad Guardian*, 9 November 1947.

66. Minutes of Executive Council Meeting, 17 February 1948, National Archives of Trinidad and Tobago.

67. *Vanguard*, 12 November 1949.

68. *Vanguard*, 4 June 1949.

69. *Vanguard*, 5 January 1946.

70. Albert Gomes, *Through a Maze of Colour* (Port-of-Spain, Trinidad and Tobago: Key Caribbean, 1974), 130.

71. Minutes of Executive Council Meeting, 27 April 1948, National Archives of Trinidad and Tobago.

72. "Note on Tubal Uriah Buzz Butler," September 1948, CO537/4903, Public Records Office, London.

73. Sir John Shaw to Sir Percy Sillitoe, 12 August 1949, CO537/4903, Public Records Office, London.

74. Memorandum, 20 December 1948, CO537/4902, Public Records Office, London.

75. Tubal Butler to Creech-Jones, 31 January 1949, CO537/4902, Public Records Office, London.

76. *Jamaica Daily Express*, 10 February 1949.

Chapter 9

1. Richard Hart to Frank Hill, 15 March 1949, No. 24, Richard Hart Papers, University of the West Indies, Jamaica.

2. Richard Hart to H. W. Springer, 19 September 1949, No. 6, Richard Hart Papers, University of the West Indies, Jamaica.

3. Richard Hart to H. W. Springer, 15 March 1949, No. 6, Richard Hart Papers, University of the West Indies, Jamaica.

4. M. Joseph-Mitchell to Richard Hart, 2 April 1949, No. 24, Richard Hart Papers, University of the West Indies, Jamaica.

5. Richard Hart to H. W. Springer, 10 April 1952, No. 6, Richard Hart Papers, University of the West Indies, Jamaica.

6. Richard Hart to Bedrich Roohan, Editor, 'Prague News Letter,' 29 November 1948, No. 24, Richard Hart Papers, University of the West Indies, Jamaica.

7. Richard Hart to Gabriel Henry, 22 January 1948, No. 31, Richard Hart Papers, University of the West Indies, Jamaica.

8. Gabriel Henry to Richard Hart, 2 September 1947, No. 31, Richard Hart Papers, University of the West Indies, Jamaica.

9. Richard Hart to E. Henny Eman, President, "Aurbaansche Arbeiders Bond," no date, No. 29, Richard Hart Papers, University of the West Indies, Jamaica.

10. Letter to Richard Hart, 3 September 1947, No. 29, Richard Hart Papers, University of the West Indies, Jamaica.

11. "Political Report of the Month of April 1949," Richard Hart Collection, National Library of Jamaica, Kingston.

12. Richard Hart to "Dear Comrade," circa 1949, No. 17, Richard Hart Papers, University of the West Indies, Jamaica.

13. Richard Hart to "Dear Comrade," 13 April 1949, No. 17, Richard Hart Papers, University of the West Indies, Jamaica.

14. F. L. Walcott to "Dear Comrade," 30 May 1949, No. 17, Richard Hart Papers, University of the West Indies, Jamaica.

15. Joseph France to Richard, Hart, 21 April 1949, No. 17, Richard Hart Papers, University of the West Indies, Jamaica.

16. *The Union Messenger* (St. Kitts), 19 February 1949.

17. Lionel Francis to Richard Hart, 27 June 1948, No. 17, Richard Hart Papers, University of the West Indies, Jamaica.

18. Richard Hart to Joseph France, 3 February 1948, No. 7, Richard Hart Papers, University of the West Indies, Jamaica.

19. Richard Hart to Harris Davis, President CSU, Quebec, 14 April 1949, No. 17, Richard Hart Papers, University of the West Indies, Jamaica.

20. "Political Report for the Month of August 1949," Richard Hart Collection, National Library of Jamaica, Kingston.

21. *The Marine Guide* (publication of the Seamen and Waterfront Workers Trade Union, Port-of-Spain), November–December 1948, No. 30, Richard Hart Papers, University of the West Indies, Jamaica.

22. "Federation in the British West Indies," PAM 321.021, 1947, National Library of Jamaica, Kingston.

23. David Lewis to Richard Hart, 22 May 1948, Reel 6, Richard Hart Papers, Schomburg Center, New York City.

24. David Lewis to Richard Hart, 24 May 1948, Reel 6, Richard Hart Papers, Schomburg Center, New York City.

25. Billy Strachan to Richard Hart, 18 September 1948, Reel 6, Richard Hart Papers, Schomburg Center.

26. Minutes, 22 May 1949, Reel 6, Richard Hart Papers, Schomburg Center.

27. Richard Hart, "Trade Unionism in the English Speaking Caribbean: The Formative Years and the Caribbean Labour Congress," in *Contemporary Caribbean: A Sociological Reader*, ed. Susan Craig, 59–96, 86, 89 (Maracas, Trinidad and Tobago: College Press, 1981).

28. *Daily Gleaner* (Jamaica), 11 October 1945.

29. Speech by Paul Southwell, 11 April 1948, No. 12, Richard Hart Papers, University of the West Indies, Jamaica.

30. *The Union Messenger*, 25 October 1948.

31. *The Union Messenger*, 17 September 1949.

32. *The Union Messenger*, 4 November 1949.

33. *St. Kitts-Nevis Daily Bulletin*, 14 June 1948.

34. Richard Hart to Grantley Adams, 22 March 1948, No. 12, Richard Hart Papers, University of the West Indies, Jamaica.

35. Report of the Executive Committee of the Ninth Annual Conference, 31 October 1948, St. Kitts-Nevis Trades and Labour Union, Labour Party International Department, Labour Party Archives, Manchester, U.K.

36. CLC Bulletin, no date, Richard Hart Papers, University of the West Indies, Jamaica.

37. *St. Kitts-Nevis Daily Bulletin*, 31 March 1948.

38. *St. Kitts-Nevis Daily Bulletin*, 5 April 1948.

39. *St. Kitts-Nevis Daily Bulletin*, 16 June 1948.

40. Whitman T. Browne, *From Commoner to King: Robert L. Bradshaw—Crusader for Dignity and Justice in the Caribbean* (Lanham, Md.: University Press of America, 1992), 141.

41. "Robert Llewellyn Bradshaw, 1916–1978," F2091, R62 1978, West Indies Collection, University of the West Indies, Jamaica.

42. Janet Higbie, *Eugenia: The Caribbean's Iron Lady* (London: Macmillan, 1993), 78.

43. *Daily News* (Jamaica), 25 May 1978, Robert Bradshaw File, National Library of Jamaica, Kingston.

44. *The Union Messenger*, 1 March 1949.

45. *The Union Messenger*, 2 March 1949.

46. *The Union Messenger*, 4 March 1949.

47. *The Union Messenger*, 7 March 1949.

48. Report from Sir Thomas Lloyd, KCB, KCMG, 25 May 1951, Richard Hart Collection, National Library of Jamaica, Kingston.

49. *Vanguard* (Trinidad and Tobago), 5 March 1949.

50. Glen Richards, "Masters and Servants: The Growth of the Labour Movement in St. Christopher-Nevis, 1896 to 1956" (Ph.D. dissertation, University of Cambridge, 1989), 388.

51. Andrew Peter Phillips, "The Development of a Modern Labor Force in Antigua" (Ph.D. dissertation, University of California–Los Angeles, 1963), 6, 11, 19, 20, 21.

52. *Daily Gleaner*, 8 November 1981.

53. Brian Dyde, *A History of Antigua: The Unsuspected Isle* (London: Macmillan, 2000), 233.

54. Vere Cornwall Bird to Richard Hart, 10 March 1947, No. 36, Richard Hart Papers, University of the West Indies, Jamaica.

55. Vere Bird to Richard Hart, 8 November 1947, No. 36, Richard Hart Papers, University of the West Indies, Jamaica.

56. Vere Bird to Richard Hart, 14 October 1947, No. 36, Richard Hart Papers, University of the West Indies, Jamaica.

57. Dyde, *A History of Antigua*, 231.

58. Vere Bird to Richard Hart, 24 May 1948, No. 36, Richard Hart Papers, University of the West Indies, Jamaica.

59. Vere Bird to Richard Hart, 10 October 1948, No. 36, Richard Hart Papers, University of the West Indies, Jamaica.

60. Vere Bird to "Comrade Hart," 19 November 1949, No. 36, Richard Hart Papers, University of the West Indies, Jamaica.

61. Vere Bird to Richard Hart, 9 April 1949, No. 36, Richard Hart Papers, University of the West Indies, Jamaica.

62. *Daily Gleaner*, 8 November 1981.

63. Dyde, *A History of Antigua*, 244.

64. Newsletter of PNP, August 1951, Richard Hart Collection, National Library of Jamaica.

65. *Daily Gleaner*, 19 June 1951.

66. Antigua Inquiry, 1951, Richard Hart Collection, National Library of Jamaica.

67. F. J. Carasco to V. C. Bird, 4 May 1950, No. 34, Richard Hart Papers, University of the West Indies, Jamaica.

68. Richard Hart to Vere Bird, 8 February 1950, No. 34, Richard Hart Papers, University of the West Indies, Jamaica.

69. Richard Hart to Vere Bird, 10 July 1951, No. 34, Richard Hart Papers, University of the West Indies, Jamaica.

70. *Daily Gleaner*, 30 June 1999.

71. *TIME*, 22 February 1971.

Chapter 10

1. Report from Sir Thomas Lloyd, 25 May 1951, Richard Hart Collection, University of the West Indies, Jamaica.

2. "Grenada Disturbances, February–March 1951," XHD 5325 G7A2 1951, West Indies Collection, University of the West Indies, Jamaica.

3. Anthony Payne et al., *Grenada: Revolution and Invasion* (New York: St. Martin's Press, 1984), 5.

4. E. A. Mitchell, President of Grenada Workers Union and Anthony Cruickshank, General Secretary of GWU, to "Dear Sir," 16 March 1951, 972.23/5, Trades Union Congress Papers, MSS 292/972.8/3, Modern Records Centre, University of Warwick, U.K.

5. *The Star*, 19 April 1966, File on Eric Gairy, National Library of Jamaica.

6. *People*, August 1979, File on Eric Gairy, National Library of Jamaica.

7. *Daily News* (Jamaica), 29 July 1973, File on Eric Gairy, National Library of Jamaica.

8. *Daily Gleaner* (Jamaica), 25 August 1997.

9. Profile of Charles Grant, circa 1947, RG 84, Foreign Service Posts of the Department of State, British West Indies, Grenada Consulate, Security-Segregated General Records, 1944–1948, 1946–1948, Box 3, National Archives and Records Administration, College Park, Maryland.

10. Profile of T. A. Marryshow, 12 July 1946, RG 84, Foreign Service Posts of the Department of State, British West Indies, Trinidad Consulate, Confidential File, 1944–1947, Box 3, National Archives and Records Administration, College Park, Maryland.

11. S. Ferguson, "Life and Work of T. A. Marryshow," F 2956. m377f4, West Indies Collection, University of the West Indies, Jamaica.

12. George I. Brizan, "The Grenadian Peasantry and Social Revolution, 1930–1951," Working Paper No. 21, Institute of Social and Economic Research, University of the West Indies, Jamaica, 29.

13. Letter from CLC-London to Editor of "The West Indian," 12 March 1951, Reel 6, Richard Hart Papers, Schomburg Center, New York Public Library.

14. E. Marese Donovan to Governor Sir Henry Bradshaw Popham, 24 August 1940, 972.23/5, Trades Union Congress Papers, University of Warwick, U.K.

15. Clarence Ferguson to Richard Hart, 7 December 1951, No. 32, Richard Hart Papers, University of the West Indies, Jamaica.

16. *The Beacon* (Barbados), 3 March 1951.

17. Clipping, 27 February 1951, Box 23, Marjorie Nicholson Papers, London Metropolitan University, North Campus.

18. *Workers' Weekly* (Basseterre), 21 April 1951.

19. "Speeches of E. M. Gairy and G. Blaize at a Meeting Held at the Market Square," 8 March 1951, "Grenada Disturbances February–March 1951," X HD 5325 G7A2 1951, West Indies Collection, University of the West Indies, Jamaica.

20. See Remarks by Robert Bradshaw, 22 March 1951; Minutes of Meeting Held in Market Square, 15 March 1951; Minutes of Meeting of the Grenada Mental and Manual Workers Union, 10 March 1951, "Grenada Disturbances February–March 1951," West Indies Collection, University of the West Indies, Jamaica.

21. *The Union Messenger* (St. Kitts), 5 December 1950.

22. *The West Indian* (Grenada), 25 March 1951; *The Union Messenger*, 27 March 1951.

23. Report from George Green, Acting Governor of Windward Islands to Commanding Office, HMS Devonshire, 23 February 1951; Governor of Windward Islands to Secretary of State for the Colonies, 11 March 1951, "Grenada Disturbances," West Indies Collection, University of the West Indies, Jamaica.

24. Report by Mr. Harold Shannon, no date, "Grenada Disturbances," West Indies Collection, University of the West Indies, Jamaica.

25. Report by the Acting Governor on 1 March 1951, "Grenada Disturbances, February–March 1951," X HD 5325 G7A2 1951, West Indies Collection, University of the West Indies, Jamaica.

26. Report, 2 May 1951, CO321/429/1, Public Records Office, London.

27. Report, 9 May 1951, CO321/429/1, Public Records Office, London.

28. Report, 21 April 1951, CO321/429/1, Public Records Office, London.

29. T. E. Noble Smith to Secretary of State for the Colonies, 20 May 1951, CO321/429/1, Public Records Office, London.

30. Report by Walter A. Knight, MBE, no date, "Grenada Disturbances, February–March 1951," X HD 5325 G7A2 1951, West Indies Collection, University of the West Indies, Jamaica.

31. *The West Indian*, 22 February 1951.

32. *The Union Messenger*, 31 July 1951.

33. *The Union Messenger*, 6 November 1951, 7 November 1951.

34. Patrick Emmanuel, *Crown Politics in Grenada, 1917–1951* (Cave Hill, Barbados: Institute for Social and Economic Research, University of the West Indies, 1978), 182, 183.

35. Paper by Ralph E. Gonsalves, in "The World of Sugar Workers: Papers Presented at the International Sugar Workers' Conference, 23–28 July 1977, San Fernando, Trinidad," British Library, London.

36. Mansraj Ramphal, "Trade Unionism and Politics in the Sugar Industry of St. Vincent: 1951–1962" (Paper submitted for M.Sc., University of the West Indies, 1977), I, ii, 2, 21, West Indies Collection, University of the West Indies, Jamaica.

37. *Barbados Advocate*, 25 January 1946.

38. *The Union Messenger*, 1 June 1950.

39. Woodville K. Marshall, ed., *I Speak for the People: The Memoirs of Wynter Crawford* (Kingston: Ian Randle, 2003), 87.

40. Albert Gomes, *Through a Maze of Colour* (Port-of-Spain, Trinidad and Tobago: Key Caribbean, 1974), 151.

41. U.S. Consul to Clara L. Borjes, Division of British Commonwealth Affairs, 12 November 1946, RG 84, Box 6, Foreign Service Posts of the Department of State, Jamaica, Kingston Consulate, Confidential File, National Archives and Records Administration, College Park, Maryland.

42. Adela Hutson, Executive Secretary, Children's Bureau of New Orleans to U.S. Consul, Jamaica, 26 August 1948, RG 84, Box 6, Foreign Service Posts of Department of State, Jamaica, Kingston Consulate.

43. Ivor O. Smith, Commissioner, Grand Cayman to Nelson R. Park, 27 September 1948, RG 84, Box 6, Foreign Service Posts of the Department of State, Jamaica, Kingston Consulate, Confidential File.

44. Nelson R. Park to U.S. Secretary of State, 1 December 1948, RG 84, Box 6, Foreign Service Posts of the Department of State, Jamaica, Kingston Consulate, Confidential File.

45. *Daily Gleaner*, 11 December 1952, 16 December 1952.

46. *The Union Messenger*, 13 January 1949.

47. *The Union Messenger*, 14 January 1949.

48. Press Release of the United American Council and American West Indian Association of Chicago, 20 July 1949, Box 7, Folder 8, Richard B. Moore Papers, Schomburg Center, New York Public Library.

49. *The Union Messenger*, 12 April 1949.

50. Richard B. Moore to Richard Hart, 30 March 1950, Richard Hart Papers, University of London.

51. Richard B. Moore to Richard Hart, 7 April 1950, No. 27, Richard Hart Papers, University of the West Indies, Jamaica.

52. Richard B. Moore to Ferdinand Smith, 31 March 1950, No. 27, Richard Hart Papers, University of the West Indies, Jamaica.

53. Report, 15 November 1947, File on Richard B. Moore, FBI Reading Room, Washington, D.C.

54. Report, no date, File on Richard B. Moore, FBI Reading Room, Washington, D.C.

55. Report, 7 November 1949, File on Richard B. Moore, FBI Reading Room, Washington, D.C.

56. Helen McDonald to Colonial Office, 27 May 1949, CO537/4314, Public Records Office, London.

57. *The Union Messenger*, 9 April 1949.

58. *The Union Messenger*, 6 August 1949.

59. *The Union Messenger*, 11 February 1950.

60. Report, circa 1950, CO321/428/4, Public Records Office, London.

Chapter 11

1. Cheddi Jagan, *The West on Trial: The Fight for Guyana's Freedom* (New York: International Publishers, 1972), 138, 177, 288, 300.

2. Report on Social and Political Forces in the Dependent Areas of the Caribbean, December 1944, RG 84, Box 1, Foreign Service Posts of the Department of State, Jamaica, Kingston Consulate, National Archives and Records Administration, College Park, Maryland.

3. R. E. R. Lovell to P. M. Lovell, 16 January 1943, RG 84, Box 2, Foreign Service Posts of the Department of State, British Guiana, Georgetown Consulate, Confidential Records, National Archives and Records Administration, College Park, Maryland.

4. "Secret" Interview with Jenaraine Singh, RG 84, Box 3, Foreign Service Posts of the Department of State, British Guiana, Georgetown Consulate, Confidential Records, National Archives and Records Administration, College Park, Maryland.

5. Jagan, *The West on Trial*, 138, 177, 300, 81, 83, 89.

6. Jagan, *The West on Trial*, 16, 17, 18, 20, 46, 47, 48.

7. David Dabydeen, ed., *Cheddi Jagan: Selected Correspondences, 1953–1965* (West Sussex: Dido Press, 2004), 1.

8. Cheddi Jagan to Dr. Orrin Dummett, 4 September 1942, "Articles by Cheddi Jagan, 1942–1954," Files 001–014, 028, 031, 070–077, Cheddi Jagan Research Centre, Georgetown, Guyana.

9. Ibid.; *Indian Opinion* (Guyana), December 1945.

10. Jagan, *The West on Trial*, 77, 78.

11. Executive Council Minutes, 17 February 1948, National Archives of Guyana, Georgetown.

12. Robert Newton to "Dear Cunningham," December 1948, CO852/941/2, Public Records Office, London.

13. Report, 23 February 1949, CO852/942/3, Public Records Office, London.

14. *Indian Opinion*, 15 August 1946.

15. Jagan, *The West on Trial*, 73.

16. Cheddi Jagan, *Forbidden Freedom: The Story of the British Guiana* (London: Hansib, 1954), 79.

17. See Executive Council Minutes, 10 July 1945: "prolonged negotiations between London and Washington concerning . . . USA bases." Executive Council Minutes, 14 May 1946: "British delegates should be requested to stipulate that the Union Jack must be flown in the Base areas." National Archives of Guyana, Georgetown.

18. Jagan, *The West on Trial*, 88.

19. Executive Council Minutes, 6 August 1946, National Archives of Guyana, Georgetown.

20. Executive Council Minutes, 20 January 1948, National Archives of Guyana, Georgetown.

21. Executive Council Minutes, 2 November 1948, National Archives of Guyana, Georgetown.

22. Executive Council Minutes, 1 June 1948, National Archives of Guyana, Georgetown.

23. Ashton Chase, *A History of Trade Unionism in Guyana, 1900 to 1961* (Demerara: New Guyana, 1964), 46, 124, 172, 173, 180.

24. H. N. Critchlow to H. V. Tewson, 7 March 1947, Mss 292/972.8/3, Trades Union Congress Papers, University of Warwick, U.K.

25. H. N. Critchlow to H. V. Tewson, 14 May 1947, Mss 292/972.8/3, Trades Union Congress Papers, University of Warwick, U.K.

26. Cheddi Jagan, "Memorandum on the Sugar Industry of British Guiana," 1948, Cheddi Jagan Research Centre.

27. Cheddi Jagan, "Bitter Sugar," no date, Cheddi Jagan Research Centre.

28. Peoples Progressive Party, "21 Years," no date, British Library, London. See also Basdeo Mangru, *A History of East Indian Resistance on the Guyana Sugar Estates, 1869–1948* (Lewiston, N.Y.: Mellen Press, 1996), 269.

29. Executive Council Minutes, 17 June 1948, National Archives of Guyana, Georgetown.

30. Executive Council Minutes, 22 June 1948, National Archives of Guyana, Georgetown.

31. Executive Council Minutes, 29 June 1948, National Archives of Guyana, Georgetown.

32. Ibid., Jagan, *The West on Trial*, 78, 97.

33. Theodore Sealy, *Sealy's Caribbean Leaders: A Personal Perspective on Major Political Caribbean Leaders Pre and Post Independence* (Kingston: Kingston Publishers, 1991), 69.

34. PPP, "21 Years," British Library, London.

35. Richard Hart, "Trade Unionism in the English Speaking Caribbean: The Formative Years and the Caribbean Labour Congress," in *Contemporary Caribbean: A Sociological Reader*, ed. Susan Craig, 59–96, 87 (Maracas, Trinidad and Tobago: College Press, 1981).

36. *The Union Messenger* (St. Kitts), 7 September 1948.

37. Richard Hart to Grantley Adams, 19 April 1950, Grantley Adams Papers.

38. "West Indies Newsletter," December 1949, Reel 6, Richard Hart Papers, Schomburg Center, New York Public Library.

39. "West Indies Newsletter," April 1950, Reel 6, Richard Hart Papers, Schomburg Center.

40. Petition, circa 1950, Co537/6152, Public Records Office, London.

41. Billy Strachan to Richard Hart, 22 May 1949, Reel 6, Richard Hart Papers, Schomburg Center.

42. Billy Strachan to Sir John Waddington, Chairman of the Commission on Constitutional Reform, 12 March 1951, CO951/68, Public Records Office, London.

43. "West Indies Newsletter," June–July 1951, Reel 6, Richard Hart Papers, Schomburg Center.

44. Report, 1 November 1949, CO537/4902, Public Records Office, London.

45. Statement by CLC-London, 2 August 1950, Reel 6, Richard Hart Papers, Schomburg Center.

46. Executive Council Minutes, 27 July 1948, National Archives of Guyana, Georgetown.

47. Executive Council Minutes, 16 May 1950, National Archives of Guyana, Georgetown.

48. Executive Council Minutes, 31 October 1950, National Archives of Guyana, Georgetown.

49. Executive Council Minutes, 16 January 1951, National Archives of Guyana, Georgetown.

50. Executive Council Minutes, 22 May 1951, National Archives of Guyana, Georgetown.

51. Commissioner of Labour to Colonial Secretary, 29 March 1951. (At the National Archives of Guyana in Georgetown, I inspected various documents—including the one cited in this footnote—that originated in London, though they were apparently brought to this site by Georgetown's Cheddi Jagan Research Centre. They had yet to be given reference numbers during the course of my January 2005 visit. As such, I will refer to these documents as "Cheddi Jagan Research Centre Papers" at the National Archives.)

52. Report from H. D. Barty-King, circa 1951, CO1031/776, Public Records Office, London.

53. Colonial Governor of British Guiana to Secretary of State, 3 May 1951, Cheddi Jagan Research Centre Papers, National Archives of Guyana, Georgetown.

54. Secretary of State to Colonial Governor, 22 March 1951, Cheddi Jagan Research Centre Papers, National Archives of Guyana, Georgetown.

55. Letter from Governor Sir C. Woolley, 2 September 1948, CO537/3785, Public Records Office, London.

56. Report, circa March 1951, CO321/429/15, Public Records Office, London.

57. "To Whom it May Concern" from Unnamed, 15 March 1949, CO537/4314, Public Records Office, London.

58. Executive Council Minutes, 23 January 1951, National Archives of Guyana, Georgetown.

59. Memorandum from Cheddi Jagan, no date, "Civil Liberties," Cheddi Jagan Research Centre, Georgetown, Guyana.

60. Sir C. Woolley to Secretary of State for the Colonies, CO537/4905, Public Records Office, London.

61. CLC to Secretary of State for the Colonies, circa 1952, Richard Hart Papers, University of West Indies, Jamaica: Re: "restrictions on travel which have been imposed on labour and progressive leaders by the Governments of Trinidad, British Guiana, Grenada and St. Vincent during the period January–May 1952."

62. Richard Hart to Grantley Adams, 14 June 1949, Grantley Adams Papers, Barbados Department of Archives.

63. Norman Manley to Secretary of State for the Colonies, 7 February 1949, CO537/4905, Public Records Office, London.

64. Minutes of Executive Committee of St. Kitts-Nevis Trades and Labour Union, 20 February 1949, National Archives of St. Kitts.

65. Memorandum to Secretary of State for the Colonies, circa 1952, Grantley Adams Papers, Barbados Department of Archives.

66. John La Rose to Richard Hart, 29 March 1952, Richard Hart Papers, University of the West Indies, Jamaica.

67. Resolution from Trinidad, 18 March 1952, Richard Hart Papers, University of the West Indies, Jamaica.

68. Letter from Richard Hart, 3 February 1948, CO537/3821, Public Records Office, London.

69. *Vanguard* (Trinidad), 21 January 1950.

70. "Secret" Report, no date, DEF 123/30/01, CO 1031-1166, Cheddi Jagan Research Centre Papers, National Archives of Guyana, Georgetown.

71. Richard Hart to "Dear Comrade," 16 July 1951, Barbados Department of Archives.

72. Letter from PNP, 30 August 1948, contained in Minutes of the Executive Committee of the St. Kitts-Nevis Trades and Labour Union, National Archives of St. Kitts and Nevis.

73. Joseph France to Secretary of St. Kitts-Nevis Chamber of Commerce, 14 September 1950, Richard Hart Papers, University of the West Indies, Jamaica.

74. Report of the Executive Committee to the 12th Annual Conference of the St. Kitts-Nevis Trades and Labour Union, 28 October 1952, No. 12, Richard Hart Papers, University of the West Indies, Jamaica.

75. Minutes of Executive Committee of the St. Kitts-Nevis Trades and Labour Union, 20 October 1950, National Archives of St. Kitts.

76. Richard Hart to "Dear Comrade," 11 March 1950, No. 41, Richard Hart Papers, University of the West Indies, Jamaica.

77. Richard Hart to "Dear Comrade," 27 October 1951, No. 41, Richard Hart Papers, University of the West Indies, Jamaica. A similar letter from Hart can be found in the Grantley Adams Papers.

78. Robert Bradshaw to Richard Hart, 8 June 1948, Richard Hart Papers, University of the West Indies, Jamaica.

79. Report of the Executive Committee to 9th Annual Conference of the St. Kitts-Nevis Trades and Labour Union, 31 October 1948, No. 12, Richard Hart Papers, University of the West Indies, Jamaica. See also Minutes of the Executive Committee of the St. Kitts-Nevis Trades and Labour Union, 2 June 1948, National Archives of St. Kitts and Nevis.

80. *Workers' Weekly* (Basseterre), 22 April 1950.

81. *Workers' Weekly*, 17 May 1952.

82. *Workers' Weekly*, 28 April 1951.

83. G. H. Seel, Comptroller of Barbados to Governor of Leeward Islands, 18 November 1950, CO311/511/6, Public Records Office, London. See also Acting Governor of Jamaica to Secretary of State for the Colonies, 23 January 1951, CO318/511/7, Public Records Office, London: This letter concerns request to repatriate to Ethiopia.

84. Benjamin Gibbons, President of Universal African Nationalist Movement, to John Dugdale, Minister of Colonial Affairs, London, 21 June 1951, CO 318/511/7, Public Records Office, London.

85. Charles O. King, Acting Secretary of State, Liberia, to "Gentlemen," 11 September 1947, CO318/511/7, Public Records Office, London.

86. Governor of Jamaica to Secretary of State for the Colonies, 28 August 1950, CO311/511/6, Public Records Office, London.

87. See "West Indies Labour for Canada," circa 1950, CO 1031/1930, Public Records Office, London.

88. *New York Amsterdam News*, 15 April 1950.

89. Report, 2 November 1951, CO1031/776, Public Records Office, London.

90. Report, 1 November 1951, CO1031/776, Public Records Office, London.

91. Report, 31 October 1951, CO1031/776, Public Records Office, London.

Chapter 12

1. Sir Hugh Foot to Secretary of State from the Colonies, 31 March 1952, Richard Hart Collection, National Library of Jamaica, Kingston.

2. *Daily News* (Jamaica), 14 December 1979, Vertical files: Richard Hart, National Library of Jamaica.

3. "Report on the Trade Union and Political Situation in Barbados," October 1945, Richard Hart Papers, University of the West Indies, Jamaica.

4. Richard Hart to Owen Rowe, 31 March 1950, No. 27, Richard Hart Papers, University of the West Indies, Jamaica.

5. "Report on the Trade Union and Political Situation in Barbados," October 1945, Richard Hart Papers, University of the West Indies, Jamaica.

6. Gary Lewis, *White Rebel: The Life and Times of T. T. Lewis* (Kingston: The Press, University of West Indies, 1999), 158, 113, 152, 163, 169–170. By way of contrast, see *Barbados Advocate*, 28 May 1960: The "forefathers" of the "Redlegs" were "brought to the island as slaves after the bloody repression of Ireland" by Oliver Cromwell, "or they were Scottish Highlanders"—at least, that was alleged. See also Thomas G. Keagy, "The Redlegs of Barbados," *Americas* 27 (No. 1, January 1975): 14–21, 17: "the word 'Barbados' actually took on a verb form, which meant to be transported to the New World by deportation or deceit." Bristol was to the "white servant market" as Liverpool was to the "slave market." The author suggests that "Redlegs"—the term given to many poorer Euro-Barbadians who were the descendants of this "white servant market"—suffered most from emancipation, they "insulated" themselves from Negroes and were "isolated by the planters."

7. Hilary Beckles, *A History of Barbados: From Amerindian Settlement to Nation-State* (Cambridge, U.K.: Cambridge University Press, 1990), 184.

8. Report of the 4th Annual General Meeting of CLC-London, 3 June 1951, Richard Hart Papers, University of the West Indies, Jamaica.

9. Richard Hart to Grantley Adams, 16 March 1950, Grantley Adams Papers, Barbados Department of Archives.

10. Rupert Gittens to H. V. Tewson, 22 January 1948, 972.9/4, Trade Union Congress Papers, University of Warwick, U.K.

11. A. S. Henderson to Morgan Phillips, 31 May 1952, 972.9/4, Trade Union Congress Papers, University of Warwick, U.K.

12. O. Nigel Bolland, *The Politics of Labour in the British Caribbean: The Social Origins of Authoritarianism and Democracy in the Labour Movement* (Kingston: Ian Randle, 2001), 499.

13. Richard Hart to H. W. Springer, 10 April 1952, Grantley Adams Papers.

14. Janet Jagan to Richard Hart, circa 1950, Richard Hart Papers, University of the West Indies, Jamaica.

15. Janet Jagan to Richard Hart, 4 October 1951, Richard Hart Papers, University of the West Indies, Jamaica.

16. D. M. Patterson to Grantley Adams, 23 August 1952, Richard Hart Papers, University of the West Indies, Jamaica.

17. Bolland, *The Politics of Labour in the British Caribbean*, 502.

18. Grantley Adams to "Dear Comrade," 5 August 1952, Richard Hart Papers.

19. Billy Strachan to "Dear Comrades," 20 September 1952, Grantley Adams Papers.

20. Richard Hart to Grantley Adams, 3 October 1952, Grantley Adams Papers.

21. Richard Hart to Grantley Adams, 11 August 1952, Grantley Adams Papers.

22. Richard Hart, *Time for a Change: Constitutional, Political and Labour Developments in Jamaica and Other Colonies in the Caribbean Region, 1944–1955* (Kingston: Arawak, 2004), 244.

23. *The Torch* (Barbados), 8 November 1952.

24. "Political Report for the Month of October 1952," Richard Hart Collection, National Library of Jamaica, Kingston.

25. F. A. Hoyos, *The Rise of West Indian Democracy: The Life and Times of Sir Grantley Adams* (No city: Advocate Press, 1963), 184. See also Interview with Richard Hart, 20 January 2005 (in possession of author).

26. Hart, *Time for a Change*, 246.

27. *The Torch*, 8 November 1952.

28. Cheddi Jagan, "Trade Unions and National Liberation," Address Before "National Union of Government and Federated Workers in Trinidad," 15 October 1976, Cheddi Jagan Research Centre, Georgetown, Guyana.

29. Cheddi Jagan, *The Caribbean Revolution* (Georgetown: Cheddi Jagan, 1979), 11.

30. "Annual Report of the Commissioner of Labour for the Year 1950," Georgetown, British Guiana: Daily Chronicle, 1952, Cheddi Jagan Research Centre, Georgetown, Guyana.

31. Executive Council Minutes, 11 March 1952, National Archives of Guyana, Georgetown.

32. Executive Council Minutes, 28 October 1952, National Archives of Guyana, Georgetown.

33. *Labor Advocate* (Guyana), 5 October 1952.

34. John Fitzgerald, Director and Secretary of Proportional Representation Society, London, to Oliver Lyttleton, Colonial Office, 17 October 1953, National Archives of Guyana, Georgetown.

35. Executive Council Minutes, 16 June 1953, National Archives of Guyana, Georgetown.

36. "The Debates of the Legislative Council of British Guiana, Official Report of Proceedings," 19 February 1953, National Archives of Guyana, Georgetown.

37. "The Debates of the Legislative Council on British Guiana, Official Report of Proceedings," 12 February 1953, National Archives of Guyana, Georgetown.

38. "The Debates of the Legislative Council on British Guiana, Official Report of Proceedings," 18 February 1953, National Archives of Guyana, Georgetown.

39. Executive Council Minutes, 23 June 1953, National Archives of Guyana, Georgetown.

40. "The Debates of the Legislative Council of British Guiana, Official Report of Proceedings," 4 February 1953, National Archives of Guyana, Georgetown.

41. "The Debates of the Legislative Council of British Guiana, Official Report of Proceedings," 27 February 1953, National Archives of Guyana, Georgetown.

42. *Thunder* (Georgetown), March 1953.

43. Executive Council Minutes, 2 July 1953, National Archives of Guyana, Georgetown.

44. Secretary of State for the Colonies to His Excellency, 4 October 1953, Cheddi Jagan Research Centre Papers, National Archives of Guyana, Georgetown.

45. Executive Council Minutes, 7 July 1953, National Archives of Guyana, Georgetown.

46. Executive Council Minutes, 16 December 1952, National Archives of Guyana, Georgetown.

47. Executive Council Minutes, 11 August 1953, National Archives of Guyana, Georgetown.

48. Executive Council Minutes, 4 November 1952, National Archives of Guyana, Georgetown.

49. Executive Council Minutes, 5 August 1953, National Archives of Guyana, Georgetown.

50. Executive Council Minutes, 14 July 1953, National Archives of Guyana, Georgetown.

51. *Daily Chronicle* (Georgetown), 18 October 1953.

52. Executive Council Minutes, 9 September 1953, National Archives of Guyana, Georgetown.

53. Executive Council Minutes, 22 September 1953, National Archives of Guyana, Georgetown.

54. Executive Council Minutes, 29 September 1953, National Archives of Guyana, Georgetown.

55. *Daily Chronicle*, 6 October 1953.

56. *Daily Chronicle*, 7 October 1953.

57. Executive Council Minutes, 6 October 1953, *National Archives of Guyana, Georgetown.*

58. His Excellency to Secretary of State for the Colonies, 29 September 1953, Cheddi Jagan Research Centre Papers, National Archives of Guyana, Georgetown.

59. Secretary of State for the Colonies to His Excellency, 4 October 1953, Cheddi Jagan Research Centre Papers, National Archives of Guyana, Georgetown.

60. Executive Council Minutes, 7 October 1953, National Archives of Guyana, Georgetown.

61. *Daily Chronicle*, 8 October 1953.

62. *Daily Chronicle*, 10 October 1953.

63. Executive Council Minutes, 8 October 1953, National Archives of Guyana, Georgetown.

64. *Daily Chronicle*, 12 October 1953.

65. *Daily Chronicle*, 16 October 1953.

66. Reprint from the *Wisconsin State Journal*, 16 October 1953, Cheddi Jagan Research Centre, Guyana.

67. *Daily Chronicle*, 15 October 1953.

68. *Daily Chronicle*, 16 October 1953.

69. *Daily Chronicle*, 18 October 1953.

70. Executive Council Minutes, 8 November 1953, National Archives of Guyana, Georgetown.

Conclusion

1. Cheddi Jagan, *Forbidden Freedom: The Story of British Guiana*, (London: Hansib Publishing, first printed 1954, 1994 edition), 10.

2. Gordon Oliver Daniels, "A Great Injustice to Cheddi Jagan: The Kennedy Administration and British Guiana: 1961–1963" (Ph.D. dissertation, University of Mississippi, 2000), 89, 90.

3. Reprint from *Wisconsin State Journal*, 16 October 1953, Cheddi Jagan Research Centre, Georgetown, Guyana.

4. H. Payne, "The Original PPP in Office–133 Days to Freedom," Paper Presented at the 16th Annual Conference of Caribbean Historians, University of the West Indies, Cave Hill, April 1984, West Indies Collection, University of the West Indies, Jamaica.

5. Remarks at Press Conference, 22 October 1953, Cheddi Jagan Research Centre.

6. Ashton Chase, *A History of Trade Unionism in Guyana, 1900 to 1961* (Demerara: New Guyana, 1964), 206.

7. "Statement to the Press by Hon. Dr. Cheddi Jagan & Hon. L. F. S. Burnham on October 22nd 1953," Cheddi Jagan Research Centre.

8. Jagan, *Forbidden Freedom*, 1994 edition, 9.

9. *Caribbean News*, November 1953, Cheddi Jagan Research Centre.

10. Richard Hart, "Trade Unionism in the English-Speaking Caribbean: The Formative Years and the Caribbean Labour Congress," in *Contemporary Caribbean: A Sociological Reader*, ed. Susan Craig, 59–96, 91 (Maracas, Trinidad and Tobago: College Press, 1981).

11. Secretary, Dominica Trade Union, to Richard Hart, 14 January 1952, Richard Hart Papers, University of the West Indies, Jamaica.

12. Sir Frank Walcott, *Frankly Speaking: Selection of Extracts from 'Union Speaks' Published in the Sunday Advocate Newspaper* (Barbados: Barbados Workers' Union, 1991), 72.

13. David Dabydeen, ed., *Cheddi Jagan: Selected Correspondences, 1953–1965* (West Sussex: Dido Press, 2004), 2. See also C. A. Nascimento and R. A. Burrowes, *A Destiny to Mould: Selected Discourses of the Prime Minister of Guyana* (London: Longman Caribbean, 1970).

14. Janet Jagan to "Dear Dick," 28 April 1954, No. 41, Richard Hart Papers, University of the West Indies, Jamaica.

15. Gerald Horne, *Race Woman: The Lives of Shirley Graham Du Bois* (New York: New York University Press, 2001), passim.

16. *Spotlight* (Jamaica), September 1961, Cheddi and Janet Jagan File, National Library of Jamaica, Kingston.

17. Robert Waters and Gordon Daniels, "The World's Longest General Strike: The AFL-CIO, the CIA and British Guiana," *Diplomatic History* 29 (No. 2, April 2005): 279–308.

18. Chase, *A History of Trade Unionism in Guyana*, 206.

19. Martin J. Baptiste to A. Philip Randolph, 30 August 1951, Reel 19, No. 824, A. Philip Randolph Papers, Library of Congress, Washington, D.C..

20. A. Philip Randolph to Stephen Mitchell, 23 November 1951, Reel 19, No. 827, A. Philip Randolph Papers.

21. R. E. Basden to A. Philip Randolph, 18 November 1953, Reel 19, No. 868, A. Philip Randolph Papers.

22. Martin Baptiste to A. Philip Randolph, 23 February 1954, Reel 19, No. 873, A. Philip Randolph Papers.

23. A. Philip Randolph to Martin Baptiste, 2 April 1954, Reel 19, No. 874, A. Philip Randolph Papers.

24. S. O. Veitch, Assistant Secretary-PNP, to A. Philip Randolph, 12 April 1954, Reel 19, No. 876, A. Philip Randolph Papers.

25. *Barbados Advocate*, 9 July 1953.

26. E. C. Loblack to H. V. Tewson, 7 March 1951, 972.22/1, Trades Union Congress Papers, University of Warwick, U.K.

27. E. C. Loblack to H. V. Tewson, 20 September 1950, 972.22/1, Trades Union Congress Papers, University of Warwick, U.K.

28. Howard A. Fergus, *Montserrat: History of a Caribbean Colony* (London: Macmillan, 1994), 146.

29. Minutes of the Conference of Delegates of the Dominica Trade Union, 16 March 1948, Richard Hart Papers, University of the West Indies, Jamaica.

30. "Confidential" Report, 1 July 1957, 972.23/3, Trades Union Congress Papers, University of Warwick, U.K.

31. Resolution by West Indian Independence Party, 14 January 1954, Richard Hart Papers, University of the West Indies, Jamaica.

32. Report, 22 September 1954, 972.23/4, Trades Union Congress Papers, University of Warwick, U.K.

33. Intelligence Report No. 6837, 16 February 1955, Department of State, Office of Intelligence Research, Federation of the West Indies: Political Outlook, Prepared by Division of Research and Analysis for Western Europe, National Archives and Records Administration, College Park, Maryland.

34. V. C. Bird to Richard Hart, 14 January 1952, Richard Hart Papers, University of the West Indies, Jamaica.

35. F. W. Dalley, CBE, *General Industrial Conditions and Labour Relations in Trinidad* (Trinidad and Tobago: Government Printing Office, 1954), HD6593, London Metropolitan University, North Campus.

36. Article by Ralph Gonsalves, "The World of Sugar Workers," Papers Presented at the International Sugar Workers' Conference, 23–28 July 1977, San Fernando, Trinidad, British Library, London.

37. Report from Maurice Mason, Provisional Secretary, Caribbean Federal Labour Party, circa 1956, Grantley Adams Papers, Barbados Department of Archives.

38. Sworn Statement by Vincent Sardine, circa 1953, Richard Hart Papers, University of the West Indies, Jamaica.

39. Ebenezer Joshua to Secretary of West Indian Independence Party, 1 June 1953, Richard Hart Papers, University of the West Indies, Jamaica.

40. *Caribbean Contact* (Barbados), March–April 1981.

41. "Confidential" Report from Arthur Galsworthy, 28 February 1951, FO371/95747, Public Records Office, London.

42. "Caribbean Federation," "West Indies Committee Draft Report," June 1956, Box CP, CENT/INT/67, Communist Party of Great Britain Archives, Labour Party Archives, Manchester, U.K.

43. V. C. Bird to Mr. H. S. L. Polak, 15 June 1950, 972.1/7, Trades Union Congress Papers, University of Warwick, U.K. See also Tom Barry, et al., *The Other Side of Paradise: Foreign Control in the Caribbean* (New York: Grove Press, 1984).

44. Claude Barnett to Herb Macdonald, 6 November 1950, Reel 6, No. 0038, Claude Barnett Papers, Columbia University, New York City. See also Terry McCoy and Charles H. Wood, *Caribbean Workers in the Florida Sugar Cane Industry*, Paper No. 2 (Gainesville: Center for Latin American Studies, University of Florida, 1982), West Indies Collection, University of the West Indies, Jamaica.

45. Stetson Kennedy, "Forced Labour in the United States," *World Trade Union Movement* No. 2 (1953), British Library, London. See also Ruslan Vidjajasastra, Assistant General Secretary of the All-Indonesian Trade Union Centre, "Developments of the Trade Union Movement in the Colonial and Semi-Colonial Countries, Documents and Decisions of the World Trade Union Congress," Vienna, 10–21 October 1953, British Library, London.

46. Ruth Siler, "Men of Gold and Men of Silver," reproduced from *This Month* (June 1946), British Library, London. See also Chester Lloyd Jones, *Caribbean Interests of the United States* (New York: Arno Press, 1970).

47. See also Howard H. Bell, ed., *Black Separatism and the Caribbean, 1860* (Ann Arbor: University of Michigan Press, 1970); Shelby T. McCoy, *The Negro in the French West Indies* (Lexington: University Press of Kentucky, 1966).

48. Article by Baseo Panday in "The World of Sugar Workers, Papers Presented at the International Sugar Workers' Conference, 23–28 July 1977, San Fernando, Trinidad," British Library, London. See also Maurice Lemoine, *Bitter Sugar* (London: Zed, 1981); George M. Baker, "Influence of the Bauxite-alumina Industry on Industrial Relations in Jamaica, 1952–1968" (M.Sc., University of the West Indies, 1970).

49. Communist Party of Great Britain, "Brothers in the Fight for a Better Life," circa 1954, CP/LON/RACE/1/3, Communist Party of Great Britain Archives, Labour Party Archives, Manchester, U.K. See also Kusha Haraksingh, "Sugar, Labour and Livelihood: Trinidad, 1940–1970," Paper Presented at the Symposium on Caribbean Economic History, University of West Indies, Mona, Jamaica, 7–8 November 1986, West Indies Collection, University of the West Indies, Jamaica.

50. "Draft Minutes of an Extraordinary Meeting of the Shareholders of the Company Held at 10 Bridge Street, Castries [St. Lucia] on Wednesday, 24 April 1957," File, Sugar, PAM 331.892 SUG, National Library of Jamaica, Kingston. See also St. Christopher and Nevis Department of Labour, "Handbook of Conditions Affecting the Sugar Industry of St. Kitts," 1954, West Indies Collection, University of the West Indies, Jamaica.

51. A. Philip Randolph to Walter Reuther, 23 March 1956, Reel 19, No. 931, A. Philip Randolph Papers.

52. Earle B. Ottley to A. Philip Randolph, 8 November 1958, Reel 19, No. 972, A. Philip Randolph Papers.

53. *Times* (London), 16 November 1948.

54. Hakim Adi, *The History of African & Caribbean Communities in Britain* (East Sussex: Wayland, 1995), 39, 42, 43. See also Marika Sherwood, *Many Struggles: West Indian Workers and Service Personnel in Britain (1939–1945)* (London: Karia, 1984).

55. *Information Booklet for Intending Emigrants to Britain* (Bridgetown: Advocate, circa 1950s), Barbados Department of Archives.

56. *Yorkshire Post*, 14 May 1955.

57. "Extract from Confidential Letter from the Foreign Office to Mr. J. H. A. Watson, Washington," 20 September 1955, CO1031/1847, Public Records Office, London.

58. Clipping, 18 March 1955, CO1031/1847, Public Records Office, London.

59. *The Union Messenger* (St. Kitts), 29 March 1950.

60. *The Union Messenger*, 18 September 1950.

61. *The Union Messenger*, 21 September 1950.

62. *The Union Messenger*, 16 March 1951. See also Rex Nettleford, ed., *Manley and the New Jamaica: Selected Speeches and Writings, 1938–1968* (London: Longman, 1971).

63. Report, 29 October 1954, CO1031/1464, Public Records Office, London.

64. S. E. V. Luke to Colonial Office, 16 December 1952, CO968/301, Public Records Office, London.

65. *Barbados Advocate*, 2 November 1954.

66. *The Union Messenger*, 20 February 1951.

67. "Confidential," 6 September 1945, Reel 4, No. 0052, Claude Barnett Papers.

68. Herb McDonald to Claude Barnett, no date, Reel 4, No. 0357, Claude Barnett Papers.

69. Claude Barnett to Herb Macdonald, 8 February 1946, Reel 4, No. 0357, Claude Barnett Papers.

70. Intelligence Report, No. 6895, 5 May 1955, Department of State, Office of Intelligence Research, Federation of the West Indies: Political Outlook, Prepared by Division of Research and Analysis for Western Europe, National Archives and Records Administration, College Park, Maryland.

71. Report from Hugh Watson, Consul General, 3 July 1939, RG 84, Box 1, Foreign Service Posts of the Department of State, Jamaica, Kingston Consulate, Confidential File, National Archives and Records Administration.

72. *Daily Gleaner* (Jamaica), 26 August 1952. See also International Labor Organization, *Labour Policies in the West Indies* (Geneva: ILO, 1952), National Library of Jamaica, Kingston.

73. *Newday*, October 1957, File on British Honduras, National Library of Jamaica, Kingston. See also "Report of Third Conference of British Caribbean Labour Officers," Barbados, 16–19 October 1950, PAM 331.1, CON., National Library of Jamaica, Kingston; Colonial Office, "Labour Administration in the Colonial Territories, 1944–1950," London: HMSO, 1951, PAM 331, GRE, National Library of Jamaica, Kingston.

74. *Daily Gleaner*, 27 February 1948; see also *Times* (London), 15 January 1946.

75. *Daily Gleaner*, 14 February 1950.

76. *The Unionist* (British Honduras), 10 April 1954, London Metropolitan University, North Campus.

77. *The Unionist*, 5 December 1953.

Epilogue

1. Colin Palmer, *Eric Williams and the Making of the Modern Caribbean* (Chapel Hill: University of North Carolina Press, 2006), 47, 48, 199.

2. "A Salute to the Federated West Indies, April 22, 1958," J1603, S3, 1958, West Indies Collection, University of the West Indies, Jamaica.

3. CPGB, "Caribbean Federation," June 1956, Box CP/CENT/INT/67, Communist Party of Great Britain Archives, Labour Party Archives, Manchester, U.K. See also "Financial Aspects of Federation of the British West Indies," 1953, HJ2479. F56, West Indies Collection, University of the West Indies, Jamaica.

4. Cheddi Jagan, *The Caribbean Revolution* (Georgetown: Cheddi Jagan, 1979), 31–32.

5. Gordon Oliver Daniels, "A Great Injustice to Cheddi Jagan: The Kennedy Administration and British Guiana: 1961–1963" (Ph.D. dissertation, University of Mississippi, 2000), 108, 109.

6. D. V. Trotman, "The Image of Indians in Calypso," in *Indenture and Exile: The Indo-Caribbean Experience*, ed. Frank Birbalsingh, 176, 177, 184–186 (Toronto: Ontario Association for Studies in Indo-Caribbean Culture, 1989).

7. *Trinidad Guardian*, 28 April 1991.

8. *Trinidad Guardian*, 10 April 1988.

9. *Trinidad Guardian*, 17 January 1975.

10. *Trinidad Express*, 8 August 1970.

11. *Trinidad Guardian*, 8 January 1975.

12. *Trinidad Guardian*, 11 January 1975.

13. *Trinidad Sunday Mirror*, 10 October 1965.

14. Clipping, 9 December 1963, Vertical File–Albert Gomes, National Library of Trinidad and Tobago, Port-of-Spain.

15. *Trinidad Guardian*, 10 March 1960.

16. "Confidential" Report, 2 December 1947, RG 84, Box 3, Foreign Service Posts of the Department of State, Port-of-Spain (Trinidad, BWI) Consulate, Confidential File, 1944–1947, National Archives and Records Administration, College Park, Maryland.

17. *Express* (Trinidad), 19 August 1981.

18. *Trinidad Guardian*, 27 April 1980.

19. Farrukh Dhondy, *C. L. R. James: A Life* (New York: Pantheon, 2001), 143.

20. Theodore Sealy, *Sealy's Caribbean Leaders: A Personal Perspective on Major Political Caribbean Leaders and Pre and Post Independence* (Kingston: Kingston Publishers, 1991), 197, 198.

21. Eric Williams, *Inward Hunger: The Education of a Prime Minister* (London: Andre Deutsch, 1969), 77.

22. Sealy, *Sealy's Caribbean Leaders*, 58.

23. *Trinidad Guardian*, 18 June 1967.

24. Ibid.; Palmer, *Eric Williams*, 104.

25. *Trinidad Guardian*, 11 December 1960.

26. *Trinidad Guardian*, 30 September 1960.

27. Richard Hart, *Time for a Change: Constitutional, Political and Labour Developments in Jamaica and Other Colonies in the Caribbean Region, 1944–1955* (Kingston: Arawak, 2004), 133. See also Angela Andrews, ed., "Reflections on Oil and Sugar," Documentation Department, CCC Trinidad Programme Centre, Port-of-Spain, Trinidad and Tobago, April 1977, HD 5345.t72r46, West Indies Collection, University of the West Indies, Jamaica.

28. *The Union Messenger* (St. Kitts), 15 October 1949.

29. Palmer, *Eric Williams*, 41.

30. See e.g. Rex Nettleford, "Manley and the Politics of Jamaica—Toward an Analysis of Political Change in Jamaica, 1938–1968," Kingston: UWI-Mona, Institute of Social and Economic Research, 1971, National Library of Jamaica, Kingston. At the same site, see also "Report by the Conference on West Indian Federation Held in London in April 1953," London: HMSO, 1953, PAM 321.021 GRE; "Caribbean Federation: Debate in the House of Lords," 4 July 1950, London: Advocate, 1950; "Memo on Draft Bill for Federation of the British West Indies and British Guiana," PAM 321.021 CAR, circa 1947.

31. Report from Jamaica Constabulary, 5 January 1967, CO1051/2767, Public Records Office, London.

32. Hart, *Time for a Change*, 205.

33. For accounts of Jamaica's often bitter negotiations with Kaiser, see e.g. *Wall Street Journal*, 10 March 1975; *Vancouver Sun*, 29 April 1975; *San Francisco Chronicle*, 28 May 1975.

34. See Reports in Carton 303, Edgar Kaiser Papers, University of California, Berkeley.

35. Ward C. Humphreys to Edgar Kaiser, 18 November 1964, Carton 296, Edgar Kaiser Papers.

36. Edgar Kaiser to John McCone, 23 November 1964, Carton 296, Edgar Kaiser Papers.

37. Ward C. Humphreys to John McCone, 19 November 1964, Carton 296, Edgar Kaiser Papers.

38. Sealy, *Sealy's Caribbean Leaders*, 41.

39. "Antigua Trades and Labour Union, Commemorative Brochure, 1939–1989," St. John's, Antigua: Hansib, 1989, West Indies Collection, University of the West Indies, Jamaica.

40. Pamphlet, "Vere Cornwall Bird," F2035, v47, no date, West Indies Collection, University of the West Indies, Jamaica.

41. Jamaica Kincaid, *A Very Small Place* (New York: Farrar Straus, 1988), 67.

42. Robert Coram, *Caribbean Time Bomb: The United States' Complicity in the Corruption of Antigua* (New York: Morrow, 1993), 5, 6, 7, 8, 36.

43. Susan Lowes, "The Peculiar Class: The Formation, Collapse and Reformation of the Middle Class in Antigua, West Indies, 1834–1940" (Ph.D. dissertation, Columbia University, 1994), 350.

44. Sealy, *Sealy's Caribbean Leaders*, 51.

45. *Daily Gleaner* (Jamaica), 3 March 1968.

46. Sealy, *Sealy's Caribbean Leaders*, 119.

47. Janet Higbie, *Eugenia: The Caribbean's Iron Lady* (London: Macmillan, 1993), 9, 10, 12, 19, 34, 60.

48. *New York Amsterdam News*, 2 March 2006.

49. *New York Amsterdam News*, 9 March 2006.

INDEX